VOM Books
The publishing division of

Serving persecuted Christians since 1967
vom.org

When he opened the fifth seal,

I saw under the altar the souls of those

who had been slain for the word of God

and for the witness they had borne.

They cried out with a loud voice,

"O Sovereign Lord, holy and true,

how long before you will judge and

avenge our blood on those who

dwell on the earth?"

Revelation 6:9-10

FOXE

VOICES

OF THE

MARTYRS

AD33-TODAY

VOMBOOKS
The Voice of the Martyrs

Cataloging-in-Publication data on file with the Library of Congress

ISBN 978-0-88264-186-7

eBook ISBN 978-0-88264-196-6

Published in the United States by
VOM Books
1815 SE Bison Road
Bartlesville, OK 74006
vom.org

Previously published by Salem Books (ISBN 978-1-68451-008-5; eBook ISBN 978-1-68451-020-7)

All Scripture quotations are taken from the ESV® Bible (The Holy Bible, English Standard Version®) copyright © 2001 by Crossway, a publishing ministry of Good News Publishers. Used by permission. All rights reserved.

Contributing writers: Mark Fackler, Dana Veerman, Neil Wilson, Kari Ziman, Brian Fidler, Cheryl Odden, Todd Nettleton, and Kameron Nettleton.

Cover design by John Caruso

Manufactured in the United States of America

"FATHER, FORGIVE THEM,

FOR THEY KNOW NOT WHAT THEY DO."

LUKE 23:34

TABLE OF CONTENTS

PART THREE
MODERN MARTYRS IN THE TWENTY-FIRST CENTURY

FOREWORD

What did you expect following Christ would be like when you first started following Him? I had read verses on suffering over and over while growing up, but somehow thought they didn't apply to me. My husband, Martin, and I did feel "called" to go overseas as missionaries, but I didn't really hear God calling us to "suffer for His sake." If I had, maybe I wouldn't have answered the call!

I was perfectly content to live in a small barrio in the Philippines with my jungle pilot husband and our three children. We loved our ministry and our life overseas. We loved each other and our Lord Jesus.

Then came May 27, 2001. Martin had to go to the southern island of Palawan to fill in for another New Tribes Mission pilot and I decided to go with him as he would have a heavy flying schedule and would need help. It would also be a chance to celebrate our wedding anniversary. We left our children with coworkers and told them we would return in one week. But life doesn't always go as planned—and we were taken hostage by militant Muslims while on Palawan. For the next year, we lived with the Abu Sayyaf in the jungles of Basilan—running from the military, sleeping on the jungle floor, starving, drinking dirty river water, watching the atrocities that these men inflicted on others, all the while wondering if we would ever see our home and family again.

In one swift moment in time, everything I had—except Martin—was taken away from me. When everything is gone and you're in an uncomfortable position, you see what is really in your heart. And what I saw in mine was not pretty.

I had always prided myself that I was a "good" Christian. After all, we had left the American dream to go overseas as missionaries, hadn't we? But in the jungle I came face-to-face with a Gracia that I didn't want to see. I saw a hateful Gracia. There were times that I really hated those Muslims for what they were doing to us—for the pain they were causing our family. I saw a covetous Gracia. When we were starving and I saw someone with food and they didn't share it with us, I coveted what they had. I saw a despairing Gracia. A faithless Gracia.

When I saw the darkness of my heart, I began to cry out to God to change me. And in His faithfulness, He did just that! As the months rolled on, we began seeing our captors as the needy men that they were. My hatred was replaced with concern and even love for them. Contentment and joy began to grow in my heart as I began acknowledging God's goodness to me on a daily basis instead of looking at the trials. God never leaves us as He finds us, and I am so grateful for His work in my life during that year!

After 376 days as hostages, in gun battle #17, Martin was killed. I was wounded but rescued that day. When I got home to America, I learned that God had been touching the hearts of countless believers to pray for us. What would we have done without the prayers of God's people?

Isn't the life of a Christian not so much "God loves you and has a wonderful plan for your life" but "If anyone desires to come after Me, let him deny himself, and take up his cross, and follow Me"? The testimonies of the martyrs in this book will challenge your faith. I don't know what the cross you are called to carry will look like. I do know that it won't be easy. As you read these stories, remember that these are not

Super Christians. They are ordinary men and women who have faced situations beyond themselves and have died to themselves and found Christ to be sufficient.

"For to this you have been called, because Christ also suffered for you, leaving you an example, so that you might follow in his steps. When he was reviled, he did not revile in return; when he suffered, he did not threaten, but continued entrusting himself to him who judges justly" (1 Peter 2:21, 23).

God calls us to carry our crosses. Jesus shows us how to do that. Follow in His steps, as these Christian martyrs have done.

Gracia Burnham
Ethnos360 (formerly New Tribes Mission)
Author, *In the Presence of My Enemies*

Introduction

n 1571, a church convocation decreed that John Foxe's *The Book of Martyrs* be chained, right beside the Bible itself, in cathedrals, select churches, and other religious buildings. Church leaders wanted Christ's followers to be reminded every time they entered the Lord's house that His words, "If anyone would come after me, let him deny himself and take up his cross daily and follow me" (Luke 9:23) were being lived out by Christians around the world.

The examples of believers giving their very lives to follow Christ sheds a new light on what it means to answer His call. "Follow Me" didn't just mean to follow Him to feed five thousand, to heal the sick, or to bask in the adoration of crowds. "Follow Me" also meant to follow Him through sweating drops of blood in the garden, through forty lashes, and on the long death march to Golgotha.

John Foxe documented the stories of those who laid down their lives for Christ. Though his stories were detailed and often bloody, his intent wasn't to scare the church. Foxe wanted the church to be encouraged by the testimonies of these saints—that in their hardest and lowest moments they found Christ present, and they found Him worthy of their sacrifice.

That calling—to tell the stories of persecuted Christians—is the same one Richard Wurmbrand had when he arrived in the West in the 1960s, freshly ransomed out of communist Romania. Immediately he began to tell the stories of his years in Communist prisons. But more than his own story, he told of the pastors and other Christians still in those prisons, still suffering and laying down their lives for the name of Christ.

The calling of Foxe and Wurmbrand is the same one that drives The Voice of the Martyrs today, and motivates and inspires this update on John Foxe's life work.

Foxe's masterpiece—originally called *The Book of Martyrs, Acts and Monuments of these latter and perilous days*—was first published in 1563. He lived long enough to see the Council of Bishops order a copy of the work to be placed in every cathedral and church in England. Foxe died in 1587. But martyrdom didn't end when he died; it has continued. The Bible says it will continue until Christ returns for His faithful ones, to take us with Him to Heaven, after the number of martyrs is complete (Revelation 6:11).

There are not enough pages in this book to tell of all those who have given their lives for Christ. In its writing we have run into the same problem the apostle John referred to in John 21:25 when talking about documenting the life of Christ: there simply aren't enough pages to tell all the stories!

The stories you will read here have been carefully researched and collected, and we offer them not as an exhaustive accounting but rather as a representative sample of lives willingly given for the Gospel message of salvation through Christ alone. There are countless others who've given their lives whose names we don't know, and will never know this side of Heaven. It is only in eternity that the complete Acts and Monuments of all the Christian martyrs will be revealed.

There were those, even in Foxe's day, who found his work offensive. To those readers, perhaps seeing only through earthly eyes, Foxe's book was a collection of murder, mayhem, and malice. But where earthly eyes see only tragedy, loss, and suffering, the lens of eternity allows us to see—as John Foxe did—courage, faithfulness, and blessing. The apostles in Acts 5 "left the presence of the council, rejoicing that they were counted worthy to suffer dishonor for the name" (Acts 5:41).

Throughout the centuries, the persecution of Christians has only increased. One reason for such an increase is the spread of the Gospel. More have placed their faith in Jesus Christ after experiencing the lostness and emptiness of false religions and atheistic political ideologies. As a result, family members and governments persecute them, viewing their decision as familial disloyalty or national betrayal. For example, the greatest movement of Muslims turning to Christ in the Middle East has occurred in the last two decades. These new followers of Christ in countries like Iran and Saudi Arabia are paying the price for their decision.

But the growth of persecution shouldn't surprise us. Jesus told His followers that the world hated Him, and that if they followed Him the world would hate them too (John 15:18-19). Paul wrote to his disciple Timothy that "all who desire to live a godly life in Christ Jesus will be persecuted" (2 Timothy 3:12). Those words are coming true right now in hostile and restricted nations around the world.

As you read these stories, there may be times that you want to turn away. In those moments, remember the rejoicing apostles and remember to read through eternity's lens. See the faithfulness of Jesus and His followers, not just the evil intent of men, and you will be encouraged to read on. And you will be encouraged, in the ways that Jesus is asking you, to follow Him more boldly and more faithfully.

May we answer His call, no matter the cost.

The Voice of the Martyrs
vom.org

PART ONE

Martyrs

of the

First Century

PERSECUTION

OF THE

EARLY CHURCH

(AD 34-98)

By the time the apostle John put the finishing touches on the book
of Revelation, he alone among the original disciples remained
alive. All of them suffered for Christ, with most dying violently
for His sake. The witnesses of the bodily resurrection of Jesus Christ
willingly exchanged their lives for the high privilege of declaring that
life-transforming miracle. As has often been pointed out, people don't
usually endure torture and painful death for something they know to be
a lie. Those who told the world, "He is risen!" stood by their claim in
the face of threats, suffering, and death. Their examples in dying left a
lasting legacy. They set a high bar of faithfulness for generations to come.

The passage of time and the proliferation of accounts make it difficult
to verify many of the specific details of the martyrdom of the original disciples and their closest companions. While the untimeliness and brutality of
their deaths are almost universally acknowledged, the locations and particu-
lars of their sacrifices are more difficult to ascertain. In the accounts that
follow, the dominant versions of the deaths of the apostles will be given, with
some reference to other possible or intriguing reports and circumstances.

Make no mistake, the shoot that grew from the root of Jesse was
abundantly watered by the blood of the martyrs—some whose names
we are honored to know, others whose stories wait to be told in the great
account of God's ways in the throne room of Heaven.

The stoning of Stephen

STEPHEN
(AD 34)

The charges were false, even ludicrous. Those who couldn't refute his arguments or silence him by threats drummed up false accusations. Stephen took control of the room with his voice, unexpectedly holding his audience spellbound. His words resonated with the kind of passion that flows from a simple man who has grasped a great idea, or has been grasped by a vision larger than himself. He told an old familiar story once again, highlighting parts of it that had been curiously overlooked and even forgotten over the years. He traced God's amazing ways down through the centuries until, like the weaver's final pass of threads in a seamless garment, Stephen confronted his audience with the truth about their condition.

Stephen presented his case, beginning with Abraham, the father of Israel and Israel's faith (Acts 7:2-53). Then he unfolded an extended history lesson highlighted by God's faithfulness despite the faithlessness of His people. Because the accusations had focused on Stephen's alleged words against the temple, his case demonstrated that even God had words of warning about the temple. That was not, after all, a place on which God had staked His reputation. Having dismantled the accusers' sham case against him, Stephen swiftly stated God's case against them. Despite all God's gifts and blessings to His people, they had ultimately rejected Him and His Son. Then Stephen's closing thunder had to provoke either a storm of resistance or an outpouring of repentance. He said, "Which of the prophets did your fathers not persecute? And they killed those who announced beforehand the coming of the Righteous One, whom you have now betrayed and murdered, you who received the law as delivered by angels and did not keep it" (Acts 7:52-53).

The crowd had gathered to judge Stephen, but history and truth passed judgment on them. They rose in rejection of the truth and killed the messenger. Stoning is perhaps one of the most effective ad hominem arguments (an attack against a person rather than an idea), but it doesn't stop or silence the truth.

Stephen must have seen the murder in their eyes. But he also saw something better when he looked up. "Behold, I see the heavens opened, and the Son of Man standing at the right hand of God" (Acts 7:56), he declared. The mob dragged Stephen out of the city and began to stone him. He didn't expect to escape, so he asked God to receive his spirit. Then, with his last breath, he prayed, "Lord, do not hold this sin against them" (Acts 7:60).

Luke, the writer of this account, was not present at Stephen's martyrdom, but he knew well a man who had been there. That man would have remembered details like the last words Stephen uttered. That man was the apostle Paul, at that time known as Saul, a fierce persecutor of Jesus's followers. But Saul didn't know he would have an appointment on the road to Damascus with the same Jesus whom Stephen had seen just before he died.

"LORD, DO NOT HOLD THIS SIN AGAINST THEM."

—STEPHEN, THE FIRST CHRISTIAN MARTYR,
AS HE WAS BEING STONED TO DEATH

James the Great
(ca. AD 44)

Arrests, beatings, and intimidation had become common. A group of believers were randomly rounded up and carted off to Herod's dungeon. Among them happened to be one of the apostles—James. The event seemed little more than the usual inconvenient harassment that the Roman leaders felt obligated to perform at the insistence of certain Jewish leaders, who seemed obsessed with the followers of Jesus. But things took a sudden turn when James was hauled out without fanfare and summarily executed by the sword. The church in Jerusalem was stunned; their opponents were elated (Acts 12:1-2).

James's death turned out to be a political experiment on Herod's part. He must have been sick and tired of the bickering in his court over the Christ-followers who seemed to be spreading like an infection. They didn't do anything wrong except provoke extreme hatred from others. But when the old politician saw the excited response to James's death among his political allies, Herod decided he could afford to eliminate a few more of these Christians. His attempt to kill Peter failed, and before he could devise a further plan, he was distracted by a crisis in another part of his kingdom. Herod died shortly thereafter when "an angel of the Lord struck him down, because he did not give God the glory, and he was eaten by worms and breathed his last" (Acts 12:23).

James, the son of Zebedee, has the noteworthy distinction of being the first apostolic martyr. His death came within fourteen years of Jesus's resurrection and ascension. Only Stephen anteceded James among the well-known early martyrs. Stephen's death and Saul's persecution must have made it clear to the apostles that things were not going to go well in the area of personal safety. After all, His presence, not preservation, had been Jesus's promise in the Great Commission, when He said, "And behold, I am with you always, to the end of the age" (Matthew 28:20).

Curiously, James and his brother John were confronted by Jesus at one point after their mother asked the Lord for a special privilege for her sons. Jesus asked, "Are you able to drink the cup that I am to drink?" (Matthew 20:22). Though they most likely had no idea to what He was referring, the brothers immediately said, "We are able." They thought they were about to get a privilege above the other ten disciples.

Jesus responded, "You will drink My cup ..." (Matthew 20:23). His words were prophetic. James was the first to die; John the last. Their deaths formed the bookends in the stories of apostolic martyrdom.

Of the three disciples with whom Jesus spent extra time (Peter, James, and John), we have the least information about James. His own brother, John, never mentions him (or himself, for that matter) by name in the gospel he wrote. James, the son of Zebedee, is called "the Great" merely to differentiate him from James, the son of Alphaeus ("the Less"), one of the other disciples.

In the context of history, fourteen years doesn't represent a large time span. But Jesus's active ministry covered only three years. The question becomes, then, what were James and the other apostles doing during those first fourteen years before James died at the hands of Herod's soldiers?

During the years following Jesus's ascension, an uneasy relationship developed between the growing movement of Christians in Jerusalem, those Jewish leaders who had rejected Christ's claims and helped to have Him killed, and the Roman authorities who were charged with keeping the peace. Order was often maintained by the use of threats and torture. The early chapters of the book of Acts provide glimpses of the ebb and flow of the persecution of believers. But Luke records a significant moment involving Gamaliel, the rabbi who was Saul's mentor. He wasn't opposed to the persecution of believers, but he cautioned his fellow members of the Sanhedrin against killing Christians. He understood the power of martyrdom. Gamaliel said, "So in the present case I tell you, keep away from these men and let them alone, for if this plan or this undertaking is of man, it will fail; but if it is of God, you will not be able to overthrow them. You might even be found opposing God!" (Acts 5:38-39). This tactic of toleration may have kept many believers in Jerusalem and thus slowed down the process of taking the Gospel to the world. Stephen's and James's deaths eventually changed all of that. (The fall of Jerusalem in AD 70 scattered the church to the winds.)

The death of Stephen almost seems like an unusual case in which things got out of hand. But packing Christians off to prison became part of life in Jerusalem. Saul apparently had success in intimidating Christians to the point that many left Jerusalem for safer places. This had the benefit of spreading the Gospel, something that Saul certainly didn't intend at that point in his life. Nor did he intend to be confronted by the Lord on the road to Damascus. But when Saul (Paul) defected as the chief persecuting official of the Sanhedrin, the situation in Jerusalem became a stalemate again for a number of years.

The apostle James (the Great) beheaded in Jerusalem, AD 44

An ancient church in Spain claims to contain at least some of the remains of James's body. This gave rise to the tradition that James may have left Jerusalem for a number of years on a mission journey to Spain before his death. There seems to be little reason why Luke would not have included some reference in Acts to that effect among his notes about outreach. But it does appeal to our pioneering view of missions that one of the apostolic fishermen would embark for a long voyage to the far end of the Mediterranean—the ends of the earth—and seek to carry out Christ's commission there.

AND YOU WILL BE HATED

BY ALL FOR MY NAME'S SAKE.

BUT THE ONE WHO ENDURES

TO THE END WILL BE SAVED.

MARK 13:13

Philip
(AD 54)

Two men named Philip occupied the stage in the early church. One was Philip the apostle, the first person called by Jesus to follow Him. The other was Philip the evangelist, one of the seven chosen by the church to help with the special needs of the growing band of believers in Jerusalem. Both men had similar evangelistic hearts, and the accounts of their lives have often been intertwined in subsequent history. Their stories are further complicated because they each appear to have fathered several daughters. Philip the apostle is mentioned several times in the Gospel of John but only once in the book of Acts (1:13). Philip the deacon appears in Acts and is instrumental in the conversion of the Ethiopian eunuch as well as in the spiritual outbreak among the Samaritans, recorded by Luke in Acts 8. Philip the deacon later hosted the apostle Paul on his last journey to Jerusalem (Acts 21:8). They may have had further contact during the two years that Paul was imprisoned in Caesarea before his journey under guard to Rome.

Philip the apostle came from Bethsaida, a town in northern Israel close to Capernaum and the Sea of Galilee. His non-Jewish name may indicate the degree to which Bethsaida was influenced by the Greek culture and government language that preceded the Roman occupation, a time when Alexander the Great had spread Greek influence across the world. The fact that Koine Greek, not Latin, was a trade and official language of the times indicates that Rome didn't rule everything.

John gives us four glimpses of Philip in action. When Jesus called Philip to follow Him (John 1:43), the young disciple immediately sought out his friend Nathanael and invited him to meet Jesus. He was clearly a young man more prone to see himself as a channel than a destination. Once he received information, he determined to act on it. Philip also spoke up in the discussion before the feeding of the five thousand, offering his estimate of what it would cost to buy food for such a large crowd

(John 6:7). His practical observation regarding the lack of means or money simply highlighted Jesus's miraculous action. Circumstances that look and are impossible do not hinder God from working. On another occasion, when a group of Greek speakers wanted to approach Jesus, they contacted Philip to act as an intermediary. John mentions Philip's connection with Bethsaida as the reason for their strategy (John 12:21).

John also remembered Philip's request to Jesus during the Last Supper: "Philip said to Him, 'Lord, show us the Father, and it is enough for us' " (John 14:8). Jesus's answer to Philip was for all the disciples: "Have I been with you so long, and you still do not know me, Philip? Whoever has seen me has seen the Father. How can you say, 'Show us the Father'? Do you not believe that I am in the Father and the Father is in me? The words that I say to you I do not speak on my own authority, but the Father who dwells in me does his works" (John 14:9-10).

Jesus told the disciples everything they would need to remember later, after the reality of the resurrection had wiped out their tendency toward unbelief. Philip's Greek name, his multilingual abilities, and his outgoing personality all combined with his vibrant faith in the risen Christ to make him an equipped messenger for the Gospel.

One of the unique features surrounding the apostle Philip is his connection with the area we now know as France. He is the only apostolic figure claimed to have carried the Gospel to the Gauls, the ancient inhabitants of that region. Philip the apostle has also been traditionally linked with Hierapolis in western Turkey. The church he led in that city was just outside the circle of seven churches mentioned by John in the first chapters of Revelation. His proximity to the apostle John may explain why John's gospel features Philip's words and actions.

Culturally, Hierapolis had a Phrygian background, and the regional religion focused on the god Sabazios, represented by a snake. Geographically, Hierapolis was the site of magnificent mineral springs—rumored to have healing powers—that drew people from many parts of the world. This gathering of various nationalities would have attracted an apostolic missionary. Historically, Hierapolis became a largely Christian city. The church may have been planted as a result of Paul's journeys, though the city is not mentioned in his itineraries. The ruins of Hierapolis today include the remains of several ancient churches. Philip may have paid with his life in order to sustain the church. The pagan priests of Hierapolis may have been delighted to profit from visitors from many places of the world, but they didn't appreciate having their religion directly challenged as Philip's message would have done.

Crucifixion was a favored punishment by the Romans, but the practice may have become even more widely known because of its prominence in the preaching of Jesus's followers. This could explain why so many of the early missionaries were themselves crucified. In Philip's case, the religious establishment apparently arranged for him to be crucified and stoned. Obviously, their tactic once again proved ineffective in stopping the Gospel.

IF YOU ABIDE IN MY WORD,

YOU ARE TRULY MY DISCIPLES,

AND YOU WILL KNOW THE TRUTH,

AND THE TRUTH WILL SET YOU FREE.

JOHN 8:31-32

MATTHEW
(AD 60)

Matthew and his brother James the Less (the son of Alphaeus) are the lesser known of three sets of brothers whom Jesus chose to be disciples. Peter and Andrew (sons of John), along with James and John (sons of Zebedee), were the other two brotherly pairs. Matthew also went by the name Levi, a thoroughly Jewish name for a man whose original career as a tax collector placed him among the despised in Capernaum and brought shame to his family. But Jesus saw something in him. One day as Matthew was collecting taxes along the main thoroughfare in Capernaum, Jesus walked by and called him to follow, so "he rose and followed him" (Matthew 9:9). Based on the existence of the gospel he recorded, we imagine that all Matthew took with him from his old life were his writing tools.

The next stop for Jesus after calling Matthew to be a disciple was a dinner party at Matthew's house. Apparently both guests and critics showed up. Since the place was packed with obvious sinners (particularly tax collectors), certain Pharisees confronted Jesus's disciples: "Why does your teacher eat with tax collectors and sinners?" (Matthew 9:11). The question reveals Matthew's reputation as well as the Pharisees' reluctance to confront Jesus directly. In this case, the disciples couldn't or didn't reply. But Jesus had an immediate answer that accomplished a number of purposes in a single statement. "Those who are well have no need of a physician, but those who are sick. Go and learn what this means: 'I desire mercy, and not sacrifice.' For I came not to call the righteous, but sinners" (Matthew 9:12-13). Jesus revealed His mission: to call sinners. He offered an invitation: those willing to acknowledge their sinfulness could claim His call. He rebuked the judgmental attitude of the critics by referring to the Old Testament Scriptures: "I desire mercy, not sacrifice." That quote also offered Jesus's listeners a subtle clue about His identity. God in Christ was demonstrating in the flesh His priorities with people. Matthew never went back to his old job.

The extent of Matthew's conversion can, in some ways, be measured by the fact that this prodigal from Israel, who had cooperated with the enemy as a taxing agent, became the author of a gospel written with his own people in mind. Matthew remained a son of Abraham. His gospel is filled with notes and highlights designed to clarify for the chosen people that their Messiah had come. One of the persistent ancient traditions about Matthew is that he was the only gospel author to write his account of Jesus's life in Hebrew.

Given Matthew's passion to reach Israelites with the good news about their Messiah, we shouldn't be surprised to discover various traditions about Matthew's ministry among the widely scattered communities of Jews throughout the Roman Empire. As an itinerant missionary, it's quite possible that Matthew visited many locations. His apostolic assignment

Matthew the evangelist pinned to the ground and beheaded in
Haddayar, Ethiopia, AD 60

was to Ethiopia. In ancient times, that name was used for two locations: the familiar African one as well as an area of Persia. Traditional consensus has leaned toward placing Matthew in African Ethiopia, where he was beheaded while carrying out Jesus's commission to reach the world.

"CHRIST OUR SAVIOR, IN THE GOSPEL OF ST. MATTHEW . . . CALLED PETER . . . A ROCK, UPON WHICH ROCK HE WOULD BUILD HIS CHURCH SO STRONG THAT THE GATES OF HELL SHOULD NOT PREVAIL AGAINST IT. IN WHICH WORDS THREE THINGS ARE TO BE NOTED: FIRST, THAT CHRIST WILL HAVE A CHURCH IN THIS WORLD. SECONDLY, THAT THE SAME CHURCH SHOULD MIGHTILY BE IMPUGNED, NOT ONLY BY THE WORLD, BUT ALSO BY THE UTTERMOST STRENGTH AND POWERS OF ALL HELL. AND, THIRDLY, THAT THE SAME CHURCH, NOTWITHSTANDING THE UTTERMOST OF THE DEVIL AND ALL HIS MALICE, SHOULD CONTINUE."

—JOHN FOXE IN CHAPTER ONE OF *FOXE'S BOOK OF MARTYRS*

JAMES THE LESS
(AD 63)

When the stones rained down on him, we don't know what he said, but he had good examples to follow. And the legacy of his death remains with us even today.

Among the "James trio" in the New Testament, James, son of Alphaeus, (or James the "Less") has the smallest profile. He receives no credit for a single question, comment, or action during his years with Christ. He was simply one of the Twelve. This James never stood out for ridicule or praise. James, son of Zebedee (the "Great"), and James, son of Joseph, both held far more prominent roles in the history of the times. James, son of Zebedee, was one of the famous Sons of Thunder among the disciples. James, son of Joseph and the half-brother of Jesus, eventually took a significant leadership role in the church of Jerusalem. But James, son of Alphaeus, lived in the background of the story.

At some point, tradition tells us, the apostles assigned themselves certain areas of the world as destinations for outreach. Syria was the appointment of James the Less. During the early persecutions of Christians in Jerusalem, one of the popular escape destinations was Damascus in southern Syria. So much so that when Saul began to run out of believers to hound in Jerusalem, he set his sights on Damascus as a concentration of Christians that he could raid for prisoners. Fortunately, God had other plans. Those who had been targeted for suffering in Damascus ended up giving shelter to Saul following his confrontation with Jesus on the road to their city.

In Jerusalem, persecution was creating what sheer obedience had not accomplished. Eventually, Paul's bold example and the successes of those like Peter and Philip, who had been drawn out of Jerusalem on specific missions, began to overcome inertia. Christ's final words, "You will be my witnesses in Jerusalem and in all Judea and Samaria, and to the end of the earth" (Acts 1:8), were coming true one way or another.

James's mission in Syria was met by three audiences: transplanted believers such as Ananias, who probably would have welcomed someone with apostolic credentials; transplanted Jews, who would suspect James as a troublemaker; and the wider mixed culture typical of territory on a major trading route. Apparently the Jews in Syria rejected James's preaching by stoning him to death.

One account says he was appointed the first overseer of the church at Jerusalem shortly after Christ's death. This account says the high priest, Ananias, summoned him before the judges to deny Jesus is the Christ. He was placed on the pinnacle of the temple where he was to deny Christ before the people. Instead, he boldly proclaimed Jesus Christ is the promised Messiah. The multitudes praised God. However, James was cast down and stoned. But the fall and stoning only broke his legs, so on his knees he prayed to God for those who were attacking him, saying, "Lord, forgive them, for they know not what they do." Then he was struck in the head and died.

James contributed to an eastern expansion of the Gospel that eventually left a lasting arm of the church on the distant end of the arched trade route that connected Jerusalem and Damascus on the west to ancient Iraq on the east. The Gospel traveled even farther east into India, pushing toward the ends of the earth.

AND THEY HAVE CONQUERED HIM
BY THE BLOOD OF THE LAMB
AND BY THE WORD OF THEIR
TESTIMONY, FOR THEY LOVED NOT
THEIR LIVES EVEN UNTO DEATH.

REVELATION 12:11

Mark

(AD 64)

O
ne of the unexpected shared characteristics of the biblical records of Jesus's life and the spread of the Gospel is the almost painful and sometimes humorous honesty of those recording the events. Mark, also known as John Mark, "signed" his gospel with an embarrassing footnote in chapter 14 when he seems to have described his own reaction to Jesus's arrest. "And a young man followed him, with nothing but a linen cloth about his body. And they seized him, but he left the linen cloth and ran away naked" (Mark 14:51-52).

We tend to justify John Mark's qualifications to record his gospel based on the tradition that he based his writings on Peter's account of Jesus's ministry. But events like the one above and the fact that Mark's home in Jerusalem was used as a gathering place for the early church certainly place this young disciple in the center of history as an eyewitness. The clipped and almost breathless format of Mark's gospel (his favorite connecting phrase is "and then") combines all the action of a storyteller's style with a young man's impatience to get the story told. Mark knew the people about whom he was writing. He may not have been part of all the events, but his personal awareness of the participants gives his gospel a ring of authenticity.

As a young man at the time of Jesus's resurrection, Mark had a long life ahead of him. Some of his learning trajectory was recorded by Luke in Acts. Mark's cousin Barnabas and his mother, Mary, were recognizable figures in the early church. Barnabas is the one who first brought Mark and Paul together shortly before the first missionary journey out of the Antioch church. Although Paul and Barnabas were specifically sent out by the church, "[a]nd they had John to assist them" (Acts 13:5). Apparently the rigors, pressures, and suffering on the road got to Mark early in the trip. By the time they reached Pamphylia in southern Turkey, he left Paul and Barnabas and returned to Jerusalem (Acts 13:13).

Mark's departure became an issue between Paul and Barnabas that led to their split as a partnership (Acts 15:36-40). Barnabas insisted that Mark deserved another chance. In the final outcome, Barnabas proved to be a better judge of Mark's character than Paul, who later acknowledged that fact by expressing his appreciation of Mark's capabilities (Colossians 4:10; 2 Timothy 4:11; Philemon 23-24). After a stint with Barnabas, Mark spent time traveling with Peter (1 Peter 5:13). These various apprentice trips took him from Jerusalem to Antioch to Babylon to Rome.

A capable evangelist in his own right. Mark had a longstanding connection with the city of Alexandria in Egypt and was instrumental in founding and nurturing the church there. As was often the case, the good news about Jesus was bad news for the existing pagan religious structures in communities. So within days of his arrival in Alexandria, Mark was a "marked" man. Though years passed before action was taken, a mob eventually exercised its demonic energy against him. Mark was tied with ropes (hooks may have also been used) and dragged through the cobblestone streets of Alexandria until his body was ripped, wounded, and badly injured. After a night in prison, the same treatment was repeated until he died. Though the crowd intended to burn Mark's body, there is a persistent account that a storm delayed the process and allowed other Christians a chance to retrieve and bury his remains.

GREATER LOVE HAS NO ONE THAN THIS, THAT SOMEONE LAY DOWN HIS LIFE FOR HIS FRIENDS.

JOHN 15:13

PETER

(AD 69)

Simon, son of John, grew up in Capernaum, on the north end of the Sea of Galilee. Raised along with his brother Andrew in a fishing family, Simon seemed headed for a career in that business. Then Jesus came walking along the shore and invited Simon to follow Him into a life of fishing for people. Simon accepted both the invitation and a new name given by Jesus—Peter (from the Greek word *petros*, meaning "a piece of rock"). For three years, Peter was Jesus's constant companion.

We find it easy to imagine Simon Peter, the rock, smiling over the immense irony of Jesus's call on his life as Peter wrote these lines: "As you come to him, a living stone rejected by men but in the sight of God chosen and precious, you yourselves like living stones are being built up as a spiritual house, to be a holy priesthood, to offer spiritual sacrifices acceptable to God through Jesus Christ. For it stands in Scripture: 'Behold, I am laying in Zion a stone, a cornerstone chosen and precious, and whoever believes in him will not be put to shame'" (1 Peter 2:4-6).

Peter knew firsthand the depth of that promise of never being put to shame. He knew the unspeakable joy that comes when, in the midst of the overwhelming facts and feelings of failure, Jesus steps in and says, "I still have work for you to do." In the biblical record, Jesus's first and last words to Peter were, "Follow me" (Mark 1:17; John 21:22). History tells us Peter did just that. From the out-of-the-way shore of Galilee to the center-of-the-world hallways of Rome, Peter followed Jesus. From laying down his nets to laying down his life, Peter learned and practiced fishing for men and women. It remains clear that Peter is one of our finest examples of what it means to be a martyr. He lived a full life and he died a faithful death for Christ.

Given the obvious leadership role that Peter had among the disciples and in the early church, it is interesting to see how faithfully the gospels record his fumbling efforts. The disciples as a group comprehended neither what Jesus was doing nor why, and Peter usually made public their lack of understanding. His impulsive nature allowed him to sometimes blurt out the truth, but more often to state the mistake. Though the resurrection of Jesus transformed an average group of disciples into a powerful force for the Gospel, those who knew them never forgot their background. The gospel writers could have easily shaped the stories of the ministry days with Jesus in order to make the first leaders of the church more heroic. They resisted that temptation. Instead, they gave us the truth—God's Word. They gave us accounts into which we can fit ourselves. The ordinary people who spent time with Jesus are people to whom we can relate. The fact that they became apostolic witnesses simply reminds us that God desires also to do something through us in order to bring glory to His name.

When it comes to Peter's missionary efforts, the first twelve chapters of Acts record the exciting events of the initial years of the movement that began with Jesus's command to make disciples throughout the world. Peter's first sermon on the Day of Pentecost seemed to open the floodgates of new believers, but the spread of the Gospel was at first limited to Jews and proselytes (those Gentiles who had become "naturalized" Jews). God used Peter's visit to a Roman soldier's household to confirm Jesus's inclusion of people from every nation as candidates for the good news of salvation. Cornelius became the test case for Gentile conversions.

Peter departs the Acts account suddenly in chapter 12. He had just been miraculously freed from prison and had briefly visited the believers who were gathered together praying for him at Mary's house. They had prayed for Peter's safety, and God had answered by having Peter knock at the door. Because he was technically a prison escapee, Peter's life was in added danger. Luke notes Peter's parting message: "But motioning to them with his hand to be silent, he described to them how the Lord had brought him out of the prison. And he said, 'Tell these things to James and to the brothers.' Then he departed and went to another place" (Acts 12:17).

The "other place" where Peter went has been the subject of both tradition and legend. Traditional accounts for Peter's travels focus primarily on time spent in Babylon (to the east) or Rome (to the west). In support of Peter's ministry in Babylon, we have the apostle's apparent location mentioned in 1 Peter 5:13: "She who is at Babylon, who is likewise chosen, sends you greetings, and so does Mark, my son." The Eastern branch of the church claims that Peter was instrumental in planting the Gospel there. In support of Peter's ministry in Rome, we have the obvious case that he did end up in Rome and was martyred there. As to his founding the church in Rome, we have little direct evidence, but someone did bring the Gospel to the Roman Empire's capital, for when Paul wrote his letter to Rome, there was already a thriving church there. But if Peter was already in Rome at the time, it seems strange that Paul didn't mention him among his various detailed greetings in that letter. What we know from Acts is that Peter was somewhere, busy sharing the Gospel.

It has often been noted that when Jesus and Peter walked on the shore of Galilee for the last time, the Lord not only reinstated His call on Peter's life, but also gave Peter an inkling of the end that awaited him.

> "Truly, truly, I say to you, when you were young, you used to dress yourself and walk wherever you wanted, but when you are old, you will stretch out your hands, and another will dress you and carry you where you do not want to go." (This he said to show by what kind of death he was to glorify God.) And after saying this he said to him, "Follow me" (John 21:18-19).

It's not where we go and what happens to us that matters all that much. What does matter is how we respond when Jesus comes to us and says, "Follow Me."

Peter's final days in Rome are not described in the Scriptures, but various traditional accounts have survived. Reportedly he spent horrific months in the infamous Mamertine Prison, a place where incarceration was often itself a death sentence. Though manacled and mistreated, Peter survived the tortures and apparently communicated the Gospel effectively to his guards. Eventually he was hauled out of the dungeon, taken to Nero's Circus, and there crucified upside down because he did not consider himself worthy to be crucified with his head upward, like Christ.

The apostle Paul was beheaded in Rome.

PAUL

(CA. AD 69)

◆

I n contrast to most of the other apostolic figures, little confusion exists about the place of Paul's death. He always had a passion to preach the Gospel in Rome, and he died there.

Paul spent time in Rome twice, on both occasions at the expense of the Roman Empire. Neither his travel arrangements nor his accommodations were first class, but they suited the apostle well. Throughout Acts and his letters, Paul conveys an unmistakable sense that his time was short, and he was grateful for every moment he was given. Paul understood God's grace, not simply as a great theological concept, but also as his own reason for living. He appreciated God's grace because he knew he needed so much of it.

His final thoughts had little to do with regrets and much to do with the satisfaction that flows from grace-drenched living. He wrote to Timothy:

> For I am already being poured out as a drink offering, and the time of my departure has come. I have fought the good fight, I have finished the race, I have kept the faith. Henceforth there is laid up for me the crown of righteousness, which the Lord, the righteous judge, will award to me on that day, and not only to me but also to all who have loved his appearing (2 Timothy 4:6-8).

While he lived, Paul certainly traveled broadly, proclaiming the Gospel everywhere he went. Perhaps his statement to the Colossians sums up his heart the best: "Him we proclaim, warning everyone and teaching everyone with all wisdom, that we may present everyone mature in Christ. For this I toil, struggling with all his energy that he powerfully works within me" (Colossians 1:28-29).

One of the greatest ironies in Paul's life is that he accomplished a lot to spread the Gospel even while he was persecuting the church. His rabid efforts to hunt down Christians in and around Jerusalem scattered believers to the wind, planting the Gospel seeds everywhere they went.

Truly God uses even the plans and efforts of evil men to accomplish His will. But once Paul turned around after his confrontation with Jesus on the road to Damascus, all the fiery intensity of his former life was now channeled into his efforts for Christ. He produced almost half the New Testament writings with the letters he sent to the churches. He set the standard for missionary living. He pioneered evangelistic practices. He planted several dozen churches. He fearlessly applied God's love and grace to the non-Jewish world, and was hounded for his faithfulness by those who should have cheered him on. The one who once persecuted Jesus Christ became the one who spent the rest of his days promoting Christ.

Fortunately, Paul has given us an idea of the treatment he received as part and parcel of his work as an evangelist in the ancient world. While the following list of highlights may make us shudder at the cost paid by God's servant, it also serves as an indicator of the common experiences of those who followed Jesus. They risked everything for the good news.

The salvation we have Jesus bought for us on the cross—a price beyond measure. The faith we claim has been delivered to us by many willing to pay the price of faithfulness.

Five times I received at the hands of the Jews the forty lashes less one. Three times I was beaten with rods. Once I was stoned. Three times I was shipwrecked; a night and a day I was adrift at sea; on frequent journeys, in danger from rivers, danger from robbers, danger from my own people, danger from Gentiles, danger in the city, danger in the wilderness, danger at sea, danger from false brothers; in toil and hardship, through many a sleepless night, in hunger and thirst, often without food, in cold and exposure. And, apart from other things, there is the daily pressure on me of my anxiety for all the churches (2 Corinthians 11:24-28).

We miss a significant lesson from Paul's life if we make suffering our goal. Suffering is not an accurate measurement of obedience or faithfulness. Disobedience and faithlessness can also bring suffering. When suffering becomes a goal, pride is often the hidden motivation. Suffering is an unpredictable byproduct of obedience and faithfulness. But it's only a small part of an even greater unpredictable aspect of life in Christ—joy! The example of the great martyrs of the faith is one of joyful, carefree living.

They didn't relish suffering, but they didn't run from it either. They learned, as did Paul, the principle of radical contentment:

Not that I am speaking of being in need, for I have learned in whatever situation I am to be content. I know how to be brought low, and I know how to abound. In any and every circumstance, I have learned the secret of facing plenty and hunger, abundance and need. I can do all things through him who strengthens me (Philippians 4:11-13).

Paul let nothing but God's Spirit hinder him from going to the ends of the earth. The timeline of his life, stories from tradition, and references in Scripture to places, such as his desire to minister in Spain (Romans 15:23-24), allow us to consider that the range of his travels took him from Arabia to the British Isles. The six years of silence between his two Roman imprisonments provide room for wide travels.

The apostle's final destination this side of eternity was a spot on the Ostian Way just outside the walls of Rome. Tradition has it that the former Pharisee was beheaded beyond the gates. He fought the good fight, finished the race, and kept the faith. He is a significant reasons why we can do the same today.

Matthias
(AD 70)

atthias was the alternate apostle. He was chosen to fill the vacancy among the Twelve created by Judas's betrayal and abrupt departure (Acts 1:23-26). Based on the requirement that each of the candidates had to meet—a long association with Jesus as a disciple—it is almost certain that Matthias was one of the seventy evangelists the Lord sent out (Luke 10:1). He was a witness to the full scope of Jesus's ministry.

After his appointment in the first chapter of Acts, Matthias is not mentioned by name again in the New Testament. But neither are most of the original twelve disciples. Luke based his account in Acts of the development of the early church primarily on the ministry of Peter and then Paul.

For Matthias's role, we rely on the general participation by the Twelve in the affairs of the church in Jerusalem, and we also turn to the various accounts from tradition that include Matthias. As one of the apostles, he was under the public pressure of persecution that broke out when Saul and others decided they needed to stamp out the followers of Jesus.

Matthias was one of those apostles whose missionary assignment took him north. Even Sebastopol (present day Sevastopol) on the northern side of the Black Sea is frequently mentioned as one of his destinations. Eventually, Matthias appears to have made his way back to Jerusalem, where he was stoned to death. Some say he would not sacrifice to the god Jupiter. Others state he was to be hung on a cross, stoned, and then beheaded with an axe for the blasphemy he had committed against God, Moses, and the Law. When Matthias would not deny Christ, he is believed to have said, "Thy blood be upon thy head, for thine own mouth hath spoken against thee."

Andrew
(AD 70)

Undoubtedly with his brother Simon's permission, Andrew temporarily left the fishing nets behind and journeyed to hear a man called John the Baptist. John was the talk of the town and wharf. He urged people to get right with God because the long-awaited Savior was coming. Andrew saw and heard something in John that he liked. This wild man was not only a scathing critic of society's flaws, but he also offered people hope through repentance. He had a knack for making people feel very bad before he showed them how they could be forgiven. So Andrew became a follower of John the Baptist. Eventually, he was likely joined by his friend John, the son of Zebedee, who recorded the initial steps Jesus took in choosing a group of disciples to train. At some point, at least five of the original apostles were in the area where John the Baptist was carrying out his ministry.

According to the biblical account, Andrew was the first of the apostolic band to discover Jesus in his unique role as Lamb of God who takes away the sin of the world. Andrew was standing beside John the Baptist when the fiery prophet pointed out Jesus as the One he had come to announce. We don't know if Andrew witnessed Jesus's baptism, but John the Baptist probably identified Jesus, who had just returned from His forty-day wilderness experience that had immediately followed His baptism.

Andrew and his unnamed companion (probably John) approached Jesus. Jesus invited them to spend time with Him. They immediately broadened that invitation to include Simon. Within a couple of days, both Philip and Nathanael joined that small group of seekers. They were with Jesus when He returned to Cana for a wedding, witnessing Jesus's first miracle. Not long after this, Jesus called Simon and Andrew to leave their nets and follow Him. Andrew never looked back.

Andrew took time for individual people. He noticed their needs and qualities and understood them. He quietly took action. He connected people with each other. He connected them with Christ. He introduced his big brother to Jesus. He was instrumental in other significant introductions, making an impact in people's lives, one by one. In the end, tradition tells us, this great quality in the first disciple got him killed.

Andrew is seldom mentioned in the accounts of Jesus's action, but he was a constant presence. His few moments in the spotlight reveal that he was always aware of what was going on and looking for ways to be helpful.

In John's account of the feeding of the five thousand (John 6:4-13), Andrew is the one who offered the quiet suggestion that he had just spoken with a lad who had five loaves and two fishes. Not much, but something! And what Jesus did with that little gift was astounding. John 12:20-26 describes a group of Greeks who wanted to meet Jesus. They singled out Philip to approach, probably because of his Greek name, but it's worth noting that Philip asked Andrew to help him make the introductions. Andrew's last appearance by name in Scripture occurs in Acts 1:13 where he is listed among the eleven disciples as they chose Matthias to replace Judas. He was doubtless present during those exciting and turbulent early years in Jerusalem, serving among the leaders of the church.

While Andrew's eventual missionary travels may have taken him as far north as Scythia (southern Russia) and included time around Ephesus with John, he likely ended up on the Greek peninsula in the city of Patras. There he began to relate to individuals and introduce them to the Savior. Among the converts was a woman named Maximilla, the wife of a high Roman official, a governor named Aegaeas, who was so angry at his wife's conversion he threatened Andrew with death by crucifixion. To this, Andrew replied, "Had I feared the death of the cross, I should not have preached the majesty and gloriousness of Christ."

Andrew was arrested and tried. Threatened, scourged, and tortured, he remained steadfast. It is said that the judge pleaded with Andrew not to cast aside his life, and the old apostle responded with equal passion, urging the judge not to cast aside his soul.

Unwilling to recant his faith in Christ, Andrew was tied to an X-shaped cross to die a slow and painful death. This particular cross is still called St. Andrew's cross. One source says that when Andrew came near it, he said, "O beloved cross! I have greatly longed for thee. I rejoice to see thee erected here. I come to thee with a peaceful conscience and with cheerfulness, desiring that I, who am a disciple of Him Who hung on the cross, may also be crucified. The nearer I come to the cross, the nearer I come to God; and the farther I am from the cross, the farther I remain from God."

Andrew hung for three days on the cross; and during this time he taught the people who stood near him, saying such things as: "I thank my Lord Jesus Christ, that He, having used me for a time as an ambassador, now permits me to have this body, that I, through a good confession, may obtain everlasting grace and mercy. Remain steadfast in the word and doctrine which you have received, instructing one another, that you may dwell with God in eternity, and receive the fruit of His promises." Only Heaven will reveal the thousands upon thousands of lives that were eventually transformed by Andrew's quiet and persistent work behind the scenes, touching one life at a time.

Precious in the sight of the Lord is the death of His saints.

Psalm 116:15

JUDAS / THADDAEUS
(ca. AD 70)

A t least three men named Judas had prominent roles surrounding Jesus. Two were disciples Jesus chose: Judas from Iscariot and Judas/Thaddaeus, son of James. The third was Jesus's half-brother, Judas, who did not believe in Christ until after the resurrection. This half-brother of Jesus wrote the letter that bears his name, Jude, in the New Testament. Our subject here is the faithful disciple Judas, also known as Thaddaeus.

Even the gospel writers sensed the need to indicate when they were talking about Judas the betrayer of Jesus or Judas the faithful disciple. Both disciples named Judas died violent deaths: the first by his own hand out of remorse (Matthew 27:3-10; Acts 1:18-20), and the second by the hands of others to whom he was carrying out Jesus's command to spread the Gospel to the world.

Although we can be sure that Judas/Thaddaeus was present through-out the Gospel accounts when the disciples are mentioned, he rarely appears on his own. John's gospel records a poignant question Judas asked: "Judas (not Iscariot) said to him, 'Lord, how is it that you will manifest yourself to us, and not to the world?' " (John 14:22). In that comment we catch a glimpse of difficulties the disciples had in grasping Jesus's purposes. Their problem wasn't that they didn't believe He was the Son of God; it was their mistaken expectations of what the Son of God would do in the world. Judas's question was basically, "How can you rule the world and not show yourself to the world?" Jesus's response made it clear again that His kingdom was not of this world: "If anyone loves me, he will keep my word, and my Father will love him, and we will come to him and make our home with him" (John 14:23).

The Great Commission in both its versions (Matthew 28:19-20 and Acts 1:8) includes the command to take the Gospel to the world. The kingdom would be global, but personal, lived out in the hearts and lives of individual men and women. Jesus gave them a monumental task and equipped them with power and understanding. At the core of their understanding of their mission was the fact that the way would not be easy. They could expect to receive the same kind of welcome their Master received. Jesus promised them victory and suffering.

The traditional accounts of Judas's ministry have him preaching north and east of Jerusalem, even as far as India. Like fellow disciple Bartholomew, Judas has a strong historic bond with Christianity in Armenia, an ancient land between the Black and Caspian Seas, spilling down into what we now call eastern Turkey. Armenia has long been recognized as the first Christian nation, based on early evangelization and the "official" declaration by the state designating itself a nation for Christ in the fourth century. But the source of that early influence for Christ goes back to Judas and then Bartholomew. Judas/Thaddaeus arrived first and carried on a ministry that lasted eight years. He was executed as a martyr with arrows or a javelin sometime around AD 70. The specific events surrounding his death are not known, but the Gospel frequently generated both faith and resistance in new lands. And when the message could not be killed, the messengers often were.

One story may explain the original reason behind Judas's journey to Armenia so soon after the resurrection. The following events have not been historically confirmed, but they provoke all kinds of curiosity about the way information traveled in the first century. According to an account recorded by a bishop and early church historian named Eusebius, news about Jesus reached as far as the kingdom of Edessa in eastern Armenia. The king, Abgar, sent a letter to Jesus, offering asylum and a more receptive audience than He was having among his own people. Abgar was also hoping Jesus could heal him from a disease. Jesus replied that though His responsibilities required Him to stay in Israel until God's plan had been fulfilled, He would arrange to send a personal emissary, one of His disciples, soon after He returned to Heaven. Tradition identifies that messenger as Judas.

Stories that come from the "silences" in the gospels or the rest of the New Testament are not inspired as are the Scriptures, but they do lead us to appreciate and pay attention to the Bible in new ways. Did Jesus receive and respond to correspondence? We have no specific examples in God's Word, but it's not difficult to imagine that such things occurred. They were simply too numerous for special attention or not considered central to the account. The ripples of good news that began in the sea of humanity with Jesus's resurrection certainly did spread a long way in every direction. And perhaps the news spread quite widely even during Jesus's lifetime. Only Heaven will reveal the extent of the original surge and the full adventures of those who first carried the Gospel to the ends of the earth.

FOR IT HAS BEEN GRANTED TO YOU THAT FOR THE SAKE OF CHRIST YOU SHOULD NOT ONLY BELIEVE IN HIM BUT ALSO SUFFER FOR HIS SAKE.

PHILIPPIANS 1:29

BARTHOLOMEW / NATHANAEL
(ca. AD 70)

artholomew came as a reluctant seeker, brought to Jesus by
Philip, who couldn't wait to spread the word about the Messiah.
Bartholomew's initial response to news about Jesus was a mixture of skepticism and sarcasm: "Can anything good come out of Nazareth?" (John 1:46).

As he had done the day before when meeting Simon, Jesus greeted Bartholomew with perceptive and challenging words. Jesus immediately let Bartholomew know that He really understood him. Imagine a person greeting you with, "Behold, an Israelite indeed, in whom there is no deceit!" (John 1:47).

Bartholomew was stunned. "How do You know me?" he blurted. Jesus had just identified his central impulse. He didn't feel complimented; he felt completely known. He was curious about how Jesus did it; to which Jesus responded with a description of Bartholomew's location when Philip found him. Jesus's perception was enough to convince Bartholomew that Philip was correct. This was in fact the Promised One. And he said so: "Rabbi, You are the Son of God! You are the King of Israel!" (John 1:49). Jesus received Bartholomew's declaration with the promise that he would eventually have many more reasons for recognizing the Son of God.

Bartholomew was one of the group of five apostles who began to follow Jesus shortly after His wilderness experience. He joined Andrew, John, Simon, and Philip in a movement away from John the Baptist toward becoming followers of Jesus. We know him under two names: Bartholomew and Nathanael. He is mentioned in the naming of the Twelve (Matthew 10, Mark 3, and Luke 6) as Bartholomew, and as Nathanael one other time as part of the group of seven disciples who went fishing after Jesus's resurrection and then had breakfast with Him on shore (John 21:2). Bartholomew is not credited with any words or actions throughout the gospel accounts of Jesus's ministry. He was simply there—watching, listening, and following. With someone around like Simon Peter, always eager to leap into the verbal breach, men like Bartholomew were content to observe and learn.

The apostolic career of Bartholomew is linked with that of the apostle Judas / Thaddaeus. Both are credited with the spread of Christianity into Armenia. Traditions have him traveling east, as far as regions called India, but the historical consensus locates his ministry and martyrdom in Armenia—a land to the northeast of Palestine, between the Black and Caspian Seas.

As has been demonstrated repeatedly during the worldwide spread of the Gospel, those who bring the message of Christ often lose their lives as a direct result of their effectiveness. Even while living peaceably and doing good, believers have often been cruelly persecuted. The mixed response by the world often parallels the response Jesus received in His own time. Some who hear the message simply decide they would have to give up too much in order to acknowledge Christ; they decide instead to eliminate His messengers.

We may long to equate faithfulness with safety and success, but there's little reason for us to do so. Some of Christ's most effective and faithful servants have suffered the same fate as their Master, being despised and rejected by the very people whom they approached with good news.

Under Bartholomew's influence, the Gospel apparently penetrated every facet of Armenian life except the stronghold of local pagan religious leaders, who rightly perceived Christianity as anathema to their belief systems and demonically energized practices. Their powers were no match for the power of God exercised by Thaddaeus and Bartholomew. Their idols were proven impotent. Believers from royal rank on down began to worship Jesus and the God of the Bible. Many were baptized, and the church grew by leaps and bounds.

Meanwhile, the pagan priests conspired with the king's brother to protect their power and system of beliefs. Underhanded maneuvers led to Bartholomew's arrest and torture. He suffered flaying, a particularly gruesome form of abuse in which a person's skin is almost entirely removed by the use of whips. He was then crucified in agony (some accounts say head down) and allowed to die a martyr's death for Christ.

One of the startling historic witnesses to the effectiveness of Bartholomew's ministry in Armenia is the obvious link between the Holy Land and Armenian tradition. Pilgrimages to the lands of the Bible became popular even in the apostolic era. Many of the biblical sites in the Holy Land are even today marked by shrines and churches constructed by Armenian believers many centuries ago.

BLESSED ARE THOSE WHO ARE

PERSECUTED FOR RIGHTEOUSNESS'

SAKE, FOR THEIRS IS THE KINGDOM

OF HEAVEN.

MATTHEW 5:10

THOMAS
(CA. AD 70)

With the exception of Peter and Paul, we have more information on the subsequent life of Thomas than on any of the other apostles. Most of the material comes from tradition. For a disciple with a doubtful reputation, he certainly left behind a variety of regions that name him among the founders of their ancient traditions of faith.

The account in John's gospel gives us the most glimpses of Thomas, but they come within the last few weeks of Jesus's ministry. Apparently his character traits became more obvious under the growing pressure of opposition. Keenly aware of the danger waiting for Jesus in Jerusalem, Thomas voiced the outlook that must have been on all their minds when he said, "Let us also go, that we may die with him" (John 11:16). Perhaps more clearly than the other disciples, Thomas thought that if their hopes of a kingdom with Jesus as the leader fell through, death would result. Jesus's frequent references to His death may have confused some of the disciples, but they seem to have unsettled Thomas.

Our next glimpse of Thomas comes during the Last Supper when he reacts to Jesus's comforting words about His Father's house. Thomas reveals that his heart is indeed troubled when he blurts out, "Lord, we do not know where You are going. How can we know the way?" (John 14:5). We can be grateful for Thomas's boldness, for it allowed Jesus to make one of His clearest claims about His role as Lord and Savior: "I am the way, and the truth, and the life. No one comes to the Father except through me" (John 14:6).

Thomas's third outburst came the evening of Resurrection Sunday (or very early on Monday). Jesus had appeared to ten of the disciples on Sunday evening, with Thomas as the only absentee. Perhaps he was reacting differently than the rest of the disciples to the news that Jesus had arisen. They gathered, but Thomas stayed away. When informed of Jesus's visit, Thomas responded with daring doubts:

> So the other disciples told him, "We have seen the Lord." But he said to them, "Unless I see in his hands the mark of the nails, and place my finger into the mark of the nails, and place my hand into his side, I will never believe" (John 20:25).

A week later, that dare was met. Jesus appeared before all of them, and Thomas's doubts vaporized as he declared, "My Lord and my God!" (John 20:28). Jesus used the occasion to make another crucial point about the nature of faith: "Have you believed because you have seen me? Blessed are those who have not seen and yet have believed" (John 20:29).

The passion Jesus awakened in His disciples drove them out to bless thousands who would not have the privilege of seeing, but would believe the testimony of those gladly willing to lay down their lives for their convictions. Once Thomas left Jerusalem, there's no evidence that he ever returned. He left his doubts behind. He headed for the ends of the earth. He undoubtedly found that Jesus was true to His promise of companionship to the end.

Thomas traveled north and east from Israel, passing through Babylon and Persia and making an impact for the Gospel as far as the southern regions of India. Longstanding traditions about his journeys far beyond the boundaries of Roman control remain even today. Many of the places and kings associated with Thomas that were thought to be merely legendary have been confirmed by independent historical and archeological studies. Undeniably, developed civilizations lay beyond the horizon to the east, and Jesus's words, "to the ends of the earth," must have constantly echoed in the apostles' minds. The trade routes he would have used have existed for thousands of years. Portuguese mariners and explorers in the sixteenth century reported evidence of Thomas's ministry, including a sizeable band of believers known as the St. Thomas Christians. The fact that Thomas has been so uniquely connected with India among the apostles makes a strong case for his ministry there.

Various versions of Thomas's martyrdom agree that he ran afoul of the Hindu priests who envied his successes and rejected his message. Thomas was speared to death. The location of his tomb can still be visited in Mylapore (Meliapore), India.

The apostle Thomas was tortured by the natives in Calamina, thrown into an oven, and stuck through with spears, AD 70.

SIMON THE ZEALOT
(AD 74)

S imon may have been the most volatile among the disciples. All of them had histories; Simon may have been a wanted man. He joined the followers of Jesus with a reputation as a Zealot. He was connected with a loosely organized resistance against Rome that today the Romans would have called terrorists. What an odd and remarkable mix! Alongside fishermen and workingmen, Jesus chose two men at the opposite ends of the spectrum: Matthew and Simon. As a tax collector, Matthew represented those who had apparently sold out to Rome and were collaborating with the enemy. As a Canaanite Zealot, Simon represented angry and frustrated Jews who were willing to kill even their own countrymen in their efforts to harass the Romans. Simon's original motive for following Jesus may have been mixed. Jesus's miracles and methods were not violent, and the people flocked to Him. Perhaps Simon felt, as most of the disciples felt in one way or another, that Jesus would usher in a kingdom and would usher out the Romans.

Other than his place in the lists the gospel writers provide, Simon isn't singled out by word or deed. As a person used to operating under cover, his inclination would have been to avoid the spotlight, even among the disciples. He watched, learned, and was gradually transformed. Interestingly, of all the disciples whose background might have led them to lash out at the guards who came to arrest Jesus, Simon is the most obvious candidate. But Peter, the impulsive fisherman, was the one who took a swipe with a blade.

The Acts of the Apostles by Luke mainly highlights the ministry of Peter and Paul, with some attention given to the contributions of other apostles and deacons along the way. Our evidence for the journeys and actions of the other apostles comes primarily from tradition. We do know that Christianity spread like wildfire during the first century. Someone had to deliver the message in a compelling way. We know that the Pax

Romana (the peace of the Roman Empire's control and infrastructure) allowed for extensive and relatively easy travel (by the standards of that day). The apostle Paul certainly traveled thousands of miles on his missionary journeys. Why not the other apostles?

The traditional account of Simon's missionary journeys has him taking the road less traveled. He went south and west from Jerusalem, crossing the full breadth of northern Africa, passing through Egypt, Libya, and Mauritania, and then up through Spain and even into the islands we now call Britain. All of these destinations fell within the boundaries of the Roman Empire. Subsequent flourishing Christian communities in far-flung places such as Carthage and Alexandria require some explanation. The grand international evangelistic explosion that occurred at Pentecost in Acts 2 may partly explain the way God's Spirit prepared the mission fields, but the apostolic follow-up best explains the wide and vibrant spread of Christianity. Another factor to consider is the presence of Jewish exiles in every direction from Jerusalem. If Paul's approach gives us a clue, those Jewish synagogues in exotic locations provided a foothold for the Gospel, for the apostles brought the good news that the long-awaited Messiah had come!

Later we pick up Simon back in the Middle East doing missionary work north and east from Jerusalem with Judas, taking the Gospel as far as Persia. Tradition has it that Simon was crucified upside down and then sawn in half.

The vivid descriptions of persecution that conclude Hebrews 11, the "roll call of faith," may well have been written with abundant examples of then-current martyrs on the writer's mind. Those verses read as an accurate sample of the suffering experienced by the followers of Jesus:

> Women received back their dead by resurrection. Some were tortured, refusing to accept release, so that they might rise again to a better life. Others suffered mocking and flogging, and even chains and imprisonment. They were stoned, they were sawn in two, they were killed with the sword. They went

about in skins of sheep and goats, destitute, afflicted, mistreated—of whom the world was not worthy—wandering about in deserts and mountains, and in dens and caves of the earth (Hebrews 11:35-38).

"Let goods and kindred go,

this mortal life also;

the body they may kill:

God's truth abideth still;

His kingdom is forever!"

—From Martin Luther's hymn "A Mighty Fortress"

Luke the evangelist hanged from an olive tree in Greece, AD 93

LUKE

(AD 93)

L uke was the official historian of the early days of the church. His account parallels the other acknowledged biographies of Jesus: Matthew, Mark, and John. We have confirmation in extra-biblical sources such as Josephus. But when it comes to the historical record, the two-volume effort called Luke-Acts gives us a carefully compiled, continuous record of Jesus's life and the immediate results of His ministry on earth.

Although Luke was not a member of the inner apostolic band, he had access to many of those individuals. In the introductory paragraphs for the Gospel of Luke and of Acts of the Apostles, Luke outlines his approach to writing: "[I]t seemed good to me also, having followed all things closely for some time past, to write an orderly account for you, most excellent Theophilus, that you may have certainty concerning the things you have been taught" (Luke 1:3-4). The intimate information that Luke includes about the birth of Jesus in chapters 1 and 2 of his gospel has the tone of an eyewitness account. In this particular case, the obvious eyewitness would have been Mary. All the things she treasured in her heart for a lifetime she recalled and shared with the gentle physician who had so many questions.

One of the characteristics of Acts involves what has come to be known as the "we" sections. When Luke narrates events of Paul's travels, he sometimes uses "we" as a subtle indicator that he was a participant. (If this is correct, then Luke first joined Paul's missionary band in Troas.) Paul calls Luke the "beloved physician" (Colossians 4:14). Having a doctor on the team would have been a real benefit. During their travels, Luke must have served as a medic for the group, not only tending to Paul's longstanding illness but also mending the occasional abrasion and contusion resulting from the beatings, stonings, and other assorted violent treatment received by those who preached the good news. Since

Luke was an assistant and keeper of the record rather than a public speaker, he may have been spared some of the harsher handling his companions suffered.

Luke, however, clearly experienced his own share of suffering for Jesus's sake. He accompanied Paul on the final journey from Caesarea to Rome.

The time of the year made a normally perilous trip even more hazardous. Describing the desperate struggle for survival by the crew of their ship as they were driven by hurricane winds (Acts 27), Luke included the details of an eyewitness and the detachment of a survivor. That two-week ordeal tested every participant. After the shipwreck on Malta, with his physician eyes Luke describes two incidents that caught his attention. Paul was bitten by a venomous serpent and escaped unharmed, creating quite a stir among the islanders. Also, he diagnosed the illness of an important man on the island as "fever and dysentery." But God provided healing through Paul's prayer. Out of that disaster came many opportunities to preach the Gospel to a new audience. The suffering had an immediate purpose.

Tradition disagrees over the manner of Luke's death. By some accounts, Luke was with Paul until the end in Rome and then carried on an extensive ministry of his own. By that account, Luke died as an old man in a place called Boeotia (which may have been a region in ancient Greece). But given the violence of the time in which he lived, the traditional echoes that point to Luke's martyrdom somewhere in Greece cannot be ignored. The beloved physician certainly brought about by his writing the healing of many more souls than he ever touched in his lifetime.

FOR TO ME TO LIVE IS CHRIST, AND TO DIE IS GAIN.

PHILIPPIANS 1:21

Jᴏʜɴ
(ᴄᴀ. ᴀᴅ 98)

U nlike his apostolic companions, John died quietly in the city of Ephesus, serving the church he loved. But he didn't live a quiet life. By the time he died, John had been part of the twelve disciples of Jesus, participated in the early life of the church in Jerusalem, traveled widely, and had written five New Testament books (the Gospel of John, the letters 1 John, 2 John, 3 John, and Revelation). John certainly had an impressive resume of accomplishments, but he would probably have been the first to point out that anything he had done in life paled in comparison to what Jesus did for him. John's character résumé tells us a lot about the ways Jesus changes a person's life.

The fact that John survived the other apostles points to the kind of unique suffering he endured. All of the other disciples suffered and died; John suffered and lived. Though not technically a martyr, John's life displayed a martyr's qualities. He was a living sacrifice worthy of imitation. And as we shall see, he only escaped actual martyrdom by God's intervention on several occasions.

John and his brother James were two of the more fiery members of Jesus's disciples. Artistic renditions and personal impressions often create a distorted picture of John. Yes, he was the disciple Jesus loved, but that didn't mean that he was particularly lovable. He was more likely a typical fisherman of his time: rough cut, hardworking, brash, and short on social graces. Jesus called John and his brother "Sons of Thunder," which was probably more a term of endearment than a compliment. Mark reports that special name early in his gospel (3:17), indicating that their character traits were obvious from the beginning. They certainly lived up to that nickname.

On one occasion, after Peter, James, and John saw Jesus transfigured on the mountain, a revealing argument broke out among the disciples over their internal pecking order: Who was the greatest? After Jesus disarmed

that argument, John reported that he and the others had confronted someone who was casting out demons in Jesus's name. They had told that man
to stop "because he does not follow with us" (Luke 9:49). If John expected
Jesus's approval, he was taken aback by Jesus's insistence that others should
be encouraged to make use of the power in Jesus's name.

But the jockeying for power and prestige were not over. Luke immediately describes the final journey to Jerusalem and an incident in
Samaria in a town where Jesus was not welcomed. John and James, eager
to flex what they might have considered heightened authority among the
Lord's followers, volunteered to take action: "Lord, do you want us to
tell fire to come down from heaven and consume them?" (Luke 9:54).
We are simply told that Jesus "turned and rebuked" them for this suggestion, raising the possibility that Jesus said nothing, but turned so they
could see his face. The look may have been a more devastating rebuke
than words. The process of discipleship Jesus practiced with the first
disciples was painstaking and time-consuming. And it continued
throughout the apostles' lives.

John learned to love the hard way. When he consistently leaves his
name out of his gospel but describes himself as the disciple Jesus loved (John
13:23), he's revealing what transformed him from a son of thunder to a son
of love. Jesus loved him. John never lost his hunger for truth. Even a casual
reading of his gospel and the three letters of John gives the impression that
the writer was a champion for truth. But an even greater impression arises
in John's writings that he was a man of love. Ancient witnesses like Eusebius
record that by the end of his life, John had simplified his message to one
gentle command: "Children, love one another." Apparently, whenever he
was asked to speak or comment, that was his chosen statement. When asked
about it, he responded that everything else necessary would be taken care
of if that one command were faithfully carried out.

That simple but profound message still describes the difference
between authentic discipleship and inconsistent following of Jesus. Since
the beginning, believers haven't been persecuted and killed just because
they held a set of beliefs. Their lives have provoked reactions. The

darkness has violently resisted and tried to destroy Christ's followers because of the awesome power that love brings into any human situation. The message of the God Who loves and Who changes people into genuine lovers represents everything the darkness abhors.

John certainly did not live a long life unscathed by pain and suffering. His emotional trials must have been considerable. He lived during times in which those who killed or abused Christians had nothing to fear from the law. In fact, they were sometimes carrying out the law. The painful death of friend after friend must have taken a heavy toll on him. Tradition holds that on one occasion, John was scheduled for boiling in oil. He escaped by divine intervention. His exile on Patmos easily could have been a death sentence. When Emperor Domitian, who had exiled him to Patmos, had died, John was brought back to Ephesus, where he was confined for two years. It is written that he was compelled to drink poison but was unharmed, and finally died in peace.

The apostle John

PART TWO

Martyrs

from the

Second

Century

to the

Twentieth

Century

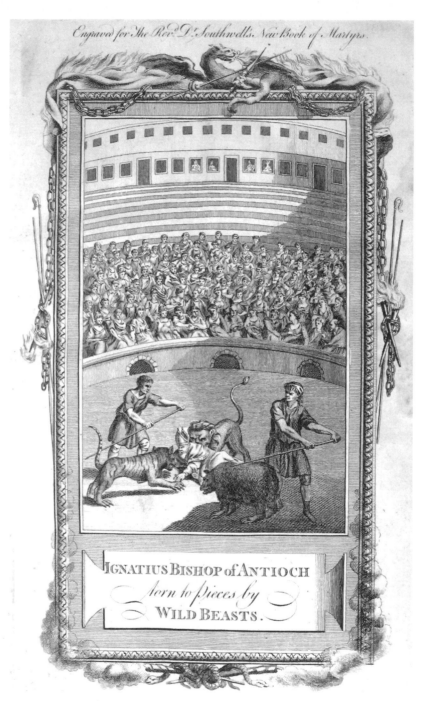

Ignatius of Antioch torn to pieces by wild beasts

Persecution

under the

Roman Empire

(AD 107-404)

Around the time of Jesus's birth, the government of the Roman
Empire changed. The older republican constitution was
exchanged for the principate, an innovation introduced by Gaius
Octavius, the adopted son of Julius Caesar. Octavius became the first
principate, ruling as Augustus (from which we get the name of our eighth
month) from 27 BC to AD 14. The principate was a lifelong appointment,
and while this person was still subject to the constitution and cooperated
with the Senate, the principate had broad powers that could easily turn
into tyranny, as happened in Nero's reign around AD 64.

Rome burned in AD 64, and Christians were blamed. Until then,
Christians had enjoyed the same privileges as Jews, who were permitted
to worship even though their monotheism challenged the cult of Roman
religion. When Paul began building churches among non-Jewish popula-
tions of Asia Minor, however, Rome felt the threat of this religion as a
challenge to its hegemony. Nero killed many Christians, including Paul.

The next great persecution came under Emperor Decius in 249-251.
Rome had lost territories, population, and power. Decius determined to

regain Rome's eminence by prohibiting cults that refused to worship the emperor. A short period of calm followed; then Valerius (257) resumed state persecution of Christians. Despite this, by the end of the third century, the majority of the residents of some areas controlled by Rome were Christian converts. The high cost of following Christ was more to be treasured than the Roman sword.

Early in the fourth century, Diocletian started the last great persecution (303), a response to the growing popularity of the faith—even among leaders and intellectuals—that centered on the Jewish rabbi named Jesus, who had been put to death in Judea centuries earlier. For eight years the church suffered a tough enforcement of Roman religious law, until the Edict of Milan (311) granted toleration to all religions. In 312, Constantine, with the cross of Christ on the battle shields, defeated Maxentius at the battle of the Milvian Bridge. In 324, Constantine became sole ruler of the empire. He encouraged the spread of Christianity and was himself baptized shortly before his death in 337. With his support, the faith took hold, and then the towering figure of Augustine (354-430) gave Christians their most elegant spokesman and convert. Christians still suffered, but mostly on the frontiers where barbarians threatened the once-mighty Roman legions. Within the empire itself, the church grew and official persecutions ended.

"NOW I BEGIN TO BE A DISCIPLE. COME FIRE AND CROSS AND GRAPPLINGS WITH WILD BEASTS, THE RENDING OF MY BONES AND BODY... ONLY LET IT BE MINE TO ATTAIN JESUS CHRIST."

—IGNATIUS OF ANTIOCH

İGПАТİUS OF AПТİOCH
(CA. AD 30-CA. 107)

◆

I hope indeed, by your prayers, to have the good fortune to fight with wild beasts in Rome," wrote Bishop Ignatius on his journey from Antioch in Syria to the Roman Empire's capital city. Around seventy years old at the time, Ignatius was one of the "post-apostolic fathers"— the generation of leaders who had been mentored in the faith by the apostles themselves; Ignatius was likely mentored by John. It is also believed that his appointment as a bishop came from Peter. Legend suggests that Ignatius was the child blessed by Jesus in Matthew 19.

After his trial and condemnation, Ignatius wrote seven letters while he traveled to his martyrdom in the Coliseum, sometime during Emperor Trajan's reign (98-117). Under military guard between Philadelphia and Troas, Ignatius was welcomed at Smyrna by fellow bishop Polycarp. There he wrote the first four letters. Later, he addressed two letters to two churches and one personal note to Polycarp.

Ignatius adopted the name Theophorus, which means "God-bearer" or "God-inspired." He wrote with a focus on Christ and the unity of the church—themes he sounded before the trial court where he faced trumped-up charges of disloyalty to Rome for failing to bow to the pagan deities. Like all Christian leaders of that era, Ignatius's treason was easy to prove. Officials had only to listen to the bishop preach, or ask him a simple question about whom he followed, or speak with the growing band of Christians to realize that a new and powerful spiritual movement was underway whose followers could never again offer Rome ultimate loyalty. For Ignatius, the heart now belonged to the triune God, and he seemed gladly to accept the punishment of the court for his crimes of faith and devotion. Readers today hear echoes of Paul's writing as Ignatius begins his letters:

Heartiest greetings of pure joy in Jesus Christ...Out of the fullness of God the Father you have been blessed with large

numbers and are predestined from eternity to enjoy forever
continual and unfading glory. The source of your unity and
election is genuine suffering, which you undergo by the will
of the Father and of Jesus Christ, our God.

Ignatius believed the "last days" had arrived. Whether he lived or
died meant little to him. Ignatius delighted in his journey to Rome,
calling it a victory, not a death march. He urged believers to "keep on
praying" and to "gather together more frequently to celebrate God's
Communion and to praise Him." In such devotion "Satan's powers
are overthrown."

Bishop Ignatius knew nothing of the wealth and power later bishops
would enjoy. In his era, a bishop was more likely to be the leader of a
single congregation rather than the head of a diocese in a well-organized
hierarchy, into which the position later expanded. Thoroughly devoted
to Christ, Ignatius was part of that great generation who taught and built
the church, buried the apostles, collected their writings, stood before the
emperor's psychotic wrath, and fought heretics and swindlers infiltrating
the movement.

Their church fathers and grandfathers had told these leaders about
the great silence of God, but Ignatius knew the "Son, Jesus Christ, who
is the Word issuing from the silence…our perpetual Life." He followed
this Word-Made-Flesh until his own flesh was torn by lions. On his way
to Rome, the old man wrote to the churches: "You deserve to be happy
in God's good news of salvation," and by every account, Ignatius was.

"Now I begin to be a disciple. I care for nothing of visible or invisible
things so that I may but win Christ. Come fire and cross and grapplings
with wild beasts, the rending of my bones and body…only let it be mine
to attain Jesus Christ."

POLYCARP OF SMYRNA
(CA. AD 70–155)

An elderly man in his eighties sat at a table eating dinner, Polycarp knew his life was in danger. A group of Christians had just been executed in the arena on account of their faith. But Polycarp refused to leave Rome. The Romans were executing any self-proclaimed Christians, and pagans were betraying those they knew to be followers of the Way. After the recent executions, the crowd in the arena had chanted for Polycarp's death.

A renowned follower of Christ and bishop of Smyrna, Polycarp had become a Christian under the tutelage of John the apostle. Recently, the Roman proconsul had been looking for him for days. After arresting and torturing one of Polycarp's servants, they finally learned where he was staying. The soldiers came into the house, but instead of fleeing, Polycarp calmly stated, "God's will be done."

Polycarp asked that food be brought for the soldiers, and he requested an hour for prayer. Amazed by Polycarp's fearlessness, especially for a man his age, the hardened Roman soldiers granted his request. He prayed for two hours for all the Christians he knew and for the universal church, and the soldiers let him.

As Polycarp entered the stadium, several Christians present heard a voice from Heaven say, "Be strong, Polycarp, and act like a man." Because of his age, the Roman proconsul gave Polycarp a final chance to live. He just had to swear by Caesar and say, "Take away the atheists" (at that time Christians were called atheists for refusing to worship the Greek and Roman gods). Polycarp looked at the roaring crowds, gestured to them, and proclaimed, "Take away the atheists!"

The proconsul continued, "Swear, and I will let you go. Reproach Christ!"

Polycarp turned to the proconsul and boldly declared, "Eighty-six years I have served Him, and He has done me no wrong. How can I blaspheme my King Who saved me?"

The proconsul urged him again, "Swear by the Fortune of Caesar."

But Polycarp replied, "Since you vainly think that I will swear by the Fortune of Caesar, as you say, and pretend not to know who I am, listen carefully: I am a Christian!"

The proconsul threatened, "I have wild beasts. I will throw you to them, if you do not repent."

Polycarp replied, "Call them! For we cannot 'repent' from what is better to what is worse; but it is noble to turn from what is evil to what is righteous."

Then the proconsul threatened Polycarp with fire, but he responded: "You threaten me with a fire that burns an hour and is soon quenched, for you are ignorant of the fire of the coming judgment and eternal punishment stored up for the ungodly. But why do you delay? Do what you want."

Finally, the proconsul sent a herald to the middle of the stadium to announce that Polycarp was confessing his faith as a Christian. The crowd shouted for Philip the Asiarch to send a lion against Polycarp, but he refused. Then they shouted for Polycarp to be burned. They moved him to the marketplace and prepared the pyre. Polycarp undressed and climbed up. But when they were going to nail him, he told them, "Leave me like this. He who gives me to endure the fire will also give me to remain on the pyre without your security from the nails." So they did not nail him but tied him up. Bravely, Polycarp prayed as the soldiers prepared the wood:

> O Lord God almighty, Father of Your beloved and blessed Son Jesus Christ, through whom we have received knowledge of You, God of angels and powers and all creation, and of the whole race of the righteous who live before You, I bless You that You considered me worthy of this day and hour, to receive a part in the number of the martyrs in the cup of Your Christ, for the resurrection to eternal life both of soul and of body in the incorruptibility of the Holy Spirit. Among them may I be welcomed before You today by a fat and acceptable sacrifice, just as you previously prepared and made known

and You fulfilled, the deceitless and true God. Because of this, and for all things, I praise You, I bless You, I glorify You, through the eternal and heavenly high priest Jesus Christ, Your beloved Son, through whom be glory to You with Him and the Holy Spirit both now and for ages to come. Amen.

The Romans had threatened Polycarp with beasts and with fire, but nothing would make him turn against Christ. After his prayer, the men lit the pyre, which sprang up quickly. But even the fire wouldn't touch him as it formed an arch around Polycarp's body. The Romans didn't know what to make of this. In the end, the Romans commanded an executioner to stab him. A great quantity of blood put out the remaining fire, and Polycarp bled to death.

SO THAT THE TESTED GENUINENESS OF YOUR FAITH—MORE PRECIOUS THAN GOLD THAT PERISHES THOUGH IT IS TESTED BY FIRE—MAY BE FOUND TO RESULT IN PRAISE AND GLORY AND HONOR AT THE REVELATION OF JESUS CHRIST.

I PETER 1:7

JUSTIN MARTYR
(ca. AD 100-165)

For all his intelligence, Justin Martyr never quibbled with the prospect that he, too, would die violently at the hands of the Roman state. In his day and time, execution was more or less the expected means of passing from this life to Heaven. After all, a Roman magistrate need only order the smallest reverence toward the emperor or the pagan deities, the shortest nod of worship, and the faithful Christian, utterly refusing, was condemned. Justin might have anticipated such a fate, but he lived into old age (for his era) before the choice confronted him.

Justin was a scholar devoted to ideas, debates, and arguments—by modern standards undramatic, yet immensely significant for the early church in the decades after the apostles. Born to a pagan family living at the site of ancient Shechem in Samaria, this bright lad mastered the writings of the Stoics and the Platonists, the best minds of Rome and Greece. Unsatisfied and yearning for the peacefulness of truth, he responded to the witness of an unknown "old man," and around age thirty committed his life and mind to Jesus Christ, who alone taught "the one sure worthy philosophy."

Thereafter Justin employed his mind to spread that truth with zeal and determination. Armed with passion for God and the tools of ancient rhetoric, he debated with Jew and Gentile the merits of the Gospel, the truth of the Messiah, and the coming judgment of the one righteous and merciful God. It is often said that Justin was the first Christian thinker after Paul to grasp the universal implications of Christian faith: God's love reached to all; the resurrection of Christ was a once-for-all answer to sin's horrendous judgment.

Strong in faith and articulate in early theology, Justin did not neglect the horizontal view. He was astute and appreciative of culture, and knew, as a sociologist might today, the times and people who comprised his dynamic world.

He taught that one can find truth in the philosophies of pagans; God had given pagan philosophers a glimpse of truth through the mercy of Christ. But the glimpse was only foretaste, not substance. The pagans cannot fully find truth until they come to Christ, as Jesus is the Reason, the Logos of the universe come to earth. Justin's breadth would pave the way for other Christians to recognize the good, the true, and the beautiful in non-Christian cultural works and writings. With courage and conviction, Justin's "apology" for the faith affirmed that only Christ was Lord and refused all compromise with lesser gods.

He resented the widespread notion that Christians were traitors, immoral, weak, or rebellious. A large part of his work described the social benefits of faith. The followers of Jesus should be admired and promoted as model citizens, he told the Roman authorities. Because of faith, because of the goodness of Christ, these Christians gave the state its noblest strength. "We are in fact of all men your best helpers and allies in securing good order." But he warned, "Don't demand that they bow before falsehood."

And just that demand sealed Justin's fate after thirty-five years of teaching and preaching (he never held an official church office). Early in the reign of Marcus Aurelius, Justin and six others were arrested and brought before the prefect Rusticus. Justin was the group's spokesperson, of course; but as soon as he began his confession and defense, the prefect, obviously bored at the prospect of a sermon, made the fatal demand to renounce Christianity and bow before Caesar. Everyone refused, and Rusticus pronounced the standard brutal sentence. Soon after, Justin and his fellows were scourged and beheaded, but the truth was not silenced. "The lover of truth ought to choose in every way, even at the cost of his own life, to speak and do what is right, though death should take him away," Justin wrote at the beginning of his First Apology. "You can kill us, but cannot do us any real harm."

MARTYRS FROM SCILLIUM
(180)

◆

I t was a hot summer day in Scillium (near the ancient city of Carthage; present-day Tunis) in the Roman province of northern Africa.
Six prisoners stood before the Roman proconsul in the hall of judgment. This was their last chance before being sentenced. Saturninus, the
proconsul, addressed the prisoners: "You can have our Lord the Emper-
or's indulgence, if you come back to a sound mind."

Speratus, the spokesman for this small band, declared their innocence: "We have never done wrong, but when mistreated we give thanks,
because we listen to our Emperor."

The proconsul tried to reassure them, "We are religious, too, and
our religion is simple: We swear by the Emperor's genius, and pray for
his health, which you should do, too."

Speratus offered, "If you will lend me your ears in peace, I will
explain the mystery of simplicity."

But Saturninus angrily retorted, "When you speak evil of our sacred
rites, I will not listen. Instead, swear by the genius of our Emperor!"

The prisoner calmly responded, "I do not recognize the empire of this
world, but rather I serve that God 'whom no one has ever seen or can see'
[1 Timothy 6:16]. I have not stolen, and I pay taxes on what I buy, because
I know my Lord, the King of kings and Emperor of all nations!"

Saturninus turned to the other prisoners and said, "Cease to be of
this persuasion."

But Speratus answered again, "It is an evil persuasion to commit
homicide, or to speak false testimony."

Ignoring him, Saturninus commanded, "Do not be participants in
this madness!"

Cittinus, another prisoner, spoke up: "We have no one to fear except
our God who is in Heaven!" One of the three women prisoners, Donata,
added, "Honor to Caesar as Caesar, but fear to God." Vestia shouted

aloud, "I am a Christian!" The third woman, Secunda, confessed, "I wish to be what I am."

Saturninus asked Speratus, the spokesman, "Do you remain a Christian?" Speratus answered, "I am a Christian." And the rest of group agreed.

Then Saturninus changed tactics. "Will you have a time to consider?" But Speratus immediately answered, "There is no deliberation in so straightforward an issue."

The proconsul inquired, "What things are in your book bag?" Speratus answered, "Books and letters of Paul, a just man." The proconsul insisted, "Wait thirty days and rethink."

But Speratus insisted back, "I am a Christian!" And the rest of the group agreed.

Finally, the proconsul read the decree:

> Speratus, Nartalus, Cittinus, Donata, Vestia, Secunda, and the rest have confessed to living by the Christian rite. Since they obstinately persist, after an opportunity to return to the Roman custom, it is decided to punish them with the sword.

Speratus said, "We thank God." Nartalus echoed him, "Today we are martyrs in Heaven, thanks to God."

The proconsul commanded the herald to announce their condemnation, along with six previously condemned prisoners. The group was executed on July 17, 180. They did not fear those who kill the body but are unable to kill the soul. Having confessed Christ before men, they were confessed by Him before His Father in Heaven (Matthew 10:28, 32).

PERPETUA, FELICITY, AND BLANDINA
(203)

Perpetua bravely held Felicity in her arms, anticipating their death together as sisters in Christ. The bull's horns had already wounded Felicity, and the crowd wanted the *coup de grace*. Then, abruptly and inexplicably, the bull stood still. The crowd hushed. This animal was not following the script. Now the crowd let loose with demands for blood, and gladiators rushed forward to finish the work. Felicity died quickly. When Perpetua's executioner hesitated, she herself helped guide his blade into her body.

The Coliseum had never before seen such a spectacle. Perpetua came from a wealthy family. Her father was pagan but her mother and brothers were Christians. Perpetua had a nursing baby at the time of her arrest for confessing Christ. Her father urged her to renounce faith, for his sake and for her family. Even Roman authorities urged her to offer a simple sacrifice to Roman power. She refused. She would not renounce Christ as Lord, claiming that the name that belonged to her was the name of a Christian.

Felicity was a slave—and pregnant. Since Roman law prohibited the execution of pregnant women, sentence was delayed. Felicity gave birth in prison to a baby girl that would be adopted by Christians. When prison guards wondered how she would handle facing beasts in the arena, especially so soon after her child's birth, she responded, "Now my sufferings are only mine. But when I face the beasts there will be another who will live in me, and will suffer for me since I shall be suffering for Him."

These two women from different classes showed fortitude, determination, and, remarkably, even joy at the prospects of public humiliation and suffering. Several times they refused offers of acquittal and ignored pleas to save themselves. Together they clung to heavenly hope, and to each other, for endurance through the ordeal. Rather than acquiesce to Roman demands, they asked to be baptized while in prison. Perpetua stated, "The dungeon is to me a palace." Amazingly, when Perpetua was told beasts would devour her, she and her companions returned to prison in high spirits at the prospect of death for the glory of God. Three men imprisoned with them were forced to run the gladiator gauntlet: two were killed by beasts; one was beheaded.

As for Perpetua, she was the picture of poise in the center of chaos and blood. When the bull tossed her but did not hurt her, Perpetua's hair came undone. She asked to be allowed to put her hair up because undone hair was a sign of mourning, but this was a day for triumph and joy.

Blandina, a slave girl, was the last to die. She was hanged from a post and exposed to wild animals, but they would not attack. She was repeatedly tortured and eventually trapped in a net, trampled by a bull. All of the martyrs' bodies were left unburied and guarded by soldiers.

Such courage made a mark on the Romans. These three women and Christians had stood together and died together. Several spectators converted to Christianity as a result, including the governor of Rome.

ORİGEN
(185-254)

An early church father, Origen was one of the first textual scholars of the Bible, one of the first Bible commentators, and one of the first to write a systematic statement of faith. Yet this early genius, an Egyptian raised by Christian parents, would do his traveling and teaching between persecutions. Indeed, the persecutions of Emperors Septimus Severus (202), Caracalla (215), and Decius (250) are markers on his life.

As a teenager, Origen felt the pain of persecution when his father, Leonidas, was captured and martyred in 215. Indeed, Origen wanted to die as well, and he would have rushed to join the martyrs had not his mother hid his clothes, preventing him from leaving the house.

Origen began teaching at a local catechetical school. Many of his students were martyred and he stood by them in their trials and sufferings, but was allowed to go free. He lived a humble life—giving money to the poor, owning only one coat, and sleeping on the floor.

To escape the persecution of Caracalla, Origen went to Palestine to preach and teach. He would return there fifteen years later to be ordained a priest.

Around the age of sixty-five, Origen was caught by the zealots of Decius, put in chains and tortured. He was eventually released, but never recovered. He died soon after.

His writings are studied today by historians and scholars, and criticized for the influence of Greek philosophy on his thought. Nonetheless, his book, *On Prayer,* reveals a heart intent on love and service to God. His life was characterized by the endurance such a heart enables.

Cyprian
(ca. 200-258)

The church was divided and angry. Believers in Carthage had stood strong against the persecution of rabid Emperor Valerius. But not all of them. Some had caved in, made their ritual sacrifice to Rome's statue gods, and renounced their allegiance to Christ. Now that Valerius was gone and his persecution done, should the cowards and compromisers be re-admitted to the church? Bishop Cyprian must decide, then lead the church toward harmony and growth—a difficult mandate made even more difficult by the fact that he himself had gone into exile to avoid persecution. Did Cyprian have the moral prestige to lead the recovery?

Little is known of Cyprian's early life. Likely he came from a wealthy Christian family and received a good education. Well respected in Carthage, he converted around age forty, but the story of his coming to faith is lost to history. Not lost, however, is the evidence of his new life in Christ. Cyprian took vows of poverty and celibacy; he gave up reading secular authors in favor of the Bible exclusively to avoid distractions as he grew in faith. He won the respect of fellow believers, for he was made bishop of the church in Carthage in 248, only two years after his conversion. But those were dangerous times for bishops everywhere.

Decius became emperor of Rome in 249, as Goths to the north threatened the empire from without as much as immorality threatened it from within. Decius would fix that by a new loyalty campaign aimed particularly at leaders of the Christian sect. He ordered that everyone do a general sacrifice, pouring out a libation to the Roman gods and eating the sacrificial meat. Roman authorities would certify compliance by issuing a *libellus*, essentially a "ticket" out of persecution.

Never before had so many Christians compromised faith as during Decius's two-year persecution, called at the time the bloodiest in the history of the church. Those who bowed to Rome (or bribed an official) carried their *libellus*, also a ticket of apostasy. In Carthage, eighteen Christians were martyred before Decius died in battle and his persecution ended. Cyprian survived by self-imposed exile. Now in 251, he was back to deal with the damage.

Another wave of persecution swept the Roman world in 258 under Valerian. This time Cyprian stayed. He was among the first arrested and ordered to reveal the roster of other Christian leaders. He refused. Awaiting his execution, Cyprian wrote to nine Christians exiled to the mines in nearby Sigua: "Let cruelty, either ignorant or malignant, hold you here in its bonds and chains as long as it will. From this earth and from these sufferings you shall speedily come to the kingdom of heaven. The body is not cherished in the mines with couch and cushion, but it is cherished with the refreshment and solace of Christ."

Cyprian used his execution to preach the greatness of knowing Christ as Lord. After kneeling in prayer, he gave his executioner a gift, and then placed the blindfold on himself, surrendering life in peace and treasuring the life to come.

VALENTINUS

(CA. 269)

The great day celebrating romantic love is named after him, yet who he really was, no one knows. Nonetheless, February 14 is his legacy, and we piece together a little fact and a lot of legend to get his story.

Three third-century martyrs all carry the name Valentinus. One was a priest in Rome, one a bishop of Interamna, and one a Christian in the Roman province of Africa. About the lives of these three we know nothing. About the death of Valentinus at the decree of Claudius II, we think the story hinges on soldiering, marriages, and a cold-hearted emperor— all the ingredients of passion and power that prompted Pope Gelasius in 496 to declare St. Valentine's Day as a replacement for the Roman pagan holiday of Lupercalia.

Apparently, recruits for Claudius's army were complaining about their long separations from wives and lovers, for the edict went forth that no soldier of Rome—may their hearts grow bloodlessly cold—could weaken his will or soften his courage in marriage. Of course, edicts do not command passions, so marriages simply went underground with an assist from the sympathetic priest Valentinus, to whom soldiers and their betrothed surreptitiously fled.

In time, the priest was caught and his treasonous disobedience duly sentenced by the Prefect of Rome. He was beaten by clubs and beheaded on February 14 in 269 or 270.

THE THEBAN LEGION
(286)

To how many loyalties can a person be loyal? How many oaths can one person keep? After the first one, all others are conditional. So the young Coptic Christians from Thebes in Upper Egypt, recruited and trained into a legion of 6,600 men in the Imperial Roman army, gave their oath of allegiance to the emperor—after they had pledged first loyalty to God.

Records of the Theban Legion are remote and sometimes contested by scholars. Evidence of their courage and sacrifice was uncovered sixty-four years after the event, in 350 by Theodore, bishop of Octudurm. Not until around 490 was their story written, at least in surviving records, by Eucherius, Bishop of Lyons. If these two bishops are dependable, the Theban Legion has given to the history of faith one of the most remarkable episodes of solidarity, duty, and hope ever told.

Commanded by Mauritius (called "St. Maurice" in Switzerland, where his memory is celebrated), the legion was ordered by Emperor Maximian to march west over the Alps to help put down an insurrection in Gaul. Of course, they obeyed. A long march followed; then a brief military campaign. Maximian was a man of immense self-importance, similar to other emperors. Wishing to celebrate the victory, he ordered all his troops to take the Oath of Allegiance, with its not-so-subtle notion that Maximian was divine, and then to help exterminate all Christians remaining in the Burgundy region.

Mauritius replied that because his own men were Christian, he would withdraw from the main encampment and permit the other battalions to reckon with their own consciences. He and his men could not kill innocents without dishonoring their first oath, taken at baptism, to love and serve God above all else.

This response from a legion commander was a slap to the ego of the commander-in-chief, who replied with an order of decimation: every tenth man in the Theban legion was to be executed.

So it was done. By picking names out of caps, 660 of the emperor's warriors were killed on his own order.

Despite their losses, still the Legion could neither take the Oath nor draw swords against brothers of faith. Maximian ordered a second decimation. Another six hundred troops were slaughtered.

The twenty-first-century reader must gasp and gather the senses to imagine the mix of faith and fury racing through the souls of these Theban survivors. They had choices to make. Defend themselves? Comply with the order? Stand by for another massacre? Mauritius and his lieutenants replied to Maximian with as clear a statement of loyalty as any soldier could offer:

> Emperor, we are your soldiers but also the soldiers of the true God. We owe you military service and obedience, but we cannot renounce Him who is our Creator and Master, and also yours even though you reject Him. In all things which are not against His law, we most willingly obey you, as we have done hitherto. We readily oppose your enemies, whoever they are, but we cannot stain our hands with the blood of innocent people [Christians]. We have taken an oath to God before we took one to you. You cannot place any confidence in our second oath if we violate the other [the first]. You commanded us to execute Christians; behold we are such. We confess God the Father the creator of all things and His Son Jesus Christ. We have seen our comrades slain with the sword. We do not weep for them but rather rejoice at their honor. Neither this nor any other provocation has tempted us to revolt. Behold, we have arms in our hands, but we do not resist, because we would rather die innocent than live by any sin.

Maximian might have been proud at their bravery and delighted that such resolute men stood ready to defend his empire. Instead, in a rage he condemned them all, the entire Legion, which order was carried out on September 22, 286. The Legion did not attempt to muster a defense or to find a hiding place. Those who were posted away from the encampment did not run. Nearly six thousand battle-hardened troops were killed for their first allegiance to Christ, by their second-in-command, Emperor Maximian.

Centuries later, in 515, a monastery was built near the site of the martyrdom through a gift from the king of Burgundy.

WE OUGHT ALWAYS TO GIVE THANKS TO GOD FOR YOU, BROTHERS, AS IS RIGHT, BECAUSE YOUR FAITH IS GROWING ABUNDANTLY, AND THE LOVE OF EVERY ONE OF YOU FOR ONE ANOTHER IS INCREASING. THEREFORE WE OURSELVES BOAST ABOUT YOU IN THE CHURCHES OF GOD FOR YOUR STEADFASTNESS AND FAITH IN ALL YOUR PERSECUTIONS AND IN THE AFFLICTIONS THAT YOU ARE ENDURING.

2 THESSALONIANS 1:3-4

ALBAN

(304)

Alban lived near Verulamium, a town in Roman Britain situated near the modern city of St. Albans in Hertfordshire on what is now park and agricultural land. A pagan and a soldier in the Roman Army, Alban became the first Christian martyr in Britain and is listed in the Anglican calendar of England and Wales as "Saint Alban."

In 303, the emperor of the Eastern Roman Empire, Diocletian, published his edict against the Christians. At some point, Alban gave shelter to a Christian priest who was fleeing the authorities. Impressed by the priest's lifestyle and devotion, and through their many conversations, Alban was converted to Christ and baptized.

Hearing that the priest was in that vicinity, the local magistrate sent soldiers to search for him. As they approached Alban's cottage, he changed clothes with the priest, wearing his hooded cloak, and was arrested instead. Alban was brought before the magistrate as he was offering sacrifices to the pagan gods. Seeing that the prisoner was Alban and not the priest, the magistrate became enraged that Alban had freely offered himself to the soldiers in place of his guest.

The magistrate ordered Alban to be dragged to the pagan gods and ordered the punishment for him that the priest would have received, if Alban had indeed become a Christian. Alban declared, "I worship and adore the true and living God who created all things."

Alban, who had voluntarily given himself up to the persecutors as a Christian, was not in the least afraid of the magistrate's threats. Instead, he openly declared that he would not obey the government's commands. Then the magistrate asked, "Of what house and stock are you?"

Alban replied, "What business is it of yours of what lineage I am born? If on the other hand you desire to hear the truth of my religion, know that I am now a Christian and devote myself to Christian service."

Angered even more, the magistrate ordered Alban to be beaten, hoping that he would recant. But Alban patiently endured the torture. Realizing that Alban was determined to confess Christ, he ordered him to be beheaded.

Alban was taken out of the town Verulamium to the top of the hill across the river. The place of his beheading is where St. Alban's Cathedral now stands. The most probable date for Alban's martyrdom is 304.

Alban thus became the first martyr in Britain. The second was the executioner that was ordered to kill him, who after hearing his testimony became a Christian on the spot and refused to follow the order. The third was the priest, who after hearing that Alban had been arrested in his place, hurried to the court to turn himself in and save Alban.

IF ANYONE WOULD COME AFTER ME,

LET HIM DENY HIMSELF AND

TAKE UP HIS CROSS AND FOLLOW ME.

FOR WHOEVER WOULD SAVE

HIS LIFE WILL LOSE IT, BUT WHOEVER

LOSES HIS LIFE FOR MY SAKE

WILL FIND IT.

MATTHEW 16:24-25

THE FORTY MARTYRS
OF SEBASTE
(320)

◆

I n 320, Constantine, the Roman emperor of the West, pressured
Licinius, the emperor of the East, to legalize Christianity in his
region—and Licinius conceded. Later, however, fearing treason
among the troops, Licinius broke his alliance and decided to eliminate
Christianity from his territory. He authorized Agricola, the commander
of his forces in the Armenian town of Sebaste (now Sivas, Turkey), to
carry out his evil intentions.

Agricola knew of forty soldiers who were devout Christians and
skilled in battle. In an attempt to force them to renounce their faith, he
announced to these men, "Either offer sacrifice to the gods and earn
great honors, or, in the event of your disobedience, be stripped of your
military rank and fall into disgrace." Then Agricola had the soldiers
imprisoned to think about what he had told them. That night they
encouraged themselves by singing psalms and praying.

The next morning Agricola brought out the forty men and tried to
persuade them with flattery, praising them for their valor and good looks.
These Christian soldiers were determined, however, not to fall prey to
the commander's empty words. So Agricola sent them back to prison to
await the arrival of an official. While the soldiers waited, they prepared
themselves for martyrdom.

When the official arrived, he again attempted to persuade the men.
Unsuccessful, he ordered the forty men to be taken to a frozen lake.
There, they were told to strip off their clothing and stand in the middle
of the frozen mass of ice. A guard watched over them while warm baths
were set up along the shore, along with fires, blankets, clothing, and hot
food and drink, in order to tempt them to turn their backs on Christ and
sacrifice to the pagan idols. One of the soldiers could no longer bear the

cold and ran to the shore. Seeing this, the remaining soldiers cried out to God to help them. Their prayer was answered as a light warmed the shivering men. One of the guards was so moved by the resolve of the Christian soldiers that he stripped off all his clothes and joined them. One version of the story reports that all the men were frozen to death by morning. Another account, however, says that in the morning the men, still alive, were taken back to the prison and tortured to death. Then their bones were crushed with sledgehammers.

Regardless of which version of the story is correct, the forty soldiers of Sebaste courageously refused to deny Christ. May we remember their courage and stand strong against anything that might lure us away from Christ. May we, like them, show God's grace even in the midst of great trials!

BUT I DO NOT ACCOUNT MY LIFE OF ANY VALUE NOR AS PRECIOUS TO MYSELF, IF ONLY I MAY FINISH MY COURSE AND THE MINISTRY THAT I RECEIVED FROM THE LORD JESUS, TO TESTIFY TO THE GOSPEL OF THE GRACE OF GOD.

ACTS 20:24

TELEMACHUS

(404)

◆

I n the Greek myths, the character Telemachus (meaning "far-away fighter") was a timid and diffident child. But as an adult he defended the honor of those he loved and became a fighter and a hero. Unlike his mythological counterpart, the fourth-century monk Telemachus was anything but a fighter. Or perhaps it can be argued that his greatest fight was his effort to eradicate fighting.

An ascetic hermit from the East and unknown except for his final act, Telemachus journeyed to Rome just in time for the victory celebrations. After years of aggressive invasions from the continent, Rome had finally defeated the Goth king Alaric in northern Italy in 403.

As was common in those times, extravagant gladiatorial contests were held in celebration of military victories. The twenty-year-old emperor Honorius decreed that this particular celebration would be held in the 50,000-capacity Coliseum, a battleground named for the colossal 130-foot statue of Nero nearby, the emperor made famous for condemning Christians into human torches. If there was one place in all of Rome that a pacifist Christian might consider avoiding, the Coliseum was it. Telemachus, a "rudely clad man of rough but imposing presence," resolved to interrupt, indeed to stop, the bloody contest in the Coliseum.

Thousands had gathered that day. Cries of "*habet, hoc habet*" erupted from the crowds—"He has had it!" they cried every time a fighter was mortally wounded. In this atmosphere Telemachus jumped from the crowd into the arena itself, no longer spectator but activist, peacemaker, preacher.

"Do not requite God's mercy," he screamed, "in turning away the swords of your enemies by murdering each other!" Certainly the crowd heard him, but the gladiators continued fighting. Telemachus ran between the gladiators, pleading with them to stop. "Sedition! Sedition! Down with him!" roared the crowd. "This is no place for preaching! The old customs of Rome must be observed! On, gladiators!" Still, Telemachus continued to turn from one encounter to another, stopping gladiators in mid-fight. Then, frustrated by the annoyance of one man interrupting the games, someone pulled a sword and, thrusting it, Telemachus fell. Joining in, the crowd threw stones down from their seats to the arena below.

News quickly spread throughout Rome that the murdered man was the hermit Telemachus. Rome was shocked, as was Emperor Honorius, that such a gentle man had been slain. Telemachus's courage and boldness to speak God's mercy and love changed the games forever. A man bent on peace, Telemachus lost his life fighting in the grandest battleground of Rome. Soon after his death, gladiatorial battles were banned from the Coliseum. Telemachus had achieved the impossible.

For to this you have been called, because Christ also suffered for you, leaving you an example, so that you might follow in his steps. He committed no sin, neither was deceit found in his mouth. When he was reviled, he did not revile in return; when he suffered, he did not threaten, but continued entrusting himself to him who judges justly.

I Peter 2:21-23

Representation of the tortures used in the Inquisition

PERSECUTION
DURING THE
MIDDLE AGES
(600-1500)

hough Emperor Julian (361-363) tried to revive paganism in the Roman Empire, that old way was doomed. Theodosius established a policy that suppressed pagan worship (392) and freed the church to expand its missionary efforts. Patrick took Christian faith to Ireland in the fifth century. Scottish monks evangelized lower England around 600. Irish monks returned to Europe as missionaries from 500 to 1000.

The Bishop of Rome came to be seen as the leader of the church, and often, when the pope was strong, the bishop was also the leader of the secular monarchs who ruled Europe. Hildebrand (Pope Gregory VII, 1073-1085) was such a figure. His papal armies fought Emperor Henry IV of the Holy Roman Empire, who eventually gave his confession and allegiance to Hildebrand.

During this era, the great Crusades were organized to roll back Muslim influence in the East, Spain, and North Africa. Jerusalem was twice won and lost by crusaders bent on holy war. At the same time, the seemingly invincible pagan armies of Genghis Khan captured much of Asia Minor.

From 1232, the church's Inquisition turned its fearsome power against "heresies" such as the Waldensians and Lollards, early "Bible-for-everyone" activists, and later, against the leaders of the Reformation.

Note: John Wycliffe (1329-1384) stands as the leading reformer of this era. Wycliffe repudiated the infallibility of the papacy, taught that the Bible was the sole authority for faith and practice, and produced the first English Bible manuscripts. An Oxford professor, scholar, and theologian, Wycliffe—and his opposition to the teachings of the Church—was known throughout Europe. With the help of his followers, the "Lollards," and others, Wycliffe produced dozens of English-language copies of the Bible. He translated these manuscripts from the Latin Vulgate, the only text source available. The pope was so infuriated by Wycliffe's teachings and Bible translation that forty-four years after Wycliffe had died, he ordered the bones to be dug up, crushed, and scattered in the river.

John Wycliffe's bones burned by papists

Boniface
(ca. 680-755)

He never lost his passion for missionary service. The archbishop of Germany, Boniface, could have enjoyed the honor of his office at an age when most men dream of a settled life. But the mission field held more purpose and challenge than presiding over monasteries or maintaining cathedrals. Boniface was seventy-five years old when he left Germany to preach the Gospel once again.

Boniface is probably the most widely known name, apart from popes and kings, of the eighth century. He was born "Winfrid" in England around 680. Early in life, to his father's dismay, he chose a vocation in the church. He took training in Benedictine monasteries and wrote the first Latin grammar in England. He was ordained a priest when he was thirty years old, but he wanted the frontier.

In 716, Winfrid set out on a missionary expedition to Friesland, or Frisia. His own Anglo-Saxon language was similar to the spoken language of the Frisians. The mission was frustrated, however, by a war raging between Charles Martel (who later stopped the "Mohammedans" from entering Europe in the battle of Potiers, 732) and the Frisian king.

In 719, during a visit to Rome, Winfrid was given the name Boniface by Pope Gregory II, who commissioned him to evangelize Germany. For five years Boniface preached and baptized in Hesse and Thuringia. In 722 he was named bishop of the Germanic territories.

A year later Boniface performed one of those simple acts of defiance that gives birth to legends. He felled a large oak tree near the town of Fritzlar in northern Hesse, a tree known to locals as Thor's Oak. Indeed, many locals were present as Boniface worked at the oak's tough base. These onlookers grew steadily more curious and angry with this foreigner who was infuriating their gods with each stroke of the axe. Indeed, they expected Thor or one of his agents to fell the bishop with a thunderclap. When the oak hit the ground, it split into four parts, so the story goes, and the people instantly knew that a superior divine power was at work. Most converted as Boniface had the wood sawn to make a chapel—today the site of Fritzler Cathedral.

Boniface made other trips to Rome, each time receiving honors and more territory to win for Christ. He was made archbishop of Germany in 732 and put his headquarters at Mentz. More structures were built and movements begun.

In 755, Boniface was restless again about the heathen in Frisia. He organized a large group of priests and lay helpers, and he preached there with extraordinary success. On Whitsun Eve (the eve of Pentecost) in 755, he called all new converts to a great meeting near Dokkum. Instead of converts, however, he was ambushed by a gang of local vigilantes, who mercilessly killed fifty-two Christians, including Boniface.

His reputation had already been won, his legacy established, his titles and honors awarded. The powers in Rome would have made his old age comfortable. Instead, Boniface chose missions, and in Frisia he died a martyr.

YOU DID NOT CHOOSE ME, BUT I CHOSE
YOU AND APPOINTED YOU THAT YOU
SHOULD GO AND BEAR FRUIT AND THAT
YOUR FRUIT SHOULD ABIDE, SO THAT
WHATEVER YOU ASK THE FATHER IN MY
NAME, HE MAY GIVE IT TO YOU.

JOHN 15:16

ALPHAGE
(954-1012)

He wanted the hermit's life: quietness, meditations, and seclusion. Instead he was given leadership, travel, international peace negotiations, and finally martyrdom. The twenty-ninth archbishop of Canterbury might have said at the end, "Not my plan, but God's."

Alphage was born to a noble English family, but early in life he chose God over temporal power and privilege. He entered the monastery at Deerhurst and then Bath, where he became abbot and was known for his piety and austerity. In 984, Dunstan (the twenty-seventh archbishop) appointed Alphage bishop of Winchester.

In 1006, Alphage succeeded Aelfric as archbishop of Canterbury. At that point, Alphage's life became more difficult as his country became more vulnerable to Scandinavian marauders. Apparently Alphage persuaded King Olaf Tryggvason I of Norway not to attack the English coast, but he did not succeed in putting off the Danes. When marauders from Denmark sacked Canterbury in 1011, Alphage was taken hostage and held for ransom at an encampment near Greenwich.

The Danes commanded, "Give us gold!"

Alphage replied, "The gold I give you is the Word of God."

On Easter Sunday in 1066, after months of captivity, Alphage was bludgeoned to death, the promised consequence of failure to pay the ransom. It is said that a sympathetic Dane ended his torment with an axe blow to the head.

Alphage (also known as Alfege, Elphege, Alphege, or Godwine) was buried at St. Paul's Cathedral, London, but his body was later moved to Canterbury. The anniversary of his martyrdom in the Anglican calendar is April 19, St. Alfege's Day.

BISHOP GELLERT
(980-1046)

◆

In one respect, Christians have no homeland on earth; our citizenship is in Heaven with Christ. However, since "the earth is the Lord's," every place is God's (Psalm 24:1). Bishop Gellert, who gave his life while teaching the Gospel to the people of Hungary, understood his dual citizenship well. He died a missionary martyr.

Gellert was born in Venice, Italy, around 980, and given the name Giorgio di Sagredo. He grew up in a noble family. While young, Gellert caught a dangerous sickness. Fearing for the boy's life, his parents took him to a monastery and dedicated him to God. Gellert recovered and joined the Benedictine order of monks. Tragedy would come to his family, though, when his father died during a religious pilgrimage. This prompted the young monk to adopt his father's name, Gellert.

At the monastery Gellert excelled in studies and prospered in life. Fellow monks elected him abbot at San Giorgio Maggiore. Around 1015, he decided to give up that honor to make a pilgrimage to the Holy Land. The trip would change his life.

Gellert's travels took him through Hungary, where King Stephen I had sought to bring the faith to his people. Stephen took note of the young teacher-traveler, and invited Gellert to tutor his son, Prince Imre. Gellert tutored the prince for seven years, and then spent another seven in solitude in the Bakony Mountains, studying Scripture and writing commentaries for the Hungarian people.

In 1035, King Stephen appointed Gellert the first bishop of Csanád. Contemplative practices, care for the uneducated Christians, and concern for the heathen marked Gellert's ministry. He evangelized the Hungarians, trained monks for missions, and established monasteries for outreach. Gellert's missionary work played a major role in converting Hungary to Christ.

In 1038, Stephen died, leaving no heir. He was succeeded by the son of his sister, whose harsh rule would lead to political revolt, uprisings by pagans, and targeting of Christians. Nonetheless, Gellert continued his missionary work until September 24, 1046. That morning, he held service near the Danube River. Crossing later, his boat was rocked in a barrage of stones thrown by pagan rebels. Gellert was caught, stabbed, his body tucked in a barrel and thrown down a hill into the river; while he prayed the prayer of the first Christian martyr, Stephen: "Lord, do not hold this sin against them" (Acts 7:60).

Hungarian Christians remember Gellert today as a father of the faith in Eastern Europe. The hill on which he prayed and died carries his name, and a monument in Budapest recalls his faithfulness in a foreign land, a way station that became his mission field and home.

WHEN THE PERISHABLE PUTS ON THE IMPERISHABLE, AND THE MORTAL PUTS ON IMMORTALITY, THEN SHALL COME TO PASS THE SAYING THAT IS WRITTEN: "DEATH IS SWALLOWED UP IN VICTORY."

I CORINTHIANS 15:54

THE GREAT SCHISM
BETWEEN ORTHODOX AND
ROMAN CHURCHES (1054)

Political power and the great geographical distances from West
(France and England) to East (Constantinople) created controversy
and division in the medieval church. When Charlemagne was
consecrated emperor in 800, the Eastern churches felt threatened. The
insertion of the term *filioque* (an effort to define the deity and humanity
of Jesus) in the Nicene Creed in 885 was unacceptable to Russian and
Greek church leaders.

In 1054, the Great Schism began in Constantinople, when delegations
from Pope Leo IX and Patriarch Michael Ceralarius parted without a treaty
or a plan for unity. Not until 1417, at the long Council of Constance (1414-
1418), did the "conciliar" efforts bear fruit. The Council of Constance
induced the Roman pope to abdicate and then deposed two other claimants.
Elected in 1420, Pope Martin IV reestablished a united papacy in Rome.

This was a time of frustration and loss for the church. The Crusades had
failed; clergy were abusing ordination vows; the papacy was so entangled in
secular power struggles that the mood was disillusionment and distrust.

John Wycliffe translated the first written English Bible from the Latin
in 1380. This printed Bible was also a threat to papal hegemony. Itinerant
preachers sent throughout England started a spiritual revolution. As
Europe became more literate, Christians sought the comfort of the Scriptures, which seemed increasingly contrary to encrusted procedures and
policies of the church. The Bible printed in vernacular languages began to
make every reader a "priest." The conciliarists who worked for papal unity
were also responsible for condemning Jan Hus (1415). After the Council
of Constance, no pope made spiritual reform a priority for a century. The
most zealous reformer before Luther, Savonarola, denounced clerical
misconduct and was condemned by the church in 1498.

THE CRUSADES
(1095-1291)

Perhaps Christendom's greatest historical embarrassment, the Crusades, at the time were a brilliant strategic move by papal leaders to unite a warring Europe against heathen enemies threatening the Byzantine church. Not that Pope Urban II in Rome cared much about Constantinople or vice versa. Each part of the church had excommunicated the other in the great schism of 1054. But internal feuding needed alternative war games, and the call to defend the Holy Land and the Eastern Church against invading Turks presented a quite legitimate target for knights and lords otherwise bent on battling each other.

The First Crusade, led by Peter the Hermit in 1095, was a military disaster. The same could be said for one of the last crusades—the Children's Crusade of 1212—when hundreds of youngsters sailed from Marseilles toward Palestine and fell into the hands of slave traders. Between these, however, many great medieval reputations were made. Richard the Lion-Hearted of England was one of many who led armies to victory, his soldiers bearing the famous sign of the Red Cross. In 1099, Jerusalem was taken. When Godfrey of Bouillon was offered the throne of Jerusalem, he refused to wear a crown of gold in the city where his Savior had once worn a crown of thorns. Instead, Godfrey took the title "Defender of the Holy Sepulchre."

But holding conquered territory was not so easy as winning it. Most of Europe's warriors returned home after winning the victory, leaving the remainder vulnerable to counterattack. The great Muslim general Saladin struck back in 1187, and a horrified Europe sent the third wave of Crusaders in response. Richard defeated Saladin in 1191, and Pope Innocent III, considered the greatest of the medieval papal leaders, launched the Fourth Crusade. His commanders wanted first to control Constantinople, so this Crusade became Christian against Christian. Pope Innocent was powerless to stop it.

Events far from Christendom, however, led eventually to the exhaustion of military resources and the settlement of disputed territories. From far away in Asia, Genghis Khan's Mongols presented an unstoppable military force, which fought against anyone and everyone with savage success. The Khan's tactic was total war, and refusal to submit to him meant extermination.

The fall of Acre in 1291 is generally regarded as the end of the Crusades; the Mongols converted to Islam. A few small Christian settlements remained, but on the Asian mainland Islam was triumphant. The Crusades had failed.

But I say to you, Love your enemies and pray for those who persecute you . . . .

Matthew 5:44

THE WALDENSIANS
(ca. 1173)

Also called the Waldenses, this movement is believed to have been founded by Peter Waldo, or Valdes, in 1173. Some sources earlier than Waldo suggest that Waldenses were active even in the ninth century. Others have claimed this movement to be the child of the early church, rejecting the infusion of power and prestige that followed Constantine's conversion.

The Waldenses sought to teach from the Bible alone and believed in voluntary poverty. They rejected doctrines of purgatory, masses for the dead, indulgences, saints as mediators, and adoration of the Virgin Mary. They were mostly pacifists, except in cases of extreme peril to family and faith. Historically, the movement favored artisan callings and avoided business as morally perilous.

Waldenses were targets of Catholic reaction and endured a long series of persecutions throughout the twelfth and thirteenth centuries. Often they were chased into mountain hideaways. New settlements outside of Europe were hounded mercilessly. As late as 1541, inhabitants of twenty-two villages in France were massacred. In 1655, the settlements in Italy's Piedmont Valley were attacked and slaughtered.

Through all these martyrdoms, the Waldensian church survived, principally in Italy. In 1893, a colony founded Valdese in North Carolina. During the Second World War, they were responsible for helping many Jews escape the Nazis. The Waldensian church is still alive today—many times joined with the Presbyterian Church—in places such as South America, Italy, Germany, and the United States.

WILLIAM SWINDERBY
(1401)

J ohn Wycliffe began the trouble. He claimed the Bible taught what the church did not, and the church taught what the Bible did not. In 1380, Wycliffe translated the first Bible from Latin into English. Others followed who called themselves Lollards. They read, studied, and preached a faith that sought genuine conversion and renewal from old forms and rituals, deposits from the past encrusted with residue of power and privilege. A stroke took Wycliffe's life in 1384. Forty-four years after Wycliffe died, the pope ordered his bones to be exhumed and burned.

But other Lollards carried on. William Swinderby was reputed to be among their ablest preachers, thus also one of Wycliffe's most dangerous protégés. Of his work little is known, except that his effectiveness and lack of conformity drew the attention of church officials five years after Wycliffe's death. Swinderby was a priest in the Lincoln diocese when a board of examiners found his teaching outrageous and ordered him to never speak again, lest his body be reduced to ashes.

Such threats would quickly silence most men, but Swinderby kept talking and teaching. In 1392, another order was issued against this persistent priest, this time by King Richard II. Swinderby was apprehended, questioned, and found wrong on matters of baptism, church policy, governance, salvation and the sacraments.

Records indicate that nine years passed between this second arrest and Swinderby's torturous death at the stake in London in 1401. What happened during those years one cannot tell, but the final chapter of his life shows that Swinderby's heart and mind were convinced that the Bible was intended to be the Christian's foundational document, that its way of salvation—God's mercy expressed in personal faith—was the Christian's hope. He surrendered neither that hope nor his integrity nor conscience during his long testing and confinement. And when his day of pain came, it was a small price for the reward of a faithful life and the sure hope of life to come.

Jan Hus
(1370-1415)

His accusers made it clear at the trial that Jan Hus would not only die, but that he would die without hope. "We take from you the cup of redemption," the prosecutors solemnly intoned before sentencing. But Hus replied, "I trust in the Lord God Almighty...that He will not take away from me the cup of His redemption, but I firmly hope to drink from it today in His kingdom."

The communion cup was key to Hus's crimes. Born in 1362 in the village of Husenic in southern Bohemia (today the Czech Republic), this son of peasants learned to pray at the feet of his mother. It was she who prompted young Jan toward the priesthood, where he might find, among other benefits, the money and prestige to escape his family's poverty. An average but hard-working student, Hus received a master's degree in theology from the university in Prague and became preacher in that city's Bethlehem Chapel in 1402. Shortly before, news had arrived from England of a certain John Wycliffe, a reformer, whose ideas soon split the university faculty. Chief among those ideas was the nature of the communion cup. Was the wine of the Lord's Supper really changed into Christ's blood during the Mass? Yes, argued the German and Roman theologians. No, countered many Czechs and Wycliffe supporters. Thus the cup would become a symbol of reform that Hus, by some accounts, would carry to his pyre.

Times were dangerous in the early fifteenth century. The church was split between two popes, one in France, the other in Rome. The so-called Great Schism (1378-1417) meant that every leader, politician or churchman must take sides and hope his pope emerged the winner. Survival and the future of the church hung in the balance.

Meanwhile, Wycliffe's influence on the preacher Hus was becoming a clear and present danger. In 1405, Hus began to speak against the sins of the clergy and denounce their hoaxes perpetrated on common

Jan Hus burned at the stake

parishioners. When the Bohemian church claimed that Christ's blood was appearing on communion wafers, Hus exposed the scheme in language sure to make its point: "These priests deserve hanging in hell" for they are "fornicators," "parasites," "money misers," and "fat swine." Strong words in a volatile church climate. "They [priests] are gluttons whose stomachs are overfilled until their double chins hang down." Later came Hus's outrage against indulgences, the selling of heavenly favor used to finance papal wars. "Shall I keep silent?" he asked. "God forbid."

Four times Hus was excommunicated. For two years (1412-14) he went into exile working in villages in southern Bohemia, writing, preaching, and keeping his head down.

Then in October 1414, Pope John XXIII convened the Council of Constance and invited Jan Hus to attend. Two grand purposes filled the Council's agenda: End the schism and eradicate heresy from Europe.

Promised safe conduct, Hus accepted the invitation, joking that "the goose [*hus* in Czech means "goose"] is not yet cooked and is not afraid of being cooked."

Within a week he was arrested. For several months Hus wasted away in a cell in the Dominican monastery on an island in Lake Constance, saved from death there only to face accusations that surely foretold a bitter death to come.

Hus's critics brought the common charges: dangerous heretic, unworthy of the name Christian, wicked man, teacher of a fourth person in the Godhead—all charges to which Hus was forbidden to reply.

On July 6, 1415, amid shouts and jeers, the church committed his soul to the devil. Hus was pushed by a crowd through the streets of Constance to the piled tinder, wrapped by the neck to a stake, and set ablaze. He died singing, "Jesus, Son of the living God, have mercy on me."

"DO NOT BELIEVE THAT I HAVE TAUGHT ANYTHING BUT THE TRUTH. I HAVE TAUGHT NO ERROR. THE TRUTHS I HAVE TAUGHT I WILL SEAL WITH MY BLOOD."

—CZECH REFORMER JAN HUS

Jerome of Prague in the stocks

JEROME OF PRAGUE
(1416)

Three months before the death of Jan Hus in Constance, Germany, a Bohemian scholar named Jerome secretly snuck into the city. He had already escaped from prison in Vienna, and had boldly made his way to Germany, without protection, to try to help his friend Hus. Jerome had translated the writings of John Wycliffe into the Czech language, which Hus had read and followed. Feeling perhaps that it was he, Jerome, who should have been arrested, he bravely wrote letters to the emperor and the Council of Constance, pleading for safe conduct and to be heard on behalf of Hus—but they refused. Having done all he could, he made his way back to Bohemia.

He never made it home. As he traveled through a small town in Germany, the Duke of Sulzbach sent an officer to illegally arrest him. Chained around the neck and shackled, he was led back into Constance as if he was the center of a parade. Surrounded by men on horseback and many more guards, they took him to a degrading prison to await trial.

Later, during which time Hus was martyred, the Council of Constance still refused to let Jerome speak. They knew he was a persuasive, intelligent scholar, and were afraid of his ability to defend the Christian faith. He asked to defend himself, and they refused again. Held against his will, with no trial or opportunity to plead his own case, he yelled out:

What cruelty is this? For 340 days I've been confined in various prisons. There is not a misery or a want that I have not experienced...and you have denied me the smallest opportunity to defend myself... You are a general council, and in you is contained all that this world can impart of wisdom, solemnity, and holiness; but you are still men, and men are often fooled by words and appearances. The higher your character is for wisdom, the more you should be careful not to fall into foolishness. The cause I wish to plead is my own cause, the cause of men, the cause of Christians. It is a cause that will affect the rights of future generations, no matter in what way the testing process is applied to me.

After accusing him on six accounts of ridiculing and persecuting the papacy, and of being a "hater of the Christian religion," they tortured him for eleven days by hanging him by his heels. Threatened with worse torture, he faltered. He verbally affirmed that the writings of Hus and Wycliffe were false. However, after returning to prison, albeit with better treatment, he retracted his statements and vowed full support of Hus and Wycliffe. The council brought 107 new charges against him, but finally let him speak before burning him at the stake.

Jerome eloquently reminded them that throughout history, men of truth have openly voiced their opinions and differences. All that Jerome had done, all that Wycliffe had done, was to unveil the misguided teachings of the Roman Church at that time to the people of their own land, and in their own language. They taught that the Gospel itself is enough to rule the life of every Christian; that the pope is no different from any other priest; that communion is not the actual blood, body, and bones of Christ; and many other doctrines that follow more Protestant lines of thought.

The Roman Church at that time had already martyred Hus, banished the teachings of Wycliffe, and now Jerome of Prague was on the pyre. Singing hymns as the pyre was lit, his last known words were, "This soul in flames I offer, Christ, to Thee."

His death was not in vain. Jerome, like Hus and Wycliffe, was simply encouraging people to know what the Bible actually said, and not to blindly follow those who claimed to have the utmost authority over Christianity. The work of Jerome, Hus, and Wycliffe led the way for men like William Tyndale to translate the Bible into English, and later into other languages, so that everyone had access to the Word of God.

John Oldcastle
(1417)

To be a friend of the king is both advantageous and dangerous. Such friendship may lead to wealth and power so long as the friendship serves the king's greater wealth and power. But friends once strong have been known to split over trifles or women. How much greater is the split when the difference is conscience—for here a man must declare himself, and no one can live long when conscience shows itself to be independent from the king.

John Oldcastle was destined for leadership. Strong, brave, and capable of devotion, he served in the armies of the English King Henry IV, a gallant soldier in an era of fighting with clubs and swords. The old king loved him. But King Henry was not immortal, and Oldcastle was not merely a warrior. The king died, and Oldcastle came under the influence of John Wycliffe and the early English reformers known as the Lollards. The Lollards opposed the church of Rome, the priesthood and its privileges, the Eucharistic sacrament and its miracle, and the veneration of saints and icons in place of the Lord Christ, to whom alone confession may be made, and who alone forgives all sinners.

Married to an heiress of title, Oldcastle entered Parliament during the reign of Henry V, and likely fought with his army in France in 1411. But he was a Lollard, and the steely archbishop of Canterbury, Arundel, wanted the English Church cleansed. The young king was finally persuaded to summon Oldcastle to a hearing, which the latter ignored until his very honor was at stake.

Heresy trials were predetermined affairs, each side aware that the debate only fixed positions. On September 13, 1413, Oldcastle presented his confession of faith to the church, including his views on the Eucharist and the confessional. Arundel condemned him as a heretic.

Execution normally quickly followed judgment. But Oldcastle was the king's friend; as a gesture, he was granted forty days to change his mind. During that time, Oldcastle escaped and became leader of a Lollard conspiracy against the crown. He devised a plot to kidnap the king, but the scheme was betrayed. Henry captured most of the conspirators; Oldcastle escaped.

Further plots developed and failed. Finally in 1417, Oldcastle's hideout was discovered and he was captured after suffering extensive injuries. He was taken to London and ordered to a double death: hanged as a traitor and burned as a heretic. The same day he was carried to the town of St. Giles's Fields, the site of his most recent failed plot. There he was hoisted by chains between two gallows and a low fire set beneath him. Throughout his agony, he is said to have praised God and commended his soul to God's keeping.

In 1598, William Shakespeare adapted an old play written when King Henry and Oldcastle were still the closest of companions. But Shakespeare knew his limits, and in his play *Henry IV* he substituted the name Falstaff for the old heretic, changing the character into someone quite unlike the Lollard leader.

The persecution of English dissenters would continue through several more King Henrys, and reach its apex when Queen Mary tried unsuccessfully but brutally to purge her island of Oldcastle's successors and compatriots.

"I AM READY TO DIE FOR MY LORD; THAT IN MY BLOOD THE CHURCH MAY OBTAIN LIBERTY AND PEACE."

—THOMAS A BECKET, THE ARCHBISHOP OF CANTERBURY, WHO WAS MARTYRED IN 1170

CATHERINE SAUBE
(1417)

By any measure, Catherine Saube was a minor player in fifteenth-century religious life. She lived in Thou, Lorraine, France. As a young girl, she presented herself to the leaders and priests of Montpelier as a candidate for life in the nunnery, essentially living as a recluse, away from the world, without contact or friend except for other nuns. Quite obviously, she felt a call to pray.

But she did more than pray. After the leaders of Montpelier led her to the nunnery on the Lates Road and "shut her" in there, Saube talked and taught so convincingly, it appears, that after only nine months she was put on trial for offenses against the faith. She no longer believed that the communion bread was made into the body of Christ or that confession should only be made to a priest. Indeed, Saube had shared these revisionist ideas with the other nuns. She had infected the entire group.

In orderly fashion, a vicar of the inquisitor, M. Raymond Cabasse, D.D., pronounced Saube a heretic on October 2, 1417, and remanded her to the bailiff for the cleansing and purifying of the church. She was burned at the stake that afternoon.

How did Saube come to her convictions? There is no record. Did she seek the nunnery as the only viable platform from which a woman living then might teach her contrary convictions? No record. Did she win converts in the nunnery? Apparently so, for the Montpelier town book records that Saube was burned, together with all the Lates Road nuns.

Apart from brief court records, no doubt kept to show the loyalty and rectitude of Montpelier parish officialdom, the story of Catherine Saube and the Lates Road nunnery would be known to God alone. How many other quiet martyrs will one day raise the choir's call when Heaven's record is opened and judgment is fairly rendered?

Martin Luther

Persecution

during the

Reformation

(1500-1600)

Martin Luther wanted to address discrepancies between theology and practice, to set right the disorder he painfully observed in the church, and to open up discussion and debate on points of doctrine encrusted by centuries of politics and mismanagement. He did not intend to start a new church. But his Disputation on the Power and Efficacy of Indulgences (known as the Ninety-Five Theses) nailed to the church door at Wittenberg on October 31, 1517, led to a massive protest against church abuses such as indulgences and church office as patronage and, finally, to the worldwide Protestant movement. Many would die for their faith in the process.

Luther was a scholar and an activist. When he was finally labeled a heretic in 1520, he took the official document and publicly burned it. Excommunicated the next year, Luther still appeared before the Diet of Worms in April, where he uttered his famous "Here I Stand" defense. The result: Luther was regarded an outlaw, and his writings were contraband. Luther owed his survival to the protection of Frederick of Saxony, his terrestrial ruler and staunch supporter.

Other centers of reform took up the movement launched by the German monk. In Zurich, Ulrich Zwingli, a parish priest, rose to prominence both supporting Luther's reforms and proposing others, primarily, that Christ's presence in the communion bread and wine was spiritual only.

The French lawyer John Calvin, in Geneva in 1536, published his Institutes of the Christian Religion, and so provided present-day Presbyterians and reformed church bodies with their first comprehensive systematic theology.

Still in the sixteenth century, the Anabaptists and Mennonites (led by Menno Simons, a Dutch priest) spearheaded the radical reformation toward adult-only baptism and pacifism as benchmarks of biblical faith.

Of course, the Reformation was more than a religious movement. It threatened economic engines and political power bases. A renewed sense of individual dignity and autonomy followed the translation of the Bible into vernacular languages. A renewed sense of wonder at God's creation emerged when science shed its accountability to the medieval church.

Blood, fire, and sword also played their painful parts in the emergence of a renewed church, or churches. To many martyrs we all—Catholic, Orthodox, and Protestant—owe a debt for a clearer vision of God's grace and truth than most medieval believers could have learned or enjoyed.

Henry Voes, Johann Eck, and Lampertus Thorn
(1523)

R eading the wrong book may cost you your life.
Throughout Europe after 1521, reading any book by Martin
Luther was a crime. Luther had presented his theological views
at Worms that year. The Church had responded with the famous Edict
of Worms, outlawing his writings. Because Martin Luther was an Augustinian monk, however, his work was widely accepted by that Order. In
Antwerp, the Augustinians enthusiastically read and preached the Gospel
as Luther taught.

But Antwerp was close enough to the University of Leuven for the
doctors of theology there to hear and react to these unlawful ideas. In
1522, the entire Order was placed under arrest and its facility demolished
as you would a building condemned for irreparable safety violations—in
this case, irreparable spiritual violations, so they thought.

The prior, James Probst, eventually escaped the dragnet; his assistant, Melchior Mirisch, recanted and joined the Inquisition. Three
Augustinian monks, among others, resolved to stand by their minds and
consciences, and so became among the first to die for disavowing the
papacy, the communion substance, and all other church regulations for
which they could find no scriptural base. Henry Voes and Johann Eck
died on July 1, 1523, without doubt or wavering. Lampertus requested
time to contemplate his recantation but eventually died, too, for a clear
Gospel of faith in Christ.

The trials of these monks were unlike trials elsewhere. Here, the
charges in the indictments were less tied to politics and were much more
a matter of theology and doctrine. The prosecutors urged that the
accused "return" to faith, and would have pardoned each one for just a
word of agreement. When told that Martin Luther had led them astray,

Henry Voes replied, "Yes, we were led astray by him, as were the apostles led astray by Christ." Asked if they had no fear at breaking the pope's edict, they answered, "We believe God's commandments, and not human statutes, save or condemn." Such responses were like sparks to the dried sticks, which eventually took their lives.

Martin Luther himself was overcome with sorrow at the news of their public and painful executions. "The cause which we defend," he said, "is no longer a simple game; it looks for blood, it seeks for life." Then he wrote "Song about Two Martyrs of Christ in Brussels, Burned by the Sophists at Leuven":

> The old enemy had captured them, terrified them with threats.
> They were told to deny God's Word, trying to trick and deceive them.
> For this purpose he gathered many of the Sophists of Loewe.
> They were impotent with all their tricks. The Spirit showed them up as fools.
> They were unsuccessful.

COUNT IT ALL JOY, MY BROTHERS, WHEN YOU MEET TRIALS OF VARIOUS KINDS, FOR YOU KNOW THAT THE TESTING OF YOUR FAITH PRODUCES STEADFASTNESS.

JAMES 1:2-3

THE ANABAPTISTS

The term Anabaptist means "rebaptizer" and was used by critics of these sixteenthcentury radical reformers. The Anabaptists believed the Bible taught "believer's baptism," while the church followed infant baptism. They did not think of themselves as rebaptizing anyone, since the first baptism done to infants, they believed, was illegitimate. The Anabaptists simply called themselves "believers" or "brethren" or "Christians." These reformers did not form a communion or church, such as the Lutherans, but were rather a collection of different movements, which today range from the Amish, Hutterites, and Mennonites (who trace from Menno Simons) to English Baptists, and in the most general sense to all who restrict baptism to adult believers. Moreover, some Christians in the first centuries followed this practice, yet the Anabaptist movement has its origins in the Reformation.

In Zurich in 1525, three men—Conrad Grebel, Felix Manz, and George Blaurock—met to continue the reforms they believed had stalled in compromises made by Martin Luther and Ulrich Zwingli. Grebel and company wanted nothing to do with an established church and its half hearted followers. For them, a commitment to follow Christ was total and meant not only belief but also practice. The sign of one's joining Christ's church was baptism, which only adults could receive. These radicals therefore refused to have their children baptized.

In the modern era, no civic authority would consider baptism to be state business, and the social response would be on the order of "live and let live; to each his or her own." But in sixteenthcentury Zurich, civil and religious authorities were not two distinct spheres. Convergence and order required the city to recognize one way of worship only. Thus the radicals presented to the city an unacceptable disunity.

The solution offered was a debate. The radicals were to meet in a public forum with Zwingli himself. Afterwards, the city council would settle the matter in law. Indeed, the debate resulted in laws expressly forbidding the "rebaptizers" from meeting, teaching, or having fellowship together. The group was to be treated as nonexistent. Obviously the passing of these laws set up a classic conflict of conscience for Grebel and the others.

Against the law, the radicals met for prayer on January 21, 1525. Thus the Swiss Brethren were born as fellows of the Reformation, yet they were rejected and made pariahs by the reformers. Succeeding generations of Anabaptists would resist the neighboring culture (Amish) or assimilate incompletely (the pacifist Mennonites). Certainly the tragic misuse of doctrine and power against Grebel and his Brethren would be repeated in succeeding centuries. The migrations of Brethren from Europe to the New World in the seventeenth and eighteenth centuries attest to their continuing effort to find a safe place to worship and raise families. And in some corners of positive Christian radicalism, the prayers of Grebel, Manz, and Blaurock are echoed today.

IF I GIVE AWAY ALL I HAVE, AND IF
I DELIVER UP MY BODY TO BE
BURNED, BUT HAVE NOT LOVE,
I GAIN NOTHING.

I CORINTHIANS 13:3

Felix Manz

(1527)

Today a disaffected churchgoer can simply choose another place to worship. Options are many; choices seem limitless. Not so in sixteenthcentury Europe, even in enlightened Switzerland, which was a bit freer in polity and conscience than any of its neighbors.

Felix Manz rose up from a difficult childhood—his father was a priest, his mother thus an unmarried woman—to become a bright, well-educated young adult. He became enamored with the teachings of Ulrich Zwingli in 1519, and associated himself with Zwingli's reform movement. But two years later, he wondered if Zwingli himself, the great teacher, was holding back, settling for compromise when he should have moved forward. Baptism was the issue. Manz and a few others—Conrad Grebel and George Blaurock—could not find infant baptism in the Bible, despite Zwingli's teachings. What was not in the Bible, they reasoned, must be human invention. Sound faith cannot be based on inference or imagination. This small group dissented, even after the Zurich City Council found in favor of Zwingli's ideas on January 17, 1525, following a public debate intended to settle the matter in their city.

Four days later Manz and his group met to pray. "Who should we follow?" they asked. What law governs one's relationship with God? At the meeting (cited as the beginning of the Mennonite Church), Grebel baptized Blaurock, and Blaurock baptized the others. Their act was a crime against the state.

For the next two contentious years, on several occasions Manz was arrested and detained. Finally authorities had suffered his defiance enough. Manz was imprisoned and ordered to cease his "radical" reforms. Of course he could not, on pain of denying his faith, so the law had its way. On January 5, 1527, he was placed on a boat, taken out on River Lammat near Lake Zurich, bound, weighted, and thrown into the water. His mother and brothers urged Felix to remain strong as he walked to his icy death. Manz left for them these words written in prison: "I praise thee, O Lord Christ in heaven, that Thou dost turn away my sorrow and sadness...already before my end has come, that I should have eternal joy in Him."

Not yet thirty years of age, Felix Manz became the first of the radical reformers to be martyred by other reformers. Manz and his group were simply known as the Brethren. (The name by which his church is known today, the Mennonites, was still a decade ahead.) Others called them Anabaptists, for they rebaptized adult believers in defiance of the law. But for Manz, church reform simply needed to go further, for "He instructs us with His divine graces, and shows love to all men."

"HE WHO IS NEAR THE SWORD IS NEAR GOD; HE THAT IS AMONG THE WILD BEASTS IS IN COMPANY WITH GOD; PROVIDED ONLY HE BE SO IN THE NAME OF JESUS CHRIST. I UNDERGO ALL THESE THINGS THAT I MAY SUFFER TOGETHER WITH HIM, HE INWARDLY STRENGTHENING ME."

—IGNATIUS OF ANTIOCH

Michael Sattler
(1495–1527)

ichael Sattler was born in 1495 and became a monk. Like many Reformation-era monks, he wrestled with his sensual passions and his love for God. Sattler broke his oath of celibacy for an equally unavailable woman named Margarita, a nun who also broke her oath for marital love. Later, the Sattlers would die for a far greater love: their bond with God.

By 1526 the Sattlers had returned to the Anabaptist movement, which Michael had been forced to renounce years earlier to avoid imprisonment. Now, with his Anabaptist convictions strengthened, Michael dedicated his life to preaching at a church in Horb, a strongly Catholic region of Austria. On February 4, 1527, in the small German town of Schleitheim, the Anabaptists met and introduced to the world a new way of understanding church and Gospel. The Sattlers traveled to Germany from Horb for the deliberations that produced the "Seven Articles of the Faith," also known as the "Brotherly Union." Michael Sattler helped write this founding document of the Anabaptist movement.

But traveling home from that meeting, Michael and Margarita Sattler were captured and their articles confiscated. They were transformed from Anabaptist advocates to Anabaptist martyrs—a twist of events that propelled the church further than Sattler could ever have imagined.

Tried before a judge on May 17, 1527, the Sattlers, nine other men, and eight women were charged with various violations of doctrine and practice. Particularly grievous were the charges against the Eucharist, baptism, unction, and the veneration of the saints.

"Michael Sattler shall be committed to the hangman," read the court's sentence, "who shall take him to the square and there first cut out his tongue, then chain him to a wagon, tear his body twice with hot tongs there and five times more before the gate, then burn his body to powder as an archheretic."

Amid cries of "Almighty eternal God, Thou are the way and the truth," the sentence was carried out on May 21, 1527. Eight days later Margarita met the same fate, burned in the city of Rottenburg near the Black Forest.

Finding completion in the love of wife and Lord, Sattler had set himself to making the Anabaptist movement a light of truth for all nations. Soon after their deaths, Anabaptists began carrying the "Brotherly Union" and an account of the Sattlers' deaths in miniature version on their persons, and no threat of torture could stop them. Something deeper than the fear of fire and mutilation burned in their souls. And this can be said about the soul of Michael and Margarita Sattler: for love they lived, and for Love they died.

REMEMBER THE WORD THAT
I SAID TO YOU: "A SERVANT IS NOT
GREATER THAN HIS MASTER."
IF THEY PERSECUTED ME, THEY
WILL ALSO PERSECUTE YOU.
IF THEY KEPT MY WORD, THEY WILL
ALSO KEEP YOURS.

JOHN 15:20

GEORGE WAGNER
(1527)

Only three matters separated Herr George Wagner from the normal life of good men. These three matters were the difference between life and death in Munich in the sixteenth century: a priest's power to forgive sin, transubstantiation of the communion bread and wine, and water baptism as a rite that saves a person from God's judgment. Wagner believed none of these tenets, having been converted to the Anabaptist movement, the radicals of the Reformation. For Wagner, what the Bible did not directly teach, he was under obligation from no human being to believe.

The prince of Bavaria who arrested Wagner for his petulance was neither a bloodthirsty man nor one to take innocent life. Rather, he preferred a simple confession and then a return to more pleasant business. Oddly, Wagner refused, even when the prince politely asked. Wagner refused again when the prince brought Frau Wagner and their child before him. For even these loves, a normal man or woman would usually admit to mistakes on a few doctrinal points so clearly taught by the church. But not this man.

George Wagner, Anabaptist, was burned on February 8, 1527, for heresy. "Today I will confess my God before all the world," he said on his way to the fire.

That very night, Wagner's executioner died in his bed. Some said it must have been the wrath of God, a sad and bitter end to a public servant's life. Wagner, on the other hand, walked to his death with a smile—a most unusual man, but a happy one at the end.

BALTHASAR HUBMAIER
(1480–1528)

He was the scholar of the Anabaptists, the radical movement that parted company with Luther on grace, and with Calvin on election, and with both on infant baptism. Hubmaier was the only Anabaptist leader to earn a doctorate in theology. His writings continue to inspire Christians around the world.

As a scholar, Hubmaier knew that most arguments had some good reasons and some notsogood ones, some logic but also some disconnects. It was perhaps his advanced learning that troubled him whenever his courage fell victim to the manifold operations of his productive mind.

For example, while in Zurich and trying to escape the army of King Ferdinand of Austria, Hubmaier was arrested for teaching against infant baptism—utterly useless, he thought. In his defense, he quoted the great reformer Zwingli, also in Zurich. Imagine Hubmaier's surprise when Zwingli refuted Hubmaier, claiming the latter had misunderstood him. Embarrassed and without an ally, Hubmaier agreed to recant. Yet the next day, his conscience in turmoil, Hubmaier retracted his recant. With those words, Hubmaier was sent to prison and put on the rack to determine if pain would clarify his theology. Indeed it did. Hubmaier agreed to his recantation after all. He was released from prison and left Switzerland. Yet his conscience was troubled. He wrote his Short Apology in 1526: "I may err—I am a man—but a heretic I cannot be...O God, pardon me my weakness."

Hubmaier did more than soulsearching, however. He preached and taught widely from his base in Bavaria, and he baptized adults throughout the region. These radical Protestant offenses had unsettled the peace of the Austrian empire, concluded King Ferdinand. When Hubmaier finally committed his views to paper, Ferdinand's forces captured him and brought him to Vienna. Eight months later, on March 10, 1528, he was burned at the stake, with his wife, Elizabeth, urging him to be strong. Three days after his execution, Elizabeth was thrown into the Danube River with a rock around her neck.

The legacy of their faith includes their writings, which taught God's love for all sinners, baptism as a witness to saving faith, and pacifism as a Christian obligation. Neither atheists nor pagans were to be tormented, Hubmaier wrote, but rather kindly confronted with God's eternal longing for their trust and obedience. Hubmaier had given the radical reformation its strongest theological statement. It cost him his life.

MY FLESH AND MY HEART FAIL, BUT GOD IS THE STRENGTH OF MY HEART AND MY PORTION FOREVER.

PSALM 73:26

GEORGE BLAUROCK
(1491–1529)

When Blaurock started a project, he went all the way.
Born in Bonaduz in the Grisons, Switzerland, Blaurock had studied for the priesthood and had been ordained. At some point before 1524, however, he abandoned his vows, took a wife, and attached himself to the reformers' movement. George arrived in Zurich that year to hear Ulrich Zwingli debate key doctrinal questions, but he found himself pulling past Zwingli's reforms toward a small group of radicals called the Anabaptists. Indeed, Blaurock was the baptizer of all the new communicants, after he himself was baptized, at the famous first meeting of the Anabaptists, or Brethren, on January 21, 1525.

Trouble lay ahead, of course. On the day Felix Manz was martyred, Blaurock, not a citizen of Zurich, was merely beaten and expelled. He went to Bern, Biel, the Grisons, and Appenzell, at each place being arrested and banished. From Switzerland he went to Tyrol and took the pastorate of Michael Keurschner, who had been burned at the stake. In August 1529, authorities in Innsbruck, Austria, apprehended Blaurock and commenced a trial.

The details of his trial are lost, except that Blaurock endured torture to extract information about the radical reform movement. On September 6, 1529, he and his pastoral associate Hans Langegger were burned at the stake.

A letter and two hymns constitute the legacy of Blaurock's writing. In the hymn "Gott, dich will ich loben," he wrote what would become his own triumph song:

Thy Spirit shield and teach me, That in afflictions great
Thy comfort I may ever prove, And valiantly may obtain
The victory in this fight.

Patrick Hamilton (1527)
and Henry Forest (1529)

No one was more surprised by the court's sentence, or treated with greater cruelty, than the early Scottish martyr Patrick Hamilton. He was royalty after all, related to the Stuart King James V. Through that relation he was educated in Paris, and knew Erasmus, one of Europe's premier scholars.

Hamilton had been appointed abbot of Ferne the same year Martin Luther posted his Ninety-Five Theses on the church door at Wittenberg. Hamilton had met the German reformer and also knew Philip Melancthon, whose written works powered the Lutheran Reformation. Patrick was a gifted musician, composing and directing in his home cathedral. This promising young man, brilliant and connected, faltered at only one life skill, so it seemed: a sense for danger.

In the summer of 1523, Hamilton returned from Europe to join the faculty at St. Andrews University. Recently challenged on the Continent to reconsider the meaning of Christian faith, he took every opportunity to teach and debate his recovery of biblical truth: God's mercy in Christ apart from indulgences and other contrived interventions. But the archbishop, James Beaton, was scrutinizing the young scholar from afar. Utterly devoted to the papacy, the archbishop would make sure this vile teaching of faith and grace at St. Andrews would not ruin the church.

Dispatching Hamilton was a quick decision and a subhumanly slow process. In late autumn 1527, just after Hamilton's wedding, he was invited to participate in a conference of learned church leaders who were gathering, so it appeared, to debate the "new doctrines." Hamilton responded without delay, anticipating a lively colloquy. Instead, Archbishop Beaton conducted a short theological examination and ordered Hamilton's arrest. The next morning the young scholar was questioned by bishops on thirteen charges of heresy, found guilty, and condemned to die that afternoon. The sentence was to be quickly carried out lest his friends exploit the heretic's royal connections and Hamilton be pardoned or acquitted. He had, of course, agreed to every charge. He very much believed what he taught. He could not deny what he and all those around him plainly knew.

Doubtless stunned by the quick turn of events, Hamilton nevertheless walked to the place of burning in a spirit of prayer. Once fixed to the stake, a bag of gunpowder was tied under each armpit and a pile of stillgreen wood and kindling placed around him. The gunpowder burst into flames but did not explode; the wood burned but with insufficient heat to kill. So there Hamilton hanged, flames smoldering, but his blistered, burned body writhing. While more wood was gathered, he begged for an end to the misery. A full six hours he suffered in front of the crowd at St. Salvator's College, who heard him cry amid the agony, "Lord Jesus, receive my spirit. How long will darkness overwhelm this land?"

Two years later, in 1529, a Benedictine monk, Henry Forest, began to illustrate his sermons with the story of teacher Patrick Hamilton, a martyr for the truth. Archbishop Beaton was no more inclined to Forest's perverse teaching than to Hamilton's. Yet Beaton had an increasingly uneasy parish to contend with. The faithful had seen uncommon courage only too recently, and Beaton feared their reaction should he move too openly against another.

Instead of confrontation, Beaton sent a friar to hear Forest's confession, always a confidential matter between sinner, priest, and God. But in this case, the confessional was really a pretext for intelligence gathering, which Beaton quickly used to condemn his mark. Instead of the stake, however, Beaton ordered Forest smothered in a cellar jail away from the people, a private affair within the church.

As the Scottish Reformation grew, Hamilton and Forest were honored as early heroes, and the man most widely known for changing the soul of Scotland, John Knox, took his place in their wake, preaching and teaching the Gospel that the abbot and the monk knew and died for.

JOHN FRITH
(1503-1533)

An English Protestant priest, John Frith lived only thirty years on this earth.

Born in 1503, Frith eventually attended Eton College and then graduated from King's College, Cambridge. After graduation, in 1525, Frith became a junior canon at Wolsey's College, Oxford. There he helped William Tyndale translate the New Testament into English. But that work earned him three years in prison.

After his release, Frith went to Marburg, where he translated Patrick Hamilton's book, *Loci Communes*. Known as "Patrick's Places," this work clearly set forth the doctrine of justification by faith and the contrast between the Gospel and the Law. The young Rev. Frith also wrote Disputacion of Purgatorye.

When Frith returned to England in 1532, he was arrested and tried for heresy. But even then, imprisoned in the Tower of London, he continued to write, formulating the Protestant views on the Sacraments.

Frith received his sentence—death—but was offered a pardon if he would say that he believed in purgatory and in transubstantiation (the Roman Catholic teaching that in the Eucharist, the bread and wine become the actual body and blood of Christ). Frith answered that neither doctrine could be proven by Holy Scriptures.

Thus, John Frith was burned at the stake on July 4, 1533, at Smithfield, London. In 1573, forty years after his death, Frith's works were published by John Foxe.

WILLIAM TYNDALE
(CA. 1494–1536)

S o great is our passion to know the truth that some seekers will give everything, even their lives, for the treasure of knowing one certain thing.

William Tyndale was a welleducated scholar who was frustrated at the distance between English education and the Bible, the source of truth. Studying at Oxford and then at Cambridge, he bristled at the barriers and longed for the nourishment his mind and heart treasured. "In the universities," he said, "they have ordained that no man shall look on the Scripture until he be nozzled in heathen learning eight or nine years, and armed with false principles with which he is clean shut out of the understanding of the Scripture." Tyndale's life would be devoted to overcoming just this obstacle. For him, the Bible "for the people" would become the answer to corruption in the church. The Bible "for the people" meant that all could drink from the truth itself, without pressure or pretext; and most clearly, without a priest to read or interpret.

Tyndale was born sometime around 1494 in Gloucester, England, near the Welsh border. Ninety years earlier the Church had banned the only English Bible in the world, the handcopied work of John Wycliffe. It was a flawed translation, based on the Latin Vulgate, but it was all English speakers had. And to have it was a crime. Tyndale's passions eventually settled on a mission as dangerous as any in his century: to work from the Greek and Hebrew texts to create a Bible in vernacular English, so readable and accurate that an Englishman could depend on it, learn from it, and find God's voice in it. All this was clear to the multilingual Tyndale by the age of thirty.

To do that work, Tyndale had to leave England. No bishop in the realm would protect him, much less encourage the project. Tyndale traveled to Germany where he completed the New Testament in 1525.

William Tyndale burned at the stake for translating the Bible into the English language

Then he went on to Antwerp, one step ahead of English agents, where the first five Old Testament books were translated and printed. In Belgium he met a community of English merchants, and though agents were searching the continent to find him, Tyndale felt secure enough to relax his guard. His lack of caution would prove fatal.

Tyndale took up a friendship with Henry Phillips, who won Tyndale's confidence but secretly sought the bounty offered for his capture. In May 1535 the trap was set. Tyndale was taken under guard to the castle at Vilvoorde, near Brussels, where he suffered in dank and cold for eighteen months before standing trial for "maintaining that faith alone justifies…that to believe in the forgiveness of sins, and to embrace the mercy offered in the gospel, was enough for salvation." The complete list of charges included direct attacks on church teaching, among them that "neither the Virgin nor the Saints should be invoked by us."

Tyndale knew how these trials ran. He would have no chance at defense, and death was the remedy. With his body shaking from cold and the winter's light dim for writing, he worked to complete the English Bible, helped by a sympathetic prison governor.

In August 1536, Tyndale was condemned as a heretic and defrocked. For two more months he was kept at Vilvoorde. Then in early October, just past dawn, he was led from prison to the stake. Formalities included placing the Mass once more in his hands, then quickly snatching it back, the offer of lastminute reprieve if he would only recant, and always the shouts of a crowd gathered to witness a "heathen" die.

Secured to the stake, surrounded by brush and logs, Tyndale was heard to pray, "Lord, open the King of England's eyes." Then the executioner snapped hard on the rope, strangling Tyndale before the blaze consumed his body.

That final prayer was for the bully King Henry VIII, whose pursuit of a male heir had already cost Anne Boleyn her life and Catherine her marriage. So full of his own power and pomp, would this king's eyes ever fall favorably on Tyndale's English Bible?

Indeed they did. Two years after Tyndale's death, King Henry authorized the distribution of the Matthew Bible, much of it Tyndale's work. And then in 1539, all printers and sellers of books were ordered by the king to provide for the "free and liberal use of the Bible in our own maternal English tongue." Tyndale's dream and his last earthly appeal had come true.

John Lambert
(1538)

Branded a "heretic" by the Catholic Church and Henry VIII's Church of England, John Lambert was burned to death on November 22, 1538, at Smithfield in London.

Lambert was born "John Nicholson" in Norwich. As a young man, he was educated at Queens' College, Cambridge. After graduation, Catherine of Aragon nominated John as a fellow at that prestigious institution. But after some theological disputes, John changed his name and went to Antwerp, where he served as a priest to English workers. There he became friends with John Frith and William Tyndale, and he joined the theologians who would meet regularly at the White Horse Tavern. This group included the future Lutherans Edward Fox and Robert Barnes and the archconservative Stephen Gardiner.

Lambert returned to England in 1531 and immediately came under the scrutiny of Archbishop William Warham. But he was not accused of anything, because the archbishop died in 1532. In 1536, the Duke of Norfolk accused Lambert of heresy, but he escaped and avoided the authorities for a couple of years. In 1538, Lambert was captured and put on trial, charged with denying the real presence of Jesus in the bread and wine of the Eucharist. He was convicted and, thus, condemned to death at the stake.

As flames consumed Lambert, he raised his hands and declared, "None but Christ! None but Christ!"

GEORGE WISHART

(1546)

Educated at King's College in Aberdeen, Scotland, Wishart the preacher became "infected" with Reformation teaching, and was forced into exile in 1538 after charges of heresy put his life in danger. He returned to Scotland in 1544.

That year Wishart was in Dundee tending to those afflicted by the plague that had consumed the city. "They are in trouble and need comfort," Wishart said about his mission, while Beaton recruited an assailant. There in Dundee, priest John Weighton, on Cardinal Beaton's orders, confronted Wishart with a cloaked dagger after listening to one of Wishart's sermons. "My friend, what would you have?" called out Wishart, as he noticed Weighton's weapon and realized his intent. Terrified, the wouldbe assassin fell to his knees pleading for forgiveness. But the congregation of the sick cried out, "Deliver the traitor, we will take him by force." Wishart rebuked them. Holding Weighton by his arms, Wishart insisted, "Whatsoever hurts him shall hurt me; for he has done me no mischief, but much good, by teaching more heedfulness for the time to come." Unfortunately, that time would come sooner than Wishart expected.

Beaton finally caught up with Wishart in December 1545, again having assigned the dirty work to another, this time the Earl of Bothwell. In a show trial, Wishart was convicted of refusing to accept that a confession was a sacrament, for denying free will, and for rejecting the idea that an infinite God "could be comprehended in one place" between "the priest's hands." Instead, Wishart proclaimed that the true church was anywhere that Christ's Word was truthfully taught.

Wishart dedicated his life to bringing the Reformation to Scotland, yet more importantly he recognized the everyman, the sick, the downand out. Wishart administered the grace of God to all equally. "I have offered you the Word of salvation," Wishart once said. "With the hazard of my life I have remained among you; and I must leave my innocence to be declared by my God." Even minutes from death, Wishart had others in mind, ironically the very people who wished him death, as he prayed: "I beseech thee, Father of heaven, forgive them that have, from ignorance or an evil mind, forged lies of me. I forgive them with all my heart. I beseech Christ to forgive them that have ignorantly condemned me." His friends were obviously not so forgiving.

On March 1, 1546, George Wishart was burned outside St. Andrews Castle in Scotland. The betrayer, Cardinal Beaton, watched from inside the castle window, thinking all was well.

"I NEED TEARS RATHER THAN WORDS TO EXPRESS THE SORROW WITH WHICH THE WOUND OF OUR BODY SHOULD BE BEWAILED, WITH WHICH THE MANIFOLD LOSS OF A PEOPLE ONCE NUMEROUS SHOULD BE LAMENTED."

—CYPRIAN AFTER THE PERSECUTION UNDER EMPEROR DECIUS HAD SUBSIDED (C. A.D. 251)

DIRK WILLEMS
(1569)

He saved the man who tracked him down, only to have the bounty hunter turn him in.

Dirk Willems was a Protestant in Catholic Holland, but the details of his faith and work are lost to history. We do know that when the authorities issued a warrant for his arrest, there was a chase— Willems running for his freedom, and a bounty hunter in pursuit. Willems took a risky path over some thin ice and made it across safely. His pursuer did not. When the sinking man's cries reached Willems' ears, the safety of the other took priority over his own. Willems turned back to rescue the man from the icy waters. Grateful for life, the bounty hunter offered Willems his chance to run. But from the far shore, a town official yelled for the deputy to perform his duty after all. Willems was brought in.

The only record of Dirk Willems's trial and punishment reads: "After severe imprisonment and great trials, he was put to death in a lingering fire by these bloodthirsty, ravening wolves, enduring it with great steadfastness, and confirming his faith."

No last words of Dirk Willems are recorded. Only two last deeds— one, saving a man's life, and then dying with dignity and faith in the God who ultimately rescues all who trust in Him.

THE NAGASAKI MARTYRS
(1597)

The Jesuits arrived in Japan in 1549, the great missionary St. Francis Xavier leading the campaign to convert the island people. Along with them came traders, whose goods were valued even if the Godwords of the priests were greeted with respectful curiosity but not much enthusiasm. Yet a small church grew.

In 1597, Japan's ruler, Toyotomi Hideyoshi, came to believe that his troubles were due to a loss of nationalistic fervor. Thus he directed the cleansing that outlawed Christian worship and led to the arrest of twenty six Christian men, nineteen of them Japanese. Following a monthlong winter march, the men were crucified on Nishizaka Hill on crosses cut to fit the dimensions of each of the condemned. It is said that when the column of prisoners saw their crosses lying in the wheat field beside the hill, they each embraced theirs, and one of the condemned asked that his hands be nailed to the crossbar. For the rest, chains and iron straps kept the men suspended until a squad of executioners finished the work by pushing spears into their chests.

The men were a mix of ages and backgrounds. Louis Ibaraki was only twelve years old. He died with a child's vision of flying from his cross into Heaven. John of Goto was nineteen, born to Christian parents who had him educated by the Jesuits. He took his first Jesuit vows the morning of his death. Paul Miki was thirty, the son of a samurai soldier. He was not ordained but was the most gifted preacher in the group. From his cross, he told spectators they could find no salvation apart from Jesus Christ. "I have committed no crime," he said. "The only reason why I am put to death is that I have been preaching the doctrine of our Lord Jesus Christ. I am very happy to die for such a cause." Brother Philip was Mexican. He died while his mother, far away, was preparing vestments for his first Mass. Brother Anthony (aged thirteen) watched his Japanese mother weeping in the crowd in front of him. All the martyrs prayed and sang together before Hideyoshi's executioners brought silence to the hillside.

For nearly two hundred years, Christians in Japan met as an underground church, and were finally discovered by French priests permitted into Japan in the 1850s. Today the Shrine of the Twenty-Six Martyrs stands in a replica of the Nagasaki church where those "hidden Christians" first emerged. The original church was destroyed by an atomic bomb in 1945.

WHOEVER FINDS HIS LIFE WILL LOSE IT, AND WHOEVER LOSES HIS LIFE FOR MY SAKE WILL FIND IT.

MATTHEW 10:39

Persecution in Sixteenth-Century England and Europe
(1553-1595)

E ngland's King Henry VIII won his battle with Rome, securing a host of wives and becoming head of his national church. When he died in 1547, his successor, Edward VI, was still a child and sickly. To stabilize power, the Duke of Somerset became adviser to the king, but he so disturbed wealthy landowners that he was executed in 1557. The Duke of Northumberland took over; and as Edward grew weaker, he plotted to bring to the throne Lady Jane Grey, also young. Northumberland forced Grey to marry his son, securing his own place in the kingdom.

Surely temporal and religious reasons combined in these plots and plans. Edward VI was agreeable to the growing Protestant movement. Grey herself was a sincere Protestant. But Edward's legitimate heir was his half-sister Mary, daughter of Catherine of Aragon, who was as devoted to Rome as anyone in Europe.

Nine days into Jane Grey's rule, Mary's army arrived in London and proclaimed her queen. Northumberland was beheaded despite his pleas to live. Archbishop Cranmer, who had instigated several reforms and had written the Book of Common Prayer, was imprisoned. The queen reversed her earlier clemency for Jane Grey and had her beheaded, along with Grey's tiresome husband.

In 1555, Parliament passed a law reinstating burning as proper treatment for heretics, and only days later the first martyrs were chained to the stake. Nearly three hundred followed, giving Mary her historical identity as one of England's most heartless monarchs. But Mary failed to lead, and angered English leaders by her unhappy marriage to Philip of Spain, son of Emperor Charles V. Many of her influential lords believed that Mary's allegiance with Rome would wreck England's independence and change the country's polity. Had Mary not died young (in 1558), many suspect that a revolution would have swept her out.

Elizabeth I (1558-1603) brought stability and calm to England. Her religious settlement in 1559 established a new day of freedom for the English Reformation, but set the stage for the persecution of Puritans and their search for a new place to worship and live. As a result, North America became home to European religious refugees.

No, in ALL THESE THINGS WE ARE MORE THAN CONQUERORS THROUGH Him WHO LOVED US.

ROMANS 8:37

LADY JANE GREY
(1554)

The morning of July 9, 1553, arrived for Lady Jane Grey just as any other summer morning in the English countryside. But much to her surprise and somewhat against her will, on that day Lady Jane was crowned queen. It was a day that her parents had dreamed of, that she dreaded, and that her cousin Mary feared and disdained.

King Edward was ill, and Jane's mother-in-law had come six days earlier to tell Grey that she had been named heir to the throne. This came as quite a shock, as Mary was closer in bloodlines than she. On July 6, Edward passed away. The news was kept a secret for several days in hopes of prohibiting the Catholic Mary from making a claim to the throne. But on July 9 the news leaked out, and Mary proclaimed herself queen.

Meanwhile, that same day Grey was brought to her father-in-law's house, the residence of the Duke of Northumberland, himself a power monger. As she walked down the familiar corridors, something unfamiliar happened. Everyone she passed curtsied or bowed. She heard murmurs of "Your Majesty" and stopped suddenly, realizing what was happening. Someone steered her toward a room which contained an empty throne. As she approached it, Grey swooned and fell, crumpling to the floor. She cried, "The crown is not my right and pleaseth me not. The Lady Mary is the rightful heir." She took a moment to gather her strength and consider what her best course of action would be as her family sought to persuade her of the imperative nature of her acceptance of the crown.

Grey did what was natural to her: She prayed for divine guidance. After a moment, she ascended the throne and allowed those present to swear allegiance to her, because she had asked God to give her "such spirit and grace that I may govern to Thy glory and service, and to the advantage of the realm."

Lady Jane Grey

But Grey's greatest challenge was yet to come. She made her state entrance into London amid few cheers, as public opinion was on the side of Mary. For several days Grey lived as queen, but soon her father-in-law, Lord Northumberland, mustered an army to meet Mary, who was encroaching on London with an army of her own. While he was gone, a royal council decided to declare Mary Tudor to be queen, which Grey herself supported. In a desperate attempt to save himself, Grey's own father swore allegiance to Mary, in spite of his previous actions to place his daughter on the throne. Lord Northumberland also quickly changed his position, but it was too late.

Grey, her father, her husband, and her father-in-law were all sentenced to the Tower of London. Grey's father was pardoned (temporarily, as it turned out), her father-in-law was executed in August, and Grey and her husband were assured of Mary's pardon. But an ill-timed insurrection of other enemies of Mary's hardened her heart, and she rescinded her forgiveness, particularly because Grey refused to convert to Catholicism.

February 11 was the date Grey and her husband were executed. Grey was brought to the block, recited the fifty-first Psalm, and asked that the deed be done quickly. Her final sentiment echoed that of her Lord's: "Father, into your hands I commit my spirit." In the end, she died a martyr for her faith. She was a political pawn from the first, acquiescing to the wishes of her family to her own detriment. Yet, her faith was firmly grounded in the truth of Scripture, and she died with the strength and dignity God provided for her.

John Bradford before being burned at the stake

JOHN BRADFORD

(1510-1555)

For saving a life, he lost his own; for owning an oath, he was condemned as a liar. A humble, sometimes timid man, this martyr gave us one of today's most frequently used quotations, yet few know of him.

The sixteenth century was one of the most religiously dangerous times in English history. Survival required changing one's color like a chameleon, depending on the whim of the monarch. Many souls, once captured by the Gospel, dared to remain loyal to God at any cost. For John Bradford, the cost was a promising career in government, and eventually his life.

Bradford was born into a wealthy family and received early training in business and law. His skill led to service in the government of the notorious Henry VIII, whose quest for a male heir forced his break with the Roman Church and the death or banishment of wives unable to bear a son.

While a law student in London, Bradford came to faith in Christ and soon afterward turned his studies toward theology at Cambridge University. He was ordained a chaplain in 1550, during the short reign of Protestant King Edward VI. As chaplain, Bradford once watched a column of prisoners being led to their execution, when he said, "There but for the grace of God go I." His words were a gift to the ages and a premonition of his own untimely death.

In 1553, King Edward died, and Mary Tudor took the throne. Known as "Bloody Mary," she condemned more than three hundred martyrs in her effort to return England to the Catholic Church. Any preacher or prelate could see the tide turning; many turned with it. Yet for Bradford, it was an act of interfaith heroism which Mary used against him.

On a hot August Sunday during Mary's first year, her loyal bishop of Bath preached a sermon critical of the recently deceased king. The crowd grew angry and threatening. One listener threw a knife at the bishop, who was shaken but unhurt. Bradford, present that day, quieted the crowd, urged them to good order, then at his own risk escorted the panicked bishop to safety. Three days later Bradford was arrested for sedition.

For two years Bradford lived inside dank English cells, preaching and writing. His word was so trusted that guards would release him occasionally at night, fully confident that he would return before daybreak. He always did. Finally examined by an ecclesial court that was determined to find fault, they asked whether he would accept the queen's mercy. Bradford replied, "I shall be glad of the queen's favor on terms that correspond with my duty to Him whose favor is life, but whose displeasure is worse than any death mortals can inflict."

The immensely popular preacher was led to the stake on July 1, 1555. Upon arriving, he asked forgiveness of any he had wronged, granted forgiveness to the soldiers around him, then picked up a nearby stick and kissed it. He was bound to the stake with a younger prisoner, who heard from Bradford this assurance as flames lifted around them: "Brother, be of good comfort, for we shall have a merry supper with the Lord this night, where all our pains will end in peace, and our warfare in songs of joy."

JOHN HOOPER

(1555)

Awaiting execution at the Newgate prison, John Hooper scribbled with coal on the prison wall: "Fear not death, pass not for bands. Only in God put thy whole trust. Death is no death, but means to live." Sentenced days earlier by a magistrate of Queen Mary of England, Hooper sat in a prison cell at the very church where he once preached, a prisoner of the Word he had so boldly announced.

Born in Somerset, England, to a well-to-do Catholic family, Hooper left home in 1515 to attend Oxford University. With a Bachelor of Arts in hand, Hooper spent the next twenty years straddling the line between overindulgence and temperance, committing himself to a monastery, only then to become steward to a wealthy family. At times admittedly a "brute beast...a slave to my own lusts," Hooper ultimately conceded that "living too much of a court life in the palace of our king" was not his calling. In the Puritan Reformation, John Hooper found his passion.

But this was unfortunate timing. Henry VIII, desperate for national solidarity in England, demanded ecclesial unity from his subjects. Puritans either went underground or faced the king's wrath. When Henry died in 1547, Hooper was made chaplain to Edward Seymour, first Duke of Somerset, where he championed the tenets of the Swiss Reformation. Then the impossible happened. John Hooper, the radical, outspoken Puritan preacher, was offered the bishopric of Gloucester by the English crown, a distinguished appointment and certainly a fortunate career move toward power and public influence. Hooper's response? He said no.

Citing the "shameful and impious form of the [acceptance] oath" and the vestments Hooper would be required to wear, he declined the position. Several months in the Fleet prison followed, until Hooper conceded various points and officially assumed the position of Bishop of Gloucester in March 1551.

Two years later, in 1553, the consummate Catholic monarch, Mary Tudor, became Queen of England. Her policy was no compromise, no concession. Defrocked and imprisoned in March 1554, Hooper had one chance left to renounce his beliefs before a Commission of Bishops in January 1555. His response was as clear as his queen's indictment of him: no compromise.

Hooper accused the pope and the entire Catholic Church of opposing the teachings of Christ. Firm in his beliefs about divorce, marriage, and the Eucharist, Hooper was condemned to death on January 29.

Charge #1: "He [a priest] had himself married and openly maintained and taught the lawfulness of the marriage of the clergy."

Charge #2: His teachings that "married persons, in the case of adultery [can be] divorced from one another."

Charge #3: Hooper's position that the Eucharist was "not truly the true and natural body of Christ and His true and natural blood under the species of bread and wine."

As noted in the execution document written by the Commission of Bishops, Hooper was "a most obstinate, detestable heretic, and, committed to our secular powers, [should] be burned according to the law." Led on February 9 from his cell to the pyre, Hooper was forbidden to speak, being a "vainglorious person [who] delighteth in his tongue." The silent John Hooper was tied to the stake and given one last chance to repent, with a box containing a pardon placed in front of him. The ban on speech lifted for a moment, and he replied, "If you love my soul, if you love my soul, away with it!"

JOHN ROGERS

(CA. 1500-1555)

L ife was a string of successes and honors for this Cambridge University graduate and rector of Holy Trinity Church in London. That is, until the death of the English king he had chosen to serve and the accession of a queen his convictions forced him to challenge. John Rogers, a minister, Bible editor, and father of eleven children, holds the dubious distinction of being Mary Tudor's first victim.

In 1534 Rogers took a post as chaplain to English merchants in Antwerp. There he met his wife, and also befriended William Tyndale, who convinced Rogers that the recovery of biblical truth, indeed the Bible itself, was the first and only foundation of God's truth. It was God's Word.

Rogers became a Protestant and helped compile the Matthew Bible, the first English edition authorized for distribution by Henry VIII himself. From Antwerp, he went to Wittenberg, where he pastored a church and studied further the doctrinal reforms sweeping Europe. In 1548, Rogers returned to England, where Edward VI welcomed reform, and leaders such as Nicholas Ridley and Archbishop Thomas Cranmer were drafting and planning a new era of Christian worship. Their efforts would be cut short, however, by Edward VI's untimely death and the subsequent reign of Mary Tudor.

By August 1553, Rogers knew that his life as leader and reformer would soon change. Early that month he preached on the foolishness of "popery, idolatry, and superstition." This was a direct challenge to Mary's vision for the future of the English church. The sermon led to John's examination and house arrest. His employment as chaplain and rector was ended and his church office stripped.

Six months later, a new bishop of London had Rogers transferred to Newgate Prison. Mary was preparing Parliament to pass her "crackdown" laws, and offenders were being put in line so that the coming legislation could be practiced and its bitter lessons taught to the people.

Rogers waited a year at Newgate without trial. Then in January 1555, he was brought before Mary's hatchet man, Bishop Stephen Gardiner of Winchester. Gardiner declared Rogers a heretic because he denied the change of substance in the communion bread and wine. Then, because Parliament had outlawed heresy and clarified its punishment, Rogers was condemned to be burned.

Treatment of the man was unnecessarily cruel. Rogers requested a meeting with his wife; he was denied. He was asked to recant; this he denied. But such stalemates and discourtesies were short-lived. On February 4, Rogers was marched to the stake. His children joined the crowd lining the street as he walked to his death. His youngest child was there, at mother's breast. All who knew the gravity of the day encouraged him to go with strength. Indeed, John's final conversation was a witness in itself.

"Will you revoke your evil opinions of the Sacrament?" the sheriff asked.

"That which I have preached I will seal with my blood," Rogers answered.

"You are a heretic then," declared the official.

"That shall be known at the day of judgment," Rogers assured him.

"I will never pray for you," the sheriff finished.

"But I will pray for you," Rogers said, moments before the flames rose.

JOHN PHILPOT

(1555)

L
ike many before him and after, John Philpot was caught in the pincers of changing worldviews, where ideas once favored become dangerous, and people who are guided by fear and ambition are placed in positions of judgment.

Philpot was privileged. His father was a knight, and his college was Oxford. With a good mind to complement a sturdy character, Philpot grew into a leader and church reformer. He traveled widely, gaining exposure beyond England's shores. He returned to his homeland in what appeared to be its prime. The boy-king, Edward VI, favored Philpot's reformational faith. And thus he became the new archdeacon of Winchester. The future appeared open, favorable, challenging.

Situations soon changed. Edward died, and after the brief and most unhappy try at queen by Lady Jane Grey, Mary I took the throne. She was a staunch Catholic and opposed the Protestant reformers as deeply as anyone in her day. Philpot, a thoughtful man, no doubt acknowledged the new difficulties confronting him. But how could he—the knight's son, the Oxford-trained church leader—have foreseen the end?

In the pogrom that Mary inspired, Philpot was relieved of duty and summoned to defend his views. He did this with conviction and intelligence through thirteen colloquies, separated by various depredations of prison and confinement. For several of these prison terms he was not allowed books or pen, as if the absence of the tools of the mind would eventually bend him to recant and join the Queen's spiritual cadre.

Intellectually defeated but politically strong, England's Privy Council convened the fourteenth examination to finally rid themselves of the Philpot pest. He had been in various prisons for more than twenty months.

His last interrogation had a stark simplicity about it. Whatever Philpot's reason for believing as he did, he could either recant or die.

Engraved for The Rev.d D.r Southwell's New Book of Martyrs.

Stothard delin.   *Grignion sculp.*

The pious and Learned Mr. JOHN PHILPOT praying at the place of his MARTYRDOM in Smithfield.

John Philpot praying at the place of his martyrdom

The realm was no longer interested in windy monologues that seemed to end in the quietude of defeat for the side that was supposed to win. Absent a complete change of heart and mind, Philpot was sentenced to be burned.

On December 18, 1555, the sheriff, escorting the prisoner across a muddy track on the way to the stake, asked if he would like the courtesy of being carried by two officers, thus avoiding the mud. He replied sharply, "Would you make me a pope? I will finish my journey on foot."

Then at the place of execution, Philpot said, "Shall I disdain to suffer here at the stake, when my Redeemer did not refuse to suffer the most vile death upon the cross for me?"

As the fire at his feet grew hot, Philpot recited Psalms 107 and 108. In moments the realm's will was done. Another voice was gone, another martyr's crown won.

BE EXALTED, O GOD, ABOVE THE HEAVENS! LET YOUR GLORY BE OVER ALL THE EARTH!

PSALM 108:5

LAWRENCE SAUNDERS
(1555)

Blood was spilled in this chaotic middle decade of England's sixteenth century. Passionate faith and politics ran strongly together, and the power of the combination was both a testament to faith and a threat to life.

Lawrence Saunders was a gifted young man. Educated at Eton and Cambridge, he obtained a license to preach during the brief reign of the boy-king, Edward VI. The king, fond of tennis and some revelry, caught a cold in the winter of 1552-53 and succumbed to tuberculosis on July 6. He and his counselors had planned that Lady Jane Grey would succeed him and thus keep Protestant faith paramount. But the people wanted King Henry's rightful heir, Mary; so nine days into Grey's patched-together queenship, Mary rode into London and took the throne for herself. Mary ordered all those involved in the Grey plot to be killed, sparing her half-sister Elizabeth. But how does one kill a church, a faith, and turn it back toward Rome? Mary's plan was to listen well to what the preachers had to say.

On October 15, 1553, Saunders delivered a sermon meant to clarify the teachings of Protestant faith and perhaps as well, to boost Jane Grey's chances for reinstatement. The sermon was theologically astute but politically futile. Whether by plan or serendipity, Saunders's sermon was heard by royal sympathizers. He was accused of treason, and the Bishop of London ordered his arrest.

The plot to bring Grey back failed completely. She, her husband, and other culprits were executed. Saunders waited in prison for Parliament to pass the law which permitted heretics to be burned. On February 8, 1555, he was marched barefoot to the fire. His last words: "Welcome the cross of Christ, welcome everlasting life."

Nicholas Ridley (1500-1555) and Hugh Latimer (1485-1555)

The fire that quenched the lives of these two pastors was lit to cleanse English soil of traitors and heretics. Instead, it silenced scholars, committed churchmen, and forceful humanitarians.

Both Nicholas Ridley and Hugh Latimer had reached pinnacles in their careers. Ridley was the bishop of London and confidant to Archbishop Thomas Cranmer. He influenced Cranmer's Book of Common Prayer, began pastoral work in inner-city London, and founded hospitals and schools.

Latimer, an extraordinary preacher, was an ardent Catholic who converted to reformation faith upon hearing of a confession by Thomas Bilney, whose confidence in the God of the Bible reduced Latimer to tears. Latimer advised the intemperate King Henry VIII and flourished under his successor, Edward VI.

But Edward died, and Mary Tudor, the daughter of Henry's first wife, took the throne. Now was the time to cleanse England of so-called reformers and restore it to Rome. Nicknamed "Bloody Mary," the new queen arrested Ridley, Latimer, and Cranmer—in all, about three hundred people met death by her decree.

Because each man refused to repent of his convictions about church and sacrament, both were condemned to be burned, a testament to the people that stature and age do not insulate a heretic from the queen's wrath (or from God's, in her view). When the queen's court passed judgment, the men were told to prepare immediately for the stake. A blacksmith approached Ridley to fix a chain around his waist. The deposed bishop replied, "Good fellow, knock it in hard, for the flesh will have its course." When executioners laid lighted wood at Ridley's feet, Latimer turned to him and said, "Be of good comfort, Dr. Ridley, and play the

Bishops Ridley and Latimer were burned together in one fire.

man. We shall this day light such a candle by God's grace in England, as I trust never shall be put out."

Latimer died quickly, but Ridley's fire waned. His lower parts burned through, but the flames barely hurt his upper body. In agony he moaned, "I cannot burn...Lord, have mercy on me." At last, flames ignited the gunpowder sack hung around his neck, and his life passed from Earth to Heaven.

Thomas Cranmer, the deposed archbishop, his own heart and mind wavering, his every sinew fearing the fire, watched his friends die from his cell in London Tower. He too was eventually burned at the stake.

FOR I CONSIDER THAT THE SUFFERINGS OF THIS PRESENT TIME ARE NOT WORTH COMPARING WITH THE GLORY THAT IS TO BE REVEALED TO US

ROMANS 8:18

ROWLAND TAYLOR
(1510-1555)

N othing in the training, preaching, or patriotism of Rowland Taylor would have led him to predict that in the prime of his life, he would be violently killed and his children left fatherless. Indeed, Taylor's own father was a distinguished rector and public servant, not wealthy but well connected, ensuring as best a man can that his lively offspring would prosper.

Taylor certainly did. By the time his father died, Taylor, at age twenty-four, had earned a degree from Cambridge University and was well on his way to a lifetime of preaching and influence.

But certain ideas were lining up for Taylor that history now reckons to be among the most dangerous of his era. For Taylor, in his education and through his royal service, had come to reject doctrines such as priestly celibacy and the miraculous transubstantiation of the wine and bread during Communion. Indeed, even Taylor's marriage might have been seen as a harbinger—his beloved Margaret is widely thought to have been the sister of William Tyndale, who was burned at the stake in 1536 for promoting an English-language Bible and other reforms.

Nonetheless, Taylor enjoyed clergy duties, and even shared the home of Archbishop Thomas Cranmer, serving as his chaplain. He maintained the parish at Hadleigh in Suffolk County, and was much beloved for his pastoral care.

Then everything changed. The friendly young Protestant king, Edward VI (successor to Henry VIII), died. Lady Jane Grey, likely with Taylor's support, took the throne but kept it for only nine days before Edward's half-sister, Mary, became queen and launched her crusade to recapture the realm for Rome.

Only a couple of days after Mary's coronation, Taylor's parish at Hadleigh was "invaded" by John Averth. He was a neighboring priest with strong Catholic sympathies; he conducted a Mass protected by armed guards, and ejected Taylor from the church when he protested. That night the die was cast.

Averth's co-conspirators wrote of the altercation to England's Lord Chancellor, Stephen Gardiner, to whom Queen Mary had given the job of enforcing her ecclesial will. A summons from Gardiner was tantamount to a death sentence, so when that summons arrived at Hadleigh, many of Taylor's churchmen begged him not to go. Some, citing Matthew 10:23, urged that he save himself for later ministry once the storm had passed. Taylor replied, "Flee yourselves, and do as your conscience leads you. For myself, I am fully determined, with God's grace, to go to the bishop, and to his face tell him that what he does to me is insignificant. God will raise up teachers after me who will teach His people with more diligence and fruit than I have done."

Rowland Taylor's interview with Chancellor Gardiner in London was bravely confrontational. He begged the bishop to remember his own vows made to Henry and Edward, vows to reform the church, to create the Church of England, to support forms recently set forth in the Book of Common Prayer. Gardiner dismissed these vows as "Herod's oath—unlawful, and properly broken." Then Gardiner turned the tables, accusing Taylor of treason (because he had objected to the Mass at Hadleigh parish) and heresy.

Taylor replied, "My lord, I am parson of Hadleigh. It is against all right, conscience, and laws, that any man should come into my parish and dare to infect the flock committed to me." And so went charge and countercharge, with the winner predetermined and the outcome grimly obvious.

Taylor was imprisoned for two years until his formal trial on January 22, 1555. The charge was heresy and schism, and the sentence cited a law revived just two days earlier in Parliament—heretics should be burned. He was taken by sheriff's escort on February 9 to Aldham Common, Hadleigh. There he was allowed a last reunion with Margaret and their children, and then chained to the pole. To his young son Thomas he gave these words, the blessing of a father about to die:

Almighty God bless thee, and give thee His Holy Spirit, to be a true servant of Christ, to learn His word, and constantly to stand by His truth all the life long. And my son, see that thou fear God always. Fly from all sin and wicked living. Be virtuous; serve God daily with prayer. In anywise see thou be obedient to thy mother, love her, and serve her. Flee from whoredom, remembering that I thy father do die in the defense of holy marriage. And another day when God shall bless thee, love and cherish the poor people, and count that thy chief riches to be rich in alms. And when thy mother is waxed old, forsake her not, but provide for her to thy power. For so will God bless thee, give thee long life upon earth, and prosperity, which I pray God to grant thee.

Taylor was only the third victim of hundreds who were burned during Queen Mary's short reign. John Hooper, her fourth, was burned later that day. Perhaps because the gruesome event was not yet well practiced and the spectators not conditioned, one of the sheriffs, as the flames were just ascending, struck Taylor's head with his halberd, killing him instantly. An unhewn stone marks the site: "Dr. Taylor, in defending what was good at this place, left his blood."

WILLIAM HUNTER
(1555)

P rovide all the incentives a young adult might want—those were the bishop's tactics. Just offer the lad what he needs and doesn't have. Offer him money. Offer him a bit of public honor. That's enough for any boy. He'll take it. London's Bishop Bonner was confident. He knew the mind of London's youth. But Bonner, trying to buy William Hunter's obedience, instead brought the judgment of history upon himself and his queen.

William Hunter's case was clear enough. Raised in a Christian home, he learned the Bible and loved it. He trusted God and distrusted the established church. The charge against him was just as clear. Queen Mary had decreed that everyone in London must take Mass. No ambiguity there. But young Hunter did not take Mass. Even in the big city, he could hide only so long.

The lawbreaker was finally caught. He explained to the sheriff that reading the Bible, even alone, was worship. He had obeyed the edict, just not in the edict's required way. Then the bishop got involved, even though he certainly must have had more important responsibilities. Who was this young boy? Why should he be petulant? Failing to coax him by money, Bonner had Hunter placed in the stocks. For two days he crouched in the wood frame without food or water. Now will you obey the queen? No? To Newgate prison then. No honor awaits you there.

For the next nine months William Hunter carried chains around the dismal prison—all for reading a Bible, for not taking the Mass, for defying the queen's express order. By February 9, 1555, Bonner had troubled himself enough with this boy. Still no? Then back to Brentwood with you, your home village, to be burned as a heretic.

On March 26, with Psalm 51 on his lips, William Hunter, Bible reader, age nineteen, died in the fire lit by bailiff Richard Ponde, acting on orders of the state.

As the wood ignited, Hunter's brother yelled to him, "Think on the holy passion of Christ, William, and be not afraid of death."

The sheriff said to his convict, "I would no more pray for you than for a dog."

"I am not afraid," Hunter replied.

Today a monument in Brentwood carries this message:

> William Hunter. Martyr.
> Committed to the flames March 26 MDLV.
> Christian Reader, learn from his example to
> value the privilege of an open Bible.
> And be careful to maintain it.

FINALLY, BE STRONG IN THE LORD
AND IN THE STRENGTH OF HIS MIGHT

EPHESIANS 6:10

Thomas Cranmer
(1489-1556)

O nly one thing did old Thomas Cranmer lack as he faced his last day of life. He had been leader of the English church, counselor to kings, writer and compiler of one of the most famous religious books ever published. The former archbishop had traveled widely, married twice, and held the hand of a dying monarch. Only one thing more he needed: courage to face execution.

Thomas Cranmer rose from a humble home to achieve renown throughout the Christian West. He was a Cambridge graduate, ordained a priest, and concluded while he was young that God had vested all earthly power in sovereign heads of state. His own sovereign at the time was the infamous Henry VIII, who would regularly return subjects' loyalty and love with the cool emotional distance of a mercenary. Indeed, Henry could watch wives and trusted friends die as traitors if it served his remote interests. Thus when Henry appointed Cranmer as the archbishop of Canterbury, he assumed the new prelate would last only as long as his usefulness.

Indeed, Cranmer did prove useful. Every marriage Henry needed, Cranmer granted. Every divorce Henry demanded, Cranmer found lawful. Finally England had an archbishop who understood the church's one true doctrine—the ecclesial supremacy of the king.

This was even more the case when Henry's successor, Edward VI, moved England closer to Protestant faith. Cranmer basked in the glow of leadership and influence. Secretly, he took as his wife the daughter of German reformer Andreas Oslander. (His first wife, before ordination, had died in childbirth.) Publicly he compiled and wrote the Anglican liturgy, called the Book of Common Prayer, which is still used today.

But history took a different turn. Edward died. The timorous archbishop threw his support to Lady Jane Grey, the Protestant great-niece of Henry VIII. She got the job, but only for nine days, when into London rode Mary Tudor, daughter of Henry's first wife, Catherine of Aragon, and a devout Catholic. The subsequent reign of "Bloody Mary" is the story of dark ages in the English church.

In November 1553, Cranmer was charged with treason and imprisoned. He stood a mock trial with reformers Nicholas Ridley and Hugh Latimer, whom he was forced to watch burn. Mary's agents wore him down, shaved his head, and scraped the tops of the fingers of his right hand—those that had been anointed in his ordination years earlier.

Then in jail on the night of March 20, 1556, Cranmer succumbed to his ultimate humiliation. Shivering with fear of the stake awaiting him the next morning, he signed decrees recanting every reformational conviction and affirming the bishop of Rome as true head of Christ's church. He quivered at how far he had fallen.

On the next day, perhaps even Cranmer himself was surprised by the calm and courage of his last hour. Asked to make public his true convictions, Cranmer clearly recanted his midnight recantations, boldly declared his faith by the Nicene Creed, clearly separated himself from Rome, and declared he would thrust his right hand first into the flames to purge the cowardice of last evening's signatures.

At nine o'clock in the morning, he was bound by a steel band to the stake. "This hand hath offended," he said, lowering it into the flames. "Lord Jesus, receive my spirit," he moaned, and then collapsed into the fire.

JULIUS PALMER

(1556)

An excellent scholar and committed Catholic, Julius Palmer could not understand how the Protestant martyrs endured their painful deaths with apparent joy and goodwill. It confounded him; it troubled him. Their faith, after all, was false and therefore groundless, he thought. Being false, they would have no reason to suffer for it, much less to suffer bearing so little ill will toward their persecutors. And not just the absence of ill will but the positive presence of peace. He watched them burn and the experience upset him.

Julius Palmer was born in Coventry, where his father was mayor. At Oxford, he became a top student and scholar of Latin and Greek. Palmer excelled in debate, and the passion to learn was so strong that he normally woke as early as four in the morning to begin research and writing. He became a reader in logic at Magdelan College, Oxford. He was heading toward academic brilliance.

The short reign of the Protestant boy-king, Edward VI, was not easy for Catholic scholars, especially debaters who projected their beliefs and taught younger scholars their ways. In early 1553, Palmer was dismissed from his post at Magdelan. Unable to find university employment, he became a tutor to a wealthy family until good fortune came his way in the early death of the sickly king and the subsequent rule of the rigorously pro-Catholic Queen Mary. Palmer was promptly reemployed at Magdelan.

But not all was well with him. Catholic as he was by practice and intellect, he did not enjoy, and, in fact, struggled greatly over the burning of Protestants as part of Queen Mary's purge of the English church. Moreover, Palmer began to study these stalwart "heretics," who seemed so convinced of their beliefs that not even the flames could budge their thinking. He inquired into their motives, and he studied the judicial records of their trials. In 1555, Palmer watched Latimer and Ridley burn and heard their strong and sure testimonies. And in his studies, Palmer himself was changing.

Because of these changes and in good faith, Palmer resigned from Oxford and became a schoolmaster in the town of Reading. Soon he was exposed as a sympathizer, however, and he left when confronted by townsmen who had discovered his Protestant bent. Out of money and without employment, he went to his mother to request his share of the inheritance his father's estate had left him. His mother replied, "Thy father bequeathed naught for heretics."

Palmer returned to Reading to gather his belongings, technically a violation of his agreement to leave the town. He was promptly arrested and offered all the goods necessary for a comfortable life, if only he would recant the errors of his new convictions. Unable to accept the bribe and now willing to follow the path of those he had so closely studied, Julius Palmer stood condemned by the court. He was burned along with two others on July 15, 1556. The last words of these courageous martyrs came from Psalm 31: "Be strong, and let your heart take courage, all you who wait for the LORD!"

Palmer's mind and then his heart led him to that place. Perhaps he himself was surprised by it; yet convinced by the truth he followed, he was obliged to accept its consequences.

One of Palmer's judicial examiners had offered this sage advice while there was still time: "Take pity on thy golden years, and pleasant flowers of lusty youth, before it is too late." But Palmer, ever the scholar, had turned the metaphor back: "Sir, I long for those springing flowers that shall never fade away." In death, he danced among them.

Hᴀɴs Sᴍɪᴛ
(1558)

hen the Spirit of God moves and people obey, the consequences belong to God alone.

Hans Smit, along with five other men and six women,
all Anabaptists, was sent on a preaching mission through the Netherlands
and into Germany. It was a short mission indeed, for only days passed
before they were arrested and interrogated in Aix-la-Chapelle, Germany,
on January 9, 1558.

Smit was the leader of the group. His own interrogation followed
questions on the conventional topics that Catholic monarchs considered most essential to the peace of the realm: baptism, the sacraments,
the nature of salvation and judgment, and the authority by which
these strangers presumed to teach about God. In every case, Smit
responded in a manner true to his beliefs, but utterly contrary to the
monarch's way of thinking. Neither did the rack seem to sway Smit's
mind on these questions, as convincing a teacher as the rack was in
many cases. No, he had come on his mission with full knowledge that
his message could lead to this; when it did, he wasn't about to doubt
the truth of it.

Apparently the leaders investigating these intruders/missionaries
were reluctant to take their blood upon themselves. Smit warned them
that they might own the gallows here, but Christ owned His judgment
throne before which they would surely stand. The leaders chose to stretch
the limbs a bit more for these malcontents; then let them go.

If only Smit had left the city quietly. Instead, he opened a loud prayer
and revival meeting. What could the authorities do? Hans was
re-arrested, along with the others.

With patience running thin, and fear of a royal backlash if they
appeared soft, authorities this time imposed a sentence that Smit seemed
all too content with. On October 22, 1558, Hans Smit was hanged and

burned. On the way to execution, Smit remarked, "Oh what a beautiful feast day we shall have. So many people are coming."

Three days later, Hendrick Adams was also hanged and burned. Three other men of the group were given three months to consider their options. They were executed on January 4, 1559. Only one came to believe the rack's teaching and was spared. The women? A scourging with rods was sufficient to satisfy their crimes. They returned home singing.

Lest torture and intimidation win the day, one other death weighed heavily on the leaders of that city. The most aggressive leader, the one most eager to see the Anabaptists dead, had received a prophecy from Adams as he was sentenced: "You yourself will not live to see this sentence carried out." Indeed, on the eve of Smit's execution, this councilman himself lay dying in mortal fear, plucking out his own beard and mumbling incoherently about fears of the afterlife. His own body was stone cold before Adams was ever burned.

"DEATH IS SWALLOWED UP IN VICTORY."

"O DEATH, WHERE IS YOUR VICTORY?

O DEATH, WHERE IS YOUR STING?"

1 CORINTHIANS 15:54-55

WALTER MILL

(1476-1558)

s he was about to be burned at the stake, Walter Mill confidently and courageously exclaimed:

> I marvel at your rage, ye hypocrites, who do so cruelly pursue the servants of God! As for me, I am now eighty-two years old, and cannot live long by course of nature; but a hundred shall rise out of my ashes, who shall scatter you, ye hypocrites and persecutors of God's people; and such of you as now think yourselves the best, shall not die such an honest death as I do now. I trust in God, I shall be the last who shall suffer death in this fashion for the cause of this land!

His words were prophetic because he was, in fact, the last martyr of the early reformation in Scotland.

Born in 1476, Mill became a priest in Angus County, Scotland. Impressed by the teachings of the reformers, he questioned the church hierarchy and theology and stopped saying Mass. So as a young man, he was condemned to death for his defiance of the church. Eventually, in 1538, Mill was arrested, but he escaped to Germany where he ministered for twenty years.

At the age of eighty-two, he returned to teach the Protestant faith and live out his remaining days in his homeland. But he was hunted down and imprisoned, even though as an old man he was not a threat. At his trial, Mill entered the courtroom at the cathedral of St. Andrews and fell to his knees in prayer. The judge, guards, and audience assumed that Mill, feeble from his imprisonment, would be unable to speak in his defense. Yet he spoke with force. And Walter Mill was condemned to be executed for heresy.

While being bound to the stake, Mill continued to speak to his captors and the assembled onlookers. Many admired his bold declaration of faith. Some complained aloud about the cruelty of his persecutors. Mill prayed quietly for a short time. Then, as the fire was being lit, he cried out, "Lord have mercy on me. Pray, pray, good people, while there is time." Then, cheerfully, he left this life to live with God.

John Knox wrote, "That blessed martyr of Christ, Walter Mill, a man of decrepit age, was put to death most cruelly the 28th April, 1558."

"THE WORLD FOR A TIME MAY DECEIVE ITSELF, THINKING IT HAS, THE VICTORY, BUT THE END WILL TRY THE CONTRARY."

—JOHN BRADFORD, WRITTEN AT THE BEGINNING OF HIS IMPRISONMENT IN 1554

PETRUS RAMUS

(1515-1572)

etrus Ramus had three strong, positive attributes that eventually put him in harm's way. First, he was intelligent. Born into a poor family in Picardy, France, not far from John Calvin's birthplace, Ramus lost his father when he was a young boy. To compensate, indeed to overcome this immense social deficit, he worked hard as a soldier, then as a servant, and eventually as a student, earning a Master of Arts degree in logic and rhetoric.

Second, Ramus was creative. His studies were not merely to fill his brain with the learning of others—whether teachers or book writers, holy men or dilettantes. Rather, Ramus was interested in finding the clue to hidden mysteries, unknown links, and in putting the ideas of others through the crucible of his own intellectual powers. Aristotle, for example, the ancient Greek revered by the church since Thomas Aquinas, received no free pass through Ramus's grid. This quality caused him no end of trouble.

Third, Ramus was loquacious. He loved debate. And he published books at a pace unequaled in France at the time: more than fifty, and some in multiple editions as his own thinking developed. No one in Europe needed to wonder what Ramus thought. He was happily telling as many souls as his tongue and pen could reach.

Two other events guaranteed Ramus a life of trouble and, finally, a shorter life than he anticipated. Ramus converted to Protestantism in the 1560s, entirely because his brilliant mind led him there. He became a Huguenot, a French believer in church reform. With that move, he lost the support of the cardinal of Lorraine, whose help was vital to Ramus's teaching career. As a result, he was forced to leave Paris and the university, spending several years in Switzerland and Germany, feasting at the table of Reformed and Lutheran theology that was spreading in those countries.

All this would have led Ramus perhaps to a reputation equal to Calvin or Luther, had not his last attribute been so prominent. As Ramus found stillness contrary to his every impulse, so also he considered hiding, cowering, or running to be a fool's errand. When he returned to Paris in 1570, he had no permit to lecture and was therefore unable to attract the large audiences his writing and education had earned. His statement, "I had rather that philosophy be taught to children out of the gospel by a learned theologian of proved character than out of Aristotle by a philosopher," angered professors and other philosophers. It was also the wrong time to be a Huguenot in that city.

On August 24, 1572, a wave of killings began, as a political tool to cement the hold of Charles IX to his crown. On this St. Bartholomew's Day eve, a spirit of massacre and bloodletting was unleashed throughout France. As a result, thousands of Protestants were slaughtered. Charles had ordered Ramus to be spared, but no one could control the Paris mob. Ramus was captured in his study at the College de Presles, where he was killed and his body mutilated, decapitated, and thrown into the Seine River.

If only Ramus had been less intelligent, less willing to follow his convictions, less talkative, a more conforming chap, and a less-determined Christian—think of the long life he might have enjoyed, the bitter end he might have avoided. Given his place and time, Ramus was like a magnet for trouble, a magnet that won him a martyr's crown.

Edmund Campion
(1540-1581)

H is best-known work, still read today in some circles, is called Campion's Brag. It is a booklet he published clandestinely, but so polished an argument for Catholic faith, so refined in its rhetorical power, that its formal title, "Challenge to the Privy Council," was replaced by detractors and admirers both with the author's name and a backhanded tribute.

For all his learning, mastery of argument, and Catholic conviction, Edmund Campion was the "most wanted" man in England in 1581. He was wanted by the Catholics to conduct masses. He was wanted by the enemy Protestants and the Protestant Queen Elizabeth I in England. And he was wanted and harassed in Ireland by the 1559 Act of Supremacy, which required all subjects to confess that the queen was supreme governor of the church.

Campion had returned secretly to England in 1580. Years earlier, he had so impressed the queen with his youthful talent that his peers believed he was destined for the highest offices of power and privilege. Indeed, Edmund had taken Anglican orders in the 1560s. But his trip to Dublin in 1569 and his work on the "History of Ireland" had shown him clearly that the faith he had celebrated as a precocious teenager during Mary Tudor's reign was his heart's passion. Thus, when Parliament passed into law the thirty-nine Articles of the Anglican Church in 1571, Campion left England for Douai, now part of France. He entered the Society of Jesus (Jesuits) and was ordained a priest in 1578. Two years later his superiors included him in a team bound for England, where Catholic families were worshiping in secret, and a small band of priests traveled from safe house to safe house, conducting Mass and offering the services of the church.

Edmund Campion hanged, drawn and quartered in England

But Campion was "wanted" by English authorities. They nearly apprehended him at Dover when he arrived, but by a narrow escape he had gotten lost in London. His "Challenge to the Privy Council" booklet had embarrassed the Privy Council. If that were not enough, his booklet, Ten Reasons (opposing Anglican worship), appeared on the seats at Oxford's commencement ceremony that June. Then, too, Campion's reappearance in England coincided with the arrival of papal military forces at Munster, Ireland—no small threat to the hegemony of Elizabeth over that isle. Edmund Campion was a very wanted man.

With a price on his head, Campion did not survive long. A bounty hunter posing as a devout Catholic caught up with him at Lyford Grange, west of London. Campion's host quickly put the priest and his two companions in a secret chamber supplied with food and water, but the small enclosure was not secret enough. Campion was discovered, captured, and taken to London Tower. There followed the usual torments and opportunities to end torment if only the prisoner would submit to the Act of Supremacy and end his rebellion, so to speak, against the queen. Edmund replied, "If our religion do make traitors, we are worthy to be condemned; but otherwise we were and have been true subjects as ever the queen had."

On November 20 the court condemned Campion, and on December 1, he was executed by one of the cruelest means ever devised: hanging, drawing, and quartering. Campion left England and life with this challenge:

> In condemning us, you condemn your own ancestors, you condemn all the ancient bishops and Kings, you condemn all that was once the glory of England.

JOHN PENRY
(1593)

◆

I f the queen and the archbishop had their way, Puritan preacher John Penry would simply and quietly disappear from the face of the earth. Why else would he be dragged suddenly, at about the dinner hour, from his cell near Old Kent Road and told to prepare for death? Why else were the gallows so quickly erected and the sheriff ordered to deny the condemned man a customary courtesy: a farewell speech affirming his innocence and loyalty? Why else, apart from sheer hatred, would the father of four young daughters be condemned as a traitor on the basis of writings never published or released to the public?

Penry was born on a farm near Llangammarch, Cefn Brith, Wales, and converted early in his life to Protestant faith. In England, to be a proper Protestant was to be a member of the Church of England, which recognized the queen as its head. An improper Protestant was part of the dissenting or free church movement, which was tantamount to disloyalty to her majesty, potentially an act of treason. That potential could be a powerful tool in the hands of political enemies, and Penry had one—the archbishop of Canterbury, John Whitgrift. Penry had indirectly criticized the archbishop for failing to provide Wales with Christian nurture in his 1587 tract entitled Equity of a Humble Supplication.

So incensed was the archbishop that he directed the Northampton sheriff to search Penry's home for incriminating papers. Indeed, the same unlicensed press that produced Penry's work was also producing the now famous Marprelate tracts, a series of satirical jabs at Church of England priests and bureaucracy. Because the Marprelate tracts were unlicensed, Elizabeth I's Star Chamber court took a serious interest in finding and stopping those very popular satires. Perhaps the sheriff could nab two birds with the same stone.

Penry slipped into Scotland to evade the sheriff, but he returned to London in 1592 to take up preaching at the Puritan meeting hall whose two pastors, Frances Johnson and John Greenwood, had just been arrested (and would later be executed). In March of the next year, Penry was captured by authorities and placed under arrest for writing such vehement criticisms of Queen Elizabeth in his journal. The journal, unpublished and simply a personal notebook, was judged to contain "feloniously devised and written words with intent to excite rebellion and insurrection in England." The one who had begged for pastors for Wales was now in a position to plead for his life, and if not for his own sake, yet for his four young daughters.

But mercy was not to come. A week after his trial the verdict was rendered; and four days after that, Penry was suddenly ordered to prepare for his execution. To his daughters—named Deliverance, Comfort, Safety, and Sure Hope—he wrote: "I, your father, now ready to give my life...do charge you...to embrace this my counsel...and to bring up your posterity (if the Lord vouchsafe you any) in this same true faith and way to the Kingdom of Heaven."

Penry was led to a quickly constructed gallows, the sheriff carrying his certificate of death by hanging, signed first, among several other names, by Archbishop Whitgrift, whose laxity toward the churches in Wales had first prompted Penry to take a public stand. Penry died a Protestant martyr killed by offended Protestants, part of the struggle for worship free of state control.

ROBERT SOUTHWELL
(1595)

◆

I n the days of Queen Elizabeth I of England, a law was passed that forbade any English-born subject who had taken priest's orders in the Catholic Church from remaining in England longer than forty days. In effect, being a part of the Roman priesthood had become a capital crime. For the likes of Robert Southwell, a devout Jesuit whose heart and mind were filled with images and emotions nurtured by Catholic faith, this law was incentive for missionary action, a journey back to England. On the eve of his installment as a priest, Southwell wrote to his superior: "I address you, my Father, from the threshold of death, imploring the aid of your prayers…that I may either escape the death of the body for further use, or endure it with courage."

Southwell had been raised a Catholic. At an early age he had left England to be educated at Douai. His young faith was strongly influenced by one of history's great Jesuits, Leonard Lessius. While a student, Southwell also met John Cotton, who operated a safe house for Catholics in London. Southwell became a priest in 1584.

Two years later he requested the dangerous English mission. Most English Catholics at the time lived in the countryside and waited for a priest to arrive for confession and last rites. Southwell traveled in disguise, providing services and succor and urging his own father and brother to return to Catholic faith.

In 1586 Southwell became domestic chaplain to Ann Howard, whose husband, the Earl of Arundel, was in prison. For three more years (six altogether) Southwell did his secretive work, until the daughter of one of his regular contacts, herself imprisoned, betrayed him. One of Elizabeth's most notorious priest-hunters, Richard Topcliffe, captured Southwell during a Mass in a private home.

The priest in full vestments was taken immediately to Topcliffe's home, and there hanged by his wrists during an interrogation intended to reveal the names and locations of Southwell's colleagues. From all reports, Southwell endured the torture, admitting only that he was a Jesuit and prayed daily for the queen, whose rule, apart from the ban on Catholic worship, he respectfully obeyed. Unable to break him, Topcliffe had Southwell's battered body transferred to the gatehouse at Westminster. A month later at his examination it was discovered that he had been so ill-treated that his wounds were infested with lice. Southwell's family, appealing to common decency, begged the queen to treat him as the gentleman he was. Mercifully, Southwell was transferred to the Tower of London, allowed a change of clothes, a Bible, and the writings of Saint Bernard. His incarceration lasted three years, during which he was put on the rack thirteen times.

Finally, in 1595, the Privy Council resolved to try Southwell on charges of treason. To break him further, if that were possible, the Council moved him to an underground dungeon called Limbo.

Three days later Southwell was brought before the court. He declared himself "not guilty of any treason whatsoever" and admitted being a priest that served Catholics who wanted the comfort of the Church. When Southwell appealed to "our Savior," the court stopped to rebuke him. When he gave his age as the same as Jesus at His trial, the court gasped at his "insupportable pride." When Southwell referred to himself as "a worm of the earth," the court ordered that the next day, February 20, 1596, he would be hanged (by the neck), drawn (before death, cut out entrails and genitalia and burned before victim's eyes), and quartered (beheaded and body divided into four parts).

From his cart on the way to the gallows, Southwell preached from Romans chapter 14, and then, *"In manus tuas, Domine"* ("Into your hands, Lord"). The court's intention was that Southwell would hang until death was near, and then be taken off the rope to have his extremities torn from their sockets; finally, his torso opened and organs removed until he died. In another moment of mercy, his agony was shortened when onlookers pulled on his legs while he hung by the rope.

Southwell left a collection of prison poems and tracts still read today, though lost for centuries after his death. His *A Hundred Meditations on the Love of God* was first printed in 1873. The famous English playwright and poet Ben Jonson said he would have willingly destroyed many of his own poems were he able to claim as his own Southwell's "Burning Babe," which depicts a vision of the suffering Christ appearing to the poet on Christmas Day:

> Alas, quote he, but newly born in fiery heats I fry,
> Yet none approach to warm their hearts or feel my fire but I.
> My faultless breast the furnace is, the fuel wounding thorns,
> Love is the fire, and sighs the smoke, the ashes shame and scorn.

"OH WHAT A BEAUTIFUL FEAST DAY WE SHALL HAVE. SO MANY PEOPLE ARE COMING."

—HANS SMIT

Indeed, I count everything
as loss because of the surpassing
worth of knowing Christ Jesus
my Lord. For his sake I have
suffered the loss of all things
and count them as rubbish, in
order that I may gain Christ
and be found in him....

Philippians 3:8-9

The Enlightenment

and the

Age of Reason

(1645-1789)

The French *philosphes* had seen enough. By the eighteenth century, Denis Diderot and other philosophers had had enough of religious faith and its institutions. Across Europe a new day was dawning. Credible evidence from the material world was replacing religious doctrine as the standard of rational belief. Intellectual leaders were tiring of the suppression of science by clerics and the dominance of a holy text over systematic observation.

The *philosphes* were but one in a series of challenges to the control of the church over commerce, politics, the arts, and the marketplace. In Germany, one philosopher (so regular that people set their timepieces at the start of his afternoon walks) revolutionized the way people in the West made moral decisions and how they understood the world of ideas. Immanuel Kant proposed a purely rational basis for value judgments and a largely humanistic basis for the origins of all ideas, including those about God and the afterlife.

At the same time, notions of "natural rights" (rights enjoyed by all people by virtue of their humanity) challenged notions of rights conferred by faith or penitence. Similarly, natural law challenged the authority of divine law. The disciplines of scientific discovery expanded knowledge of disease, mechanics, and the Earth as part of a vast uncharted universe. Yet despite this shift from faith to philosophy, followers of Christ were still dying for the privilege of knowing Him.

BUT GOD CHOSE WHAT IS FOOLISH IN THE WORLD TO SHAME THE WISE; GOD CHOSE WHAT IS WEAK IN THE WORLD TO SHAME THE STRONG.

I CORINTHIANS 1:27

MARY DYER

(ca. 1611-1660)

C onvinced that the intolerant law of Massachusetts Colony
banishing Quakers violated God's law, Mary Dyer would not
stay quiet or stay away. Dyer was a Quaker, and Quakers
believed that God could communicate directly to us and that salvation
could be assured. This was considered heresy by the Puritans in Massachusetts, so they banished her from the colony.

Dyer challenged that law with a persistence that finally led authorities to a critical decision: Agree with Dyer and change the social structure
of the colony, or silence her. Mary Dyer died on the gallows on June 1,
1660, affirming her stand against the government that persecuted her
Quaker faith. "Nay, man," she said at the last, "I am not now to repent."

Dyer had other alternatives. For one, she was married to a respected
colonial official, William Dyer, who more than once had rescued her
from a Massachusetts jail through his political connections. He too was
a Quaker but less militant than she, who never dodged a fight over religious freedom, especially when her "inner light"—God's voice to the
soul—bade her confront the secular powers.

For another, Dyer had the testy patience of Massachusetts Governor
John Endicott on her side. When her fellow Quaker "lawbreakers," William Robinson and Marmaduke Stephenson, were hanged in 1658, Dyer
stood right behind them, awaiting the same fate. To her complete surprise, she received a last-minute reprieve and was ordered never to return.
She left under guard, with her husband's promise that she would comply
with the Massachusetts edict of banishment.

Finally, Dyer had a mission to Native Americans on Shelter Island,
teaching and converting them to the Quaker faith. Had she been content with her work and obedient to the law, she might have seen the
last of her eight children reach adulthood. But she was neither content
nor submissive.

Mary Dyer hanged for heresy by the Puritans

In April 1660, Dyer returned to Boston, led by her conscience and fully aware of her danger. She didn't tell her husband, who nonetheless wrote a moving letter to Governor Endicott asking again for mercy toward his driven wife. This time, however, the stakes were too high.

At issue was more than Quaker nonconformity. To survive in the New World, settlers had learned to build strong communities. If food security, weather, the forest, disease, and hostile Indians were not enough, tough-souled London businessmen had given up on the colonies, leaving them to their own wits and devices. Religious nonconformity was a further strain on the social system, and defiance of law was finally a capital offense. Who could waste precious resources maintaining a prison system? Dyer wanted religious freedom; Massachusetts wanted order and survival. Leaders such as Roger Williams in Rhode Island had found middle ground, granting wider freedom of expression in and around the city of Providence. Dyer and her husband lived there for a while, but she was not a person to take refuge there.

Thus, on May 31, 1660, the General Court of Massachusetts summoned Mary Dyer and convicted her of willful violation of the banishment decree. Replied she, "I came in obedience to the will of God, desiring you to repeal your unrighteous laws, and that is my work now and earnest request."

The next morning she was escorted to the gallows, a troop of drummers in front and behind to keep Dyer from preaching to the gathering crowd. She left behind engraved on the wall of her jail cell: "My Life not Availeth Me / In comparison to the Liberty of the Truth."

In 1959, on the 300th anniversary of her death sentence, the Massachusetts General Court decreed that a bronze statue of Mary Dyer be erected in her memory on the grounds of the State House in Boston, recognizing the truth and social value of her "earnest request."

THE SCOTTISH COVENANTERS

The late sixteenth and early seventeenth centuries were times of immense religious and political upheaval for England and Scotland. Politically, the English kings were desperately trying to roll Scotland into a single unified British state. Religiously, battle lines were being drawn between competing models of worship and governance.

The Scottish Covenanters were named for a series of covenants made during the late sixteenth and early seventeenth centuries that preserved the Presbyterian doctrine as the only religion of Scotland. At first, the Covenanters merely promoted and developed Presbyterianism as a form of church government favored by the people, in contrast to Episcopacy, which was favored by the crown of England. Later they came to represent a rallying cry for complete Scottish independence—a cause worth dying for.

The first of the covenants was made in 1557 in opposition to the Catholic faith, when Scotland was ruled by Mary of Guise, the Catholic queen-regent. After her imprisonment, a relatively peaceful time followed when James I became king. He was more religiously tolerant, and in 1581 the King's Covenant was signed, which allowed for the continued existence of Catholicism in England and Scotland, Calvinism in Scotland (to which the Scottish Covenanters subscribed), and the growth of Puritanism in England.

Problems for the Covenanters began in the early 1600s, when James I tried to unify Scotland and England with "high-church" Protestantism by appointing his own bishops over the church in Scotland. Later, James's son, Charles I, was less tolerant and sought to move the Church of England toward a high-church form and away from Calvinism. Rebels and men of action, the Scottish Covenanters established the National Covenant in 1638, denouncing the pope and all rule by the king's bishops. Charles I saw this as a direct challenge to his royal authority, as did his son, Charles II. They both sought to crush the "rebellion." A period of time followed, from 1679-1688, called the "Killing Time." Most Covenanters that were captured during these years were executed by hanging, with hands and sometimes heads displayed on pikes for all to see. A few were even sentenced to be slaves in American plantations.

However, the Scottish Covenanters boldly clung to their faith. Rebel ministers preached at secret services or "conventicles" in the fields, despite the harsh persecution that followed. Anyone associated with the Covenanters was subject to arrest and consequent execution. Because of the fierce oppression and heavily biased trials that took place, Covenanters eventually organized to take up arms and tried to fight back. Unfortunately, they were no match for British forces and their rebellion was crushed, first at the Battle of Drumclog in 1679, and then at the Battle of Bothwell Brig a year later.

WHO SHALL SEPARATE US
FROM THE LOVE OF CHRIST?
SHALL TRIBULATION, OR DISTRESS,
OR PERSECUTION, OR FAMINE,
OR NAKEDNESS, OR DANGER,
OR SWORD?

ROMANS 8:35

JAMES GUTHRIE
(1612-1661)

James Guthrie was born into a wealthy Scottish family in 1612, at a time and place fraught with risk for trusting souls. Power was shifting and realignments created quicksand that could surprise and swallow the cleverest person.

While attending St. Andrews University, Guthrie met the esteemed theologian Samuel Rutherford, whose reformational convictions won Guthrie's heart, soul, and trust. He became a Presbyterian minister.

When the King of England, Charles I, tried to impose his bishops on the Scottish church, Guthrie opposed it, along with many of his countrymen. He signed the National Covenant, a document sure to be reckoned as political rebellion, despite its focus on the church as God's house, free from the state and ruled by Christ alone. Those who signed this National Covenant were known as "Covenanters." Given notions of kingship in the seventeenth century and King Charles's need to tap the wealth of his entire realm, only heretics or traitors would dare propose a church independent from the crown.

Guthrie guided his parish through the Puritan Revolution, which led to the beheading of King Charles I in 1649 and Oliver Cromwell's decade of power. But the monarchy was again restored in 1660, when Charles's son, Charles II, became king. Consolidation of power was the order of the day. Certainly churches were subject to the realm. Obviously the king's bishops would be the church leaders.

Guthrie had come to trust Charles II. During Cromwell's reign, the heir apparent, safe in Scotland, had taken an oath to uphold the National Covenant and promote Presbyterian polity. Now this same man, sitting at last on his father's throne, was demanding that the Scottish church become Anglican. This new king had given his promise, had he not? Even on Scottish soil he had made his solemn pledge. Guthrie joined a group of twelve Scottish pastors who made a formal petition to Charles II to uphold the National Covenant. But power finds its own purposes. The entire band of Scottish Covenanters was imprisoned.

Guthrie, forty-nine years old, was sentenced to be hanged. His head was fixed to a pole for public humiliation and his belongings confiscated. Guthrie's trust had been tragically misplaced. Facing the loss of life and family fortune, Guthrie gave these words to the crowd gathered on June 1, 1661, to watch him die.

> I take God to record upon my soul, I would not exchange this scaffold with the palace and mitre of the greatest prelate in Britain. Blessed be God who has shown mercy to me such a wretch, and has revealed His Son in me...Jesus Christ is my Life and my Light, my Righteousness, my Strength, and my Salvation and all my desire. Him! O Him, I do with all the strength of my soul commend to you. Bless Him, O my soul, from henceforth even forever. Lord, now lettest Thy servant depart in peace, for mine eyes have seen Thy salvation.

For almost three decades, James Guthrie's severed head was spiked above the Netherbrow Port in Edinburgh. But Guthrie, not Charles, had come to know the One Whom he could trust, and so died in confidence and hope.

HUGH McKAIL
(1666)

He was young and brave, a Scotsman who believed that no human, peasant or king, was head of Christ's church, but Christ alone. Hugh McKail said so in the last sermon he preached, on the Sunday before all Presbyterian Covenanters were deposed in favor of Charles II's episcopacy. His words that day were food to the people but poison to the state. Young Pastor McKail fled to Europe and safety.

Virtually nothing is known of McKail's birth and growing years. After studying at the University of Edinburgh, he was ordained at the age of twenty, only a year after Charles II had rejuvenated the monarchy following Oliver Cromwell's failed experiment in popular sovereignty.

McKail was a Scotsman. He could neither travel forever nor ignore his calling to the Scottish church. Four years in hiding was enough. He returned to Galloway to watch and wait. When his fellow Covenanters took up swords and clubs against the British, he couldn't be content sitting quietly at his hearth.

Whether McKail became a fighter is uncertain, but certainly he knew the Covenanter captains and likely traveled with them. In November 1666 he was captured and tortured for information, which apparently he withheld despite a metal wedge being hammered into his leg, shattering the bone.

A month later, on December 18, he was tried with other prisoners and sentenced to be hanged. During the next four days he prepared for death, composing an eloquent gallows farewell and asking his father, who was with him for a last dinner on the night before the hanging, "I desire it of you, as the best and last service you can do me, to go to your chamber and pray earnestly to the Lord to be with me on that scaffold; for how to carry there is my care, even that I may be strengthened to endure to the end." Then he asked his father to leave him, or else he would stir emotions that would deflect his purpose the next day.

At the gallows, McKail spoke at some length, begging the audience to listen to his "few words," as his years on earth were few as well. At the end of his testimony and admonition to courage, he said:

> And now I leave off to speak any more to creatures, and turn my speech to thee, O Lord! And now I begin my intercourse with God, which shall never be broken off. Farewell father and mother, friends and relations; farewell the world and all delights; farewell meat and drink; farewell sun, moon, and stars. Welcome God and Father; welcome sweet Lord Jesus, the Mediator of the new covenant; welcome blessed Spirit of grace, and God of all consolation; welcome glory; welcome eternal life; welcome death.

Then McKail climbed the ladder to the waiting rope and prayed for some time before the executioner released him to gravity and Heaven.

It was said that Charles II had sent a letter of reprieve, which Archbishop Burnet of Glasgow had hidden so that McKail and other Covenanters would die. It was a dangerous decade to be a free-church Christian in Scotland.

RICHARD CAMERON
(1680)

Zeal was his hallmark, passion his shield, and a prophetic sense his special gift. The eldest of three sons to a small shopkeeper in Scotland, Richard Cameron was converted by Covenanter preachers as a young adult. Leaders of this movement quickly realized what a gifted preacher he was. They urged him to quit teaching school and licensed him to preach. They soon came to regret this decision, however, for Cameron was more radical than any Covenanter before him. He felt they were timid, shortsighted, and fearful of the implications of their doctrine, and he said so. This resulted in being censured in 1677 by the Presbyterian clergy in Edinburgh. This experience put Cameron into a depression, for his gifts were great and his passion for an independent church knew no bounds. He went to Holland to cool down.

In the Netherlands, Cameron caught the attention of free-church ministers, who laid hands on him, ordaining him to the Gospel ministry. His spirits recovered, Cameron returned to Scotland in early 1680 and immediately began to preach sermons that moved the crowds gathered in fields to hear.

"Will you take Him? Tell us what you say! These hills and mountains around us witness that we have offered Him to you this day. Angels are wondering at the offer. They stand beholding with admiration that our Lord is giving you such an offer this day. They will go up to the throne to report everyone's choice," he proclaimed.

Cameron was also busy with plans of sedition against Charles II, king of England—at least that's how Charles saw it. King Charles's indulgences and additional restraints to worship practices had many Christians more willing to suffer than to resist. Richard Cameron refused to give in to King Charles. When Cameron and his followers met in Sanquhar Town on June 12 to read and declare that Charles was a tyrant, without any right or title to authority in Scotland, Charles needed no further evidence. He issued a writ to arrest them with suitable bounty attached, and Cameron fled to the hills to hide.

On June 20, 1680, Richard Cameron was camping with his brother Michael and twenty others at Meadowhead Farm, owned by William Mitchell. That morning he carefully washed at a stone trough and then said to Mrs. Mitchell, "This is our last washing. I have need to make [my hands] clean, for there are many to see them." At 4:00 that afternoon, a troop led by Bruce of Earlshall appeared at the farm. Cameron quickly gathered his band at the ready, loudly pleading with God "to spare the green and take the ripe." Outnumbered, the Covenanters were no match. Cameron and his brother were killed. A half dozen escaped. The rest, taken captive, were hanged in Edinburgh.

Richard Cameron's head and hands were carried to Edinburgh and there placed high on Netherbow Gate, an example to others of the terrible cost of defying the king. Before putting them on display, the sheriff pulled Cameron's head from the bag in front of another prisoner, the old Alan Cameron, Richard's father, mockingly asking if he recognized the parts. "I know, I know. They are my son's, my own dear son's. It is the Lord. Good is the will of the Lord, who has made goodness and mercy to follow us all our days."

Cameron's hands were tied fingers upward at the sides of his head, as if he were praying. The display intended to show his weakness, even the futility of his protests. But Richard Cameron is known to history as the "Lion of the Covenant," and King Charles, apart from his title, was only one in a line of Stuarts easily forgotten.

Donald Cargill
(1681)

Who should govern the church? Bishops appointed by a monarch? Or elders and deacons called by God and endorsed by the church itself? Who is head of the church, Christ or king? This question, along with the role of Scripture and the path of salvation, were critical issues during the Reformation, fought over with argument and sword.

Donald Cargill was a fighting Scotsman, a preacher, and a warrior. Educated at the distinguished universities of Aberdeen and St. Andrews, he was appointed minister to the parish of Barony in Glasgow in 1655. A Covenanter, Cargill was starting his ministry in the calm eye of a hurricane. Ill winds would soon carry him into exile and eventually to his death.

Scottish Covenanters were Presbyterians devoted to church leadership by elders. Thus they were utterly opposed to a church led by bishops, who were titled with a religious mandate but empowered by the English crown. King Charles I of England had sought to impose the Anglican Church in Scotland since 1625. But Charles had met his own doom at the hands of Cromwell's army in 1649. When Cargill started preaching, England was without a king. Yet the Glorious Revolution was unwinding, and Charles II would ascend the throne in 1660. Cargill thus had five years of peace.

Charles II clearly had territory to recover and an island empire to regain. He must suppress the Scots, and that meant placing his bishops in charge of the Scottish church. Enough of the independents, the elder-ruled churches, and their pastors who, to his thinking, mixed salvation with too clear a hint of political liberation. Charles II declared Covenant-ers to be traitors, their churches illegal, and the church's new leader—himself—the sovereign of state and of church.

Cargill responded by "excommunicating" Charles II and his bishops, saying, "The church ought to declare that those who are none of Christ's are none of hers." For such carefree boldness, Cargill's capture now carried a bounty, and the preacher was urged to find refuge in the Scottish lowlands where the king's agents had fewer allies.

Even during this internal exile, however, Cargill preached and taught, kept moving, and avoided sheriff and hunter. Finally in 1662, Cargill fled to the remote north of England, away from danger.

But could he stay away? He had inspired people with such words as, "If believers loved Christ as He loves them, they would be more in haste to meet Him." Was that a sermon to preach in exile, fleeing the king's agents?

Cargill's conscience said no, and his exile was short. Returning to Scotland again as an outlaw, he resumed his itinerant ministry, careful to keep his whereabouts within the counsel of close friends. Twice he escaped capture; once he suffered wounds during the getaway. Finally in 1679, he joined in a showdown of force at the Battle of Bothwell Bridge where Covenanters were viciously defeated. Cargill again fled, this time to the Netherlands.

Within months he was back, committed to a more open confrontation with the king. Cargill and fellow Covenanter Richard Cameron issued the Sanquhar Declaration, calling for war against Charles II and resistance to his brother, James II, who stood in line of succession.

On July 10, 1681, Cargill preached an inspired sermon in County Lanarkshire in southern Scotland, the site of battles lost against English forces. Before sunrise the next morning, he was seized and taken to Glasgow. He and several other Covenanters received a trial and sentence of death.

When Cargill mounted the scaffold on July 27, he said, "The Lord knows I go up this ladder with less fear and anxiety than I ever entered the pulpit to preach. Farewell all relations and friends in Christ; farewell all earthly enjoyments, wanderings, and sufferings... Welcome joy unspeakable and full of glory." A moment later the executioner's axe severed his head. Cargill was again absent from his beloved Scotland, this time home with his beloved Savior.

ISABEL ALISON AND
MARION HARVIE
(1681)

To young Scottish women were caught in the British wars of religion and executed for little more than being present at a Covenanter's open-air revival meetings. Both women were uneducated. Marion Harvie was a servant to the wealthy, and so little is known of Isabel Alison that she is described simply as "living in Perth." Their deaths signaled no victory for the British crown, no gain in the battle to suppress the Scottish spirit. Caught in events to which they were quiet observers, nonetheless they went to the gallows singing.

The first of the Scottish covenant bands appeared in 1557, and for a century these religious dissenters preached a clear Gospel, while simultaneously mounting a military campaign for independence from England. A "killing time" followed the 1679 assassination of the king's archbishop, James Sharp. Charles II had restored the monarchy in England in 1662, and was not about to allow another rebellion like the one that severed the head of Charles I. The Covenanters must be stopped—annihilated. So in late 1680 the crown's agents conducted raids against commoners who had any association with the likes of Donald Cargill or Richard Cameron.

Alison was taken from her home in Perth and Harvie from Borrowstounness. Each was interrogated concerning the Sanguhar Declaration, a Covenanter creed, and other differences of doctrine and practice. Of these matters the women knew little beyond the preaching they had heard. But they did strongly affirm that their sins had been forgiven through faith in Jesus Christ. Credited by the court with good sense and uncommon intellects, they were nonetheless condemned as traitors and rebels, and then further condemned to hell by the king's churchmen.

On January 26, 1681, Alison and Harvie were led with five other female criminals to the Grassmarket, Edinburgh's outdoor gallows. Alison testified: "So I lay down my life for owning and adhering to Jesus Christ, He being a free king in His own house, for which I bless the Lord that ever He called me." Harvie wrote before her hanging: "I die not as a fool or evildoer, or as a busybody in other men's matters; no, it is for adhering to Jesus Christ, and owning Him to be head of His church."

Together on the platform they sang Psalm 84. As the winter wind carried their voices to Heaven, the hangman pushed them over the edge. The king had won a short moment of silence at Grassmarket Square, but many more voices were singing in the angelic choirs above them.

"BLESSED ARE THOSE WHO SPREAD JOY THAT ARISES OUT OF THEIR OWN SUFFERING. HE WHO DENIES HIMSELF FOR OTHERS CLOTHES HIMSELF WITH CHRIST."

—PRINCE VLADIMIR OF THE ROYAL HOUSE OF GHICA, WHO WAS IMPRISONED IN A HARSH DUNGEON

JOHN DICK
(1684)

The Scottish Covenanters were ever-present pests to Charles II, king of England. His cavalry and the Covenanters' militia played cat-and-mouse in the highlands for years. But in 1679, the battle of Bothwell Bridge was a full-fledged military encounter, and the Covenanters lost badly. A year later, Richard Cameron and others signed the Sanguhar Declaration—a declaration of independence from England based on two claims: The head of the church was Christ alone; and Charles, usurping that position, was no longer the head of Scotland. Charles saw treason in the statement and sent his army to find Covenanter leaders.

John Dick was among the Bothwell battle veterans who were rounded up and put in two cells of the Canongate Tollbooth in September 1683. None of the prisoners expected to see the sun again, except on their march to the gallows. But in one of the cells, the men managed to obtain a file and saw, enough to cut through a bar to the outside. Slowly they worked the metal, concealing their work, then fitting the displaced bar in place until the appointed day. When it came, all twenty-five men escaped.

John Dick thus enjoyed six months of freedom until a peasant woman, eager for the crown's reward, betrayed him. Dick was the only escapee to be recaptured. Within a day or two, he was taken to the scaffold, where he spoke to the crowd:

> I am come here this day, and would not change my lot with the greatest in the world. I lay down my life willingly and cheerfully for Christ and His cause, and I heartily forgive all mine enemies. I forgive all them who gave me my sentence, and them who were the chief cause of my taking; and I forgive him who is behind me [the executioner]. I advise you who are

the Lord's people, to be sincere in the way of godliness, and you who know little or nothing of the power thereof, to come to Him and trust God. He will not disappoint you. I say trust in the Lord, and He will support or strengthen you in whatever trouble or affliction you may meet with. Now blessed be the Lord, here is the sacrifice and freewill offering. Adieu, farewell all friends.

İNDEED, ALL WHO DESİRE TO LİVE A GODLY LİFE İN CHRİST JESUS WİLL BE PERSECUTED.

2 TİMOTHY 3:12

JOHN PATON
(1684)

Captain John Paton, a legendary Scottish soldier and Covenanter, is best known for his stirring testimony delivered from the scaffold on May 9, 1684. He fought bravely for Gustavus Adolphus in Germany, and also for his Covenanter brethren against the English crown in pitched battles going back to 1644. His last testament to faith has become Captain Paton's gift to the ages:

Dear Friends and Spectators,

You are come here to look upon me a dying man...I am a poor sinner, and could never merit but wrath, and have no righteousness of my own; all is Christ's and His alone; and I have laid claim to His righteousness and His sufferings by faith in Jesus Christ; through imputation they are mine; for I have accepted of His offer on His own terms, and sworn away myself to Him, to be at His disposal, both privately and publicly. Now I have put it upon Him to ratify in heaven all that I have purposed to do on earth, and to do away with all my imperfections and failings, and to stay my heart on Him...I now leave my testimony, as a dying man, against the horrid usurpation of our Lord's prerogative and crown-right...for He is given by the Father to be the head of His church...Oh! Be oft at the throne, and give God no rest. Make sure your soul's interest. Seek His pardon freely, and then He will come with peace. Seek all the graces of His Spirit, the grace of love, the grace of holy fear and humility ...

Now I desire to salute you, dear friends in the Lord Jesus Christ, both prisoner, banished, widow and fatherless, or wandering and cast out for Christ's sake and the Gospel's; even the blessings of Christ's sufferings be with you all, strengthen, establish, support, and settle you...Now as to my poor sympathizing wife and six small children upon the Almighty Father, Son, and Holy Ghost, who hath promised to be a father to the fatherless, and a husband to the widow, the widow and orphans' stay. Be Thou all in all to them, O Lord...And now farewell, wife and children. Farewell all friends and relations. Farewell all worldly enjoyments. Farewell sweet Scriptures, preaching, praying, reading, singing, and all duties. And welcome, Father, Son, and Holy Spirit. I desire to commit my soul to Thee in well doing. Lord, receive my spirit.

TRULY, I SAY TO YOU, THERE IS NO ONE WHO HAS LEFT HOUSE OR WIFE OR BROTHERS OR PARENTS OR CHILDREN, FOR THE SAKE OF THE KINGDOM OF GOD, WHO WILL NOT RECEIVE MANY TIMES MORE IN THIS TIME, AND IN THE AGE TO COME ETERNAL LIFE.

LUKE 18:29-30

MARGARET WILSON AND MARGARET MACLACHLAN
(1685)

Eighteen-year-old Margaret Wilson could see the older woman, Margaret MacLachlan, roped to a stake, waiting for the tide to cover her. This slow, methodical death by drowning was ordered by the court at Wigtown for their refusal to swear allegiance to Charles Stuart, King of England, and to his church. Wilson, too, had refused the oath, yet her stake was deliberately closer to shore so that she, witnessing the death throes of the other woman, might think better of her Covenanter convictions and save her own life.

The elder Margaret, MacLachlan, farmed the pitiful soil granted to peasants near the small village of Wigtown, Scotland. Not educated, yet intelligent and full of wisdom, widow MacLachlan had been convinced by Presbyterian preacher James Renwick that the Church of England had surrendered its integrity to the corrupted English king. It was a lost church, loyal to the Stuarts above all, not to be confused with Christ's church of the Gospel and true sacrament. Against both tradition and law, MacLachlan declined to worship in her parish church but met with Covenanters in her own home. For this she was a marked woman.

Margaret Wilson, a teenager, was the oldest of three children of a prosperous farmer near Wigtown named Gilbert Wilson, who had complied with the law and worshipped where and how the king demanded. His two daughters and son, however, were religious rebels. When the children were too frequently absent from Sunday worship, officials used intimidation and threats so intense that the children fled to nearby mountains for safety. The boy, Thomas, was not heard from again, at least in history's records. But the two sisters, cold and hungry, sought refuge in the home of fellow Covenanter Margaret MacLachlan. All three were betrayed by neighbors, arrested and imprisoned.

Their trial was a farce of justice. The court, perhaps all too aware that it had become a laughingstock, demanded that the three criminals sign the Oath of Abjuration, certifying that they were not aligned with the Cameronians (led by Richard Cameron), who had challenged Charles II both politically and as head of the church. In effect, the Oath was a pledge of loyalty to the king. All three refused.

Frantic, Gilbert Wilson raised enough money to buy his younger daughter's freedom, but not Margaret's, who was sentenced on April 13, 1685, to be "tied to stakes fixed within the flood-mark in the water of Blednoch…there to be drowned." As for MacLachlan, the crown was simply glad to be rid of her. "Don't speak of that damned old bitch," one accuser said. "Let her go to hell."

At low tide on May 11, the two condemned Margarets were each fixed to their stakes. MacLachlan, weak from prison, was put furthest from shore. She died first, after a short struggle for life. Guards allowed the surf to nearly quench Wilson's life before they pulled her from the sea. They demanded again she pledge fealty to the crown. She replied, "May God save the king, if He will."

Tied once more to her stake, guards pushing her under the tide, Wilson died singing.

REMEMBER NOT THE SINS OF MY YOUTH

OR MY TRANSGRESSIONS; ACCORDING

TO YOUR STEADFAST LOVE REMEMBER ME,

FOR THE SAKE OF YOUR GOODNESS,

O LORD!

PSALM 25:7

JOHN NESBIT
(1685)

John Nesbit was a fighter, a soldier in the Thirty Years War on the Continent, a warrior among the Scottish Covenanters. But he suffered scars and wounds of the heart nearly more severe than those of the body. By the time he was captured and tried, he was already taking leave of the struggles he had seen on Earth and was eager for Heaven.

When Nesbit returned from war in Europe, King Charles II had begun to impose his will on Scotland and the Scottish church, a will opposed by the determined free-church Covenanters. They resisted any king as church-head and the king's priests as intermediaries. The Covenanters believed with equal ferocity in Christ alone as head of the church and armed resistance as the right of all who seek to worship that way. The Covenanters would not bow to Charles without a fight.

But Nesbit had other business, too. He married Margaret Law and they raised a family. He kept a handwritten New Testament passed on to him from a great-grandfather who was one of the barefoot preachers sent to England in the fourteenth century by John Wycliffe. He studied, learned, worked, prayed, and often hid from Charles's dragoons.

But he couldn't hide forever. Severely injured on the field at Rullian Green, Nesbit was left for dead, but escaped and recovered. He fought again at the Battles of Drumclog and Bothwell Bridge, both Covenanter disasters, which Nesbit survived after a brave fight. By then he was marked and a bounty was put on his head.

To draw him out from hiding, the king's troops forced Margaret and the children out of their home. Unable to secure shelter that winter, she died of exposure. A daughter and son followed her. Nesbit apparently found them as his daughter was being prepared for burial. His surviving son later wrote this account of it:

Friends were putting his little daughter in her rude coffin. Stooping down, he kissed her tenderly, saying, "Religion does not make us void of natural affection, but we should be sure it runs in the channel of sanctified submission to the will of God, of whom we have our being." Turning to a corner where two of his sons lay in a burning fever, he spoke to them but they did not know him. He groaned, saying, "Naked came I into this world and naked I must go out of it. The Lord is making my passage easy."

He buried his family and quickly went into hiding again. For two years he evaded his captors, despite the growing price on his head. Then one day, in the company of three others, a squad of dragoons led by a Captain Robert, Nesbit's cousin, surrounded them. A brief fight followed. Nesbit's three colleagues were injured, then executed. Nesbit, however, was worth more alive than dead. He was taken to Edinburgh, where he told his prosecutors that he was more afraid to lie than to die; that he was more willing to give his life than even they were to take it.

Quickly convicted, Nesbit was sentenced to be hanged. In prison he wrote his Last and Dying Testimony:

> Be not afraid at His sweet, lovely and desirable cross, for although I have not been able because of my wounds to lift up or lay down my head, yet I was never in better case all my life. He has so wonderfully shined on me with the sense of His redeeming, strengthening, assisting, supporting, through-bearing, pardoning, and reconciling love, grace, and mercy, that my soul doth long to be freed of bodily infirmities and earthly organs, that so I may flee to His Royal Palace.

On the gallows he recited from the eighth chapter of Romans, then dropped and was gone. A warrior's heart was home at last.

JOHN BROWN
(1685)

John Brown was a Scottish farm lad full of passion for Christ. He came from the homeland of the Lollards, the Shire of Ayr. Reared in reformational and free-church faith, Brown was a close friend of Richard Cameron, called the Lion of the Covenant, and Alexander Peden, the Prophet of the Covenant. At Brown's wedding in 1685, Peden told the new Mrs. Brown: "Ye have a good man to be your husband, but ye will not enjoy him long. Prize his company, and keep linen by you to be his winding sheet, for ye will need it when ye are not looking for it, and it will be a bloody one."

A speech impediment kept Brown from becoming a preacher, but in his humble cottage he ran a Bible school where he taught youth in what may have been the first regular Sunday school.

The year 1685 has been called the worst killing time in a terrible era. Scottish Covenanters were relentlessly pressed, harassed, and murdered, as recorded by historian Lord McCauley and author Daniel Defoe. When troops arrived at Brown's door that year, they were seeking Peden, whom they believed was nearby. They ransacked Brown's cottage and found a few papers. They wanted to know about these writings and to know Peden's whereabouts. Instead, Brown gave them prayers and lessons, cut short by the commander's order to assemble a firing squad.

Brown turned to his wife, "Now, Isabel, the day is come."

She replied, "John, I can willingly part with you."

"That is all I desire," he said. "I have no more to do but die." He kissed her and his child, saying he wished Gospel-promise blessings to be multiplied upon them.

The six soldiers ordered to shoot Brown were apparently so moved by the scene and its disregard for law that they lowered their muskets and refused to fire. Their officer placed his own pistol at Brown's head and ended his life, just outside his cottage.

Isabel Brown set her child on the ground, took her linen, and wrapped her husband's body. She mourned alone until neighbors, told of the murder, gathered to support her and to remember anew their own losses of that terrible year. Scotland was fighting for its identity and for freedom to worship in the form and fashion its people deemed right. Brown's murder was simple cruelty, yet the reason for it eventually won the day.

BLESSED IS THE MAN WHO REMAINS STEADFAST UNDER TRIAL, FOR WHEN HE HAS STOOD THE TEST HE WILL RECEIVE THE CROWN OF LIFE, WHICH GOD HAS PROMISED TO THOSE WHO LOVE HIM.

JAMES 1:12

JAMES RENWICK
(1662-1688)

K ill a martyr; make a follower. If only England had known what the deaths of Scottish Covenanter leaders would do for the movement, and how those courageous men and women would light a fire of faith among the next generation. So it was for nineteen-year-old James Renwick, a graduate of the University of Edinburgh despite his family's humble means. Renwick had watched Donald Cargill die, had heard his stirring last words, and had seen his head and hands strung up on Netherbow Gate. That day Renwick determined to carry the mantle, to be a Covenanter preacher.

He turned out to be a very good one. He was clear, sincere, and passionate. In the meetings he held along hillside heather and valley stream, hundreds would hear him preach about a gospel centered on Christ, a church free of state control, and a destiny of joy that God had prepared for each person who trusted the Savior. Cargill would have been proud to hear him and see him evade capture time and time again.

One time, Renwick traveled to Newton Stewart for a series of outdoor meetings, called conventicles. During his stay at the town's inn, an officer of the king's army, also passing the night at the inn, engaged him in conversation. The two talked into the night, each equally delighted by the lively interchange. At length they retired. When the officer inquired the next morning about his new friend, he was told the man named James Renwick had left early to escape capture. The stunned officer simply returned to his barracks, convinced that such a winsome, harmless young man as Renwick was not worth arresting.

On another occasion, Renwick sought a hiding place in a shepherd's cottage from which he had heard loud singing. He surmised it to be a Covenanter's cottage because of the exuberance of the music. But no, this shepherd was merely drunk and free-spirited. Still Renwick spent the night. In the morning while his own clothes were drying, Renwick used one of the man's old plaids for a morning walk, roaming the valley to pray and enjoy the early hour. Suddenly, a troop of soldiers appeared. They stopped the plaid-draped Scotsman to ask the whereabouts of the preacher they were hunting. Satisfied with the old man's empty-headed innocence, the soldiers rode on. Another narrow escape for Renwick.

Finally, in 1684, a frustrated Privy Council issued an edict naming James Renwick and all who gave him aid as enemies of the state. To withhold information or to hide him was tantamount to collusion in his crimes. Even then, three years would pass before the king's men would catch him.

In December 1687, Renwick was seized in Edinburgh when an officer heard praying inside a house and recognized the voice. The charges against him were three: refusing to accept the king's authority, refusing to pay the tax, and counseling his listeners to attend outdoor meetings with arms. Renwick pleaded guilty to all three and declined offers of pardon. On February 17, 1688, he was hanged in the Grassmarket, Edinburgh, and his head and hands hung on Netherbow Gate.

Who might have been watching that day in the Grassmarket? What young Christian might have been inspired when they heard him say, "I go to your God and my God. Death to me is a bed to the weary. Now, be not anxious. The Lord will maintain His cause and own His people. He will show His glory yet in Scotland. Farewell."

THE FRENCH HUGUENOTS

Who would rule sixteenth-century France, and how would the nation worship? These questions were eventually settled after a century of warfare and persecution. At the beginning of the century, however, was the immense influence of French exile John Calvin, who trained a cadre of missionaries and sent them back into France. These French Protestants were known as Huguenots. They built up the Protestant movement and also served as a magnet for political forces dueling for control of the crown.

The House of Bourbon favored the reformers. The Chantillon family, notably Gaspard de Coligny, joined forces with them and split French culture along religious affiliation. Civil war resulted. The Huguenots, while still a religious reform movement, became more and more dominated by secular princes bent on power. Violence was part of the movement from 1560 until Henry IV came to the throne in 1589. He was a Huguenot sympathizer, but converted to Catholicism in 1593. In 1598, he issued the Edict of Nantes, which made Catholicism the official religion of France, but permitted Huguenots freedom of worship and rights to keep a militia for self-defense, especially at their fortified city, La Rochelle.

In 1685, however, Louis XIV revoked the Edict of Nantes. Protestantism was now illegal in France. Four hundred thousand Huguenots sought refuge from persecution in Prussia, Holland, Britain, Switzerland, and North America.

Later, the French Revolution eventually destroyed the Catholic Church as a political power in France. Full religious liberty was finally guaranteed by the Napoleonic code of 1802.

For I am sure that neither death nor life, nor angels nor rulers, nor things present nor things to come, nor powers, nor height nor depth, nor anything else in all creation, will be able to separate us from the love of God in Christ Jesus our Lord.

ROMANS 8:38-39

Theophane Venard imprisoned and beheaded in Tonkin (Vietnam)

PERSECUTION

DURING THE

INDUSTRIAL REVOLUTION

(1790-1902)

A s communication and transportation technologies began to shrink the world, Catholics and most of the Protestant movements engaged in the evangelization of North and South America, the vast malaria-plagued African continent, and the Hindu-Asian subcontinent. Clearly, missionaries from different movements overlapped, but the broad expanse of these territories seemed like limitless opportunity to missionary-sending agencies and churches.

There were plenty of obstacles though. Missionaries often followed in the path of colonizing armies, and frequently they bore the brunt of tribal and regional backlash. The church too often shrank from urban centers where destitute workers were put in virtual slavery to work the factories of industrial growth. And the era's towering intellectual giants—Karl Marx, Charles Darwin, and Sigmund Freud—each took aim at the full orbit of Christian belief. They believed the age of faith was finished and done as a kitchen floor is swept clean of dust and crumbs.

In the Christian West, the age of martyrdom was over. Democratic governance would not tolerate every religious idea and teaching, but state-sanctioned killings of religious non-conformists largely ended. Certainly some sects saw persecution. The Namugongo martyrs died at the order of the Buganda king in East Africa. Disease more than martyrdom was the great killer of Christian missionaries who took the Gospel to the Southern hemisphere. We must also pause to acknowledge uncounted deaths for faithful discipleship in the movement that outlawed slavery.

The Industrial Revolution redirected Western religious aspirations from world evangelism to wealth, from sacrifice to a regime of efficiency, and from geographic churches to widespread acceptance of the notion that people must live and work together with different faiths in order to reap the benefits of progress and products promised by new machines.

"LOVE YOUR ENEMIES...PRAY FOR THOSE WHO SPITEFULLY USE YOU AND PERSECUTE YOU."

—Bishop Hannington's last words as he was killed by the Ugandan cannibals he tried to reach with the Gospel of Jesus Christ

John Smith
(1790-1824)

Demerara was one of three counties in the Caribbean colony of British Guiana (now Guyana). Slavery was the rule in Demerara, the way of life, the engine of its sugar cane economy. Whatever else happened there, slavery was never to be questioned or threatened. Of those who might do so, missionaries were the most culpable.

The London Missionary Society (LMS) sent John Smith to British Guiana in March 1817. In Demerara he took over from the Reverend John Wray, who had been transferred to neighboring Berbice County. Such transfers helped keep relations transitory between the missionary preacher and the slave population. Bonds of sympathy were dangerous to the economy.

Smith's first interview with Governor Murray made it quite clear: Teaching the African slaves to read was forbidden. The job of the mission station was to teach contentment, not to educate, nor to "insinuate anything which might...lead them to any measures injurious to their masters." In British Guiana, sugar cane was lord and king.

So the honorable Reverend John Smith set about his work in one of the most thankless, humid, and oppressive mission stations in the world—far from the British homeland where William Wilberforce and other Christian leaders were challenging the foundation of slavery and mapping out its legalized extinction.

Smith did his job perhaps too well. For one, he became a friend and counselor to his congregants, not merely their preacher. Second, he distributed books sent by the LMS for worship and nurture. One can hardly distribute books if the writing inside remains undecipherable. Teaching church leaders to read was a natural consequence of his teaching them the responsibilities of Christian discipleship.

Five years into his work, Smith was caught in a crisis that he and others must have seen coming. Certain slaves, having acquired reading skills and aware of Britain's anti-slavery movement, came to believe that plantation owners and the colonial government had already received orders for their emancipation but had suppressed them. With injustice piled upon wretchedness, a slave revolt was planned. Then an old slave named Quamina, a deacon at Smith's church, rose to advise that a work strike was the better alternative to bloody rebellion. Quamina wanted the advice of the preacher before he or others took up arms.

Smith advised patience. If new laws were coming, let them come. Even the governor himself would be obliged to enforce Acts of Parliament. After all, Britain was a civilized country. But counseling patience when freedom was in the air was unsuccessful. About thirteen thousand of the seventy-four thousand slaves in Demerara rounded up plantation managers on August 20, 1823, and put them under house arrest. The governor mustered his militia, however, and quickly disarmed the disorganized rebels, with enough loss of life to teach the required lesson. Quamina was hunted down and killed. Smith was arrested at the urging of plantation managers. They figured that he must have known about it, had failed to warn the governor, and thus was, in their eyes, a co-conspirator as guilty as an African slave carrying a gun or club.

Smith was tried by a military tribunal, which included officers who had directed field operations against the slaves. They sentenced Smith to be hanged.

Outraged that a British missionary might be executed by the British military after a mock trial on British soil, the LMS and others tried to save him. But before calmer minds from the homeland could send his commutation to Governor Murray, Smith was dead, the victim of pneumonia, caught in the stink and stench of the Guyana jail awaiting word from London.

Smith's journal quietly acknowledges his guilt:

Guilty of distributing Christian literature to slaves: "The Bibles and Testaments were sent from the Bible Society in allowing me a discretionary power in the disposal of them."

Guilty of befriending slaves: "No missionary can properly discharge his sacred functions without having some intercourse with his people besides that of public teaching."

Guilty of discouraging fieldwork on Sunday: "What crime have I committed? Are their masters greater than God?"

Guilty of sacrifice and service to the Gospel: After his death, the African workers called him the Martyr of Demerara.

Parliament stopped the British slave trade in 1807. All African slaves in the Empire were granted freedom in 1833.

HENRY LYMAN
(1809-1834)

The life change for Henry Lyman was dramatic. A fellow alumnus of Amherst College described him as "one of the worst, boldest in wickedness, defying the authority of God." But after his conversion, "he became as ardent and bold for Christ as before he had been in opposition to all good."

After studying theology at Andover Seminary and medicine in Boston, Lyman became one of the first missionaries sent to Indonesia by the American Board of Commissioners for Foreign Missions. Less than a year into his service, Lyman and his companion, Samuel Munson, met some Batak warriors near Tapahuli in northern Sumatra. Servants traveling with the missionaries reported that each was speared and then eaten by the Batak.

Lyman's intense, shortened, but dramatic life ended in violence, but work among the Batak continued. Today the Batak worship Christ and train others for missionary service in the region.

JOHN WILLIAMS
(1796-1839)

John Williams was an unlikely missionary. He apprenticed with an "ironmonger" as a teenager—a suitably rough and difficult trade for a lad whose life was skidding away from the faith he had been taught by pious parents near London. At age eighteen, however, John was converted so enthusiastically that he determined to go to the earth's remote corners, and the London Missionary Society agreed. But the LMS had misgivings. Williams was not schooled in theology, and his enthusiasm for searching out remote tribes exceeded prudent considerations.

To his credit, Williams was a good mechanic and problem solver, and he was gifted at languages and preaching. He excelled at team building, always leaving trained nationals behind to follow up his initiatives. Those efforts constitute a remarkable record of adventure and achievement. He brought Christian faith to the Hervey Islands after starting a mission on Raiatea. He preached on Rurutu and Rimatara. When he ran out of money, he sold his schooner, the Endeavor, and built his own, the Messenger of Peace, to get to Samoa and Tonga, then back to Raiatea and Raratonga, where he worked to revise the New Testament.

After eighteen years of missionary work, Williams and his wife, Mary, returned to England with their two sons in 1834. Their public meetings drew great interest. Another ship, the *Camden*, was purchased and fitted. Meanwhile, Williams wrote one of the most popular accounts of the region, plainly titled Narrative of Missionary Enterprises in the South Sea Islands. He was able to state that every known island along a two-thousand-mile line had received the Gospel.

The Williamses returned to Polynesia in 1837. Two years later, he was exploring the New Hebrides, where traders had recently exploited the natives. When Williams landed, trouble was imminent. He and his companion James Harris were attacked and killed at Erromango, their bodies eaten by the islanders.

News of his death inspired many new missionary voyages. Chalmers from Scotland, whose death so closely mirrored Williams's, and the Gordons from Canada are but two examples of those who went to fill the space made empty by Williams's murder. Eventually the Martyr's Church was built on Erromango as a memorial to the many, including Polynesian pastors and teachers, who gave their lives for the Gospel there.

I HAVE SAID THESE THINGS TO YOU, THAT IN ME YOU MAY HAVE PEACE. IN THE WORLD YOU WILL HAVE TRIBULATION. BUT TAKE HEART; I HAVE OVERCOME THE WORLD.

JOHN 16:33

ANDREW KIM TAEGON
(1820-1846)

A ndrew Kim Taegon was the first Korean to be ordained a Catholic priest. He died at age twenty-six in a wave of persecution intended to cleanse Korea of foreign intrusions threatening its customs and traditions.

Born to Christian parents, Taegon was baptized at age fifteen. Determined to work in the struggling Korean church, he traveled 1,300 miles to study in a seminary in Macao, China, and was ordained in Shanghai. He secretly re-entered Korea in 1845.

Only nine months later, he was arrested, kept in prison for three months, and then beheaded along the Han River near Seoul. His father also had been martyred years earlier.

While awaiting his execution, the priest sent this letter to his parish:

> My dear brothers and sisters, know this: Our Lord Jesus Christ upon descending into the world took innumerable pains and built the Holy Church through His passion...I pray you to walk in faith, so that when you have finally entered into heaven, we may greet one another. I leave you my kiss of love.

"I LEAVE YOU MY KISS OF LOVE."

—ANDREW KIM TAEGON

Allen Gardiner starved to death off Tierra del Fuego.

Allen Gardiner

(1794-1851)

H is mother knew there was no stopping the youthful Allen Gardiner. He had always dreamed of adventure on the seas. But at fourteen he seemed so young. Surely his mother knew, despite her prayers, that his heart was turning away from God.

Gardiner left home, still an adolescent, but with a heart so primed for travel that he moved successfully through Britain's Naval College at Portsmouth, and began a long career that took him to China and South America.

During these journeys, Gardiner searched and made three discoveries: first, the pursuit of the divine through Buddhism was futile; second, God did indeed love him; third, he would be transformed from captain in the Royal Navy to missionary to the world's most remote tribes. All his youthful energy still intact, Gardiner set out to take the Word of God to people and places where no missionary had ever succeeded.

In 1838, he crossed the Andes Mountains on muleback, searching for people who could understand his language and hear the Gospel. The results? No converts at all. He went to preach among the Zulu in southern Africa (where he founded Durban). He traveled to Indonesia but was rebuffed as an enemy.

In 1850, Gardiner turned his attention to the Yagan peoples of Patagonia, a tribal group that Charles Darwin encountered and judged too savage to ever be civilized. Gardiner recruited a doctor, a fellow missionary, and four hardy Cornish sailors to join his party. They spent twenty months trying to make contact with the Yagan people. But the Yagans chased them from their shores, stole their provisions, and left the band with one boat wrecked and digging in for the winter at Spanish Harbour on Picton Island, off Tierra del Fuego. Every man died of scurvy or hunger. The results? No meaningful contact with the Yagan, no converts, nothing accomplished.

Gardiner was the last to die, at least the last to write a journal entry. Considering his ordeal, one might expect a message less buoyant. But to the last, he was thinking of the next journey. In the journal, he urged that the Patagonia Missionary Society be renamed the South American Missionary Society (it was!) and that Christians from Britain return to bring the Gospel to these people. (They did, and more died. Altogether, fourteen missionaries gave their lives before any Yagan came to the faith.)

Following the death of John Maidment, who had been searching for food for the two of them, with his strength at last waning, Gardiner wrote:

> Lord, at your feet I humbly fall. And I give you all I have. All that your love requires. Take care of me in this hour of test. Do not let me have the thoughts of a complainer. Make me feel your power, which gives me life. And I will learn to praise you…Wonderful grace and love to me, a sinner.

Gardiner died of starvation at age fifty-seven in August 1851, beside his boat named *Speedwell*. The British ship *Dido* discovered his camp in January 1852. Anglicans celebrate September 6 as Allen Gardiner Day, remembering these saints and heroes of the faith.

John Mazzucconi
(1826-1855)

issionaries traveling to the South Seas in the early nineteenth century said their goodbyes, knowing full well that returning home was unlikely. Distance over water, the islands' suspicious peoples, and tropical diseases constituted a triumvirate of risk. Father John Mazzucconi's goodbyes came with this added burden: His father begged him to stay home, to find his calling near native Milan. The old man had already lost three children in their infancies; another six children had entered religious life. Why did this one have to go so far away to serve God?

But Mazzucconi convinced his father, Giacomo, that the risk was no match to the reward. His mission would be to evangelize remote islands around present-day Papua New Guinea, places few Westerners were willing to explore. Mazzucconi asked how those islanders would find their way to Heaven if not by the Gospel brought through God's chosen servants.

Mazzucconi graduated from the Pontifical Institute of Foreign Missions, founded in 1850. He would be traveling with four other priests and two brothers. Seven years earlier a group of thirteen priests and brothers had ventured to Melanesia. Malaria and islanders had battered and beaten that first group. Mazzucconi was going as part of the second wave. God's will be done. His father finally consented.

In late summer 1852, the new missionaries arrived in Sydney, then on to Rook Island. On Mazzucconi's first night there, he contracted malaria. Soon all the missionaries on Rook were sick.

As malaria comes and goes, taking its toll of strength and sometimes of life, the first missionary fatality occurred in March 1855. Apparently Mazzucconi had recovered from his first bout, but then the worst of malaria put him down. His Father Superior ordered him back to Sydney. There he recuperated and purchased supplies for the mission.

Not long after, a spate of deaths in the families of local chiefs caused the islanders to conclude that their "spirits" were angry because of these white invaders. Their decision to exterminate the missionaries led to an evacuation at the same time Mazzucconi was leaving Sydney to return. His ship probably passed his fleeing colleagues at sea.

Thus on September 25, 1855, a group of natives, led by a man known to dislike missionaries, met the ship, the *Gazelle*, in Woodlark Bay and offered to help guide and unload. Under their few clothes were knives and hatchets. The black-robed Mazzucconi was their first target. One thrust of the hatchet split open his skull. The natives finished off the ship's crew quickly.

A setback to evangelization in the South Pacific? Certainly. A grief to a father in Milan? Indeed. But today two-thirds of the population of Papua New Guinea is Christian, a blessing that John Mazzucconi could not have imagined as he wrote in his journal before he left for his mission station:

> I do not know what He is preparing for me in the journey I begin tomorrow. I know one thing only—If He is good and loves me immensely, everything else, calm or storm, danger or safety, life or death, are merely passing expressions of eternal love.

THEOPHANE VENARD
(1829-1861)

The young French boy, on a hillside near his home, watched his father's goats grazing. He saw the wind sweep through distant trees and nearby grasses. He watched clouds take shape and move along. He wondered about life. And he read from the *Propagation of the Faith Review*, a missionary magazine, about the story of Father Cornay, a French priest who had died as a martyr the previous year in far-away Tonkin (Vietnam). On that hillside, nine-year-old Theophane Venard said, "I want to go to Tonkin. I want to die a martyr too."

Such youthful quests are so rarely completed, but Venard meant it, and set about his schooling to achieve it. He would also need to convince his family, especially his father, who would not want the oldest child, the son, to abandon France for a mission so distant. In all this, Venard persisted, first at a minor seminary in Montmorillon, then a major seminary in Poitiers, then with his family. At his last dinner with them on February 27, 1851, he asked for his father's blessing. Through tears the old man said slowly, deliberately, "My dear son, receive this blessing from your father, who is sacrificing you to the Lord. Be blessed forever in the name of the Father, and of the Son, and of the Holy Spirit."

Venard had strength of will and purpose, despite a weakened body. He suffered typhoid fever, seasickness, and later pneumonia and asthma. Yet people around him could not fail to see his deep inner joy that carried his spirit through the goodbyes to family and France and into the port of Hong Kong and then Tonkin.

Tonkin at last—from hillside reverie to reality. Yet the same dangers awaited missionaries in 1854 as Cornay had faced in 1837. Here and there were pockets of Christians and functioning parishes. Politically, however, the situation was dangerous, leaning toward desperate. By 1859, Emperor Tu-Duc determined that the "Jesus religion" and all people associated with it must go—and go permanently. Tu-Duc's edict called for death to Christians and their accomplices and rewards for informants and betrayers. Venard took refuge in the home of a Christian widow, but the woman's cousin went to the authorities, who came for him on November 30, 1860, and put him in a narrow, short wooden cage.

During the interrogations and trials that followed, Venard gathered admirers even among the emperor's guards. God's mercies came in the form of paper to write letters home, a slightly larger cage, a mosquito net, an occasional visitor, and a secret confession to a priest.

Finally, on February 2, 1861, Tu-Duc signed the death warrant. Venard was beheaded that day. At the place of death, the executioner asked him what it was worth to kill him quickly. Little did he know that for this priest, the next moment would be the fulfillment of a boyhood vision and reunion with his beloved mother and father, the fitting end of an earthly calling. Venard had written his bishop: "My heart is like a calm lake." And so he sang the Magnificat as the half-drunk executioner swung his heavy sword.

George and Ellen Gordon (1861)
James Gordon (1872)

The South Sea Islands were there for the taking, if only the takers could survive disease, cannibals, and loneliness. The legendary explorer Captain Cook noted how barbaric the islanders had become and how unlikely the Christian Gospel would ever be adopted there. His words only challenged the bravest souls to come. So to Erromanga Island they went.

The first to die, John Williams and James Harris, were likely the victims of revenge killings directed against white-skinned people who had been selling, cheating, and exploiting the Erromangans for years. That these two had come to build a church was a distinction lost on local chiefs. Yet their deaths inspired nearly forty national Christians from neighboring islands to come. Perhaps these brown-skinned Christians would escape the hatred felt toward whites. But most of these people either starved to death or were also killed.

Then a Canadian linguist and doctor, George Gordon and his wife, Ellen, sailed for Erromanga, arriving in 1857. On the way, they learned all they could of the island's four languages—simple phrases and greetings—but enough to get them on shore and ease their entry. For four years they taught the Bible and tended the sick. Then in the spring of 1861, a measles outbreak took the lives of two children under Gordon's care—two children of a chief. On May 20, George and Ellen were clubbed to death.

Back in Canada, George's younger brother James heard the news and knew he must take his brother's place. When he finished theological training in Halifax in 1864, James sailed to the strange, exotic, and treacherous mission station where his brother and sister-in-law had served and perished. To his surprise, he found a church there.

It was small, to be sure, but nonetheless a church had taken root on Erromanga in the three years since the Gordon murders. So James was welcomed by Christians. Single and eager, he traveled widely, translated the Bible into two island languages, and sent back to Canada detailed reports of the island cultures and history.

For eleven years James Gordon invested his mind and heart on Erromanga Island. Then on March 7, 1872, for reasons unknown, he was killed by a blow from a stone axe as he sat translating Stephen's words in Acts 7:60: "Lord, do not hold this sin against them."

Eight years later, a church building at Dillar's Bay was named the Martyr's Church, and by the century's turn, nineteen of every twenty islanders identified themselves as Christians. Captain Cook had miscalculated by far the power of God's message to take root and grow in the South Seas. And few could have calculated the cost of its planting.

AND WITHOUT FAITH IT IS

IMPOSSIBLE TO PLEASE HIM,

FOR WHOEVER WOULD DRAW NEAR

TO GOD MUST BELIEVE THAT HE

EXISTS AND THAT HE REWARDS

THOSE WHO SEEK HIM

HEBREWS 11:6

John Kline
(1797-1864)

When the American Civil War began to divide families and make soldiers out of farmers, Brother Kline saw his role as a reconciler and healer, as a peacemaker and pastor. He offered medical help and pastoral counsel to men of both armies, North and South, traveling freely through contested areas and past each sentry line. A pacifist who preached against violence, his mission was to spread the word of the Prince of Peace and to administer balm to pain and loss. After twenty-nine years of itinerant ministry on horseback and four years of work during America's most vicious conflict, bullets finally took his life.

John Kline was born in Dauphin County, Pennsylvania, in 1797. He grew in the faith taught by the German Baptist Brethren, a "plain people" much like the Amish and Mennonite with whom the Brethren shared a common heritage in the Reformation.

Kline's family moved to Virginia in 1811 when he was fourteen years old, setting the stage for the difficult decisions he would have to make as an adult: between the union or slavery; discerning the proper power of government as an instrument of God's power; and the most important question: what does faith require in time of war?

Selected by the Linville Creek congregation for diaconal work in 1827, Kline was appointed to a preaching ministry in 1830. The Brethren did not normally build churches; instead, they met in homes spread throughout their farmlands. Kline's horse thus became his daily companion. He rode, it is estimated, more than 100,000 miles preaching, teaching, and offering elemental medical skills to Brethren congregations throughout the region. Each day Kline would record in a small journal his travels and reports—the basis for an unusual historical record published years after his death.

Kline rose in Brethren leadership. He was moderator of the Annual Meeting during each of the Civil War years. His gentle strength no doubt kept the Brethren united, as other Christian communities divided between North and South. Kline also led the Brethren in reaffirming their central doctrine of Christian pacifism. In 1864 the Annual Meeting report included this statement, "We exhort the brethren to steadfastness in the faith, and believe that the times...strongly demand of us strict adherence to all our principles, and especially to our non-resistant principle, a principle dear to every subject of the Prince of Peace...and not to encourage in any way the practice of war."

Kline was not indifferent to the nation's struggle. He opposed slavery and taught obedience to the law "which does not conflict with the Gospel of Christ." During Grant's Wilderness Campaign, close to Kline's home, he secured permission from commanders on both sides to offer medical relief and spiritual aid. Riding home one night from his pastoral duties, he was ambushed near his house. His bullet-ridden body was discovered the next day. Most accounts accuse Southern sympathizers who were most offended by Kline's views against slavery. Only a few months later, Kline's Brethren neighbors would lose their farms and homes during Sheridan's torch-and-burn campaign through the Shenandoah Valley.

For John Kline, trust and obedience to God's call meant enduring the trials that tested faith. In a sermon from Psalm 45, Kline said, "Although iniquity bears rule in the present, God still hates wickedness. God does not acquiesce in the injustice and wrong that is being perpetrated in the world. From this we are being saved."

ROBERT THOMAS
(1839-1865)

A n isolated Asian government, an aggressive American skipper, and a Welsh missionary armed with Bibles all came together at one spot in September 1865. The foreigners had come too far, their supplies were too thin, and they were overwhelmed. They all perished, including the missionary-interpreter Robert Thomas, the first Protestant to minister in Korea, and the first Protestant to die there.

Thomas was born in Wales in 1839, the son of an independent church minister. He studied at London University, and with his wife, Caroline, he was commissioned by the London Missionary Society for work in Asia. A five-month-long voyage put the young missionaries in Shanghai, where Thomas quickly learned Mandarin. He was assigned as a schoolteacher in Beijing. But the Hermit Kingdom, as Korea was then called, was on his heart.

Thomas found a way. In 1864 or early 1865, he slipped into Korea loaded with Chinese-language Bibles provided by Scotland's National Bible Society, and as many Korean language as he could obtain from contacts in China. For four months he traveled and preached, though heavily disguised. Only a year earlier, the Korean king had turned against Christians, killing about eight thousand Roman Catholics in a purge of "foreign religions." Robert's successes brought joy, but his heart sank when Caroline suddenly became ill and died.

In the summer of 1865, an American entrepreneur, W. B. Preston, with the help of a British business firm, launched an expedition designed to open trade with Pyongyang. They supplied a former U. S. navy ship, renamed the *General Sherman*. Thomas offered his services as translator and packed cases of Bibles for his second expedition to this tightly controlled kingdom.

The journey was a missionary's nightmare. The ship captain, under pressure from Preston, ignored Korean orders to turn back. Instead, at high tide, the *General Sherman* steamed upriver. It appeared to be a direct threat to the already testy Dae Won Kun, who apparently believed the ship was an effort by Catholics to reestablish their mission. He ordered his army to kill the ship's crew.

Now stuck on a sandbar, the crew of the *General Sherman* had cannon and rifle in their favor, but time favored the Koreans massed on the banks of the river. Captain Page even took one of the Korean negotiators as hostage, but to no avail. After two weeks of gunfire, Korean troops sent burning barges against the American ship. Its crew fought the blaze, but unable to contain it, they jumped overboard into the waters and the waiting swords of the Koreans. Some reports claim that Thomas made it to shore with Bibles, which he offered to the soldier who killed him.

The *General Sherman* sank into the river, its iron ribbing and anchor all that remained. Thomas's executioner did indeed take that Bible offered to him, and used it to wallpaper his house. Amazingly, guests read the writing of that strange book so casually displayed. The soldier's nephew was converted and became a pastor.

Today, 40 percent of South Korea is Christian. However, little is known about the church in Pyongyang. North Korea is as isolated and closed to public worship as in the day of Robert Thomas. But that too will change. Then, stories of the martyrs of Pyongyang will be told for the first time, and Thomas's sacrifice—his kneeling on the shore to offer a Bible—will be among the stories of faith gratefully recalled and remembered.

JUST DE BRETENIERES

(1838-1866)

E ven as a youngster, Just de Bretenieres dreamed of faraway places and missionary service. He was born in the Burgundy region of France to devoted Catholic parents. One day at the age of six, de Bretenieres was playing with his younger brother, digging holes in the ground. Suddenly he shouted, "Quiet, I hear the Chinese, I see them. They are calling me. I have to go to save them." De Bretenieres never forgot this incident, and as his devotion to faith grew, so did his sense that his life must be given to carrying God's salvation to foreign soil.

Not yet twenty, de Bretenieres entered "minor" seminary in Paris, then went on to the Foreign Missions Seminary. Childhood dreams may have taken him there, but those dreams had to grow up, deepen, mature. In 1861 he wrote to his parents: "I sense quite well the road I am taking is rough and difficult. I am not deluding myself about its obstacles and sufferings, nor to the dangers I will meet. I place myself entirely in God's hands."

Graduates of the seminary were never told beforehand where they would be sent. A priest was to simply follow orders, adjusting and accepting his assignment, aware that the ticket to foreign service was often "one-way" and that few places would be welcoming. When de Bretenieres heard his post would be Korea, his sense of calling and youthful joy of adventure came together. "I believe that our Lord has given me the best portion. Korea, the land of martyrs!" he wrote.

Just de Bretenieres sailed from Marseilles on July 19, 1864. He entered Seoul, the capital city, on May 29, 1865, secretly, taken to shore under cover of night in the same way that a spy might approach an enemy country. The government of Korea had in fact declared war on the church.

De Bretenieres learned the language and culture, and he began working covertly. Operating mostly at night, he heard confessions, blessed

Just de Bretenieres tortured and beheaded in Korea

marriages, gave confirmation, and administered last rites. He had baptized about forty adult converts when in February 1866, his location, along with his bishop's, was betrayed by one of the bishop's servants. De Bretenieres was arrested while celebrating Mass and taken to court tied in red rope, the symbol of a serious crime.

De Bretenieres's crime was being a priest and a missionary at a time when the regime had decided that foreign influences must be swept away. When he responded in his defense—"I came to Korea to save your souls"—he was actually testifying of his guilt and leading the court even more quickly to its preordained conclusion. After two weeks of ceremonial proceedings and daily tortures, de Bretenieres and his bishop, along with others, were carried away (tied to chairs, for their legs were no longer capable of bearing weight) to the sandy beach that would absorb their blood.

The party of priests testified and preached as the heavily guarded caravan reached its destination. The prisoners were each held up by poles placed under the arms and paraded before the gathered witnesses. Executioners then performed the death dances, swinging swords and inciting the crowd's bloodlust. Each man was stripped of clothing and made to kneel; then quickly the swords fell, and lives spent mostly in study, prayer, and preparation were cut violently short. De Bretenieres was twenty-eight years old.

Upon hearing the news, his father wept; his mother raised her eyes toward Heaven. The boy who had heard a call to missionary service while digging in the ground had finished his mission as a man, a priest, a martyr.

John Patteson clubbed to death with a hatchet

JOHN COLERIDGE PATTESON
(1827-1871)

issionary John Patteson knew every missionary initiative carried risk. He understood nothing could be won for God without a daring faith that trusts God in every circumstance. Patteson was a planner, a trainer, an activist for social justice, a preacher, and an evangelist, courageous to the end in his effort to plant churches and schools in Melanesia. He died at the violent hands of Nukapu islanders, who sought revenge on white men for stealing their people and making them slaves.

Educated at Eton and Balliol College, Oxford, Patteson was ordained in 1853. His tutor at Eton, George Selwyn, became the first bishop of New Zealand and convinced Patteson to pursue a missionary career in the South Seas. From 1855 until the time of his death, Patteson toured the islands of Melanesia on a ship called the Southern Cross, opening schools funded by his private fortune. In 1867 he founded the Melanesian Mission with headquarters on Norfolk Island, where the climate allowed school during winter months and year-round farming. In his travels, he learned twenty-three local languages and prepared the first grammars as connected language families became clearer to him. Patteson became the first bishop of Melanesia in 1861.

Besides the dangers of disease, sea travel, and immense cultural differences, Patteson also had to work in the face of the region's most profitable but illegal business—the slave trade. Some islands, he noted, were becoming depopulated to the point where subsistence was precarious. Many islanders were taking up crude but effective arms for self-protection against the light-skinned people who would steal their wives and sons. While Patteson was widely known, he was quite aware that he shared with the slave traders their most identifiable trait: skin color.

Thus he wrote en route to Nukapu, only four days before his death:

How I pray God that if it be His will, and if it be the appointed time, He may enable me in His own way to begin some little work among these very wild but vigorous islanders. I am fully alive to the probability that some outrage has been committed here...I am quite aware that we may be exposed to considerable risk on this account... But I don't think there is much cause for fear.

On September 20 he landed alone on Nukapu, and was clubbed to death. His body delivered back to the ship revealed five hatchet cuts to the chest, one for each islander recently stolen by traders. England was stunned by his death. At last, Parliament passed the Kidnapping Acts of 1872 and 1875, outlawing the slave-trade terror that led to Patteson's martyrdom.

A Melanesian Christian who had been trained by Patteson offered this tribute to the slain bishop: "As he taught, he confirmed his word with his good life among us. His character and conduct were consistent with the law of God. He did nothing carelessly. White or black, he loved them all alike."

James Hannington
(1847-1885)

On a hill to the west of Kampala's city center stands the dome of Namirembe Cathedral, with its bronze cross clearly visible to the crowded capital of Uganda. It is one of two cathedrals of the Province of the Church of Uganda (Anglican), one of the strongest Christian movements in East Africa. Beside the church rests a small cemetery, and just inside the gate is a simple stone marking Bishop James Hannington's grave. The epitaph contains his last words: "Tell the Kabaka I die for Uganda."

Born in Hurstpierpoint near Sussex, England, Hannington was a precocious, adventurous child. (He blew off one of his thumbs with black powder in a childhood prank.) He studied at Oxford, and then went into business and the British Army. Dedicated to Christ, he entered the ministry, and at age thirty-seven he was appointed by the Church Missionary Society to Uganda to lead the first expedition of Protestant missionaries to the East African interior. But he never arrived in Uganda; malaria and dysentery forced his return to London.

In 1884 he tried again, this time as the first bishop of Eastern Equatorial Africa. His goal was the Buganda kingdom, west of the source of the great River Nile, discovered by British explorer John Speke just two years before. This time Hannington might have completed the long journey but for a rumor passed to the Buganda king (Kabaka Mwanga), warning him to beware of white men approaching from the east—they were aggressors intent on a takeover.

Indeed, Hannington's expedition was stopped near Jinja in late July. Bugandan warriors apprehended the bishop, sending word back to Kampala of whites held prisoner. Hannington wrote in his journal on July 22:

Starvation, desertion, treachery, and a few other nightmares hover over one's head in ghostly forms...let me beg every mite

James Hannington speared to death after months in captivity

of spare prayer. You must uphold my hands, lest they fall. If this is the last chapter of earthly history, then the next will be the first page of the heavenly—no blots or smudges, no incoherence, but sweet converse in the presence of the Lamb.

Not until late October did the Kabaka's order make its way back: "Kill him." Today, Bugandan leaders will say that in the Luganda language, "release him" and "kill him," sound remarkably similar, but in 1885, warriors holding Hannington could not worry if they had heard the Kabaka correctly. On October 29, Hannington read Psalm 30 and recorded in his journal that it brought him "great power." Later that day he was speared.

Reports of Hannington's death sparked a wave of missionary recruits from England. Within a year the church was growing and Mwanga's own court included several young Christian servants. Even the Kabaka himself, after further bloodshed (see the Namugongo Martyrs), confessed his faith in the same Lord who had called Bishop Hannington to Africa. Today, the Church of Uganda worships in every part of the nation, including the war-torn northern provinces, where the story of martyrdom is still being written.

JOSEPH MUCOSA BALIKUDDEMBE
(1885)

The arrival of Catholic and Protestant missionaries in modern-day Uganda occurred during the reign of Kabaka Mutesa I (the king of the Buganda kingdom). Mutesa allowed his people free choice among the competing missionary alliances, including Muslims, while he remained neutral and died a traditionalist. He died in 1884, leaving power in the hands of his younger and less adroit son, Mwanga II.

The Christian movement in Uganda required a definitive break from African traditional religion. Converts were taught new behaviors (polygamy, for example, was forbidden) and new loyalties (God first), which upset the traditional religious view of the Kabaka's ultimate sovereignty. Thus Mwanga could afford a certain fascination with the European's faith while he was prince. However, when he succeeded to his father's throne, he came to regard their teaching as subversive.

Certainly the missionaries' teaching was subversive to Mwanga's own personal pleasure, for when he made sexual advances upon his young male servants, they expressly refused in the name of the Christian God Who now held their ultimate loyalty. Even though homosexuality was abhorrent among the Buganda people, the refusal of subjects to obey the will of Kabaka had never before happened. Mwanga was caught in a power crisis, without the diplomatic skill or personal maturity to resolve it apart from confrontation and violence.

Only a year after becoming king, Mwanga ordered the execution of his first Bugandan martyrs. Seven years later, Anglican Bishop James Harrington, while approaching the Buganda kingdom through the southern route, was speared on Mwanga's orders.

Joseph Mucosa Balikuddembe, a Catholic convert who was an adviser to Mwanga, criticized the order to kill Harrington. It was customary to give a condemned man opportunity to explain himself, Balikuddembe asserted. This traveler from Britain—an important man with title and mission—had been executed while still outside the kingdom because of superstitions about the route he traveled. Balikuddembe's criticism was emblematic of the trouble Mwanga faced, his loss of authority and esteem among his own people, and his failure to live up to images of his father's greatness.

Balikuddembe, meaning "man of peace," knew where his advice would lead. He had directly confronted Kabaka's long-held authority to take life at his pleasure. He had encouraged faith among young converts in Kabaka's court, urging them to observe conscience against enemies, to refrain from wanton killing, and to resist Mwanga's sexual aberrations. Though Balikuddembe had been a royal page since age fourteen and a loyal servant since, his faith presented a threat to the new king.

Balikuddembe had been baptized at age fifteen, one of the first converts of Catholic missionaries. When his mentors retreated to the south side of Lake Victoria, he became the leader and teacher of the other Catholic pages. At the same time, he was Mutesa's most trusted attendant.

When Mwanga became king, Balikuddembe was appointed majordomo and given permission to reprove the king for inappropriate conduct. He was the king's conscience, as it were, and an adviser and tutor. It was a dangerous position, ripe for intrigue and prevarication. But Balikuddembe approached his work from his growing faith.

Following Harrington's death and Balikuddembe's criticism, Mwanga fell ill. Balikuddembe administered the medicine, probably opium. Mwanga experienced side effects and accused Balikuddembe of attempting to poison him.

In late October 1885, Balikuddembe was summoned to account for allegations of subversion and treason. He replied simply, "I am going to die for God." Condemned to burn, he refused to be bound. "Why bind me? Do you think I shall flee? Flee where, to God?" He was taken to the Nakivubo River near the Nakasero hills on November 15. His executioner so admired him that before the fire was lit, he beheaded Balikuddembe. Before his death, Balikuddembe forgave the king and other enemies.

More martyrdom followed, including many of the king's pages. At the Catholic and Protestant sites commemorating these deaths, guides will say that much later in life, Mwanga made his peace with the Church, even adopting the faith of those he killed.

"I HAVE HAD MANY STORMS IN THIS WORLD, BUT SOON MY VESSEL WILL BE ON THE SHORE IN HEAVEN... JESUS, I BELIEVE."

—THE LAST WORDS OF THOMAS BILNEY, A LAW PROFESSOR AT CAMBRIDGE UNIVERSITY, WHO WAS ARRESTED FOR "HERESY" AND BURNED AT THE STAKE

ΠAMUGONGO ΠARTYRS
(1886)

The Uganda martyrs were young men who were recruited in the Kabaka's service (the Buganda king), but who had also embraced the Christian faith as presented by the Catholic fathers and the Protestant missionaries who were resident in the King's court.

In 1875 the great adventurer-journalist Henry Morton Stanley wrote in the *London Telegraph*, requesting missionaries to come to Uganda. Kabaka Mutesa I had made this request. When missionaries arrived in Uganda in 1877 and 1879, some of their first converts were these young men in the king's service. When they embraced the Christian faith, they insisted that God was sovereign. This, of course, was treason in the Buganda kingdom where the Kabaka held all power. When the king made homosexual advances on these youth, they refused. Such insubordination was an unprecedented threat to the king.

Both Catholics and Protestants were beaten, rolled tightly in combustible leaves, and then placed in fire. Forty-five men, from age twelve, were burned in a place called Namugongo, near Kampala. Many others were killed in the towns of Busega, Nakivubo, Munyonyo, Lubowa, Mengo, Old Kampala, Mityana, and Ttakajjunga.

Years later the executioner—whose nephew was among those killed— turned to the Christian faith. He tried to explain his actions, pleading that he had only done what the king ordered. A local proverb said that the "queen ant in an anthill feeds on its ants"; thus Kabaka Mwanga executed these martyrs because their allegiance was to God and not to him.

In memory of these young men who gave their lives for God, a shrine was constructed in 1969 at the sight of the execution. Today that structure is a basilica. Near the Catholic site is a Protestant seminary, which recreates the scene of the blaze and tells the story of young faith that would not quiver at the prospect of death by fire. Thousands gather in Namugongo every June 3, a national holiday in Uganda.

Bernard Mizeki speared to death in Rhodesia (Zimbabwe)

BERNARD MIZEKI
(1896)

◆

I n the frontier of Christian missions always stands a spiritual no-man's land—contested territory claimed by pagan faiths and practices where resistance to the Christian invasion is often violent. These territories have casualties of war—saints who sacrifice safety for the sake of establishing a sure testimony to the power of God, defying the pagan spirits, and claiming ground for the Gospel by the blood of Christ, made real and visible by their own.

Bernard Mizeki was born Mamiyeri Mitseka Gwambe in Portuguese-controlled Mozambique, sometime around 1861. Before his teenage years, he left home for Capetown, South Africa, to search for work and education. He landed at a school operated by the Society of St. John, an Anglican order. In March 1886, Mizeki was baptized, adopting the name Bernard. For five years he worked as a lay leader doing translations and providing other assistance. Then Bishop Knight-Green asked Mizeki to join him in Southern Rhodesia (now Zimbabwe).

During the next few years he helped open schools, begin translations, and conduct worship. Gifted at languages, Mizeki learned Shona and several others. In 1891 the bishop placed Mizeki in Nhome, the village of the paramount-chief Mangwenda. The chief gave permission to build a mission complex near a grove of sacred trees. Mizeki cut down some of these trees to build, and claiming others for Christ, he notched them each with a cross. Mizeki's less-than-reverent treatment of those trees was a serious affront to local witch doctors.

Mizeki was fully aware that tampering with the African traditional religion was like waving a red scarf before a raging bull. According to the witch doctors, this act would not only challenge their social status, but also their beliefs, causing the spirits to become restless or angry. Mizeki was facing the enemy, engaging in the spiritual battle.

All the while, another battle was simmering, and in 1896 it exploded. A rebellion against colonial masters threatened all who followed their ways. So the Shona-land westerners took refuge back in South Africa. But Mizeki stayed, despite threats on his life.

On June 18, 1896, loud knocking warned him of enemies at the threshold. Mizeki was taken outside and speared. As he lay gravely injured but alive, his young wife, pregnant with their first child, ran for help. She then claimed to have seen a bright light over his body. When she returned, the body was gone. Had his killers taken the body into hiding? Had a miracle occurred? In any case, Mizeki's body was never discovered, but his witness and the faith he taught lived on among the Shona.

Today Bernard Mizeki College stands near a monument recalling his sacrifice. Churches in Pretoria, Botswana, Capetown, and Swaziland bear his name. Most important, the daughter born after his death was named Masiwa, "fatherless one," and was later baptized Bernardina. The church grew as martyrs chose trust and courage over fear and flight.

THEREFORE, MY BELOVED BROTHERS,
BE STEADFAST, IMMOVABLE, ALWAYS
ABOUNDING IN THE WORK OF THE LORD,
KNOWING THAT IN THE LORD YOUR
LABOR IS NOT IN VAIN.

I CORINTHIANS 15:58

BOXER REBELLION in CHINA
(1900)

Europeam powers were carving China into trading zones, as they had done to sub-Saharan Africa a decade earlier. When the United States acquired the Philippines in 1898, President McKinley and his Secretary of State, John Hay, devised an alternative to the European plan called the "Open Door" policy. This policy would ensure the United States an entry into the vast Chinese market by declaring rather simply that trading zones be abandoned in favor of open competition. The dowager empress, Tsu Hsi, saw the obvious danger to her Ch'ing Dynasty and fostered an informal reaction in an imperial message to all Chinese provinces: "The various Powers cast upon us with tiger-like voracity, hustling each other to be first to seize our innermost territories...If our millions of people...would prove their loyalty and love of country, what is there to fear from any invader?"

In drought-stricken Shandong province, a secret society called the Fists of Righteous Harmony recruited thousands of new members. Called by foreigners the "Boxers" because they practiced martial arts, this militant society taught that thousands of "spirit soldiers" would rise from the dead to join their cause.

That cause, promoted by Empress Tsu Hsi as a way to unite her empire, was to rid China of all "foreign devils." Diplomats fled to a compound in Beijing near the Forbidden City. Missionaries in the outer provinces had few choices. Many wives saw their husbands beheaded, and children their mothers. The Boxers took the lives of adults and children alike—Catholics, Orthodox, and Protestant. Diplomats and others who reached the Beijing compound were nearly at the end of their food and bullets when American sailors and Marines fought their way from Shanghai to rescue them.

The empress, who escaped the city disguised as a peasant, returned a year later but never regained the power of the Ch'ing dynasty. John Hay's Open Door policy opened China's market until the Japanese invaded China in World War II.

Ia Wang

O ut of the 1,000 Orthodox believers in Beijing, three hundred were killed. On the evening of June 11, 1900, leaflets were posted in the streets calling for the massacre of Christians and anyone who dared to shelter them. That night, gangs of Boxers with torches attacked Christian houses, seizing believers and demanding that they disavow Christ. Those who remained faithful were gutted and then beheaded or burned alive. One Orthodox schoolteacher, Ia Wang, died twice. First, the Boxers slashed her with swords and covered her in a shallow grave. Her groans, however, alerted nearby terrorists. She was exhumed and tortured again. Eyewitnesses reported she died confessing Christ.

Mr. Farthing

A n English Baptist missionary named Farthing was the first to be led from his house. His wife clung to him, but he put her aside. Farthing knelt before the soldiers, and his head was severed with one swing of the sword. He was followed by Hoddle, Beynan, Lovitt, and Wilson, each of whom was beheaded. Then Stokes, Simpson, and Whitehouse. When the men were dead, the women were taken. Mrs. Farthing held the hands of her small children, but soldiers separated them, beheaded the mother, then all the children quickly. Mrs. Lovitt was wearing glasses. A soldier took them and then beheaded her as she held the hand of her small son.

After the Protestants were killed, the Roman Catholics were led out. The bishop asked the governor why he was ordering these killings. Without answering, the official drew a sword and split the bishop's face. Priests and nuns followed him in death. The bodies of forty-five victims—all

Christians, including Chinese—were left in the street that night so that clothes, rings, and watches could be stripped from the corpses.

John and Sarah Young

John and Sarah Young had been married fifteen months when the evacuation order arrived. They joined others hurrying to escape. On the way, Chinese soldiers met them and offered to protect them if they would agree to stop preaching their foreign religion. The missionaries could not agree because they had been called to share God's good news with everyone, including those speaking to them. The soldiers killed them immediately.

Carl Lundberg

A small group of Christian and Missionary Alliance missionaries continued their work in remote northwest China. When news arrived that Boxers were coming, they attempted to flee into Mongolia. Bandits intercepted them and stole their clothing and supplies. For two weeks, the group survived by eating roots until some Catholic priests came to rescue them. But they were too late. The Boxer army was close behind. Missionary Carl Lundberg wrote:

> I do not regret coming to China. The Lord has called me, and His grace is sufficient. The way He chooses is best for me. Excuse my writing; my hand is shivering.

The Boxers killed everyone.

HORACE TRACY PITKIN
(1869-1900)

H orace Pitkin was an American East Coast blueblood. He was a distant relative of Connecticut's colonial-era attorney general and also kin to Elihu Yale, founder of the great Yale University from which Pitkin graduated in 1892, at the height of America's Gilded Age. It was also the era of "muscular Christianity"—a mix of robust physical and spiritual development coupled with nearly unlimited optimism that the new century just ahead would be the Christian century, the fulfillment of the Gospel mandate to all the world.

For Yale men like Pitkin—strong, charismatic, and gifted—the arena where all virtues would meet their test was China. Indeed, Horace organized Yale's first Student Volunteer Band for foreign missions. He then went on to Union Seminary in New York, married Letitia Thomas, and set sail for Hunan Province in central China.

Pitkin was an organizer, but not blind to the risks. He was, after all, in charge of the station in Hunan for the American Board of Commissioners for Foreign Missions. As news from Beijing arrived and the Boxers began to show restless aggression, Pitkin sent his wife and child back to the United States.

On Saturday, June 30, 1900, the Presbyterian compound on the north side of Paoting was attacked. The missionary surgeon, Dr. G. B. Taylor, went out to plead the missionaries' good will. He was killed immediately, and his severed head was raised for display in a nearby temple. The remaining Presbyterians were burned inside one of the houses.

News traveled quickly to the south side of the city, where Pitkin and two staff women were trapped at the American Board office. By 9:00 a.m., the Boxers arrived. Pitkin was killed trying to defend the others.

Back at Yale, four friends created a missionary society in 1901 (that still exists today). Their work, honoring Pitkin and others, included a hospital and a school in Hunan Province.

LIZZIE ATWATER
(1900)

◆

I n June 1900, a fierce nationalist reaction in China against Christian missionaries and churches claimed more than thirty-two thousand lives. The worst massacres occurred in the northern province of Shanxi. The pregnant Lizzie Atwater wrote a memorable letter home before she and six others were martyred.

> Dear ones, I long for a sight of your dear faces, but I fear we shall not meet on earth. I am preparing for the end very quietly and calmly. The Lord is wonderfully near, and He will not fail me. I was very restless and excited while there seemed a chance of life, but God has taken away that feeling, and now I just pray for grace to meet the terrible end bravely. The pain will soon be over, and oh the sweetness of the welcome above! My little baby will go with me. I think God will give it to me in heaven and my dear mother will be so glad to see us. I cannot imagine the Savior's welcome. Oh, that will compensate for all these days of suspense. Dear ones, live near to God and cling less closely to earth. There is no other way by which we can receive that peace from God which passeth understanding. I must keep calm and still these hours. I do not regret coming to China.

On August 15, 1900, soldiers took Atwater and ten others away from the relative safety of a nearby town and hacked them to death with their swords, tossing the bodies into a pit.

James Chalmers killed by cannibals in New Guinea

JAMES CHALMERS
(1841-1901)

He loved the sea, this rebellious Scottish lad. The fishing village of Ardrishaig was his home, and the fishermen his friends. The sea was wild when the wind blew strong, like young Chalmers himself. He breathed the sea air and wondered what lay beyond the rolling waves. Later, when God's call to missionary service touched his heart, he spent many perilous days on the sea, searching out peoples who had never heard God's story.

Chalmers was eighteen when he converted to Christ in an evangelistic meeting led by two preachers from Ireland. Chalmers had come with friends to break up the meeting, to mock the zealots, to make sport of the timid who sought their peace in religion. Perhaps the heavy rain that night dampened the youths' recklessness, but Chalmers listened and believed. The message was from Revelation 22:17: "The Spirit and the Bride say, 'Come.'" It was an invitation to make his heart's home in God; Chalmers gladly accepted. "I was thirsty, and I came," he said later.

A few years later he received pastoral training and a commission by the London Missionary Society to serve in the Pacific Islands. Chalmers and his wife, Jane Hercus, were standing at water's edge in New Guinea. Suddenly a mob of painted warriors surrounded them, demanding gifts and weapons.

Chalmers knew the danger, for he had come to a part of the world where killing was honored, where warriors bit off the noses of their victims as a sign of triumph, and where eating human flesh was common. Were those dangers not enough, the waters were infested with snakes and crocodiles, and the entire area filled with malaria and fevers.

"Give us tomahawks, knives, and beads or we kill you, your wife, your teachers and their wives," the leader said, ready to strike with his stone club.

"You may kill us," Chalmers replied, "but we never give presents to persons threatening us. Remember we have only come to do you good."

The mob retreated, threatening to return at dawn's light. Missionaries came to New Guinea with daily prayers for survival and converts. But on this particular evening, waiting for dawn, survival was the small group's chief concern.

Inside their quarters, Chalmers asked the group, "What shall we do? Men stay, women escape? The boat is too small for all of us." Jane replied, "We have come here to preach the Gospel. We will stay together." The teachers' wives agreed, "We live together or die together." They prayed, and gradually fell asleep. Chalmers wrote that night in his journal: "The Spirit and the bride say, 'Come!' We came at thy bidding to this land to point these wretched people to the same cleansing, refreshing, healing Fountain. Protect us, that we may fulfill the mission." And God did protect them.

For ten years Chalmers and Jane helped build the church on Rarotonga, training pastors and teachers. They constantly reached beyond the established churches and schools to uncover new peoples not yet reached.

In the fall of 1877, they moved to New Guinea, where they found villages filled with disease, sorcery, filth, treachery, and weapons. Slowly, patiently, they told the Gospel story and made God's invitation plain. Often they slept as guests in a village's *dubu*—the main lodge and trophy room of human skulls. Most of the people they met had never seen white skin. Chalmers would introduce himself by taking off his black boots, revealing then his white arms and chest to the laughter of some and the shrieks of others. His name there was Tamate, the closest sound the natives could make to Chalmers. Wherever Tamate went, the threat of the warrior with the stone club was never far away.

Jane grew sick in 1878 and sought recovery in Australia. Five months later she died. Chalmers, who had remained in New Guinea, was devastated. He wrote in the journal: "Oh to dwell at His cross and to abound in blessed sympathy with His great work! I want the heathen for Christ!"

In 1886, Chalmers returned to England to tell his stories of twenty years. There he married Sarah Harrison, who would also die of fever later in the Pacific after remarkable and courageous service. And Chalmers turned down a government appointment that would have guaranteed his safety as a missionary-diplomat. His position: "Gospel and commerce, yes. But remember this: it must be the gospel first."

Chalmers returned to New Guinea in the fall of 1887. He was never content to manage a mission station; he wanted new contacts, far up the unmapped rivers, down the inland trails. On one such journey a year after Sarah's death, warriors armed for piracy and murder surrounded his boat near shore. Chalmers decided, as was his custom, to demand a meeting with the local chief as the best way to escape the mob. His young colleague, Oliver Tomkins, insisted on accompanying the sixty-year-old veteran.

Together they approached the village dubu, hoping for a council and anticipating a shared meal. Once inside, however, the stone clubs fell, the strangers' heads were severed and their bodies cooked, mixed with sago, and eaten. The day was April 8, 1901, at the dawn of what was then called the "Christian Century."

Chalmers, two heroic wives, and many co-workers and their families gave their lives to bring the Spirit and Bride's invitation to Pacific Island peoples. "Let him that is athirst come," read the words in Chalmers' Bible, "and whosoever will, let him take the water of life freely."

JOHN KENSIT
(1902)

J ohn Kensit was not someone to go about "business as usual" when truth and reform were at stake.

Kensit was raised by a pious, prayerful mother who focused the young lad's mind on *Pilgrim's Progress*, the Book of Common Prayer, and the Bible. Then, as often happens in youth, two odd events created a conflict, which was later resolved by Kensit's lifelong devotion to reform within the Church of England.

The first event was his recruitment to the choir of St. Ethelburgh's, a high-church parish where worship was decidedly more Catholic than Protestant. At the same time a nearby evangelical vicar began preaching reformation doctrines. Kensit went to those meetings, and was positively convinced that the Bible alone was God's Word and that Jesus alone was the sufficient sacrifice for sin.

The second event was a visit to London in 1859 by Giuseppe Garibaldi, the Italian nationalist who sought a republic led by citizens rather than a theocracy led by priests. Garibaldi, a man of action, and not one to avoid conflict, made an indelible impression on young John.

Until 1898, Kinset's personal campaign to recover the heart of faith in the Church of England was accomplished by selling books and teaching Sunday school. But in that year, he literally made headlines when he disrupted a Good Friday service at St. Cuthbert's Church. He seized a cross from the people who were kissing it—treating it as an icon—and proclaimed to the crowd, "In the name of God, I denounce this idolatry— God help me." After a sound beating by the crowd, he was arrested. At that moment John Kensit left the life of the quiet soldier and became a public debater— some would say a public nuisance—in the cause of church reform. At every opportunity, he confronted church officials with his probing challenges to return to the faith of Ridley, Latimer, and other English reformers.

Kensit founded the Protestant Truth Society and sent out a corps of lay evangelists he called the Wycliffe Preachers to awaken people to biblical faith. He held public meetings, frequently in parishes dominated by Catholic sentiment. His last meeting was at the Claughton Music Hall in Birkenhead, on September 25, 1902, which was conducted without incident. Later, however, as he was walking to the ferry, a youth hurled a heavy metal file at Kensit and his group. It found its mark on Kensit's brow. He was rushed to an infirmary and seemed to recover, but he contracted pneumonia and died on October 8.

Kensit's crusade for reform, some say, was never realized in the Church of England. He died nonetheless for his reformational faith, one of the last martyrs in England.

"CHEER UP, MY BROTHERS,

AND LIFT UP YOUR HEARTS TO GOD, FOR

AFTER THIS HARSH BREAKFAST WE SHALL

HAVE A GOOD DINNER IN THE KINGDOM OF

CHRIST OUR LORD AND REDEEMER ....

THIS IS GOD'S ARMOR, AND NOW I AM A

CHRISTIAN SOLDIER PREPARED

FOR BATTLE."

—ANTHONY PARSONS, AN ENGLISH PRIEST,
WHO WAS BURNED AT THE STAKE

Chet Bitterman's grave in Colombia

Persecution

During the

Twentieth Century

(1914-1999)

B y 1914 the century that was to be the "Christian century" had turned instead into the beginning of the bloodbath of World War I. This caused many people to ask, "Where is God now?"

Notable martyrs died as violence erupted around the globe, linking their blood with millions of other victims of imperialism, fascism, rebellions, pogroms, and the indiscriminate annihilations of modern warfare.

However, beyond the trenches of World War I and World War II, the Holocaust, the killing fields of Southeast Asia, and China's Cultural Revolution stand the dominant secular ideologies that have replaced a "Christian climate of opinion" in places where the church was once strong. Pragmatism, existentialism, and the post-modern mood have drawn the once sacred-leaning climate of Europe decidedly away from Christian moorings. Indeed, the constitution of the European Union makes no reference to deity or to the church at all.

In the United States, commercialism and a widening appetite for toleration had softened Christian convictions to the point where many believers were bewildered as to why anyone would surrender their life for their faith convictions. Martyrdom no doubt still occurred. Many Christian Hutus died trying to save Tutsi neighbors in the Rwanda genocide. Bombings of Christian churches in the Middle East took the lives of courageous believers who met for worship at their peril. Christian converts in Afghanistan were put under an automatic sentence of death.

The demographic center of the Christian church was shifting to the southern hemisphere—Latin America and Africa—with strong movements in Asia as well. The examples of Dietrich Bonhoeffer, Maximilian Kolbe, Janani Luwum, and others whose stories are told here continue to instruct the church on the meaning of steadfast faith in God's promises to heal all wounds and wipe away all tears.

> "WITH HIM, MY BELOVED MASTER, IT IS GOOD EVERYWHERE. WITH HIM I HAVE LIGHT IN THE DARK DUNGEON. I HAD ASKED HIM TO BE WHERE I AM NEEDED, NOT WHERE IT IS BETTER FOR THE OUTWARD MAN, BUT WHERE I CAN BEAR FRUIT."
>
> —FROM A LETTER WRITTEN BY A RUSSIAN PASTOR AFTER HE WAS IMPRISONED FOR THE FIFTH TIME

CHRYSOSTOMOS
(1922)

ationalism and ethnic loyalty, normal bonds of a community, also hold potential for evil. This was the case at the turn of the twentieth century in Asia Minor. Bishop Chrysostomos was living in a time of genocide, but refused the safety offered to diplomats and dignitaries.

From 1894 to 1923 in Asia Minor, Turkish nationals purged minorities and Christians in a "pure blood" campaign that rivaled the Nazis' New Order a decade later. In 1922, the pogrom came to Smyrna, the largest city in the Pontus region, a cosmopolitan hub populated by Greeks whose education and energy had created a thriving middle class. Chrysostomos was the Metropolitan (bishop) of Smyrna, serving thousands of Greek Orthodox Christians who lived there. He was urged to leave the city as Turkish forces approached. Instead, he gathered the faithful for worship. He said in his final sermon:

God is testing our faith, our courage, and our patience at this time. But God will never abandon Christians. It is during the high seas that the good sailor stands out, and it is during the time of tribulations that the good Christian does the same. Pray and all these will be gone. We shall again see happy days and we will praise the Lord. Have courage as all good Christians should.

At the conclusion of the Mass, a police officer informed Chrysostomos that he had been summoned to the Turkish garrison. That night, death came slowly. The Turks first gouged out his eyes, and then dragged the blind bishop by his beard and hair through a Turkish neighborhood, where he endured the abuse of the crowd and further cruelties of the soldiers. One of those troops confessed a month later:

We hit him, swore at him, and cut off pieces of his skin. He neither begged, screamed, nor cursed while he endured all the tortures. His pale face, covered with blood, was constantly looking towards the sky as he mumbled barely audible words, which I could not understand. Every now and then, he would raise his arms and bless the persecutors. One of the troops became so furious that he drew a sword and chopped off the bishop's hand. Then I felt so sorry for this man that I shot him twice in the head to finish him off.

To allay his guilt, that Turkish soldier secretly led a Greek university instructor and students to safety, hoping the rescue would purge his conscience. Chrysostomos died by his hand; others would live.

In 1997, on the seventy-fifth anniversary of the burning of Smyrna, a Resolution was passed by the 105th Congress of Greece to commemorate the genocide, citing the martyrdom of Chrysostomos and other persecutions against the church.

It is the privilege of politicians to note the world's disapproval of long-ago crimes. Chrysostomos was pleased to face them with his people. "The duty of the priest is to stay with his congregation," he had said to those who begged him to flee. Those standing near that day saw him wave farewell to the rescue ship, his last hope. As the ship weighed anchor and set to sea, Chrysostomos turned to the duty of preaching the Word and praying for forgiveness for his enemies.

Manche Massemola
(1913-1928)

The life and death of this young African girl would be completely forgotten had not the church of the Province of Southern Africa (Anglican) declared her a martyr soon after her death.

Too young to have attained the honors of university degrees or ordination, Manche Massemola endured beatings and ridicule from her own family for simply attending pre-baptism classes with her cousin. Massemola represented financial stability because her marriage to a man of means would have brought a considerable dowry. But the girl's pursuit of the Christian life threatened those familial intentions. When the beatings proved ineffectual, or perhaps because they grew in severity and frequency, the young girl's body succumbed. In childhood faithfulness she died by the hand of her closest would-be caregiver, her own mother.

Martyrdom is losing one's life because of loyalty to Christ. In most cases, the martyr stands against ruthless power and chooses death over compromise. That was true for Massemola as well, though her young world was smaller, and her murderer so close to home.

JOHN AND BETTY STAM (1934)

etty Stam held the baby in her arms, singing softly to this infant child, all too aware that this was their last night together. Her husband, John, tied to a bedpost, could not sleep either. Only two weeks ago they had arrived at their mission station with three-month-old Helen Priscilla, full of hope, eager for ministry. But on this winter night, their quiet lullabies were parting sorrows, for tomorrow they would die.

Betty Scott, daughter of Presbyterian missionaries to China, graduated from Moody Bible Institute in 1931. She had already accepted the call of God to service with the China Inland Mission. The bond she felt with John Stam, whom she had met at a prayer meeting for China, and their mutual decision to serve Christ in the middle of a dangerous civil war, could not—did not—hold her back. When she was assigned to a mission station in the interior, she left for China. She wrote, "When we consecrate ourselves to God, we think we are making a great sacrifice, and doing lots for Him, when really we are only letting go some little bitsy trinkets we have been grabbing; and when our hands are empty, He fills them with His treasures."

Stam, meanwhile, finished his training at Moody in 1932. He gave the graduating class address that year, urging, "Dare we advance at God's command in face of the impossible?" In the fall he sailed for Shanghai, expecting an assignment too dangerous for a family. He arrived to discover that the Communists were gaining ground, missionaries were on the move, and his beloved Betty, to his great surprise, was in Shanghai, recuperating from illness. They were soon married, and in September 1934 their daughter Helen Priscilla was born. The young family moved to Anhui Province near the town of Ching-te. The local leader assured their safety.

It was a surprise to everyone when the town magistrate appeared at the missionaries' door only three months later to warn them of the approach of Communist troops, but it was too late. Before the Stam family could get out, the troops got in. John was taken first, bound and pleading for the safety of his wife and child. Soon the troops returned for them. That night in jail, the baby cried. When guards threatened to kill her, an older Chinese man, also a prisoner, intervened. Guards asked if he were so bold as to die for the foreign baby; he assented. The man was hacked to death on the spot.

That night Stam was ordered to write to mission leaders, demanding a $20,000 US ransom. He concluded the note, fully aware that ransoms were never paid: "The Lord bless and guide you. As for us may God be glorified, whether by life or by death."

The next day soldiers marched the Stams to the nearby town of Miaosheo, where they were placed in the office of the local postmaster, who asked where they were going. By this time Stam must have known the soldiers' intentions, for he replied, "I don't know where they are going, but we are going to Heaven."

The next morning, the Stams were led to their execution. A local Christian doctor approached the soldiers to plead mercy for the missionaries. He was threatened, and John then pleaded for the doctor. The Communist leader had heard enough. He ordered John to kneel, and with the flash of a sword decapitated the young missionary. Betty fell on her husband's body, and the sword fell again.

What then happened to baby Helen? A Chinese evangelist, Dr. Lo, found her wrapped in a sleeping bag, with a change of clothes and money pinned to her diaper. Betty, during her sleepless last night, had done her best to comfort and care for the child she knew she was leaving behind. Lo concealed the child in a rice basket and eventually brought Helen to her grandparents, still serving in China. Helen became a teacher and raised a family in the eastern United States. She chose a private life: no interviews or public statements.

What happened to the church in China? In response to news of the Stams' deaths, several hundred new missionary recruits volunteered for service. The Chinese church went underground for many years. Today it is emerging, stronger than anyone expected; stronger than Mao's forces, whose day has already passed.

Maximilian Kolbe died by a lethal injection of carbolic acid on August 14, 1941.

Maximilian Kolbe (1894-1941)

T en Polish pigs will die for the one who escaped." A normal day at the Auschwitz extermination camp in 1941, and a normal punishment announced by the SS commandant, "Butcher" Frisch. He then called the ten names of the condemned. All the prisoners were weak and dehydrated, having stood in the sun without food or water all day, waiting for the escapee to be caught. None wanted to die. One of them, Polish sergeant Francis Gajowniczek, cried out for mercy for his young wife and child, and for himself—just the sort of weakness the SS relished. Then in the line of prisoners someone stirred, moved, spoke up. It was forbidden.

"Who are you?" demanded Frisch.

"I am a Catholic priest. I wish to die for that man."

Frisch hesitated. A hero in the camp? No matter. Better to rid the place of such heroes. Better for the hopelessness that breaks the spirit. In any case, none of these prisoners would likely live long anyhow. Frisch accepted the fool's offer. The ten, including Father Maximilian Kolbe, were marched to the camp's starvation cells.

Raymond Kolbe was born to hard-working Polish nationalists near Pabianice on January 8, 1894. His father died later, executed by the Russians for fighting for the independence of a partitioned Poland. His mother, a pious Catholic, saw her prayers for her son answered when Kolbe was only twelve. In that year, his "wild youth" gave way to lifelong Christian devotion. In a vision, he had seen two crowns from which to choose. The first was white for purity, the second red for martyrdom. Young Kolbe asked for both. From that day, his life was given to study, missionary work, evangelism, and care for the oppressed. Everything he attempted prospered.

At age thirteen Kolbe and his brother, Franciszek, illegally crossed the Russian-Austro-Hungary border to join the Franciscans at Lwow. At seventeen he professed first vows, and took his final vows at twenty, when he also took the name Maximilian Maria—to denote his veneration of the Virgin. Maximilian aimed high and he received a doctorate of philosophy at the Gregorian University at age twenty-one, and a doctorate of theology at twenty-four. His other accomplishments include missionary service in Japan; the opening of a seminary near Warsaw; a start-up of a radio station, newspapers, and magazines; and the founding of an Order, the Militia of the Immaculata, which grew from 650 friars under Kolbe's leadership, making it the largest Catholic religious house in the world.

Kolbe was a vibrant leader, but to be a Polish leader in 1939 was neither safe nor prudent. He could see the storm gathering. Indeed, Kolbe's media outreach began to assail the dangers of Germany's militarism, and his monastery took in Jewish refugees. Before his arrest by the Gestapo, Kolbe kept nearly 1,500 Jews under cover.

On February 17, 1941, the German war machine caught him. Kolbe knew what he believed. In a well-known statement he said, "No one can change the Truth. What we can do is to seek truth and serve it when we have found it...There are two irreconcilable enemies in the depth of every soul: good and evil, sin and love. And what use are victories on the battlefield if we are defeated in our innermost personal selves?" When Kolbe was sent to Auschwitz in May, he was prepared for his innermost battle.

During Kolbe's two weeks in the starvation cellblock, a Nazi guard in charge of the prisoner log made note that he led in prayers and hymns. When he grew too weak to speak, he whispered. Kolbe and three others survived those two weeks, but the Nazis needed their cells for other miscreants. So the end came by a lethal injection of carbolic acid on August 14, 1941. Francis Gajowniczek lived to an old age, dying in Poland in 1997.

Maximilian Kolbe had the kind of devotion to Christ that stands up to evil and takes a condemned man's place. He wrote about his relationship with Christ: "You come to me and unite Yourself intimately to me under the form of nourishment [the Sacrament]. Your Blood now runs in mine; Your Soul, Incarnate God, penetrates mine, giving courage and support. What miracles! Who would have ever imagined such!"

JOHN WILLFINGER
(1942)

◆

I n the summer of 1942, the Empire of Japan planned to capture a
perimeter of defense and oil reserves that extended from its islands
south to Australia. Borneo was to be a land of strategic occupation,
and foreigners operating there, especially North Americans, must be
captured and controlled.

Missionary John Willfinger and his Bible translator partners, the
Lenhams, knew the danger. But their work was critical—producing the
Murut New Testament. In July 1942, they learned that Japanese forces
had captured missionaries to the south, so instinctively they moved
north, to the dense jungle and isolated villages of the Murut. But they
underestimated Japanese persistence.

On September 19, a Murut messenger arrived in the village where
these three missionaries were waiting out the Japanese occupation. The
word he brought was worrisome. All three missionaries were named on
the "most wanted" list. Anyone harboring or aiding the three would be
severely punished.

Still the Murut people were confident they could successfully hide
the missionaries. It would require deception of the kind already used by
European Christians and others hiding Jews from the Germans. But this
deception the Lenhams and Willfinger were not willing to impose on
their Murut friends. Instead, they decided to surrender themselves to the
Japanese, trusting God for whatever lay ahead.

The Lenhams went north to the nearest Japanese encampment.
They managed to keep copies of Murut Gospels intact throughout the
war. Willfinger, who had anticipated a reunion with his fiancée prior
to the danger, chose to visit several tribal churches in eastern Borneo
before surrendering himself. How far he traveled is not known, but
eventually he encountered his captors and was executed three days
after Christmas. At the end of the Pacific conflict, Willfinger's body

was recovered and his Bible was also found. On the inside cover John had written this poem:

> No mere man is the Christ I know
> But greater far than all below.
> Day by day his love enfolds me
> Day by day his power upholds me.
> All that God could ever be
> The man of Nazareth is to me.
> No mere man can my strength sustain
> And drive away all fear and pain.
> Holding me close in his embrace
> When death and I stand face to face.
> Then all that God could ever be
> The unseen Christ will be to me.

And underneath the poem his own comment: "Hallelujah, this is real."

SO EVERYONE WHO ACKNOWLEDGES ME BEFORE MEN, I ALSO WILL ACKNOWLEDGE BEFORE MY FATHER WHO IS IN HEAVEN....

MATTHEW 10:32

DIETRICH BONHOEFFER
(1906-1945)

H e could have escaped the Nazi dragnet, but he chose to return to his troubled country. To stay in New York would be to abandon the mission—a mission he would not survive.

Dietrich Bonhoeffer was born into a prominent Berlin family. His father, Karl, was a renowned psychiatrist and neurologist. Bonhoeffer himself was a gifted child. Skilled at piano, his parents once thought he would become a professional musician. At age fourteen, quite to his scientific family's surprise, Bonhoeffer announced that he would study to become a theologian. By the age of twenty-one, he had earned his doctorate in theology from the University of Berlin.

But Bonhoeffer was as much a pastor as a scholar. In 1932, he taught catechism to the youth in one of Berlin's poorest neighborhoods. He actually moved there to spend more time with some of the boys. In Spain he pastored a German-speaking church. Later in London, he helped build an international base that would play significantly in his efforts to end World War II.

But in New York City in 1939, he faced his crisis of conscience. It was a lecture tour arranged by American friends who wanted to give Bonhoeffer sanctuary from the Nazis. Only one month into the visit, he knew he could not fail to struggle with the German church against the National Socialists, who were already showing their hostility toward humanity and especially the Jews. Indeed, Bonhoeffer had already led an "underground" seminary (closed by the Gestapo), and he knew of plans forming in the Abwehr (German intelligence) to depose Hitler by whatever means. In effect, the theologian knew too much for his own safety and the well-being of his family and friends. Still, he hastened back to work with the "confessing church" (those who proclaimed that Jesus alone is Lord and that allegiance to Hitler was idolatry).

Back in Germany, Bonhoeffer was forbidden to teach, preach, or to publish without prior approval. He was ordered to report regularly to police officials. But an odd assignment gave him reprieve from Nazi surveillance. He was recruited to the Abwehr. Pastor Bonhoeffer, with his British and American connections, was to be a spy for Hitler. At least so his orders read. Actually, the anti-Hitler plotters, led by Admiral Canaris, recruited him. His assignment was to use every means possible to negotiate terms of surrender with the West. Of course, this dangerous double-agentry must also do away with German leadership.

On April 5, 1943, the Gestapo caught up with Canaris and his double agents. Bonhoeffer was sent to Tegel prison in Berlin, where he continued to preach and write among guards and inmates. Two years later, April 9, 1945, after conducting a worship service in prison, with Allied troops approaching, Bonhoeffer was hanged by direct order of the faltering Fuhrer. His last words: "This is the end—for me, the beginning of life."

Bonhoeffer's writings continue to challenge the church today. His notions of "cheap grace" and the "cost of discipleship," life in community, and radical Christian social responsibility are still relevant, vibrant, and widely studied. The personal struggles and faith issues he faced were many: the taking of life (he helped with two failed attempts on Hitler's life), prayer and peace under duress, and love unfilled (he postponed his engagement to Maria van Wedemeyer because his secret negotiations could have been dangerous to her.)

Bonhoeffer died as a traitor to Nazi Germany. The camp doctor who witnessed the execution noted, "I have hardly ever seen a man die so entirely submissive to the will of God." Three weeks later, Hitler committed suicide in his Berlin bunker. In less than a month, the European war was over.

Maurice Tornay
(1910-1946)

aurice Tornay was the seventh of eight children born to a Catholic family who lived high in the Swiss mountains near Valais. The family was united in the work required to live and the faith they lived by. Tornay recalled his mother at the fireside telling the story of Saint Agnes, virgin and martyr. "You are virgins," she told her children, "but to be martyrs, that's more difficult. You must love God more than anything else, and be ready to give your life, to shed the last drop of blood for Him." Young Tornay never forgot his mother's lesson.

After secondary school, Tornay joined the Canons Regular of Grand St. Bernard, best known for their rescue work in the Alps and the famous Saint Bernard dogs they breed and train as "assistants." As Tornay progressed, the Canons were asked by the church to send missionaries accustomed to living at higher elevations to begin evangelizing people in the Himalayas, or "the Asian Alps," as they were called in Europe. Tornay volunteered, but he was kept back until surgery cured an ulcer. In 1936 he arrived in Weixi Province near the Tibetan border, where he finished theological studies, learned Chinese, and was ordained a priest. Tornay wrote: "And now I've almost made a world tour. I've seen and felt that people are unhappy everywhere, and that real happiness comes in serving God. Really, nothing else matters. Nothing, nothing."

Work on the China-Tibet border, difficult on any day, was made more dangerous by the invasion of Japanese forces in 1939. Tornay was in charge of a boy's school, and every life need—food, clothes, heat—was in very short supply. Add to that the antagonism of local Buddhist lamas, especially one Gun-Akhio, who sensed that missionaries would erode his power base. Gun-Akhio was not averse to threats and force against the foreigners.

In 1946, Tornay was made priest of the Yerkalo parish in southeast Tibet. Only days later forty local lamas broke into the priest's residence, looted it, and at rifle-point, forced Tornay out of town. He went to Pame in Yunnan Province, China, there to provide whatever help he could for his people—prayer, correspondence, comfort, and care for the sick that made their way to him. By May he was sure that the risk of returning was less than the risk of waiting further. "Leave a parish without a priest…and the people will be worshipping animals," he said.

At the edge of Yerkalo, Gun-Akhio waited. Again Tornay was kept out of his parish. By now, however, he had a plan: a direct appeal to the Dalai Lama for permission to conduct his mission, for religious tolerance rather than belligerence and intimidation. Tornay began the two-month journey to Lhasa, Tibet's capital.

But Gun-Akhio had his agents, and Tornay could not make a move without his knowledge. The lamas intercepted Tornay's caravan and forced him to retreat. On August 11, at the Choula gorge near the Chinese border, Tornay was ambushed and shot along with his companions. Chinese authorities eventually convicted members of the Karmda lamasery for the killings.

Maurice Tornay had written as a teenager, "Death is the happiest day of our lives. We must rejoice in it more than anything, because it is our arrival in our true homeland." Tornay, the priest who rarely walked on level ground and never served a day in comfort or ease, was finally home.

Jim Elliot, Pete Fleming, Ed McCully, Nate Saint, Roger Youderian
(1956)

A news flash alerted the world: "Five Men Missing in Auca Territory." The date was Monday, January 9, 1956. A team of missionary pioneers trying to make peaceful contact with an infamous tribe of Indians in Ecuador, the Waodani, had failed to make a scheduled radio call. For almost a full day no word had come from their camp on the Curaray River, which they named "Palm Beach." Then a hovering pilot reported the badly damaged plane at the camp. This was followed by a gruesome confirmation on Wednesday, January 11, when the first body was spotted in the river. Though a search and rescue team was quickly formed, the discovery of more bodies quickly changed the mission from rescue to retrieval and burial.

By Friday of that week the team reached the missionaries' campsite and hurriedly buried four of the bodies. The men had died violently from repeated spear wounds and machete cuts. The fifth body (Ed McCully) was never located after being identified on the beach but then washed away by the river. Five widows and eight orphans mourned the deaths and looked to God for comfort and direction. The world witnessed in stunned amazement.

Shockwaves from the tragedy traveled around the globe. Eventually, thousands of Christians identified the news of the deaths of five young men as the turning point in their lives. In her book, *Through Gates of Splendor*, written a year after the deaths, Jim Elliot's widow, Elisabeth, described some of the remarkable early results from what seemed like a tragic waste of life. The places of service vacated by those men were filled many times over by young men and women moved and motivated by their selfless sacrifice. Fifty years later, the effects continue to be felt.

Within two years of their deaths, Elisabeth Elliot and Nate Saint's sister made a friendly and lasting contact with the Waodanis. Bible translation into the Waodani language began. One by one, the men who committed the murder became believers in the One who sent the missionaries to reach them. Steve Saint spent much of his childhood among the Waodanis. Despite the fact that they had killed his father, Steve became an adopted son of the tribe and eventually took his own family to live for a time among them. The painful arrival of the Gospel among that violent people worked a miracle of transformation.

While martyrdom has always been part of the great battle between good and evil in the spiritual realms, the death of believers has not always resulted directly from those seeking to silence their witness. Violence has often been an expression of fear, suspicion, ignorance or timing rather than a conscious rejection of the message. The five men who died in Ecuador had spent months contacting the Waodanis through over-flights and gifts exchanged via an ingenious bucket drop devised by the team's pilot, Nate Saint. Though the tribe had a history of violent encounters with outsiders, the men had decided they had established some degree of mutual trust that would support a direct contact. At first, their cautious optimism had been rewarded by a visit from three Waodanis. That had occurred without incident. They had expected further contact. Little did the missionaries know that they had stepped into an intra-tribe squabble.

When the attack party killed the five men, their actions weren't personal or even driven by what or who the white men represented. The violence was almost a diversion from internal issues the Waodanis couldn't handle. Two of the three who had visited the camp at Palm Beach reported that the missionaries had mistreated them; the third person argued otherwise. Though others in the group recognized the false accusations, it seemed easier to eliminate the cause (the missionaries) than to address the internal issues. Once the possibility of killing was raised, the general tone in the tribal group shifted to well-established patterns of preparation for battle. They knew the white men had guns;

they didn't know they wouldn't use them. Several of the Waodanis reported hearing strange supernatural voices and seeing moving lights in the sky during the attack, as if God sent an angelic choir to celebrate the faithfulness and the homecoming of His loyal servants.

Steeped in generations of horrific hand-to-hand combat, combined with the heightened memory that tends to characterize verbal cultures, the Waodani display an amazing capacity for remembering the details of battles. Lengthy conversations among the Waodani often consist of show-and-tell descriptions of spear and machete scars and gruesome minutiae of the deaths of enemies. But it wasn't until years later that Steve Saint heard the full story of the raid. Reminiscing by a fire late at night, the aging warriors gave an account of the event, still amazed that the white men had done nothing to defend themselves. Steve learned that Mincaye, who had since become a father to him, had actually been the one who had dealt the deathblow to his father. As soon as he knew, Saint realized it didn't really matter. What mattered was that God had used an amazing mixture of spiritual weapons, including the deaths of five servants, to defeat the power of fear and violence that had kept the Waodani captive as far back as they could remember.

In his book *The End of the Spear*, Saint reports that he has been frequently asked over the years about the struggle he must have experienced to forgive those who had taken his father from him. He has always responded that it was never a struggle for him. Even to his grieving five-year-old mind, the death of his father and friends had been a part of God's plan. You don't have to forgive someone whom you have never held responsible for an act.

True to the Maker and Mover behind the scenes, the story of the Waodani displays God's ways. Those who were once the impossible-to-reach are now taking their place among those who reach out. Believers among the Waodani have suffered for Christ and at least one has experienced martyrdom. Their long history with violence makes them keen observers of the state of the "modern" world, where the increasing fascination and practice of hatred, violence, and killing appear all too familiar for those recently freed from that life of despair. God's deeper purposes take time to come to light. Occasionally, those who are paying attention get to see those purposes shine and are amazed.

"BEFORE BEING SHOT BY YOU, WE WISH TO THANK YOU HEARTILY FOR WHAT YOU HAVE MEANT TO US. YOU BAPTIZED US; YOU TAUGHT US THE WAY OF ETERNAL LIFE, YOU GAVE US HOLY Communion WITH THE SAME HAND IN WHICH YOU NOW HAVE A GUN ... GOD BLESS YOU, AND REMEMBER THAT OUR LAST THOUGHT OF YOU WAS NOT ONE OF INDIGNATION AGAINST YOUR FAILURE. EVERYONE PASSES THROUGH HOURS OF DARKNESS. WE DIE WITH GRATITUDE."

—Two Christian girls, Chiu-Chin-Hsiu and Ho-Hsiu-Tzu, who were killed by their pastor, whom the guards had promised to release if he shot them

ESTHER JOHN
(1929-1960)

E sther John was born in British-ruled India with the Indian name of Qamar Zia. She was educated in a Christian school where Bible reading and her teachers' vibrant faith led to her conversion as a teenager. When Qamar gave her heart to Jesus Christ, she began a life of service and growth in which each new day was a gift.

When India was partitioned, Qamar moved with her family to Pakistan, where she was pledged to a Muslim husband. Unwilling to accept this family decision, Qamar fled to Karachi. There she found a missionary, Marian Laugesen, who provided a Bible, encouragement, and a job working in an orphanage. At this time Qamar took the name Esther John.

Still under family pressure to marry, John relocated to Sahiwal, where she lived and worked in a mission hospital under the protection of Pakistan's first Anglican bishop, Chandu Ray. In 1956, Esther enrolled in the United Bible Training Centre. Completing that course of study, and well aware that her faith was not something her family could ever accept, John moved to Chichawatni, thirty miles west of Sahiwal. She lived with American Presbyterian missionaries and took up evangelism among rural women, teaching them the Scriptures and working alongside them in the fields. Her life had taken on a second dimension of danger through her evangelism.

On February 2, 1960, John was brutally murdered in her bed in Chichawatni. No investigation was conducted; no one was indicted for taking her life. She was buried in a Christian cemetery in Sahiwal. As a tribute to this brave woman, a chapel bearing her name was built on the grounds of the hospital where she had worked. Although her life was suddenly taken away, it still impacts the Christian community where she worked and lived, and she is remembered with devotion today.

Paul Carlson gunned down in the Congo

PAUL CARLSON

(1928-1964)

W hen trouble broke out in the Congo, Paul Carlson took his wife, Lois, and two children across the Ubangi River to the Central African Republic. When he left them there to return to the Congo, the missionary doctor with the Evangelical Cove- nant Church assured his family that he had several escape routes mapped out. He would leave if the Simba rebels got too close to the hospital at Wasolo, deep in the Congo where this family from California had lived for a year. Soon, on a radio contact, Carlson told her, "I must leave this evening." It was not soon enough.

In 1960, Belgium granted independence to its diamond-rich colony, the Congo. No government had mastered its terrain and tribal differ- ences, and now, in the early fall of 1964, a rebel movement called the Simbas had captured Stanleyville (Kinshasa) and were moving to con- solidate their gains. Carlson feared for the safety of his family and his patients at the eighty-bed hospital in this jungle town "at the edge of the world."

Carlson did not fit the profile of a hero. A quiet man deeply commit- ted to healing, he was a graduate of North Park College, Stanford Uni- versity, and the George Washington University medical school. Then he signed up with the Christian Medical and Dental Society for a six-month term in the Congo. That was 1961. The African service appealed to him, but he had a young family and had planned on a normal medical career; so back they went to Redondo Beach, California, to set up a practice.

Soon, however, he knew where his heart lay. "I can't stand hernias and hemorrhoids anymore," he told a friend. Returning to the Congo in 1963, the family was stationed in Wasolo to care for 100,000 regional people and to help build the church.

A year later, on September 9, 1964, Paul was captured by Simba rebels. He was accused of being a spy, and transported three hundred miles to Stanleyville as rebels negotiated for his release. Weeks went by while rebels made sport of killing foreigners. Carlson was routinely marched to face a firing squad, blindfolded, kicked, pushed, and hit, but never shot. Ransoms remained unpaid. Tension mounted. Finally in mid-November, a joint command of American-supported Belgian paratroopers dropped outside the city in a daring effort to rescue diplomats and hundreds of other trapped expatriates.

That morning, Carlson and fellow hostages at the Victoria Hotel were quickly ordered into the streets. Young Simba soldiers, eyes turned upward at the descending rescuers, guns turned level at the massed foreigners, went blank with fear and rage, firing indiscriminately into the hundreds huddled in the street.

Around him, children were falling, women were covering their babies, and men were bleeding and dying. A small group including Carlson at the back of the crowd saw their chance for escape and ran toward a house just past a seven-foot cement wall. Carlson arrived first and helped missionary Charles Davis over the wall. Then Carlson grabbed for Davis's hand to pull himself over, but one of the Simba machine gunners fired a volley. Carlson slumped to the ground dead.

Minutes later, paratroopers secured the house where the missionaries had taken refuge. Photographers documented Paul Carlson's riddled body lying in the street. *Time* and *Life* magazines featured his story—the self-giving doctor who almost got away. Carlson was sure, however, where his true refuge lay. Earlier he had scribbled in his New Testament the date "November 24" and the single word "Peace."

The Paul Carlson Partnership still works to assist the people of Wasolo, and a memorial at North Park University in Chicago remembers the quiet hero who kept his humor and trusted his Lord during a too-short career as "Mongonga Paul," missionary doctor.

Yona Kanamuzeyi
(1964)

The terrible genocide of the 1990s focused the world's attention on Rwanda, but it was not the beginning of violence between Hutus and Tutsis there. The animosity had simmered for decades by then. In 1960, the Rwandan government began to resettle people left homeless by the tribal violence into the Nyamata district in southern Rwanda. The area—made up of swampy land and crocodile-infested rivers—didn't have many people, so had lots of room for resettling the displaced.

It was to this area that Yona Kanamuzeyi felt the call of God to go and minister. He knew it would not be an easy assignment.

Of his birth and early life almost nothing is known, not an uncommon circumstance for rural Africans, who frequently date their birth around seasons and record their lives in oral history only.

Kanamuzeyi was born to a mixed marriage, Hutu and Tutsi, and raised in the Christian faith. Eventually, he served as pastor in the Nyamata district of Rwanda. There he was responsible for twenty-four churches with about six thousand total members.

In addition to pastoring, Kanamuzeyi helped to distribute relief supplies to the displaced. The first time he met with the Christian refugees, they met in the shade of a large tree. Kanamuzeyi read passages from the Bible that reminded the refugees that the Lord was their shelter and shade.

He moved to the area first by himself, and then later when he got a house his wife, Mary, and their children joined him. Those around marveled at the love for each other this couple showed. Women would ask Mary, "Doesn't he ever beat you or curse you?" And Mary would explain that no, he didn't. "Sometimes he asks my forgiveness, and I ask his. And Jesus forgives us. And we pray together." A husband that modeled such love was rare in that area.

In the early 1960s, Tutsis who had fled into surrounding countries began to use terrorist tactics to try to fight back against Hutu control in Rwanda.

The terrorists were called *inyenzi*, or cockroaches. As the terror grew, any Tutsi might be suspected of being a terrorist.

Late in 1963, rumors flew around Nyamata that the *inyenzi* were going to invade Rwanda from the south. Twice they actually tried to invade, but were repelled by the Rwandan army. From then on, anyone with suspected *inyenzi* connections was arrested by the army. Some were executed. Some were thrown into prison, where many died from the overcrowding and lack of medical care.

Amid all that turmoil and trouble, Kanamuzeyi continued his ministry work. One night he went out after curfew to bury the body of a Christian worker who had been gunned down in the street. He welcomed Christians to come to his house—in spite of the curfew—for late-night prayer meetings.

In January 1964, a friend warned Kanamuzeyi that he was going to be killed. When Yona asked why, the friend said it was because of his belief in the Word of God and the way he loved everyone.

"The Word of God and the love of God are two things I can't live without," Kanamuzeyi replied.

He told Mary about the threat, and the couple prayed together. "God," Kanamuzeyi prayed, "You called me and sent me here. You know me, the days I've already lived and the days which remain. If it's Your will to call me home, I'm ready."

On the evening of January 23, five Rwandan soldiers arrived in an open jeep at the Kanamuzeyi residence, demanding he come with them for questioning. They knew that when the soldiers came for someone at night, that person was never seen again.

Two other people were also forced aboard the jeep. The soldiers drove north until they reached the bridge over the Nyaborongo River. They ordered the prisoners out of the jeep and put all of their possessions in a pile. Before he laid down his journal, Kanamuzeyi wrote inside it, "We are going to heaven."

Kanamuzeyi spoke with the other two prisoners about their salvation, then together they began to sing, "There is a happy land...where saints in glory stand."

Kanamuzeyi asked the sergeant to return his diary and money to his wife. The man replied, "You had better pray to your God." He did, with these words: "Lord God, You know that we have not sinned against the government, and now I pray You, in Your mercy, accept our lives. And we pray You to avenge our innocent blood and help these soldiers who do not know what they are doing."

Kanamuzeyi was tied up and marched out onto the bridge. He sang as he marched, "There's a land that is fairer than day. And by faith, we can see it afar. Where the Father waits over the way. To prepare us a dwelling place there."

The soldier ended the song with a gunshot. Kanamuzeyi's body was dumped in the river.

His friend, Andrew Kayumba, also tied and ready to be shot, was instead driven home with a stern warning to never speak about Pastor Kanamuzeyi's execution. Kayumba escaped from Rwanda and told what he had seen, and about the courage of his friend, who prayed for his executioner and walked singing to his death.

"BEFORE PRISON WE HEARD ABOUT GOD. BUT IN PRISON WE EXPERIENCED GOD."

—PASTOR SZE, A CHINESE HOUSE-CHURCH LEADER WHO WAS IMPRISONED FOR HIS FAITH

WATCHMAN NEE
(1903-1972)

W atchman Nee was unique, committed, controversial, and effective. Despite the ongoing controversy concerning his teaching and orthodoxy, the spiritual movement he founded in the 1920s—the Little Flock—certainly helped to stabilize Chinese Christianity during the Mao years and beyond.

Nee was born in 1903 into a family of teachers and evangelists. His mother named him Shi-Tsu, and later changed his name to "bell ringer" or Watchman. This was a sign of the work Nee would do: calling forth a vigorous Christian movement that contained elements of Pentecostalism and the Plymouth Brethren movement and was based on the teachings of English pastor Robert Govett and Theodore Austin of London's Honor Oak Christian Fellowship.

Following Nee's conversion at age seventeen, he taught that churches were properly organized geographically, one to each city. Nearly seven hundred churches eventually considered Nee their pastor-teacher. He emphasized the inner life: God speaks to each person's intuitive sense. He insisted that the eschaton, specifically the Rapture of the church (emphasized in John Darby's Plymouth Brethren teaching), would involve the pre-tribulation "taking up" of mature believers, while those who still need development must endure the Great Tribulation. These ideas and the call to disciplined faith were promoted in his teachings. A collection of these are found in books that are still known throughout the world: *The Normal Christian Life* and *Sit Walk Stand*.

In 1942, Nee took over management of his brother's chemical factory, hiring Little Flock members and channeling profits to the movement. In 1947, he became active in church planting and training Christian workers. He also became involved in migration evangelism, based on the church in Jerusalem in Acts 8. His work founded hundreds of house-churches throughout China. He sought to make the church in each city and village self-propagating, self-supporting, and self-governing.

Nee was zealous, idealistic and studious, refusing to become a part of Chinese nationalism. When Chairman Mao came to power in China in 1949, Nee was considered an imperialist and was imprisoned on made-up charges of espionage, licentiousness, and stealing church funds. He was imprisoned up until just before his death when the officials released him so that they wouldn't be held responsible for it.

Commentators examining his writings and those of his followers (especially Witness Lee) are divided on Nee's strategy, biblical interpretation, and the eclectic mosaic of his sources on spiritual development. But no one questions Nee's commitment to Christ and the courage he showed throughout more than twenty years of persecution under Mao.

God used Watchman Nee's work in China to create a system of underground churches that have survived and grown over the past thirty-five-plus years. Through the ministry of Watchman Nee, more than 150,000 people have come to follow Christ, and the number continues to grow through his ministry, the Little Flock.

"YOU CAN HELP OTHERS IN PROPORTION TO WHAT YOU YOURSELF HAVE SUFFERED...AS YOU GO THROUGH THE FIERY TRIALS, THE TESTING, THE AFFLICTION, THE PERSECUTION, THE CONFLICT...LIFE WILL FLOW OUT TO OTHERS, EVEN THE LIFE OF CHRIST."

—WATCHMAN NEE, WHO WAS IMPRISONED IN CHINA FOR HIS FAITH

WANG ZHIMING
(1907-1973)

K illed by the Communist government, Wang Zhiming holds two distinctions. He is the only Christian executed during the Cultural Revolution to have a memorial built in his honor in China. Second, he is one of ten representative martyrs noted on the Great West Door of Westminster Abbey in London.

Wang was born in Wuding County, in the Yunnan region just a year after the first missionaries arrived there. He became a teacher in the Christian school and the pastor to the 2,800 Christians living through one of China's most difficult decades. The Cultural Revolution intended to remake China into a modern state by casting off all things ancient and traditional. Wang signed on to the Three-Self movement but refused to participate in the public denunciation meetings, claiming the hands that had baptized should not now berate and humiliate those same people.

In May 1969, midway through the Revolution, Wang and members of his family were arrested. Local Red Guards knew he was their critic. Wang's leadership in a "foreign religion" was public and therefore dangerous, they asserted. Wang waited four years in prison before his sentence and the spectacle of his own denunciation on December 29, 1973. He was executed at a mass rally in a stadium before ten thousand spectators. Some of his last reported words were: "You should follow the words from above and repent." (Encouragement to follow God above all.)

Wang's wife was held in prison for three years and two of his sons for nine years. A third son died while in detention. The Chinese government eventually recognized the wrong done to Wang Zhiming and paid a reparation of $250 US to his family—a paltry sum in relation to the value of a man's life. Meanwhile, the church in the Wuding area grew tenfold, as Wang would have wanted.

Minka Hanskamp and Margaret Morgan
(1974)

Two nurses, one from Wales and the other from Holland, were conducting a leprosy clinic in Thailand. In 1974 the political situation worsened, and they were kidnapped by guerrillas and held for ransom. Overseas Missionary Fellowship (OMF) was ordered to pay $500,000 US for their release and to write a letter to the government of Israel supporting Palestinian rights.

Minka Hanskamp was a Dutch citizen who grew up in Indonesia. During World War II she and her family were sent to separate internment camps following the Japanese invasion of Indonesia in 1939. Hanskamp saved many lives as a nurse in the camp and was reunited with her family after being released. She then went to New Zealand, where she attended Bible college. After graduating, she was accepted to serve with OMF in Thailand, where she worked both as a midwife and in a rural leprosy clinic.

When Margaret Morgan felt the call to missions, she was already a nurse. She took further missionary training at the Mount Hermon Missionary College. Then she sailed for Thailand, supported by the Tabernacle Baptist Church in Porth, Wales.

For eleven months Minka Hanskamp and Margaret Morgan were missing, presumed to be held somewhere near Pujud, Thailand. In March 1975, BBC radio reported two bodies had been found in the jungle, with evidence that one was Morgan. She had been shot five months earlier. A Malay informant confessed to killing the two women. The former insurgent reported to officials that when the women were told they were to be killed, they said calmly, "Give us a little time to read and pray."

Janani Luwum
(1922-1977)

Janani Luwum was killed by the president of the Republic of Uganda, Idi Amin, on February 16, 1977. That same year the Christian church in Uganda marked 100 years of existence.

Luwum was born in Northern Uganda and began his career as an ordained minister in the Anglican Church in 1956, in the Northern Uganda diocese. Later he trained in theology at St. Augustine College in Canterbury and at the London College of Divinity in the UK. He rose through the ranks from a priest to become archbishop. An active member of the East African Revival Fellowship since 1948, Luwum is remembered as one who always told his congregations, "God does not have grandchildren. He only has sons and daughters." He always urged people to have a living personal relationship with God through Jesus and not depend on one's parents' faith. The East African Revival also taught, and Luwum certainly believed, that God is never absent, no matter how difficult life becomes. When Luwum was accused of treason—death sure to follow—he replied to Amin, "We must see the hand of God in this."

Luwum became archbishop of the Anglican Church of Uganda, Rwanda, Burundi, and Boga-Zaire in 1974. Trouble started when he began criticizing the gross human rights abuses perpetrated by the Amin regime, including public executions, disappearances, and expulsions. Property was regularly confiscated without due process. As head of the Church of Uganda, Luwum publicly confronted this lawlessness in the pulpit. Very few critics of Idi Amin who did not flee for their lives survived his eight-year reign of terror.

After Luwum was killed, his family and some of the bishops of the Anglican Church fled the country, but his death certainly strengthened opposition to Amin's brutality. The church continued under intense persecution until two years later in April 1979, when the regime fell to a combined force of Ugandan rebels and the Tanzanian troops.

Life was cheap in Idi Amin's Uganda. People lost their lives for small things such as having a nice car or a beautiful wife. These were the ills Janani Luwum had the courage to say were against the will of God. Today he is honored as one voice crying in the wilderness when few dared to speak out. His sacrifice is remembered every February 17. The Church of England recognizes him as a martyr of the twentieth century, and a statue in his honor was erected on the front of Westminster Abbey in London. In Kampala a street is named after him.

"MORE LOVE, O CHRIST, TO THEE. MORE LOVE TO THEE."

—SUNG BY NORTH KOREAN CHRISTIANS AS THEIR CHILDREN WERE BEING HANGED BY THE COMMUNISTS BECAUSE THE PARENTS REFUSED TO DENY CHRIST

CHESTER A. "CHET"
BITTERMAN III
(1952-1981)

C het Bitterman went in with his eyes open. He knew that sharing the Gospel could be costly. It could cost everything. But he willingly went to Colombia to bear the Good News. " ... I find the recurring thought that perhaps God will call me to be martyred for Him in His service in Colombia. I am willing." Bitterman penned those words in his diary before he and his wife, Brenda, arrived in Colombia. Bitterman's devotion to his Savior was evident: "I am willing."

When the gunmen came into the Wycliffe Bible Translators guest house in Bogotá, Colombia, early the morning of January 19, 1981, they were looking for the mission's leader, a more high-profile hostage whose captivity could somehow help their cause. Who they got instead was Chester A. Bitterman III, "Chet" to his friends. The next day President Ronald Reagan took the oath of office, and American hostages left Iran after 444 days in captivity. Their ordeal was over, with the Bittermans' just beginning.

They hadn't been in Colombia long. Their mission career and their translation work lay before them. They had gone to language school and helped in various tasks for Wycliffe, including managing the guest house, serving as buyer for goods needed by mission workers and even as radio operator. Finally, it seemed God was opening the door for them to move into the jungle with the Carijona Indian tribe to begin language study and eventually translation work. In the days before M-19 terrorists kidnapped Bitterman, he had been scouring hardware and building-supply stores, stockpiling materials for their move to the Carijonas.

The terrorists' demands were twofold. First, they wanted their views printed in several of the world's leading papers. The second demand was that all Wycliffe mission workers be out of Colombia in thirty days, or Bitterman would die.

Wycliffe's stand was clear: The work God had called them to in Colombia was not complete, and they could not desert the effort. Bitterman wouldn't want them to leave with so many people still unable to read God's Word in the language of their heart.

Negotiations went on in fits and starts. Brenda and her two young daughters—one barely old enough to walk—waited and prayed and hoped. They prayed Bitterman would remember the Scriptures that he had faithfully memorized. The guerrillas maintained their stance that Wycliffe must leave; Wycliffe agreed to leave when their translation work was done, more than a decade into the future.

His captors released a letter from Bitterman. His words carried not discouragement and worry, but an exciting sense of mission and possibility:

> The Lord brought II Corinthians 2:14 to mind: "But thanks be to God, who always leads us in triumph through the Lord Jesus Christ." The word for "triumph" was used for the Roman victory parades, when the soldiers were received back at home by the cheering crowds after a successful battle…I have had a lot of free time to think about such things as Daniel's three friends…and Paul and Silas' experience in the jail at Philippi.
>
> In the case of Daniel's friends, God did something very unusual through His power for a specific purpose, so that through everything, all concerned would learn (i.e., have their misconceptions corrected) about Him. The result of the experience was that everyone learned who He was. Remember Paul and the Praetorian Guard. Keep this in your thoughts for me. Wouldn't it be neat if something special like this would happen?

Brenda was thrilled to see that her prayers were being answered. Bitterman was remembering the Scriptures.

Even as he was held hostage, the Lord's work was being accomplished. Colombian media reports about Wycliffe's work included reference to the Gospel message and shed a positive light on Christian workers. Bible verses Bitterman had mentioned in his letter were printed in Colombian newspapers. The Word was going out.

On the morning of March 7, forty-eight days after Bitterman's abduction, his life was ended by a bullet to the chest. His body was left on a bus. A sedative in his blood suggests he may have felt no pain.

And still the message went out, even after his death. A radio interview with Bitterman's parents was broadcast numerous times across the country. "I'm sorry I won't see Chet again in this life," his father said, "but I know I'll see him again in Heaven." He went on to say how much Bitterman loved the Colombian people. His mother said that even though her son had been killed, she still had love for Colombia and its people. "We're hoping the guerrillas come to know God," she said.

Bitterman was buried at Loma Linda, the Wycliffe base where he'd lived and worked. His burial in Colombian soil carried its own message of his love for that land and its people.

At memorial services around the world, men and women stepped forward to answer God's call to full-time service, to take Bitterman's place on the dangerous front lines of ministry work. Applications to Wycliffe skyrocketed in the months after his death.

Wouldn't it be neat if something special like that would happen? Bitterman's words carry the echoes of prophecy. Something special did happen. God's Word went forth; people's hearts were touched and changed. Through one man laying down his life for his Savior, many lives were changed. The avalanche of blessing and ministry began with three words: "I am willing."

✠

Haik Hovsepian and Mehdi Dibaj

(1994)

B rother Haik Hovsepian was on his way to Mehrabad airport in Tehran to meet a friend on January 19, 1994, when he was abducted. His wife, Takoosh, and their four children waited in suspense for the next week and a half for any news regarding his whereabouts, fearing the worst. They didn't doubt that he had been abducted and possibly killed for his Christian faith.

As the General Superintendent of the Assemblies of God Church and Chairman of the Council of Protestant Ministers of Iran, Hovsepian was a respected, influential evangelical leader with a heart for bringing Christ to Iranian Muslims. He had refused to comply with government restrictions on Christian worship, which included the prohibition of preaching in the official Persian language and restricting Muslims and Muslim converts from attending services. An activist for religious freedom, he spoke out openly against discrimination and persecution of Christians, and refused to sign a declaration falsely stating that Christians received full rights of religious freedom in Iran. Hovsepian was a musician as well and composed several songs and hymns for the church in the Persian language.

A suspicious aspect of his disappearance was that it occurred just three days after a well-known Iranian pastor was released from jail. Hovsepian had been instrumental in bringing international attention to the unjust, almost decade-long imprisonment of Pastor Mehdi Dibaj, who had been tried for apostasy and sentenced to death.

An Iranian Muslim who converted to Christianity as a teenager, Dibaj had a passion for God's Word and wished to share it with others. He joined the Assemblies of God Church in Iran, becoming a pastor and evangelist. In 1983, he was arrested for his beliefs and held in Sari Prison in northern Iran for nine years. During that time he was tortured, beaten, and held in solitary confinement. His wife was forced to divorce him and marry a Muslim man. Through it all he displayed remarkable courage and faith, choosing to believe in God's divine plan and protection during his time in prison. He later said about his experience, "The God of Job has tested my faith and commitment in order to strengthen my patience and faithfulness. During those nine years He has freed me from all my responsibilities so that...I would spend my time in prayer and study of His Word...and grow in the knowledge of my Lord. I praise the Lord for this unique opportunity."

Finally, in December 1993, Dibaj was tried before an Islamic court and received the death sentence for the crime of apostasy, or leaving the Islamic faith. At that point he had been a Christian for forty-five years. His execution date was set for the following month. Hovsepian, learning of Dibaj's story, led a campaign to free the pastor. He began speaking out against the unjust court ruling, publicizing the events, and bringing international attention to Dibaj's plight. Because of increased pressure from human rights groups in the West and the U.N., the Iranian authorities released Dibaj on January 16, 1994. But just three days later, Hovsepian disappeared.

For eleven days Hovsepian's family was kept in suspense about his status, and on January 30 they were finally informed of his death. He had been stabbed to death and then buried in a Muslim cemetery. Takoosh and her children gained permission to exhume the body and rebury it in a Christian cemetery. His death was devastating to Hovsepian's family, but they knew that he understood the risk he took daily to bring truth and hope to Iran. In a letter that he wrote just a day before his abduction, Hovsepian said, "I am ready to die for the cause of the Church so that others will be able to worship their Lord peacefully and without so much fear."

Because of his sacrifice, Dibaj was finally free after nearly ten years in prison. But he was soon to follow in his friend's footsteps. Five months after his release, on June 24, 1994, Dibaj was also abducted under mysterious circumstances and disappeared for days. He had been attending a Christian retreat in Karaj and was returning to Tehran for his daughter's sixteenth birthday when he disappeared. On July 5 his body was found in a park in Tehran. He had been stabbed to death and had rope burns on his neck. No group or individual ever claimed responsibility for either death.

These men are just two among many Christians who have been similarly persecuted and killed for their faith in Iran. Christians constitute a severe minority in Iran at less than 1 percent of the population. Persecution and discrimination of Christians intensified after the 1979 Iranian revolution. It has included the expulsion of foreign missionaries from the country, church closings, the closing of the Iranian Bible Society in the 1980s, a prohibition on the printing of Bibles and Christian literature, regular police inspections of church buildings, and government-imposed restrictions on church gatherings and worship, as well as personal threats and intimidation by authorities. Intimidation is especially pressing for Muslim converts to Christianity.

Bishop Haik Hovsepian and Mehdi Dibaj worked against the odds every day to bring the hope of Christ to Iran. Their lives exemplified what it means to be a living sacrifice for God, and they carried that sacrifice all the way to death. As Dibaj said during his trial, "Life for me is an opportunity to serve Him, and death is a better opportunity to be with Christ. Therefore I am not only satisfied to be in prison for the honor of His holy name, but am ready to give my life for the sake of Jesus my Lord and enter His kingdom sooner, the place where the elect of God enter everlasting life."

ABRAM YAC DENG
(1998)

The Bible was small and barely holding together, but it effectively delivered God's Word through the preaching of Abram Yac Deng. With only minimal training, he faithfully shepherded his large congregation near Turalei, Bahr El Ghazal Province in Sudan. He taught the church of four hundred Sudanese with the only Bible of the entire congregation. Although many of the people were illiterate, his desire was to provide literary classes for men, women, and children. When a Christian ministry brought in hundreds of Bibles, Deng was thrilled that every member of his congregation would have access to the Scriptures.

Four days after receiving the Bibles, radical Islamic raiders invaded the village. Deng was shot in the head at close range, killing him instantly. The church was torched and many people made it out just in time. Almost one hundred villagers were killed that day and many people were kidnapped and forced into slavery. The newly delivered Bibles that brought them such hope and joy were destroyed in the fire.

One of Deng's favorite verses was Romans 6:23: "For the wages of sin is death, but the free gift of God is eternal life in Christ Jesus our Lord." Today, he is reaping that free gift in eternity.

By Western standards, the possessions of a Sudanese family would be considered scant and primitive. The grassroofed "tukel" they live in contains almost nothing of value. But it is not for earthly possessions that these brothers and sisters are willing to make such great sacrifices: It is for what they will possess in Heaven. They will someday experience the promise of Hebrews 10:34: "For you had compassion on those in prison, and you joyfully accepted the plundering of your property, since you knew that you yourselves had a better possession and an abiding one." The price that Sudanese Christians pay is very high, but their reward will be great. It is this "better and lasting" possession that gives them courage to withstand such brutal assaults on their faith.

Antonio Revas
(1998)

The sound of gunfire echoed down the hall in the early-morning hours of January 23, 1998, waking the Revas family. Wearing sombreros, army fatigues, and T-shirts, a small squadron of the FARC guerrillas (the Revolutionary Armed Forces of Colombia) armed with revolvers, Uzi machine guns, and AK-47 rifles burst through the door. They demanded to escort Pastor Antonio Revas and his oldest son, twenty-two-year-old Roberto, to a meeting with one of the local FARC commanders. Revas and Roberto kissed and hugged their families good-bye for the last time.

At the time, Revas's wife, Rosa, wasn't worried or fearful. The men had visited her home before, demanding that her sons join the rebel movement. She began talking with the men and told them she needed to dress Roberto before he left for the meeting. While in an adjacent room, Rosa quietly whispered her suspicions to Roberto. Roberto assured his mother that he would be all right, reminding her of God's continual presence.

Rosa, along with her daughter-in-law and several of her children, waited all night for Revas and Roberto to return. When morning arrived and the two men were still absent, Rosa's daughter-in-law and two grandchildren headed out to search for them. Not long afterward, they returned shouting, "Mom, we need some sheets! We need some sheets! They've been shot! They've been shot!"

Only one block from their home, Revas and Roberto had been shot and killed. One bullet had pierced the back of Roberto's head. Revas had been shot in the back of his neck and through his forehead.

Why did the FARC guerrillas target Antonio and Roberto Revas? The family had stood up to the guerrillas on many occasions. When the guerrillas would come to the house and demand that their sons join their Marxist movement, Revas and Rosa would refuse, explaining that they were born-again believers and did not support Marxist ideology.

Revas also refused to make the payments required of all the farmers, quoting the book of Malachi 3:8, saying the tithes go to the house of the Lord and not to the rebels.

Even after these deaths, the FARC guerrillas weren't finished with the Revas family. Shortly after the assassination of Revas and his son Roberto, the FARC guerrillas occupied the family farm and seized their harvest. The Marxist guerrillas kidnapped Rosa's younger son Juan. Juan failed to return home after several weeks, so Rosa traveled into town to meet with a known leader of FARC.

Snarling in disgust, the man pulled out a revolver, looked Rosa in the eye and said: "You don't need to be asking about your son. You don't need to be telling anybody where he is. And if you tell anybody that he's gone, you're going to suffer the consequences."

Rosa and her family were eventually driven from their land. They are now living in a small house in another village, far from their ancestral home.

The Revas family stood strong in the Lord. Revas and Roberto suffered for Christ and gave up their lives for His name's sake. The impact of their lives continues in Colombia and across the world.

FOR NONE OF US LIVES TO HIMSELF, AND NONE OF US DIES TO HIMSELF. FOR IF WE LIVE, WE LIVE TO THE LORD, AND IF WE DIE, WE DIE TO THE LORD. SO THEN, WHETHER WE LIVE OR WHETHER WE DIE, WE ARE THE LORD'S.

ROMANS 14:7-8

GRAHAM, TIMOTHY, AND PHILIP STAINES
(1999)

Raised in Queensland, Australia, Graham Staines took his medical skills to a leprosy hospital in Orissa State, India. His wife was a nurse and they had a daughter and two sons. Along with his medical work, Graham participated in evangelistic crusades, notably the *JESUS* film campaign in the predominantly Hindu area where they lived.

In January 1999, Graham was conducting a five-day open-air evangelistic "jungle camp" in Orissa. His sons, Timothy (nine) and Philip (seven), were with him. A few days later, after Graham and the boys had retired for the night in their station wagon, a group of militant Hindus attacked them with clubs and set fire to the vehicle. Trapped inside his car by the mob, the missionary died holding his boys, while rescuers were threatened by the mob to stay away.

Nearly four years later, the leader of the militants, widely known for his radical hatred of Christians, was convicted in an Indian court along with twelve others. In May 2005, the leader's death sentence was changed to a life sentence and the others were acquitted.

Graham Staines had been working for thirty-four years in India. K.R. Narayanan, president of India, denounced the "barbarous killing" of Graham and his sons. Lepers at the hospital operated by his Evangelical Missionary Society buried the three victims two days after the killings. His widow Gladys and daughter Esther consoled the mourners with their complete trust in God. All together they sang:

There's not a friend like the lowly Jesus
No not one, no not one.
None else could heal all our souls' diseases,
No not one, no not one.

Graham Staines and his sons Timothy and Philip

There is not an hour that He is not near us—
No night so dark, but his love can cheer us.
No not one, no not one.

Later Gladys told friends and reporters that ten days before the killings she had been urged in prayer to give to Jesus all she had. She meditated and then tearfully prayed, "Lord Jesus, yes, I am willing. Take all that I have. I surrender them all to you."

Gladys remained in India to assist at the lepers' hospital before returning to Australia in 2004 for her daughter Esther's studies. She and Esther speak to each other in Oriya, the local language in Orissa. Most of her friends, she reports, are Hindus. The Evangelical Missionary Society continues to operate the leprosarium established in 1897. She was given a civilian award from the Government of India in 2005, which aroused protests from right-wing organizations in the country.

THEREFORE, SINCE WE ARE

SURROUNDED BY SO GREAT A

CLOUD OF WITNESSES, LET US ALSO

LAY ASIDE EVERY WEIGHT, AND SIN

WHICH CLINGS SO CLOSELY, AND LET

US RUN WITH ENDURANCE THE RACE

THAT IS SET BEFORE US.

HEBREWS 12:1

TRULY, TRULY, I SAY TO YOU,
UNLESS A GRAIN OF WHEAT FALLS
INTO THE EARTH AND DIES,
IT REMAINS ALONE; BUT IF IT DIES,
IT BEARS MUCH FRUIT. WHOEVER
LOVES HIS LIFE LOSES IT, AND
WHOEVER HATES HIS LIFE IN THIS
WORLD WILL KEEP
IT FOR ETERNAL LIFE.

JOHN 12:24-25

PART THREE

Modern Martyrs

in the

Twenty-First

Century

While many rejoiced over the fall of Communism in the Soviet Union and Eastern Europe toward the end of the twentieth century, terrorist attacks by Islamic extremists increased significantly at the beginning of the twenty-first century. Islamic extremism became a global movement, and, after the September 11, 2001, attacks in the U.S., the Taliban, al-Qaida and Osama bin Laden became household names. The oppression and violence that Christians and other non-Muslims had experienced for centuries under Islam in the Middle East was beginning to capture the world's attention, as extremist groups spread their acts of terror throughout the world using mass media to further their cause.

In the east African country of Nigeria, an Islamic extremist group called Boko Haram formed in 2002, increasing the persecution that Christians were already experiencing in the northern part of the country. And in Somalia a few years later, an extremist group called al-Shabaab began waging jihad, or "holy war," against the "enemies of Islam." The group seeks to eradicate all Christians from the country and has even crossed Somalia's borders into Kenya to target Christians.

In the Middle East, the self-proclaimed Islamic State (ISIS) gained worldwide notoriety in 2014 with its invasion of Mosul, Iraq, where ISIS fighters went door to door identifying homes of Christians and spray-painting a red Arabic "N" on their houses. The "N" (or *noon*, as pronounced in Arabic) stands for *Nasara*, a term used in the Quran to identify Christians — followers of Jesus of Nazareth. ISIS gave Christians in Mosul an ultimatum: Convert to Islam, pay an exorbitant tax called a *jizya*, abandon their homes and property to flee Mosul, or be killed. Nearly all chose to leave, but some, such as those unable to travel, were killed.

ISIS expanded its reign of terror to Syria, forcing Christians out of towns and imposing its extremist form of Sharia, or Islamic law. Despite and, in part, because of the surge in global Islamic extremism, the twenty-first century has seen one of the largest movements of Muslims turning to Jesus Christ in history.

Hindus are also turning to Christ in great numbers in India, where Christian converts face increased persecution for turning away from Hinduism's thousands of false gods. In 2018, Christians in India experienced an average of one attack every 24 hours, a dramatic increase over past years. Under the country's leadership by Prime Minister Narendra Modi, the Rashtriya Swayamsevak Sangh (RSS) Hindu nationalist organization has seen a 20 percent increase in membership. And the group's emboldened base now hopes to further bolster India's Hindu identity among the country's great diversity of languages, cultures and religions.

While the focus of Christian persecution has shifted from communist nations in the last century to the Middle East and South Asia in this century, it persists in the few remaining communist strongholds. Communist governments in China, Vietnam, Laos, North Korea and Cuba continue to actively persecute Christians; in 2018, the Chinese government imposed new restrictions that resulted in the arrest and imprisonment of pastors and the closure of churches.

Amid this century's increasing extremist violence, we take inspiration from believers like Pastor Gideon Periyaswamy of India, Li Xinheng and Lu Ling Lina of China, Terry Tumba of Nigera and the twenty-one Christians executed by ISIS in Libya. All have taken their place among the countless number of martyrs who remained faithful to Christ to the end.

2000—2006

YESU DASU
(SEPTEMBER 11, 2000)

They were avoided by people from India's higher castes. These dalits, the so-called "untouchables," were the lowest caste in the Hindu culture. To be a dalit is to be without hope for a future. Someone cared for them, however, and was willing to risk it all to help them.

Yesu Dasu loved the untouchables, and put that love into action by befriending and helping them. When others ran away, he came closer. He gave them back their dignity. As a mirror of Christ's love, the fifty-two-year-old Christian preacher came to bring healing to their souls.

The roaring of the motorcycle engine outside disrupted their quiet family dinner. As Dasu rose to look out the window, two men began pounding on the door. "Yesu Dasu," they shouted. "Open up! There is someone who wants to speak to you, and you must come with us now."

Dasu slowly opened the door and looked at the men. "Who?" he asked.

"There is no time to talk. You must come with us now," they responded. They grabbed his arm and ushered him to the motorcycle. Dasu's wife and children stared out the window as the motorcycle raced away. After putting the children to bed, his wife patiently waited for her husband to return. She read her Bible as she waited, and eventually fell asleep.

The morning sun streaming through the window awoke her with a start. She struggled to remember the events of the night before and why she had been sleeping in the chair. Filled with dread, she realized Dasu had never come home. Waking her children, she got them dressed, and together they searched the village for their father.

Dasu's wife heard her name called and looked up to see one of her village neighbors hurrying toward her. He wrapped his arms around her. "I'm so sorry," he said. "They found his body. He's dead."

Near a cattle barn on the outskirts of town, Dasu lay in a pool of blood, his head and other parts severed from his body. Four members of a radical Hindu group had tied his hands and cut him with an axe.

Dasu had been threatened numerous times by members of a radical Hindu group, and he had been warned not to preach in the area. But he had ignored the threats. God had called him to preach, and he would answer that call.

He was a simple and humble man who served society and was respected by the villagers. His ministry to dalits, touching the untouchables, reflected his desire to reach all of God's people. Yesu Dasu not only preached the truth of Christianity, he lived out his faith. Through his life and work, many have come to know the Truth and now spend their lives ministering to others. Dasu demonstrated God's love to the least of those around him without regard for his own well-being. In doing so he earned the highest honor—a martyr's crown.

"Jesus."

—The final word of Roy Pontoh, a fifteen-year-old boy attending a Bible camp in Indonesia that was attacked by a Muslim mob. Pontoh was killed with a sword.

Liu Haitong
(October 16, 2000)

The government does not wish to create martyrs." The government official in Beijing, China, spoke privately and quietly. "They make religion uncontrollable." Perhaps this officer of a government bent on controlling and abating the growth of the church within its borders knew the effect of suffering and martyrdom upon the Kingdom of God: It expands it.

He might very well have been speaking of nineteen-year-old Liu Haitong.

Liu was a member of an underground Protestant house church in the city of Jiaozuo in Henan Province. Because of Henan's thriving house-church movement, the province had been at the center of a two-year campaign by the government against unregistered church groups.

Police discovered and raided an underground worship service at a private home on September 4, 2000. Liu was targeted for his simple faith in Christ. He was arrested, taken into custody, and beaten.

"At any one moment," explained one underground house-church leader, "there are probably well over a hundred Christians detained for their faith and receiving severe beatings from sadistic policemen."

Liu was left without adequate food or provisions for hygiene. Within days he began vomiting and developed a high fever, but jail officials refused to provide medical care. On October 16, Liu died of injuries sustained during his beatings and from neglect.

Liu Haitong's death was "a bad mistake," according to government officials who want to suppress Christianity. Because of his faith and the faith of others like him, the Kingdom continues to expand throughout the country like a wildfire, unrestrained and uncontrollable by those who fear it.

Zhong Ju Yu
(August 3, 2001)

The family members of imprisoned Christian Zhong Ju Yu had been invited to a restaurant by the Public Security Bureau (PSB) in the city of Zhong Xiang, China. Zhong's family had waited for months for news of her condition, and had heard nothing. They hoped to learn something—any news of their loved one—from this meeting.

Their feelings were doubtless mixed as each of Zhong's family members entered the restaurant. Would she be released to them? Had she been killed? Would she be sentenced to death, as other members of her church group had been? What news would the PSB officers bring, those who arrested Zhong during a roundup of underground church members in May 2001?

Once inside the restaurant, the family was given an equivalent of $8,000 US by the PSB as they told them in cold finality of Zhong's condition: She was dead. The announcement came with the threat that anyone who shared publicly what had happened to Zhong would be arrested just as she had been.

Zhong had chosen to participate in an underground church because it was where she had found Christ. To fellowship with others of like mind and heart, to "contend for the faith" (Jude 1:3), became so crucial for her she was willing to risk imprisonment and death. Her fellowship didn't end with her arrest or even with her death. She now joins in fellowship with other saints who surround us as a great cloud of witnesses (Hebrews 12:1), cheering us on as we too run the race of faith.

JAMES ABDULKARIM YAHAYA
(AUGUST 6, 2001)

James Abdulkarim Yahaya had grown up in a Muslim family in Nigeria, a country where 50 percent of the population follows Islam. He had fully embraced that religion and its prophet until a few years before his death, when he decided to follow Christ.

Yahaya may not have read C. S. Lewis, but he fully experienced what Lewis described as being "seized by the power of a great affection." It was an affection he had never known or found in following Muhammad. Yahaya was seized by this affection and gave his life over to seeking and serving the Lord. His conversion was neither a subtle nor a quiet one. He became an itinerant preacher who traveled throughout the country preaching the Gospel and the "fragrance of the knowledge of him everywhere" (2 Corinthians 2:14). In his vital work he made, at the same time, many friends and many enemies. There were, of course, those for whom Yahaya was the aroma of Christ, but there were also those for whom he was the stench of death. In a Muslim-dominated country, abandoning the religion of Muhammad to follow Christ is a dangerous venture. At the least it usually means rejection by family and community. In Yahaya's case, it also meant open hostility from fundamentalist members of his former religion, since Sharia Law states that anyone who converts from Islam must be killed.

On August 6, 2001, Yahaya had retired for the night to the bedroom in his apartment in Abuja, Nigeria's capital city. It was common for him to leave the apartment door open, as his roommate explained, "because of the unbearable heat and the poor ventilation." Four heavily armed gunmen burst into the apartment and shot the evangelist while he slept.

Christian leaders and friends throughout the country mourned Yahaya's death, but they also remembered the power and effect of his life lived fervently for God, and his desire for others to know the same "great affection." The fragrance of the knowledge of God still spills out, as his life and memory stand as a testimony to the love of God and the invitation of the Gospel.

Emmanuel Allah Atta
(October 28, 2001)

P raises echoed off the walls of St. Dominic's Church just before 9 a.m. on October 28, 2001. Catholics shared the church building with the Church of Pakistan, and the Protestant praise and prayer time was running late. Thus, the start of the Catholic service would be delayed.

Pastor Emmanuel Allah Atta had concluded his sermon on the importance of prayer during the turbulent times facing Pakistani Christians, when three terrorists forced their way into the church. They were dressed in black *shalwars* (a long, loose-fitting shirt common among Pakistani males) and armed with AK-47 automatic weapons.

One of the gunmen marched to the pulpit and ordered Atta to throw his Bible to the ground. "I will not!" he replied. He turned away from the terrorist pressing his Bible close to his heart. The gunman shouted, *"Allahu Akbar!"* ("Allah is great!") and opened fire on Atta. He shot the pastor in the back, the bullet piercing his heart. As his body dropped to the floor, Atta captured one last glance at the almond-shaped eyes of his precious four-year-old daughter, Kinza.

The radical Islamic terrorists opened fire on the congregation for six minutes, emptying more than five hundred rounds. Fifteen of the seventy-five congregants attending the service perished in the attack, as well as a Muslim security guard standing watch at the church gate. The body of a two-year-old girl was found riddled with forty bullets, and one woman miraculously survived thirteen bullets piercing her arm and abdomen.

Shortly after the assault, Atta's wife, Sarapheen, publicly spoke of forgiveness for the attackers, stating that it was an honor and a privilege that her husband was chosen to be a martyr for Jesus. Little Kinza, who witnessed her father's death, simply said her daddy had gone to Heaven.

U Maung Than
(March 2002)

You are of our blood, and unless you return to our traditions, I will take back your blood myself!" shouted the uncle of U Maung Than.

When Than decided to leave his family's traditional religion and become a follower of Christ, he immediately became a marked man by his own family in his homeland of Myanmar. He was soon arrested and imprisoned on trumped-up charges. The military dictatorship used the uncle's hatred of Than's faith to sentence him to death.

In March 2002, Maung Maung and Kam Lian Ceu, two Christian friends of Than, came to visit and encourage him, not realizing their friend was in prison. Maung and Kam learned of the seriousness of Than's case, as well as the intense hatred against his faith in Christ. For two days the men diligently sought permission to visit him in prison but were continually rejected. On the third day, military police in that area finally allowed Maung and Kam to see Than, but they were ordered not to speak to him.

After traveling with Than and the police escort to a wooded area, Maung and Kam were surprised to receive permission to talk with Than. Before they could say anything, Than pleaded with them, "Please go to my area and share the Gospel. This is our responsibility: that the Gospel covers the entire neighboring area. You must be faithful unto death."

Suddenly one of the police shouted at Than, "You have said too much!" He drew out his pistol and shot Than in the head. The two Christian friends stared in shock and disbelief. The tears began to flow as they stared at the bloodied body of their dear brother in Christ. Than's friends were sternly warned to recant their Christian faith or the same would happen to them.

Than's dying wish was for his friends to be "faithful unto death." With his sacrifice he proved qualified, on behalf of his Savior, to make such a request.

Mohammed Saeed
(June 2002)

ohammed Saeed was twenty-seven when he began searching for something spiritual outside of his family's Islamic faith. In that search, he attended an evangelistic healing festival with a sick friend in the nearby village of Bail Ahata, in his homeland of Pakistan.

Saeed had never experienced anything like the Christian festival. He was amazed at the joyful spirit and the incredible healings that he saw taking place. The evangelists there prayed for Saeed's friend. Days later, the friend was pronounced cancer-free, and Saeed was convinced he needed to discover more about this Jesus who had healed his friend. Soon he accepted Christ, was baptized, and started attending church regularly. He had finally found the joy and contentment he had never found in Islam.

Saeed's faith grew and he became more vocal and aggressive in sharing Christ with others. In his neighborhood, he would knock on doors and pray with those he met. But his bold witness drew hostile reactions from some family, friends, neighbors, and even some church members who feared for his safety. He was now viewed by the Islamic community as an infidel, and co-workers and customers at the restaurant where Saeed worked refused to eat food he had cooked or even touched. His parents and relatives wouldn't give him food or allow him to touch kitchen utensils. He lost his job, and his wife took their two sons and moved in with her parents.

In June 2002, four years after his conversion, a Muslim relative asked Saeed to stop by his shop, saying he wanted to learn more about Jesus. Saeed arrived at the shop carrying his nine-month-old son in his arms. The relative closed the door and urged Saeed to return to Islam or he would be killed immediately. Saeed stood firm, insisting he would not renounce Christianity. If necessary, he was prepared to die for Jesus. The relative pulled out a knife, stabbed Saeed in the stomach, and slit his throat, lips and tongue. Later, Saeed's infant son was discovered sitting in a pool of blood beside his martyred father's body.

Jesus said, "Do you think that I have come to give peace on earth? No, I tell you, but rather division. For from now on in one house there will be five divided, three against two and two against three. They will be divided, father against son and son against father, mother against daughter and daughter against mother, mother-in-law against her daughter-in-law and daughter-in-law against mother-in-law" (Luke 12:51-53). Mohammed Saeed experienced these words in a most horrific manner. But he also experienced another of Jesus' promises: "the one who endures to the end will be saved" (Matthew 10:22).

"WE HAVE LEARNED THAT SUFFERING IS NOT THE WORST THING IN THE WORLD . . . DISOBEDIENCE IS."

—A VIETNAMESE PASTOR WHO WAS IMPRISONED FOR HIS FAITH

Martin Ray Burnham
(June 7, 2002)

◆

I f I have to go, I want to go out strong for the Lord." Those were some of forty-two-year-old Martin Burnham's last words before he was killed.

It was supposed to be a relaxing and romantic time, celebrating their eighteenth wedding anniversary at a beach resort in western Philippines, but it soon turned into a nightmare. Abu Sayyaf, a Muslim extremist group, ransacked the resort and kidnapped the guests, including New Tribes missionaries Martin and Gracia Burnham. The hostages were threatened and forced to march with their captors through the steaming jungles, trying to avoid the Philippine army that was tracking them. Burnham was forced to carry bags of rice through the rain. The months of being in captivity and trudging through the jungles had worn down his boots and he slipped often. Burnham never complained. He picked himself up and kept walking, even offering to help others along the way.

He and Gracia refused to give in to despair. They spent their time in prayer, thanking the Lord for this opportunity to minister to the other hostages and to suffer for His sake. They led the group in singing inspirational songs, and Burnham even tried to share the Gospel with the guerrillas. Burnham risked his life for Christ and His mission to help others.

After hearing of the capture, the Philippine army increased its search for the guerrillas. As they got closer, Abu Sabaya, the leader of Abu Sayyaf, ordered his subordinates, "If the Philippine soldiers come any closer, I want you to kill the American missionaries." Bullets flew through the air between the guerrillas and the soldiers. When the smoke cleared, Burnham and a Filipino nurse, Ediborah Yap, were dead. Gracia had a bullet in her thigh.

Burnham wasn't afraid to die. During his time in captivity, he encouraged and strengthened the hostages, praying with and for them.

Martin Burnham sharing the Gospel with his killers

He was thankful in all circumstances. While all the hostages prayed to be released, Burnham was also sending up prayers of thanksgiving. Both he and Gracia were steadfast in their faith. Despite all the tremendous difficulties, they kept their faith in Christ.

Just days before his death, Burnham felt the need to write a letter to his three children—Jeffrey (fifteen at the time), Melinda (twelve), and Zachary (eleven). He wanted to tell them how much he loved them, how proud he was of them, and how he desired for them to keep their faith no matter what happened. He gave the letter to Gracia; it was lost in the firefight, but was eventually recovered by troops who went back to look for it.

Martin Burnham was an example of generosity, love, and faith. He generously lived his life to share the Gospel at all costs. As the news of his death and the story of his life were shared around the world, Burnham's strong faith inspired Christians everywhere to share the ultimate gift of Christ's salvation. Gracia carried on that ministry, writing books and speaking to thousands. She and her family committed to pray for members of Abu Sayyaf to come to know Christ personally; they saw it as their own little "holy war." She encourages Christians around the world to go to war on their knees for the souls of Muslims, to carry on the work that her husband lived and died for.

CORNELÏO TOVAR

(AUGUST 17, 2002)

◆

In many rural villages throughout Colombia, Saturday night is known as the "night of the assassins"—the night when those who oppose the Marxist rebel group known as FARC (Revolutionary Armed Forces of Colombia) are targeted for death. But the church members refused to cower in fear at the guerrilla threats, and the Christian and Missionary Alliance Church was packed with three hundred worshipers who heard Pastor Cornelio Tovar talk about staying focused on Jesus. He urged them to resist temptations and distractions and to remain steadfast in Christ. The praise and worship time was electrifying, and the attendees were filled with the Holy Spirit and determination, despite the danger outside. No one was worried—the FARC guerrillas had not made any threats against Tovar or any of the leaders of his church.

It was a sweltering night in Algeceris, Colombia, as Tovar and his wife began the familiar walk home after church. They traveled with five other believers, full of joy from the night service. They talked excitedly about the attendees at the service who had decided to trust in Christ as Lord and Savior. Five blocks from the pastor's home, two men leaped from the shadows, and gunfire rang out in the night.

Panic and confusion reigned as people frantically ran in circles, trying to escape the gunfire that exploded all around them. When the shots ceased and the believers began to move around again, Tovar's wife, Nelly, looked around and found her husband lying on the ground in a pool of blood. She fell down next to her husband's dying form, her anguished screams piercing the night.

As the two masked gunmen fled, Nelly closed her eyes in prayer asking the Lord to bless those who had violently attacked her husband. Later, as doctors tried in vain to somehow revive him in the emergency room, Nelly again lifted her eyes toward Heaven asking, "Why is this happening to me? Please don't let this happen!" Like Jesus, Nelly prayed and asked God to "let this cup pass…" (Matthew 26:39). She wrestled with God in that hospital, but peace came as she finally submitted to Him, saying, "Not as I will, but as you will."

Nelly surrendered her emotions and her hopes to God's will, and He reminded her that one seed had to fall to the ground in order for the Gospel to be spread. She knew her husband was the seed and he had been willing and ready to give his life for the Gospel. She determined in her heart not to lose hope, but instead to work toward a bountiful harvest.

Although Nelly was probably not aware of the famous words of the third-century scholar Tertullian, his words continue to ring true: "The blood of the martyrs is the seed of the church."

BE FAITHFUL UNTO DEATH,

AND I WILL GIVE YOU

THE CROWN OF LIFE.

REVELATION 2:10

Bonnie Witherall
(November 21, 2002)

Operation Mobilization (OM) missionary Bonnie Witherall was up early on that fateful morning of November 21, 2002. Her husband, Gary, remained in bed, and she did her best not to disturb his sleep. It was not unusual for her to get an early start to get the tea and snacks ready at the clinic where she volunteered. But not long after Witherall left, Gary was awakened by the persistent ring of the phone.

It was difficult for Gary to understand the frantic words he was hearing. But one thing was clear: something terrible had happened, and he had to get to the clinic right away.

When Gary arrived, he rushed up the stairs of the clinic building to the front door. He barged past the soldier there but was tackled by two others and forced into a separate room, away from the body lying on the floor—the body of his beloved wife. Sobs overwhelmed him, and he began to tremble as the realization sunk in—Witherall was dead.

She had been met at the clinic by a Muslim extremist with clear intentions. He mercilessly fired three shots into her head at close range. A man full of hate killed a gentle Christian woman who'd come to his country to share about love and forgiveness.

In deep anguish, Gary moved to the wall separating him from his wife of six years. He stretched out on the cold tile floor, pressed himself against the wall, and tried to get as close to her as possible. With tears streaming down his face, he felt as though his heart had been ripped from his chest as he mourned the death of his best friend and life partner.

Images of Witherall's warm, sunny smile and sparkling eyes, her love and compassion for all people, floated through Gary's mind. He remembered her serving in the clinic, giving pre- and post-natal care to Arabic refugee women. He remembered how diligently she had worked to learn the Arabic language but still struggled with certain words and expressions and was often lovingly teased by her patients. She had spent many nights in tears for these women whose religion kept them in bondage with very little compassion or hope. The couple had prayed daily for the clinic to meet not only short-term physical needs but also the deeper, spiritual needs of these lost and suffering women. Witherall's sole desire was to bring them the message of eternal life, love, and hope.

Only a year and a half earlier, the Witheralls had begun serving the Lord in Sidon, Lebanon. They quickly saw God's plan in action as they worked together to share Christ and to love the Lebanese.

They made a great team. She was peaceable, fun-loving, and a perfect counterpart for her unconventional husband. Gary was a seemingly fearless, out-of-the-box evangelist, who would spend his days roaming the streets of the noisy, busy town, building relationships with his predominantly Muslim neighbors and taking every opportunity to tell them of his God—a God who was merciful, loving, and forgiving; a God who could be known.

As the pictures of the past surfaced, Gary found a song running through his mind. He and Witherall had sung it often.

I surrender
All to You, all to You.
I surrender
All to You, all to You...

In that moment, the Lord spoke to Gary with these words: "A seed has been planted in your heart today. It is a seed that will turn either from anger to hatred or from forgiveness to love. You need to choose."

Instantly, Gary chose to reject the temptation to hate his enemies and seek revenge on his wife's murderer. Instead, God gave him an unprecedented opportunity to appear live on television across Lebanon and proclaim forgiveness for the assassin from himself and from God.

At Witherall's funeral back home in the U.S., Gary addressed the crowd: "I know we are all very sad, and we all miss Bonnie. But Bonnie is not in a box! She is in the presence of the God she loved and died serving. She isn't sad or afraid or in pain; she is dancing and rejoicing in Heaven. We should be celebrating for her!"

Gary opened the huge curtains at the front of the sanctuary. As they were drawn back, the room was flooded with light, and there, framed in the picture window, was a magnificent view of Washington state's Mount Baker, snow-capped and dazzling in the sunlight. Though mournful at first, the ceremony became a celebration of Witherall's life, a time of giving glory to her Lord and Savior.

The service formed a picture of Gary's emotional and mental decision. He was choosing to look past the dark, physical curtain and to focus instead on the glorious beauty of the spiritual realm. It hinted at the reality that persecuted Christians seem to understand better than most. Sharing in Christ's sufferings and being found worthy to be beaten, imprisoned, or even killed for His sake is not a tragedy, a punishment, or an accident. Instead, it is the greatest privilege that a Christ-follower has. Neither is such sacrifice wasted in God's eyes.

"THE CHURCH HAS BEEN AND ALWAYS WILL BE PERSECUTED. EVERYONE WATCHES US. IF WE DIE IN FAITH, HOPE, AND LOVE, IT CAN CHANGE THE HISTORY OF NATIONS."

—A missionary who works in China and North Korea

Bitrus Manjang
(December 2002)

She could hear the continued gunfire and screams everywhere as she frantically searched for a place to hide, the tears freely flowing down her cheeks. Feeling helpless and afraid, she huddled behind a door, waiting for her turn to die. She covered her ears so she couldn't hear the screams echoing down the street and prayed, "Lord Jesus, help us."

Eventually it was quiet. Garos Manjang slowly crawled out of her hiding spot and made her way to the front door, where she had last seen her husband alive. Opening the door she looked out onto the destruction—people walking the streets in shock, bodies either hurt or dead on the ground, and numerous houses destroyed. Looking down the stairs, she saw her husband, sixty-nine-year-old Bitrus Manjang, lying next to his car, keys beside his still body. Garos became dizzy and quickly sat down.

Manjang was a well-known Nigerian church leader who had retired five years earlier as senior pastor of the three-million-member Church of Christ. He was a gifted evangelist and had helped translate the Bible into several Nigerian tribal languages. Although retired, he was still actively involved in the church and continued to attend numerous church meetings.

The day of the attack, Manjang had graced several church meetings about thirty miles away. He returned home and hurriedly made his way up the front porch steps toward his beloved wife. He had a wide smile on his face as he wrapped his arms around her and kissed her. Realizing he had left some materials in the car, he took the keys out of his pocket and made his way back to the car.

Garos watched in horror as a mob of Fulani Muslims approached and opened fire on her husband. She saw his blood splatter onto the car

Bitrus Manjang shot by Muslims

and watched the keys slip out of his hands as he fell to the ground. In fear for her own life, she turned and ran.

By the time the Islamic extremists finished raiding the village, nineteen people were dead, and eighteen injured. One hundred twenty-six homes were destroyed; but not the faith of the people. Despite the loss, the church grew stronger.

Garos and the other Christians could have been angry and bitter at the militants and even with God. But just as Jesus had forgiven her, Garos chose to forgive her husband's murderers. She knew that the Islamic extremists believed they were doing Allah a service, but they did not know the Father or His Son Jesus. She prayed that they would come to know Jesus and become His followers.

On the day he was killed, family and friends were preparing a party to mark the fifth anniversary of Manjang's retirement. They didn't plan a time of mourning, but a time to celebrate his ministry and life, a life finished on earth but now continuing in Heaven with Jesus. They mourned their loss, but they celebrated the pastor's eternal victory.

"IF I DIE, I WILL BE VERY HAPPY BECAUSE I WILL LEAVE AN EXAMPLE FOR OTHER CHRISTIANS TO FOLLOW IN MY WAKE."

—KUWA BASHIR, A SUDANESE YOUTH PASTOR, WHILE STANDING BEFORE HIS MUSLIM GUARDS AS THEY POURED ACID ON HIS HANDS

REV. JOSE JUAN LOZADA
CORTEZA (January 27, 2003)

◆

n 2001, the Revolutionary Armed Forces of Colombia (FARC) guerrilla commander Mono Jojoy announced that all evangelical ministers in the country would become targets due to their resistance to the group's movement and ideology. Within five years of Jojoy's announcement, more than 100 pastors had been killed. Largely as a result of its activities and those of the smaller ELN (National Liberation Army) and the paramilitary group known as AUC (United Self-Defense of Colombia), pastors who continue to bring the Gospel to Colombia live under constant threat.

Well aware of the danger of his ministry, Rev. Jose Juan Lozada Corteza continued to follow Christ in the calling he had been given—to shepherd the Lord's people in a war-torn nation of unrest, uncertainty, and suspicion. He served as the pastor of the Evangelical Christian Church in the small town of San Antonio in the central Colombian state of Tolima.

On January 27, 2003, Rev. Lozada Corteza was traveling on a public bus between his home in San Antonio and Chaparral, a city farther south. Uniformed men suspected to be a part of FARC stopped and boarded the bus. Scanning the faces of the passengers, they landed on the clergyman and a member of his church traveling with him, singled them out, and forced them off the bus.

From inside, the passengers watched in horror as the assailants dragged the men to the side of the bus and shot them both in the head.

As a pastor, Rev. Lozada Corteza was targeted by the guerrillas for both his resistance to their ideology of corruption and extortion, and his insistence that the Lord God is the source of life and power. The FARC learned quickly that young people reached with the Gospel message of love and peace could not be recruited into their violent cause, and they acted violently to shut up—permanently—any witnesses for Christ. Lozada Corteza's death backfired for his killers, for as a martyr his life and death stand as an unshakeable testimony to the truth of the Gospel and of the life found in a relationship with Jesus Christ.

Sunday Madumere
(April 22, 2003)

W e are not surprised at all about this incident," said Bishop Nyam of the Church of Nigeria. "We saw it coming."

It was a peaceful April night when Pastor Sunday Madumere and his family were suddenly awakened by the strong smell of smoke. Madumere looked around the room but could hardly see anything. His eyes filled with tears from the smoke as he crouched to the ground and crawled toward his wife. His breathing became heavier, his vision blurred; finally he collapsed to the floor.

Madumere was a zealous preacher in Nigeria whose effective ministry often angered Muslim militants. His powerful preaching led many Muslims to convert to the Christian faith. The militants found a way they could retaliate.

Madumere and most of his family died in the house fire. His son, Daniel, was the only one who managed to escape the flames. He survived, but he sustained serious injuries. It took over two hours for the Nigerian Fire Service to get the fire under control.

Similar incidents have happened in the northern part of Nigeria, where Muslim fanatics have killed numerous Christians and church leaders. Years before, a Christian man, Gideon Akaluka, was killed and extremists carried his severed head through the streets. The government appeared unable or unwilling to make a difference.

Christians in Nigeria are aware of the dangers they face daily. Though the number of those killed increases, so does the faith of surviving believers. The testimonies of those who have sacrificed their lives for their King gives His still-living followers courage to face the future, whatever it may hold.

REDOY ROY

(APRIL 23, 2003)

H is purpose was to bring as many people to Christ as he could—to point them to the Savior. It didn't matter the danger. God had called him to this work, and he would follow to the end. So he packed up his belongings and began working in an outreach ministry with Campus Crusade for Christ in his native Bangladesh.

Redoy Roy walked quickly up the stairs to his home in the late evening of April 23, 2003, after being dropped off by the rickshaw. It had been a wonderful evening as he showed the *JESUS* film to almost two hundred villagers. He loved to watch the audience and the beautiful expressions of fascination and hope that showed on their faces. And he loved even more when the film finished and some in the audience chose to follow this Jesus—their newfound Friend and Savior.

Roy turned the handle, pushed the door open to his rented home, and made his way through the dark house. Before he could reach the light switch, he was hit in the face and knocked to the ground. Angry radical Muslims grabbed him and dragged him over to his bed. A couple more held him down as they tied his hands and feet to the bedposts. Roy screamed in pain as the men hit him repeatedly. The knives followed. He uttered a final prayer and departed this earth to spend eternity with his Savior.

Neighbors who heard the screams called the police, who quickly made their way to the scene. The police were eager to make an arrest, so they arrested the two Christians from the home where the film had been shown that night, as well as the rickshaw driver who had taken Roy home from the screening. None of them had anything to do with the murder. But in the eyes of the police it showed "progress" in the investigation.

The murder came as no surprise to other Christians in the area. Several times Roy had been threatened and told to stop showing the *JESUS* film. He refused to stop. He was willing to pay the price for using this tool to reach people with the Gospel message.

The Christians could have gotten angry with the police and the murderers, but God has used the persecution to strengthen their faith. Just like Redoy Roy, they decided to be faithful to Christ's call, no matter what the cost. The ministry grew immensely. Many Muslims heard about the case and were curious to see the film that this murder victim had given his life to show. They wanted to know more about Jesus and how to follow Him. God used the attack to spread His word.

Roy and his co-workers did not pray that the persecution would go away. They prayed that God would find them faithful. Roy passed the ultimate test. And through his example, others committed to do the same.

FOR I DECIDED TO KNOW NOTHING AMONG YOU EXCEPT JESUS CHRIST AND HIM CRUCIFIED.

I CORINTHIANS 2:2

JAMIL AHMED AL-RIFAI
(MAY 6, 2003)

A smile spread across Jamil al-Rifai's face as he watched yet another person walk away with a New Testament in his hand and the Word of God on his mind. He tried to pray for each one—by name if he could—as they walked away.

The past ten days had passed in a blur. There were so many people in Lebanon who needed to hear about Christ, and al-Rifai was thrilled about the number of people he spoke with. He'd given out almost three thousand New Testaments! "After all that God has done for me, it's the least that I can do," he said. The highlight of his day was telling others about Christ. He was active in Campus Crusade for Christ, multiple Bible studies, and evangelism. *God has really blessed me and provided for me the past few years,* he thought.

Al-Rifai grew up in a high-class Jordanian Muslim family. Just a few years earlier, he became a Christian through the ministry of Trans World Radio. When his family heard he was a Christian, they angrily told him that he was no longer allowed to live with them. Al-Rifai packed up his belongings and left his family in exchange for following Christ. He moved around several times, finally ending up with a couple, Anna and Frank Marsden, and their three children.

Living with the Marsden family was an incredible encouragement to al-Rifai. Frank Marsden was a powerfully anointed evangelist who spent his days sharing the Gospel with neighbors or whomever the Lord brought to him while in town. Anna was a prayer warrior. She tended to the home and children and constantly took opportunity to pray for the place and people she loved. It was no surprise that they took in the twenty-nine-year-old al-Rifai when he approached them about living arrangements. He became a part of the family.

Two nights after al-Rifai finished handing out New Testaments at the Exhibition, Marsden and Anna were reading in the living room.

Anna looked up from her book and noticed that it was 11:30 p.m. She pulled herself out of the chair and got ready to go to bed. As usual, she looked in on the children on her way. The two younger ones slept in their parents' bedroom, and she paused to tuck the blanket around one of them. As she turned away, a movement outside the window caught her eye. Looking out, she saw a man walking past the house, inside their garden. He turned the corner, and through the other window Anna saw him pass along the back of the house.

Rushing back to the living room, Anna alerted her husband, who hurried into the kitchen to investigate. Lifting the curtain, Marsden too saw the man, who was now crouched down with his back to the door. The man tried to force open the door, but Frank quickly closed it. Then he and Anna summoned al-Rifai.

The two men returned to the kitchen and opened the door. On the patio, just a couple of feet from the door, was a bomb. With his bare hands, Marsden attempted to extinguish the fuse; then he and al-Rifai tried to push the device away from the house. They were able to shift it to the opposite end of the patio, about six feet from its original position.

Thinking the immediate danger had been averted, Marsden and al-Rifai quickly searched the property for the intruder. There was no sign of him, so Marsden re-entered the house. "We need to call the police," he told Anna, leading the way into the hall. Almost before he had finished the sentence, a huge explosion rocked the house. If they'd been in the kitchen instead of the hallway, they likely would not have survived the blast.

Running to the children's rooms, they were amazed and relieved to see that all three of them were safe. Gathering them up, they hurried outside the house, where a crowd of onlookers was rapidly assembling. The police arrived and began to take control of the situation. But where was al-Rifai?

The rest of the night was spent at the police station, going over and over the events of the day, trying to make some sense of what had happened.

They heard that a body was found in the garden, but it was some time before the awful realization dawned that it must be al-Rifai.

No one knows exactly what happened. Perhaps al-Rifai had simply been too late following Marsden back into the house. Maybe he realized they had not been successful in extinguishing the fuse and was trying again when the bomb exploded. There was little doubt about what the motive was; a Dutch missionary said it was "almost 100 percent certain" that the attack was religiously motivated—an angry Muslim striking back at effective witnesses for Christ. Even in their grief, the couple realized that this was no surprise to God. Several people reported that they'd had prophetic dreams and visions in the weeks prior to the incident.

Perhaps the most significant was by a friend who saw a vision of al-Rifai in eternity. It was so powerful that he told al-Rifai about it, just a few weeks before the explosion, saying, "Jamil, I saw you in the presence of the Lord. I saw you in eternity! If this is going to be, that you will be with the Lord, what is your advice for us—what are the words that you are going to leave with us?"

With a rare opportunity to choose his epitaph, Jamil Ahmed al-Rifai answered with simple clarity, "Run the race; finish the race that I have started."

REVEREND WAU
(JUNE 9, 2003)

Local Indonesian Muslims told him to stop holding church services. They warned of the danger if he continued his Christian activities. But Rev. Wau chose to ignore the warnings. He wasn't ashamed of his faith in Christ.

The day their threats were carried out started like any other Lord's Day. Wau led Sunday services in the morning, challenging and encouraging his fellow believers in their Christian walk. Afterward, he and his family spent a relaxing afternoon at home.

Around 5:00 p.m., a man knocked on the door. He didn't say much, only that he needed the pastor to go with him for a short while. Saying little, Wau picked up his Bible and followed the man out the door. When Wau didn't return home after a couple of hours, his wife began to worry. It wasn't supposed to take long. Also, aware of the many threats to her husband's life, she knew that being absent for that amount of time with someone they didn't know couldn't be good.

She asked her neighbor for help, and together they began searching for her husband in the surrounding neighborhood. After searching for several hours and finding nothing, they made their way home. As they neared the house, Mrs. Wau noticed something lying in the front yard. Running toward her house, she began screaming as she realized it was her husband's body. He was covered with bruises, and the deep wounds around his neck indicated that he had been strangled.

Rev. Wau knew the consequences of his very public faith and witness, but he had courageously chosen to speak about it to the people of Sumatra. He knew that every day he walked fearlessly with Christ was a day more people would come to know Christ and grow in their faith; he also knew that it was a day closer to the escalating danger. His last Lord's Day was truly the best one for him, as it was the day that he entered for eternity into the Lord's presence.

PASTOR MARIANO DÍAZ MÉNDEZ AND PASTOR JAIRO SOLÍS LÓPEZ

(OCTOBER 2003)

ariano Díaz Méndez was a minister of the indigenous Tzotzil Evangelical Church in San Juan Chamula, a small town in the central highlands of Chiapas, Mexico. He was traveling near the village of Botatulan early on the afternoon of October 24, 2003, when a group of heavily armed men stopped his car. As a pastor in a tumultuous area, Méndez was well aware of the threat against his life and intimately familiar with the increasing attacks aimed at evangelical Christians from the *caciques*, or community chieftains, in the area.

Since Christianity's advent in the Chiapas Highlands in the 1960s, the *caciques* have used violent tactics to discourage its spread. Scores of evangelicals have died and hundreds more have suffered injury by groups who practice "traditionalist" religion, a semi-pagan mix of Mayan and Roman Catholic beliefs.

Méndez bolted from his car in an attempt to evade his attackers, but they overpowered him with their weapons, their bullets piercing his body and bringing the pastor to the ground. The assailants shot him to death.

The deadly assault against Méndez had occurred exactly one week after a pastor in the city of Mapastepec, namely Jairo Solís López, had also been killed by the *caciques*.

Both Méndez and López had given their hearts to serve Christ in the face of formidable challenges in Chiapas. Together, they embody what God promises in Revelation, that "they loved not their lives even unto death"; rather, they overcame "by the blood of the Lamb and by the word of their testimony" (12:11).

Zhang Hongmei
(October 30, 2003)

Mrs. Zhang Hongmei was thirty-three years old when she was arrested by local Chinese police in the village of Dong Maio Dong, China, for her Christian witness and for participating in so-called "illegal religious activities."

The afternoon of her arrest, October 29, police approached her family and demanded a bribe of 3,000 RMB (about $400 US) in order to release Zhang. The family was unable to raise the money, so later that day her brother and her husband, Xu Feng-hai, went to the police station to request her release. What they found there shocked them.

Zhang was bound to a bench with heavy chains. She was badly wounded and unable to speak. In spite of her deteriorating condition, police refused to let her go. Her husband and brother were forced to leave without her.

The following day, her family returned to the station where they were notified that she had died at noon that day. The autopsy report showed that she had died from internal injuries sustained from vicious beatings.

Affected by Zhang's life and outraged by her death, more than 1,000 people joined in a protest the next day in front of the city offices.

Zhang Hongmei was ready to die rather than deny Christ. In her life, she touched many in her community. In her death, she offered a challenge and example to believers around the world.

MUKHTAR MASIH
(JANUARY 5, 2004)

Tears streamed down the aging cheeks of Parveen Mukhtar as she detailed the final days of her husband's life. She clutched his Bible tightly in her hands as she told how Pastor Mukhtar Masih had loved the Lord and wanted to share the Gospel with all who would listen.

Masih had led more than two hundred people to Christ during seventeen years of ministry in his homeland of Pakistan. He started a church in the year 2000. Though his church was small, Masih was convinced that the fifty-member congregation would grow as a result of their daily morning prayer services, which were broadcast throughout his predominantly Christian neighborhood via several loudspeakers atop the church steeple. Muslims blasted their calls to prayer into the streets of Khanewal five times daily; Masih thought Christians should do the same.

The fifty-year-old pastor had studied the Koran and was prepared to discuss matters of faith and religious doctrine with Muslim scholars. He was a convincing debater and an effective speaker, and Muslim leaders grew disgruntled at his growing popularity among Christians and non-Christians alike.

One day, a Muslim *mulvi* (mosque leader) came to the church during the children's Sunday school. He demanded that they halt the Sunday school and immediately discontinue the loudspeaker broadcasts, saying the noise was interfering with the Muslim prayers. Church members tried to calm him, but he wouldn't listen and kept shouting angrily.

Masih was then summoned to the police station after Muslims lodged a formal complaint against the church. He was told the loudspeaker broadcasts were too loud. Masih apologized and willingly lowered the volume of the loudspeakers. Days later, some elderly Muslims came to the church and warned him that he would be killed if he continued his loudspeaker evangelism. Masih didn't fear death and continued the broadcasts.

The morning of January 5, 2004, Masih rose to catch a 4 a.m. train to Lahore to visit his eldest daughter, Esther, and his grandchildren. The morning air was cold and damp. A thick fog had settled in, making it very difficult to see. Despite the conditions, Masih slowly made his way down the winding roads leading to the train station.

The pastor was only a few blocks from his destination when his assailants appeared. Due to the fog, Masih may never have seen them or even heard the first shot come ripping through the air toward him. Later that morning as the fog lifted, Masih's body was discovered in a pool of blood. Beside him was his travel bag with clothing, a few of his possessions, and his Bible.

The day before his murder, Masih preached his last sermon to his Church of God congregation. He urged his church family to love one another, pray regularly, and remain united. "I may not be among you for a long period; therefore, be united and be a congregation of faithful believers," he said. He encouraged them to spread the good news of Christ just as the early church did after Jesus's resurrection. The early disciples were told,

> Remember the word that I said to you: "A servant is not greater than his master." If they persecuted me, they will also persecute you. If they kept my word, they will also keep yours (John 15:20).

Timeless words for those who follow Christ.

SERGEI BESSARAB
(JANUARY 12, 2004)

T he shots rang through the air and shattered the glass window of Pastor Sergei Bessarab's front room the evening of January 12, 2004. The first bullet hit the hand that was gently strumming his guitar while singing songs of praise to God. The second shot got him in the leg and the third in his chest, ending his life on earth.

Bessarab's wife, Tamara, heard the shots and frantically ran into the room. She stared in disbelief at the scene before her—the shattered glass and blood spattered on the chair, carpet, and on her husband's guitar. She dropped to the floor to avoid additional bullets and began to sob as she lay next to her husband's body.

Tamara could smell the acrid scent of gunpowder as the shooter continued his rampage, firing into the house and at Bessarab's car. Finishing his task, he finally turned and fled down the narrow, dusty alley behind the house, disappearing into the darkness.

Suffering wasn't new for Sergei Bessarab, and he was prepared to die for Christ. Just five years earlier, however, the idea would have been inconceivable. Bessarab had gone to prison five different times as a leader in Tajikistan's organized crime underworld. A fellow prisoner who had come to know Christ through a prison ministry began to minister to Bessarab as he served one of his sentences. This prisoner continually prayed that Jesus would become real to him.

"Pray for someone else," Bessarab would growl. "Don't waste time praying for me." But the man persisted and prayed every day that he would come to accept Christ as Savior and Lord. Finally, three years later, in August 2000, his prayers were answered. Bessarab began walking with the Lord and eventually began a Bible study in the prison. After his release in November 2001, he returned often to bring Christ's message to the inmates who remained.

Bessarab traveled all over Tajikistan. He was a passionate preacher with a great love for people. He planted a church in Isfara, a city with no Christian presence but a strong, radical Muslim one. Accompanied by his wife, Tamara, Bessarab would travel to Isfara on Sundays to hold services; in early 2003 they moved to the city permanently. The church began to grow, and new people were accepting Christ, but their ministry did not go unnoticed by enemies of the Gospel. A week before his death, the local paper carried the headline: "What's going to be done about Sergei Bessarab?"

Bessarab's life for Christ was like an exploding star, burning hot and fast and spreading much light. Even after his death, Tamara received numerous letters from prisoners all over Tajikistan. They had either heard her husband speak or heard about the remarkable way Christ had changed his life. They were challenged to know God more, and to rely on Him.

Bessarab was a man of prayer. For two hours every morning and two hours every evening, he spent time with the Lord. He read his Bible, prayed, and sang praise songs while strumming his guitar. His favorite passage was John 12:24: "Truly, truly, I say to you, unless a grain of wheat falls into the earth and dies, it remains alone; but if it dies, it bears much fruit."

Those four hours of daily prayer were the source of Bessarab's continual spiritual fervor. In fact, in the weeks before his death, he had been asking the Lord to open up two more hours—in the middle of the day— for him to commune with God. God answered his prayer in a way no one expected—not just two more hours, but an eternity with Christ.

Before Bessarab's death, he and Tamara prayed alone for Isfara, and then with a small group of believers in Tajikistan. One of their requests was that God would raise up an army on their knees for the city He had called them to. God answered their prayer, using the death of one prayer warrior as a seed to raise up a bountiful harvest of prayers for Isfara from around the world.

AHMAD EL-ACHWAL
(JANUARY 21, 2004)

When a person's faith is true, and they realize that their suffering doesn't go unnoticed by God, they see that they're doing something for the cause of Christ and furthering his kingdom...then they grow with more courage...and still the work goes on." These words, spoken by a West Bank evangelist, reflect the life of Ahmad El-Achwal of Palestine.

A cook at a Jerusalem fast-food stand and father of eight, El-Achwal was born a Muslim. And in Palestine, if one is born a Muslim, he is expected to remain a Muslim or face the consequences.

While serving time in prison after the Palestinian Authority accused him of dealing in stolen gold, Ahmad met Christ. He was later acquitted of all charges, and word quickly spread of his newfound faith in Christ. But his decision to turn his back on Islam and embrace the One born in neighboring Bethlehem came with a generous dose of consequences, including one that would cost him his life.

Ahmad was repeatedly harassed and abused. Palestinian Authority security forces would search his home, confiscate his Bibles and Christian books, interrogate him for days, and arrest and hold him for long periods of time. However, members of the Palestinian Authority promised an end to his suffering. Their offer? Return to Islam. They would even give him a job—financial security for his wife and eight children. Ahmad rejected the offer, so the suffering continued.

The assaults intensified. Repeatedly, El-Achwal was beaten. He and his family received death threats. Men affiliated with the Palestinian National Security Forces fire-bombed his home. Then El-Achwal livelihood was threatened when the landlord of the building where he ran his fast-food restaurant refused to renew his rental agreement. This forced El-Achwal to work in distant Jerusalem.

In the face of the beatings, losses, arrests and threats, he kept professing his faith in Christ. His home was converted into an informal Christian center where he held Bible studies, handed out Christian literature and shared the Gospel with others.

His body began to bear the scars of Christ (Galatians 6:17). Burns from hot pieces of sheet metal that were pulled from a fire and held to his skin covered him. But the Muslims' hatred of his faith in Christ and persistent witnessing soon went beyond torture to murder.

On January 21, 2004, El-Achwal heard a knock on his door. Ready to greet his guest, he turned the knob and pulled the door open only to be met by a flood of bullets.

The persecution of Palestinian Christians has increased over the last century. Christians have fled the West Bank and Middle East due to political insecurity, economic adversity and human rights violations. In 1914, the Christian population in Israel, Syria, Lebanon, Jordan, and the Palestinian Authority was 26.4 percent; in 2006, it was less than 10 percent. Because Islamists dominate the Palestinian Authority, Christians are treated as second-class citizens in the Holy Land. Christians are forced, along with everyone else, to abide by Islamic laws and teaching.

However, many Christians have chosen to stay in the Holy Land during this era of turbulence and uncertainty. And for this they have, like Ahmad El-Achwal, paid dearly—even with their lives. But like the West Bank evangelist said, these brave believers know God has taken note of their suffering; He is the God who sees (Genesis 16:13). They consider it a joy, an honor, to bear His scars.

Pastor George Masih shot by Muslims

Pastor George Masih
(April 2, 2004)

George Masih was an elder in a Church of Pakistan congregation in Lahore. When he and his wife, Aniata, felt called to relocate their family to the small, predominantly Muslim village of Manawala to plant a church, they willingly went.

For two years, Masih pastored the church based in his home. Filled with the love of Christ, he ministered house-to-house, reaching out to his neighbors and praying for the sick—even if they were Muslims. He and his wife became well known in the village for the worship songs that could be heard pouring from their house. Their desire was to know God and to make Him known to those in their community.

Their work drew the anger of a Muslim neighbor named Shokat Ali. Ali was irritated by the Christian meetings in the Masih home, and urged the landlord to kick the family out. On more than one occasion Ali threatened to kill Masih if he continued preaching.

But Masih remained steadfast. Around noon on Friday, April 2, 2004, Masih, his wife, and their four children were watching the *JESUS* film in their home. When the movie finished, Aniata got up to go out of the house. When she opened the door, two masked attackers burst in. One grabbed Aniata and covered her mouth, threatening her with death if she tried to cry out for help. The other attacker fired a shotgun point-blank at Masih's face. As the Christian man lay dying, the assailant hit him in the head with the butt of the gun. Then both men fled, dropping the stunned Aniata to the ground. Neighbors ran toward the home when they heard Aniata cry. Shokat Ali was one of the few neighbors who did not show up to offer aid.

George Masih had a boundless passion for the Lord God and a deep compassion for people. His mark on the community was immense, as evidenced by those gathered for his funeral. Around three hundred people crowded into his brother's home to remember Masih and express gratitude for his life, including many Muslims who had been blessed by his ministry. "He was a true and passionate believer," said Pastor Mukhtar, the man who led George to Christ, "and he always tried to win the souls with his preaching."

"MORE PERSECUTION ...
MORE GROWING!"

—PASTOR SAMUEL LAMB, A CHINESE HOUSE-CHURCH PASTOR
WHO SPENT TWENTY YEARS IN PRISON FOR HIS FAITH

Samuel Masih
(May 28, 2004)

The blasphemy law in its present form has become more of an instrument of persecution and vendetta than of justice," a Pakistani newspaper editorial stated. Blasphemy means showing extreme irreverence toward something sacred, and for centuries Christians have been accused of blaspheming Islam. Often in Pakistan, contrived witnesses with false accusations have spoken out against believers, sending them to jail and even to death. Such was the case with Samuel Masih, whose body was found bloodied and battered, his skull smashed.

Masih spent his days as a whitewasher and painter. He had just finished a job and stopped at the local mosque in order to use the restroom. As he returned outside, bystanders grabbed him and shouted accusations. Masih's accusers, knowing he was a Christian, claimed that he had spit on the walls of the mosque; two false witnesses confirmed this story. Samuel was immediately arrested and put on trial.

Under the maximum penalty for violating Section 295 of the Pakistani penal code, Masih could have been jailed for two years and fined, if convicted of "defiling a place of worship with the intent of insulting the religion (Islam)."

The pungent odor of urine and sweat filled the dirty prison. The sounds of coughing and scuffling feet echoed along the walls. Just down the hall lay Masih, struggling to breathe and continuously coughing up blood. Although the head of the prison deeply resented his Christian prisoner, he sent Masih to the hospital to treat his advanced tuberculosis.

During his stay, a policeman was posted near his bed. When Masih should have been safely recovering, a horrible crime occurred.

Early one morning, the police constable entered the room and swung a hammer down on Masih's head. Bleeding profusely from his wounds, Masih fell into a coma and was rushed to the emergency neurosurgery ward, where he died a few days later. The Pakistani police constable who took his life claimed, "I wanted to earn a place in paradise by killing him."

"This is a case that brings out, like nothing else, the myriad contradictions that these [blasphemy] laws have infused in this state and society," a *Daily Times* newspaper editorial stated the day after Masih's death. "The fact is that it is a bad law both in its conception and its implementation, and the legislation has created a psyche that encourages vigilante behavior."

Samuel Masih was arrested for a crime he never committed. His only crime was following the call of the one true Savior, Jesus Christ. Masih's murderer thought killing him would earn him a place in paradise. Samuel Masih, however, knew the one true way to get to Heaven, through Jesus Christ, and he is now with his Savior.

"I WOULD RATHER HAVE THE
WHOLE WORLD AGAINST ME,
BUT KNOW THAT THE ALMIGHTY
GOD IS WITH ME."

—MEHDI DIBAJ, IN HIS DEFENSE TO AN IRANIAN COURT
AFTER BEING CONVICTED OF APOSTASY AND SENTENCED
TO DEATH IN 1993

Jianc Zoncxiu
(June 18, 2004)

She was arrested for handing out Christian materials in a village marketplace. She was not a threat to anyone, certainly not a threat to the great nation of China. Yet thirty-four-year-old Sister Jiang Zongxiu would never taste freedom again. Instead, she was beaten until she died. It happened at the Public Security Bureau (PSB) office of Tongzi County, Guizhou Province—a neighboring province of her hometown.

The previous day, Jiang and her mother-in-law, Mrs. Tan Dewei, went to the marketplace of Pusdu Town, Tongzi County. The women had been active in their local house church for ten years and were distributing Bibles and other Gospel tracts in the street. They were arrested by the local PSB, who bound their hands with one set of handcuffs on the way to the county detention center. Tan was kicked repeatedly during her interrogation. She noticed that Jiang's treatment was even worse. They took off Jiang's shoes and beat her. They told her mother-in-law they would beat her too if she didn't obey.

Both Jiang and Tan were accused of spreading rumors and "disturbing the social order" by the PSB. They were sentenced to fifteen days of "administrative detention." In the police report, they were described as having "seriously disturbed the social order by distributing Christian literature to the masses in the market."

In the early-morning hours of June 18, they were taken to the Tongzi detention center. The police took their fingerprints and sent them to separate cells. Tan protested that they had not broken any laws and were being held illegally, but it didn't matter. Tan also remembered seeing a person's feet lying on a bed across from her cell, and officers later came in to take pictures. She asked an officer what had happened, but he told her it was not her concern.

Tan asked to see her daughter-in-law, but was told she was resting. When she inquired again, she was told Jiang was very sick and in serious condition. Tan kept asking to see her, but the officers refused and cursed her. Then without notice or explanation, they released her. She again inquired about her daughter-in-law but Tan was forced onto the train back to her village. She learned of Jiang's death after she arrived home, and only then realized why they were taking pictures at the detention center and why they wanted her to leave so quickly.

The family received the autopsy report later that month. It stated that Jiang died of natural causes, of heart failure. There was no mention of her wounds from the beatings, no mention of the brutal treatment at the hands of a government that claimed to have freedom of religion. The family asked for a second autopsy. They were refused. They went to their local court to tell how Jiang was beaten to death and were again refused. PSB officials then pressured the family to cremate Jiang's body, destroying any evidence of her murder.

The surviving members of Jiang's family naturally sought justice. They were not afraid of a government that persecuted its citizens for preaching the Gospel of Jesus Christ. They were shocked at the assault and murder of Sister Jiang, a loving wife and mother.

The PSB killed Jiang because she was caught sharing her faith. How could a young peasant woman threaten the "social order" of China? A simple act of handing out Christian literature resulted in a brutal death.

Jiang's sister-in-law asked permission to take pictures of her body, but was refused. So she rented a camera and snuck into the detention facility. From the pictures she took, it was easy to see the wounds on Jiang's body, the scars on her neck from the beatings. One PSB officer even told the family secretly they didn't need another autopsy; it was "easy to see that she was beaten to death."

Jiang's family sought justice, but it was not to be granted in this life. Jiang now joins the martyrs written about in the book of Revelation. Her family joins in asking, "How long?" (Revelation 6:9-11)

The Lord is my light and my salvation;
whom shall I fear?
The Lord is the stronghold of my life;
of whom shall I be afraid?
When evildoers assail me to eat
up my flesh, my adversaries and foes,
it is they who stumble and fall.
Though an army encamp against
me, my heart shall not fear; though
war arise against me, yet I will
be confident.

Psalm 27:1-3

MULLAH ASSAD ULLAH
(JULY 1, 2004)

The sun reflected off ripe fruit laid out in the market stalls in Ghazni Province, Afghanistan. Mullah Assad Ullah breathed in the clean air, thankful to God for the beautiful day. He made his way through the market, picking out ripe fruit and crisp vegetables. He loved the market, with the rush of people and the easy conversation. Some of those conversations had led to discussions of faith, discussions where Assad could quietly share that he was no longer a follower of Muhammad but of Jesus Christ.

As Ullah stopped at the next booth and reached for some fruit, there was rushed movement behind him. He looked up and briefly saw the faces of his attackers before the knife swung across and slit his throat.

People in the market began to scream as the Taliban fighters dragged Ullah's now-lifeless body down the streets of the market. "This is what happens to Christians who seduce people, and to the people who listen to their teachings," the men shouted as a warning. "This is what happens to people who convert Muslims to Christianity." The Taliban even called the media so they could brag about murdering Ullah.

His passion was to tell people about the Gospel of Christ. He spent his time getting to know people and living a life that reflected God's love. Of course, his family was a priority. Ullah made sure his wife and four daughters, ages seven to fourteen at the time, were growing in their faith as well.

As a former mullah, Ullah knew the Muslim law. He could speak knowledgeably about the Koran and Muhammad's teachings, which made his witness for Christ even more effective. He came to know Jesus Christ as Lord and Savior after receiving a New Testament five years before his murder. He was baptized secretly two and a half years later under the brutal rule of the Taliban regime.

There were others killed not long after Assad Ullah. Each left behind a wife and children. They did not live in fear, nor did they die in vain. Their deaths have shown the power of Jesus and the strength of faith in Him, even in a land where so few choose Christ.

The men were accused of studying the Bible, praying in the name of Jesus, and converting people to Christianity. No better epitaph could be written for a follower of Christ than that he or she was "guilty" of those charges.

WE ARE AFFLICTED IN EVERY WAY,

BUT NOT CRUSHED;

PERPLEXED, BUT NOT DRIVEN TO

DESPAIR; PERSECUTED, BUT NOT

FORSAKEN; STRUCK DOWN,

BUT NOT DESTROYED;

ALWAYS CARRYING IN THE BODY

THE DEATH OF JESUS, SO THAT

THE LIFE OF JESUS MAY ALSO BE

MANIFESTED IN OUR BODIES.

2 CORINTHIANS 4:8-10

SUSIANTY TINULELE

(JULY 18, 2004)

At twenty-six years old, Reverend Susianty Tinulele was one of the younger leaders within the Presbyterian Christian Church of Central Sulawesi in Indonesia. Only two weeks after being ordained, she had earned a reputation as an outstanding Bible preacher who would speak the truth in love, even if that truth was unpopular.

When "Susi," as friends called her, was invited to speak at a nearby church, nobody expected it would be her last sermon. She was just finishing it when the gunmen arrived—radical Muslims, their faces wrapped in black jihad masks, with automatic weapons in their hands. One of them stood in the entryway to the church and fired, blowing out the back of Tinulele's head as she stood at the pulpit. Four other worshippers were also wounded in the attack; the gunmen fled on motorbikes and in a car.

Just two days earlier, Tinulele had delivered food to an imprisoned pastor and encouraged him to remain strong in his faith. She was a vocal supporter of justice in the region, calling for local authorities to give fair treatment and equal protection to Christians.

Her ministry and her life had just begun; now both were over. She had been scheduled to be married in a few weeks; now she would never be a bride.

Yet Tinulele's final sacrifice was not made blindly. She knew that to stand up for Christ and for justice in Muslim-dominated Indonesia made her a target. Only the night before, a Christian woman living nearby had been stabbed to death in her front yard. Witness reports from that crime were very similar to the reports of the jihadis who invaded the church.

Her ministry may seem short to human eyes, but in God's eyes it lasted exactly the right amount of time. Her days had been numbered before the world was created; however, it is not the number that matters but how we use those days. Tinulele used her short time on earth to build something for eternity.

JOSEPH MONDOL
(SEPTEMBER 18, 2004)

◆

I t had been a long day at the pharmacy and the walk home for Dr. Joseph Mondol was a lengthy one. The night air was crisp and cool, and Mondol faithfully used this time in prayer. He would have been deep in thought when the men approached.

Mondol, a Bangladeshi pharmacist, had made the decision two decades earlier to leave Islam and follow Christ. He found joy in following Christ and wanted to bring glory to Him. He was known as a faithful follower of Christ in his village and often provided medicines to poor families without charge. He was a living example of God's love.

Mondol, who was still known by his former Muslim name of "Dr. Goni," was employed by the government health department and also had a small pharmacy of his own. He rose to leadership in the Bangla desh Baptist Fellowship (BBF), becoming secretary of one of the BBF districts. His area of responsibility included sixteen churches, made up almost entirely of former Muslims who had chosen to follow Christ.

At 9:30 p.m. on September 18, 2004, while walking home from his pharmacy, Mondol was passing under a banyan tree when he was attacked by four radical Muslims. As instructed in the Koran on how to deal with Muslims who leave the faith, they slit his throat from one side to the other, almost decapitating him. His dead body was left lying on the road. The radicals thought they had silenced his witness for Christ.

The next day Mondol's wife, Teresa, buried his body in the village over the objection of Muslim leaders who didn't want a memorial to the Christian martyr so close to their soil. Teresa stood firm, wanting her husband's grave to be a reminder and testament to Christians in the village that they need not fear being a witness for Christ. She hoped the grave would remind Christians in the village of the words of Christ, "And do not fear those who kill the body but cannot kill the soul. Rather fear him who can destroy both soul and body in hell" (Matthew 10:28).

Francisco Montoya
(December 8, 2004)

Squeals of delight from the children could be heard from down the street. Father Francisco Montoya was laughing with them, grinning from ear to ear. The local priest was performing illusions for the kids, reveling in the smiles that radiated from their faces. This was Montoya's favorite time of day.

Montoya called the kids closer and had them sit down as he pulled out his clarinet. The children sat mesmerized as the beautiful music pierced the air and touched their souls. The adults also gathered around and allowed the sounds to wash over them.

Putting down the clarinet, Montoya began telling the story of Jesus Christ. The people of Quibdó, Colombia, needed to hear the Gospel message more than the music. God used the music to draw people closer and to open their hearts, and Montoya was now prepared to share the good news with them.

The next day, Montoya rose early to attend services and began his trek from Quibdó (the capital city of Chocó Department) to the village of Nóvita. He traveled on foot all around the region, carrying necessary belongings in a typical indigenous basket. The time passed quickly as Montoya walked steadily down the road.

Suddenly, a man raced toward him and grabbed his right arm. Montoya pulled away but soon another man arrived, grabbing his other arm. Others appeared and there was no hope for Montoya to escape.

The area he was visiting was under the control of the FARC guerrillas, and he had entered the area with their authorization. The guerrillas knew he was a religious worker, but they also suspected him of being an army informant. Through the diverse terrain, they force-marched Montoya from town to town and eventually to a mountain base in another region of the country. Forcing him to his knees, the men stared at him and pointed a gun, shouting false accusations and insults at him. Without any proof or even investigation of his alleged spying, Montoya was killed with a single bullet to the head.

When they had not heard anything from him days later, his congregation grew worried. A group from the church was sent to look for him and encountered the FARC guerrillas, who blatantly confessed to shooting him. The guerrillas had buried his body in the mountains. No one would be permitted to see his grave.

Under the control of the FARC guerrillas, organized church services were not permitted. Many church leaders had tried to negotiate with the guerrillas, telling them they had no intention of stirring up problems. They simply wanted to minister to the people. Their pleas fell on deaf ears.

Knowing the possible fate that awaited him, Montoya still asked the church to send him to minister in this dangerous region. The risk was great, but the need for people to hear the Gospel was greater. Armed only with God's love and a conviction to serve, he left the safety of the city to minister in rural, guerrilla-controlled communities. Faith had overcome fear as Francisco Montoya demonstrated the greatest love of all.

Sunday Nache Achi strangled by Muslims

Sunday Nache Achi
(December 9, 2004)

P
assionate, sincere, faithful, and loving—those are some of the words used to describe Nigerian Christian Sunday Nache Achi. Despite the opposition to Christian evangelism on the campus of Abubakar Tafawa Balewa University, Achi passionately shared his faith openly with other students. While studying architecture at the University, he served as president of the campus ministry of the Evangelical Church of West Africa (ECWA). Despite the tension between Muslim and Christian students on the university grounds, Achi continued his ministry and Bible studies—people needed to hear the good news of Jesus Christ. Achi was at one of these meetings when men showed up at his room looking for him.

Achi closed his Bible and looked around at the people gathered in the small room. It had been a good turnout, with some new students, and everyone was eager to hear the Gospel. Even though three of their members had recently been expelled from the school for distributing leaflets contrasting Jesus's teachings with Islamic beliefs, they continued to meet. Achi bowed his head and led the group in prayer, unaware of the turmoil back at his room in the student hostel.

Idakwo Ako Paul, Achi's roommate, stared at the papers in front of him, wishing he was praying with the others instead of studying for his exam the next day. The stillness was broken as the door burst open and Paul jumped out of his chair. Three Muslim students dressed in Islamic jihad clothing rushed into the room and demanded: "Where is the Christian leader? Where is Sunday?" "I don't know where he is," said Paul. The men angrily stormed out of the room and continued their search.

A few hours later, Achi returned and Paul shared what had happened. Though his life was in danger, Achi simply smiled, thanked Paul for telling him, and took a seat at his drawing board to work on some drafts for his architectural class the next morning. Paul lay down on his bed and went to sleep.

"Wake up, Paul! Wake up!" Achi screamed. Paul jumped out of bed and saw masked Muslim men dragging Achi out of the room. Paul ran toward the door, but one of the kidnappers pointed a pistol at him, forcing him back into the room and locking him inside. Paul pounded on the door and screamed. The Muslims living in the hostel stayed in their rooms. Paul slumped to the floor, exhausted. No one came to help.

Paul was awakened the next morning by one of the Christian students unlocking the door. Paul told him about Achi and made a plan to tell the other Christians of the danger they faced. They ran out of the room, down the stairs, and right into another Christian brother who knew what had happened to Achi.

"He's dead," he said, tears streaming down his face. He collapsed into the men's arms as he began to tell them about Achi's body, which was found next to a mosque, near the home of the university's vice chancellor. His neck was broken from being strangled, and bruises covered his body. The men wept as they shared their grief over the loss of a strong, brave, and faithful friend who was now gone.

The persecution didn't end with the death of Sunday Nache Achi. It grew stronger. The offices of the Nigeria Fellowship of Evangelical Students (NIFES) were burned down, and authorities closed Abubakar Tafawa Balewa University.

One of the Christian students from the university said it best:

> Evangelism is something we must be prepared to die for. I see
> in the Bible examples of many who had to lay down their lives
> for the sake of the Gospel. Why not me?

DULAL SARKAR

(MARCH 8, 2005)

D ulal Sarkar was a thirty-five-year-old lay pastor and evangelist with a local branch of the Bangladesh Free Baptist Church in Jalalpur village, in the southwest division of Khulna. As a lay worker, his desire was not only to care for his church but also to plant churches in other areas. His goal was to minister to all the people of Bangladesh.

On March 8, 2005, Sarkar was slowly walking toward his home. God had given him a strong love for the people and he spent most of his spare time in prayer for them. He looked forward to his time at home with his wife, Aruna, and their five children. "Thank you for my family, Lord God. I am so blessed," prayed Sarkar daily.

That day Sarkar spent hours talking about his faith with many of the villagers. The week before, several Muslim villagers had accepted Christ as their Savior. He made sure they came to church so they could continue to be discipled and grow in their faith.

Suddenly, ten Muslim extremists, armed with knives, surrounded and threatened the native evangelist. "We know that you have led many people to believe in this Christ of yours. Stop preaching or we will kill you right now," said the men. But Sarkar stood firm and replied, "I will not stop the ministry God has called me to perform." With that answer, the men attacked. Sarkar's throat was cut so deeply that his head was separated from his body.

Sarkar's wife immediately filed a police report and officers arrested three of the ten attackers. However, local Christians reported that the remaining seven, who had connections with the Jamaat-e-Islami political party, had tried to bribe the police to get their friends out of jail. After filing the police report, Aruna was also threatened by Islamic extremists and forced to move numerous times to protect herself and her children.

Dulal Sarkar left a legacy for his family and church members. He fulfilled the highest mandate in demonstrating faithfulness as a good shepherd who laid down his life for the sheep.

TAPON ROY AND
LIPLAL MARANDI (JULY 28, 2005)

The screams echoed down the hallway and woke neighbors from their sleep. The closest ones tried to rush out of their homes to see what was happening, but their front doors were chained closed and they were unable to get out. Neighbors farther away got out of their houses and ran toward the screams, but they were too late to prevent the carnage.

It was July 28, 2005, and Tapon Kumar Roy and Liplal Marandi were sound asleep in the calmness of the night. A loud noise woke the two men as their door came crashing in and eight Muslim men rushed into the room. They held Roy and Marandi down while they tied and bound their hands with strips of the sheets they ripped apart. Then they began to viciously stab them.

Soon the neighbors' footsteps and voices could be heard outside. The assailants quickly fled the scene after stabbing Marandi fourteen times and Roy twelve. The two severely wounded men were rushed to the nearby Boalmari Health complex in a van. Roy died in transit, and Marandi died immediately after reaching the hospital.

Roy and Marandi began their ministry in Dhopapara in April 2005. They rented a small room to share and began showing the *JESUS* film. They were warned by local Muslims more than once to stop showing the film. Roy and Marandi knew their God was greater than any threats, so they continued in the ministry He had called them to, showing the film.

Only a few days before their murder, a mob of people rushed to their house around noon and demanded that they leave Dhopapara village immediately. "If you fail to obey, then we will make sure that you will be gone forever while your JESUS film will be left behind." Once again, the men followed God's call and remained in the village. They knew the danger they faced and were prepared to die if it was God's will. Roy and Marandi left behind more than a film. They left behind a witness of a Savior Who chose to face the cross that all might be saved.

Ezzat Habib

(October 24, 2005)

The taxi's tires screeched as it careened into Pastor Ezzat Habib, his son Ibram, and a friend as they were crossing the street in Cairo. The men were thrown across the street as the taxi raced away.

People hurried to the scene and Habib was rushed to the hospital, suffering from internal bleeding and a broken skull. He underwent surgery, but it didn't help; he died the next day. The friend suffered a broken leg, and Ibram had severe bruising on his legs and persistent lower back pain.

While he was still stunned and in shock, the hospital had Ibram sign an incident report after Habib arrived, even though he was unable to read it clearly at the time. Later he saw the report contained a completely different set of facts than what had actually happened. The taxi driver went unpunished.

This was no accident. The Habib family was frequently threatened, and faced physical abuse from neighbors and from Egypt's national security police. In June 2003, Habib was arrested for supposedly "disturbing the neighborhood." He was put in an underground cell that was so narrow he couldn't sit down. He was physically and sexually abused by the police officers, yet he never rejected his Lord Jesus Christ.

After being in prison for five days, an officer bandaged his eyes, chained his hands, and interrogated him. Two police officers, one on each side, hit him, kicked him, and insulted his wife. He was warned to stop his Christian meetings and to forbid non-Christians from attending. The source of the abuse was clear: Police knew that Habib had been sharing the Gospel with Muslims; he'd been encouraging them to leave Islam and follow Jesus Christ. This could not be tolerated.

In spite of repeated threats, Habib's congregation continued meeting. Later, two trees smashed through the windows of the Habibs' apartment building. There was a man in the front yard chopping the trees with an axe. The phone line was cut, and the front door was blocked from the outside. The man claimed a police officer told him to cut down the trees.

"Didn't I tell you to stop doing your meetings?" the officer told Habib. "Look what is happening to you."

In spite of harassment and continued threats from police and neighbors, Ibram and the family resolved to continue the house fellowship after Habib's death. They had seen him stand firm in his faith, even unto death; they were determined to do the same.

REMEMBER JESUS CHRIST, RISEN FROM THE DEAD, THE OFFSPRING OF DAVID, AS PREACHED IN MY GOSPEL, FOR WHICH I AM SUFFERING, BOUND WITH CHAINS AS A CRIMINAL. BUT THE WORD OF GOD IS NOT BOUND!

2 TIMOTHY 2:8-9

Theresia Morangkir, Alfita Poliwo, and Yarni Samube

(October 29, 2005)

Four teenage girls walked down the path leading to Poso Christian High School. The sun was shining in a cloudless sky and the girls looked forward to another day of classes. It was a holiday for the Islamic schools in the area, celebrating the holy month of Ramadan. But Christian schools like the one the four girls attended were still in session. Their friendship and fellowship brought smiles across their young faces as they enjoyed the peacefulness of the early Saturday morning.

The stillness of the air was broken as six men dressed in black and with veils covering their faces jumped out of the bushes and ran toward them. Before the girls could move, the men surrounded their young victims and viciously began swinging machetes. Screaming for help, the girls fought for their lives. Only one, Noviana Malewa, was able to escape. Covered in blood from cuts mostly on her face, she ran to find help. The bodies of Theresia Morangkir and Yarni Samube (both fifteen years old), and Alfita Poliwo (seventeen), were left on the ground, their heads severed from their bodies and missing.

A couple of women walking to the nearby market heard the girls screaming for help. Filled with fear, the women ran toward the military post, reporting what they heard. The Indonesian soldiers began looking for the source of the screams but instead discovered the three decapitated bodies.

The attackers put the girls' heads in a sack and dumped them in different areas around the county. Two of the heads were found near a police post, while the third was discovered outside a local church.

It wasn't enough for the radicals to attack churches or Christian leaders. They purposely targeted young Christian girls who refused to recognize the Islamic holiday of Ramadan. Girls who would never be able to be forced into marriage with Muslim men. They also made a deliberate statement by taking their heads and leaving them by a police station and a church. The message was clear: Neither the church nor the government could stop their cowardly attacks on young girls in the area.

These teenagers knew of the dangers they faced, but with confidence and joy they made their daily trek to school. They chose to rise above fear and trepidation. Though their lives were mercilessly taken that Saturday morning, their faith lives on. Word of their testimony traveled worldwide, giving encouragement and hope to others to possess lives full of youthful joy in Christ, and a sober reminder that we are all just visitors in this corrupt world.

EVEN THOUGH I WALK THROUGH THE VALLEY OF THE SHADOW OF DEATH, I WILL FEAR NO EVIL, FOR YOU ARE WITH ME; YOUR ROD AND YOUR STAFF THEY COMFORT ME.

PSALM 23:4

COLLIN LEE
(NOVEMBER 5, 2005)

The smoke billowed as flames engulfed the jeep. Hedwig Unrau Lee's face was flushed not only from the heat of the flames, but also from dragging her wounded husband, Collin, away from the disaster. What had started as a typical day for the couple working for International Aid Services (IAS) quickly turned to fear and turmoil.

The Lees and their driver, Karaba Juma, were driving along the Ugandan border in Sudan toward the town of Yei when they suddenly came upon a roadblock. Juma spotted twenty militants—members of the brutal Lord's Resistance Army (LRA)—and tried to reverse the jeep to avoid it, but it was too late. Bullets flew through the air, hitting Lee's chest and neck as he sat in the jeep's passenger seat.

Despite her own injuries, Hedwig refused to leave her bleeding husband. She begged the gunmen to let her remove him from the vehicle before they set it ablaze. Struggling with his seatbelt as tears streamed down her face, she eventually pulled Lee from the car. The pregnant thirty-five-year-old woman draped her husband's arm around her and made the hour-long trek to the closest village.

Hedwig's minor wounds were treated and Lee was immediately taken to Yei hospital, where doctors unsuccessfully tried to keep him alive. Six hours after the shooting, Lee was pronounced dead.

It was only a couple of years earlier that Lee had felt a call from God to begin working for IAS doing trauma counseling for war victims in Somalia, Sudan, Ethiopia, and Uganda. He joined his wife, who had worked for IAS before. Together, with urgency, they worked diligently to counsel the victims and share the Gospel of Jesus Christ.

Over a million lives in Uganda and surrounding nations have been affected by attacks of the Lord's Resistance Army (LRA). Children have been kidnapped by the LRA and used as soldiers, porters, and sex slaves. Many walk up to ten miles every day just to find a place to sleep securely.

A large part of the Ugandan rural population has left home and taken refuge in large cities.

These were the conditions where the Lees felt called to minister. Lee worked strategically to help these victims, putting his concerns for his own safety aside. Hedwig stood with her husband in this service. Hundreds have come to know Jesus through their work, and only God knows how many more have been reached because Lee followed God's call and glorified Him.

NOW I REJOICE IN MY SUFFERINGS FOR YOUR SAKE, AND IN MY FLESH I AM FILLING UP WHAT IS LACKING IN CHRIST'S AFFLICTIONS FOR THE SAKE OF HIS BODY, THAT IS, THE CHURCH.

COLOSSIANS 1:24

GHORBAN DORDI TOURANI
(NOVEMBER 22, 2005)

◆

I t was a late November afternoon when the phone rang. "Ghorban," the caller began, "I heard you speak at the meeting last week and was moved by the testimony of your Christian faith. I want to hear more about your beliefs. I prefer to meet somewhere other than your house, so that others don't see me. Can you meet me at a park in the city so we can talk more about Christianity?"

Pastor Ghorban Dordi Tourani eagerly agreed to meet with the caller and made his way quickly out of the house and to the park. Someone wanted to know about Jesus!

One week earlier, Tourani had been contacted by the head of religious leaders in his area of northern Iran. He was invited to a meeting held by the ethnic Turkmen Islamic leaders in the area so he could answer their questions about his faith. Tourani believed it to be an opportunity to share the Gospel of Jesus Christ with these Islamic leaders.

But when he arrived at the meeting, he was disappointed to find that it wasn't a time for questions and open discussion. The Islamic leaders' goal was far more direct. They wanted Tourani to return to Islam and strongly advised him to give serious consideration to what they were saying.

"We are well aware that your ancestors and your parents have been dedicated followers of Islam," they told him. "And you are supposed to be a committed Muslim too. Why have you turned to Christianity? We are giving you one more chance to deny your Christian faith and return to Islam."

"I am not going to deny Jesus," he replied.

Now a week later, Tourani thought about that meeting as he hurried to the park, excited that his words seemed to have touched the heart of at least one of his listeners. He knew it could be a trap, but then again, the caller could be sincere and Tourani would not want to miss the

Ghorban Dordi Tourani knifed by Muslims in Iran

opportunity to speak about Christ. He waited for some time, but no one showed up. Deciding that the man must have gotten scared, he began making his way home. At the end of the alley leading to Tourani's house sat a car with three people inside.

One of the three got out of the car and called to him. Hesitantly, Tourani approached the man, who quickly pulled out a knife and thrust it into Tourani's stomach. The second person out of the car attacked him with a knife to his back. The third slit the pastor's throat.

Standing over the body of the slain pastor, the men shouted a warning to all who could hear. "This is the punishment of those who become infidels and reject Islam."

Tourani's path to the true God began when he and his family moved from Iran to Turkmenistan in 1983 to find a better job. Things didn't turn out as they planned. Tourani got into a heated argument and killed someone with a knife. As a result of his crime, he was arrested and sentenced to fifteen years imprisonment. His time in prison was difficult and he soon earned a reputation as the most evil prisoner.

A Russian Christian in prison for his faith was eventually transferred to Tourani's cell. He befriended this "most evil" prisoner and shared the message of the Gospel. For a long time Tourani opposed his cellmate's message. But the more he got to know him, the more he was impressed by the Christian's love and peace, in spite of the prison conditions.

Tourani, unable to deny the truth being revealed, gave his life to Christ. Shortly after his conversion, he boldly asked the head of the prison if he could hold evangelistic meetings. The prison warden, amazed at the changes in Tourani's life, miraculously agreed. "Because the God you worship has changed your life in such a dramatic way, I will give you permission to have meetings in the prison."

Tourani was finally released from prison and went back to Iran and to his city, Gonbad-e-Kavous. He shared with his family and friends and relatives the faith that had transformed his own life. He also shared with them the Christian teachings he had learned and all that the Holy Spirit had revealed to him as a result of his study of the

Word of God in prison. Twelve ethnic Turkmen gave their lives to Jesus within the first couple of years of Tourani's ministry. He then moved to another large city in Iran, as he needed further training to better disciple and teach these new converts. He eventually met a key leader in one of the churches in that city who was willing to help him in his ministry among the Turkmen.

Tourani attended a Bible training program to become more equipped for pastoral and teaching ministry. Over the next seven years, God's work among the Turkmen people grew, and at least thirty-five Turkmen became Christians as a result of his ministry.

Tourani was a fearless Christian leader and would boldly share about Jesus on the streets and in shops and bazaars. He was convinced that true faith in Christ was not to be kept silent, and he shared it with others everywhere he went.

Several times Tourani was threatened by the Islamic religious leaders in his community. His own brother slashed Tourani's face with a knife for his Christian witness. In spite of these oppositions, he continued to share about Jesus, no matter what it cost him.

Tourani's wife, Afoul Achikeh, had learned from her husband's boldness. After finding him dead on the street, she shouted to those crowded around his body, "O people, remember that Ghorban is a Christian martyr who laid down his life for the sake of Christ!" She repeated the words in a loud voice several times, not wanting death to end her husband's powerful witness.

After the murder, the secret police took all Tourani's family members and the other believers for interrogation. They asked a lot of questions and told them they were trying to identify the three murderers. They also took all the Christian materials (books, videos, Bibles, etc.) from their homes.

Afoul and her children also came under extreme pressure from Tourani's brothers, urging them to turn back to Islam. But she and the children have stood firm in their Christian faith and have told those who ask that they will follow Jesus, no matter the cost.

Before meeting Christ, Ghorban Dordi Tourani was an angry, violent man, a murderer and a prisoner. But his anger and violence died long before he did; Tourani had become a man of inner and outer peace. No three attackers—indeed, not three hundred—could take that from him, no matter what.

BUT THANKS BE TO GOD, WHO in CHRIST ALWAYS LEADS US in TRIUMPHAL PROCESSION, AND THROUGH US SPREADS THE FRAGRANCE OF THE KNOWLEDGE OF HIM EVERYWHERE. FOR WE ARE THE AROMA OF CHRIST TO GOD AMONG THOSE WHO ARE BEING SAVED AND AMONG THOSE WHO ARE PERISHING, TO ONE A FRAGRANCE FROM DEATH TO DEATH, TO THE OTHER A FRAGRANCE FROM LIFE TO LIFE...

2 CORINTHIANS 2:14-16

Aroun Voraphorn
(December 2005)

Metta Voraphorn answered the door with dread in her heart, already sure of what the men were going to say. Grief and pity filled their eyes as they looked at her and said the two words she feared most, "He's dead."

Her husband, Aroun Voraphorn, had been missing for two days when these same friends first came to visit. They were supposed to join him for a Christmas service in another part of Borikhamxai Province in Laos. Metta told them she assumed her husband had been called on short notice to preach at another church, but it had been awhile since she'd talked with him. She shared her concerns about his whereabouts due to some recent unusual events.

Three unidentified men came to their house the day before Voraphorn's disappearance. Metta didn't know the men or why they were there, but assumed they wanted to know about the church or Jesus. Voraphorn left home the next day to preach a Christmas service about ninety kilometers south. The three men arrived at the end of the service and entered the church. Voraphorn introduced the men to the pastor of the church and told him that two of them were his relatives. They all ate together, and then he and the men thanked the pastor and left. Metta talked with Voraphorn later that afternoon. He told her he would be late for their youngest daughter's birthday party because he was going to buy a cake on his way home. That was the last time she spoke with him. Voraphorn never returned.

After hearing Metta's story, Voraphorn's friends left the house and started toward their preaching engagement. On the way, they stopped by the church where Voraphorn had preached a few days before and asked the pastor if he had heard from or seen him. The pastor hadn't. The men thanked him and made their way down the jungle road. About twenty meters into the jungle, the friends saw some policemen in a huddle. As they moved closer, the men covered their mouths and clutched their stomachs as they saw the body. It was Aroun Voraphorn.

The men turned away so they could compose themselves, then approached the body. It was bloody and mutilated, but the friends would recognize that peaceful face anywhere. Voraphorn's hands were tied tightly behind him and he had been stabbed numerous times. The rock lying next to his body had been used to smash his head, and his throat had been cut.

The two friends asked permission to take Voraphorn's body back to their church in Vientiane.

Aroun Voraphorn preached the Gospel fearlessly, always aware of the danger surrounding him. At his funeral service the day after the body was discovered, Metta encouraged the Christians in Laos to do the same—to preach the good news without fear.

When Laos became a Communist republic in 1975, the government severely restricted Christian activity. Pastors, evangelists, and anyone associated with the Christian church were often harassed and beaten by police and local officials. Christians have been tortured and imprisoned for refusing to sign documents renouncing their faith. Ten years before his death, Voraphorn had been imprisoned for his faith.

Aroun Voraphorn knew there would be consequences for his faith on both sides of eternity. Yet he chose to follow Christ no matter what the consequences would be here on earth. At his funeral, held on Christmas Eve, Metta pleaded with Christians in Laos to continue preaching the Gospel fearlessly, just as her husband had done.

"WE DON'T PRAY TO BE BETTER
CHRISTIANS, BUT THAT WE MAY
BE THE ONLY KIND OF CHRISTIANS
GOD MEANS US TO BE: CHRISTLIKE
CHRISTIANS; THAT IS, CHRISTIANS
WHO WILL BEAR WILLINGLY THE
CROSS FOR GOD'S GLORY."

—A NOTE SMUGGLED FROM THE UNDERGROUND CHURCH
in Communist Romania

Pastor Jimendra Nayak
(January 1, 2006)

Thirty-five-year-old Pastor Jimendra Nayak was accustomed to threats for witnessing to his Hindu neighbors. As a pastor for two years in the Indian Church Assembly in the northern village of Baliguda, Kandhamal district, he preached God's Word to his community. His proclamation of the Truth angered radical Hindus. They wanted him silenced. But it was Nayak's love for Christ that compelled him to continue reaching out to them.

That devotion led Nayak to the nearby Beradakia church for a New Year's Day service. Here he was to preach the Word in his desire to lead the hearers deeper in their relationship with God, in hopes that they would believe and call upon the Lord as Paul expressed to the church in Rome (Romans 10:13-14). He didn't know it as he prepared, but this would be his last sermon.

The afternoon had dwindled into evening before Nayak left the church building to head home for the night. As was customary, he hired an auto rickshaw taxi to navigate through the streets of the village and drive him to his house. The pastor never left the vehicle alive. His body was later recovered from the cabin of the rickshaw. Death had apparently come through a severe blow to the head.

The police insisted that the pastor had died in a strange automobile accident, but investigation into his mysterious death reveals several major discrepancies that allude to a more sinister story—one of premeditation and murder at the hands of those opposed to his message and witness.

Nayak was among the impassioned who sought out God's Kingdom with intense desire, and sought to share its light with others as well. Through him, the kingdom advanced forcefully. His work is completed, his race run. Now others take the torch and carry the light of the Gospel of Christ as a beacon for the lost and dying in Nayak's community.

Andrea Santoro shot during morning prayer

ANDREA SANTORO
(FEBRUARY 5, 2006)

Sun streamed through the stained-glass windows onto the pews. Only the soft murmurs of prayers disturbed the peaceful silence. The morning Mass at Santa Maria Church in Turkey had subsided. Father Andrea Santoro could take his time in fellowship and conversation with God.

Suddenly the back doors of the church flew open. Before Santoro could even turn around, two bullets had pierced his body, hitting his heart and liver. In an instant, he went from simple conversation with God on Earth into eternal fellowship with Him in Heaven.

"Allahu Akbar!" ("Allah is great!") cried the Muslim assailant as he fled the church and escaped down the road. This phrase is an Arabic exhortation used as a rallying cry by Islamic militants. Police later launched a major manhunt and found him hiding in a relative's home near the city center. He was only sixteen years old, already filled with enough hate and deception that he could kill an innocent priest in cold blood, believing he was doing Allah a favor.

Prior to his murder, Santoro was threatened numerous times by Muslim militants about his ministry of converting Muslims to Christianity. The priest never requested police protection. He did not want it to hinder his ministry.

There are numerous theories about why Santoro was killed, but the constant theme running through them is that he was a Christian—one who dared to share his faith with Muslims. Had he confined his ministry to his church, he may have avoided the assault.

The Santa Maria Church was built in the second half of the nineteenth century to serve foreign Christians visiting the city. Santoro was a member of the Sons of Divine Providence, a Catholic religious order in Italy. He came to Turkey in 2000 to live and work, and eventually to die for his commitment to bring "church" outside the safety of its four walls.

EUSEBIO FERRAO
(MARCH 18, 2006)

B roken and splintered, the wooden cross lay upon the grass outside the church. Clearly written on one of the wooden pieces were the words *"Shri Pardesi"* ("Mr. Foreigner"). Christians were seen as unwanted foreigners by radical Hindus in India. A priest's robe was found covered with a mosquito net, hanging on a tree branch in a park near a church where another cross had been destroyed.

A couple of weeks later, those threats became reality. In Macazana, parishioners of St. Francis Xavier Church arrived around 6:30 a.m. for morning service. The church seemed unusually quiet and their priest, Father Eusebio Ferrao, wasn't at his usual spot by the door to welcome his parishioners. The early arrivers crept quietly toward the front of the sanctuary—and then the silence was broken as their screams filled the air. Lying on the floor in a pool of blood was the body of their beloved priest. Some of them fell to the floor and began weeping as they looked at Ferrao's beaten, stabbed, strangled, and smothered corpse.

Police soon arrived at the scene and ushered the parishioners out of the church. They began searching for clues about why Ferrao was murdered. Nothing was taken from the church, so theft wasn't the motive. It was clear that someone with a great deal of anger against the church had committed the crime. On the last night of his life, Ferrao had dinner with two young men; police suspected they might have been the killers.

Hindu extremists have created tension between Hindus, Muslims and Christians. The extremist group Rashtriya Swayamsevak Sangh (RSS) was accused of crusading for an all-Hindu state, and they targeted areas with a high percentage of Christians. Riots had broken out between Hindus and Muslims, leaving two policemen and two civilians severely injured. The rioters also looted eighteen shops and a gas station, and damaged twenty-four vehicles owned by Muslims. About a month before his death, Ferrao had written articles for two local newspapers about the recent rioting. As an outspoken Christian unafraid to address the needs of a nation, Ferrao became a target of extremist hatred. He was aware of the danger of his words, but knew the truth must be spoken. Without fear for his life, he defended not only his faith but also human rights for all his countrymen.

Father Eusebio Ferrao could have chosen a path of safety and silence. But he chose to speak out, and in doing so he brought an end to his ministry on this earth. His testimony rings loud of boldness and courage.

AS FOR YOU, ALWAYS BE SOBER-MINDED, ENDURE SUFFERING, DO THE WORK OF AN EVANGELIST, FULFILL YOUR MINISTRY. FOR I AM ALREADY BEING POURED OUT AS A DRINK OFFERING, AND THE TIME OF MY DEPARTURE HAS COME. I HAVE FOUGHT THE GOOD FIGHT, I HAVE FINISHED THE RACE, I HAVE KEPT THE FAITH.

2 TIMOTHY 4:5-7

PREM KUMAR
(JUNE 8, 2006)

hen God imparted the Ten Commandments to Moses, He told him, "For I will cast out the nations before you and enlarge your borders ..." (Exodus 34:24). Such was the ministry of sixty-seven-year-old Pastor Prem Kumar, whose effective outreach extended beyond the boundaries of his church in Nizamabad, India. He taught at prayer gatherings, corner meetings and conventions. However, his fruitful work of expanding God's kingdom did not go unnoticed.

On Thursday, June 8, 2006, Kumar left for his regular prayer service at the local church in Kotagiri. Afterward, an unidentified, well-dressed man arrived at Kumar's house and asked his wife if this was indeed his home. He told her he had come from Nizamabad to take Kumar to lead a service. Since he had already left, the man wrote down Kumar's cell phone number and went away.

At about three o'clock in the afternoon, Kumar called his son Sunil saying he was going with a man on his scooter to lead a prayer service in Rampur Thanda, in Kotagiri Mandal.

Around nine o'clock that night, Kumar again called his son, this time saying he was at the Bodhan bus stop and was accompanying four unidentified people to another prayer service. He mentioned he was scared to go with them and asked Sunil to call him every half hour. He was scheduled to arrive in Kotagiri in thirty minutes.

A little later when Sunil tried calling his father, he could not reach him, as his cell phone was in an area without service. He called again and again, still with no answer. After learning that his father's cell phone was turned off, family members began to panic.

Kumar's sons called their friends in Kotagiri to find out if they had seen their father. They had not, so the sons immediately left for Kotagiri.

After searching all night, they gave up and started again early the next morning, asking many if anyone had seen their father. One person said they had seen a dead body and a scooter in an open space nearby. They rushed to the spot and found a pair of glasses…then slippers…and then a scooter and a Bible. To their utter shock, they found their father dead in a pool of blood in the hills near Rampart in Kotagiri Mandal, of the Nizamudeen district. Kumar's body was mutilated beyond recognition, forcing the Kotagiri sub-inspector to identify the remains from a description of the clothes he'd been wearing.

The family took his body home. At ten o'clock that night, they said goodbye to Kumar in a funeral.

A pair of local landlords and some villagers were very annoyed because one of Kumar's family members had been sharing her faith with her family and drawing not only them, but also others, to belief in Christ; the landlords are suspects in Kumar's murder. A police official stated that personal rivalry was more than likely the motive. "There is definitely no religious angle," he insisted, adding that Kumar was one of the accused in a separate murder case and that relatives of the victim could be behind the killing. He also claimed that one of Kumar's sons had been involved in a kidnapping some time before, and after the kidnapped woman was released, she had threatened him.

However, one of Kumar's sons said his father had no enemies, and he strongly suspected the hand of Hindu extremists. He also said he could identify the person who invited his father to hold the prayer meeting in Rampur Thanda.

In the face of persecution and threats from Hindu radicals, believers in Jesus are standing strong and continuing to witness the love of Christ. Like Prem Kumar, God is enlarging the borders of their outreach, gathering more into His kingdom daily.

A Nigerian Woman
(June 28, 2006)

Release her to us!"
"Release her or we will burn down the building!"
"She deserves death!"

By now the mob had fully surrounded the police station, and their demands for the officers to hand the woman over to them had grown to a deafening level. Several held rocks of various sizes in their hands, ready to release them at the first sight of the woman—the infidel—while others held clubs and sticks.

The police had only moments ago found the bruised and bloodied woman and brought her into the station to protect her from Muslim extremists who were beating her with clubs and fists.

Earlier that day, this unidentified woman had been evangelizing in the streets of Izom, Nigeria. She had entered into a conversation with some Muslim youths, sharing the Gospel and handing them some Christian literature to read. Her encounter had not gone unnoticed.

Muslim elders standing nearby had seen the exchange and approached the youths to find out what she had told them. They were infuriated to learn that she had shared the Gospel with them. They claimed she had insulted the prophet of Islam, Muhammad, and insisted that the woman be killed. Their rage and allegations incited hundreds of other Muslims to pour through the streets to track down the woman. They finally caught up with her near the River Gurara and began beating her.

That's when the police intervened and brought her into protective custody at the Izom police station.

The mob stormed the premises, demanding she be released to be stoned to death in accordance with Shariah, Islamic law. The Islamic legal system was implemented in several states of Nigeria in 2000, making it illegal to speak out against Allah or the prophet Muhammad.

The police had persistently refused to hand her over and were now faced with the real threat that the mob would burn down the police station. In an effort to protect the woman and get her to safety, the police tried to smuggle her out through a back door, but the angry Muslims had blocked all escape routes. Fleeing for their lives, the police abandoned the woman at the door, and members of the mob clubbed her to death.

In the panic, the police did not have time to identify the woman before she was killed. All that is known of this courageous young woman is her actions of love in reaching others for Christ and bringing them the Good News. Although nameless in death, she unashamedly pointed others toward the true Name above all names, Jesus Christ, and it is certain that He was ready to welcome her by name into eternity.

"A CHURCH WiTHOUT MARTYRS IS A CHURCH WHiCH iS DYiNG."

—ORiGEN, MARTYRED iN AD 254

Y NGO ADRONG
(JULY 13, 2006)

A Montagnard Degar Christian named Y Ngo Adrong, age forty-nine, from Dak Lak Province was tortured to death in the police interrogation room at Ea H'leo district of Vietnam. ("Montagnard" is French for "mountain dweller" or "mountain people," and "Degar" is how Montagnards in Vietnam refer to themselves.)

On July 13, 2006, Adrong was summoned to the police station, where officers interrogated him about his Christian house-church activities.

At about eleven o'clock that morning, the police went to Adrong's village of Buon Le. They told his family he had hanged himself at the station. On July 14, 2006, his body was transferred to the morgue; then one of his relatives brought his body to the village of Buon Blec, the village of his birth.

But Adrong's family's grief did not end with the news of his mysterious death. Dozens of police surrounded the village, preventing residents of nearby villages from attending the funeral. The police also refused to allow his family to inspect the body or to remove his clothing. Even though family members wanted to see his wounds to try to understand the cause of his death, police refused to permit relatives to get near the body.

Added to the restrictions on inspecting Adrong's body and attending the funeral, the police gave his family fifteen million Vietnamese dong in compensation, and admitted they were wrong in causing his death. However, the police refused to provide details of what happened in the interrogation room.

Like Adrong, Montagnard Degar Christians are carrying on in their ministry, sharing the Good News of Christ throughout Vietnam. They know well the risks they face—risks of imprisonment and even death—yet the message they carry is so valuable, so important, that they willingly take any risk to share it.

Pastor Irianto Kongkoli
(October 16, 2006)

◆

I t is God's will," Rita Arianti Kopa exhaled. "He gives life."
Her memory flashed back to the last moments her husband, Irianto Kongkoli, spent on earth. The two of them and their five-year-old daughter had gone to the hardware store in Central Sulawesi, Indonesia, to buy ceramic tiles, a trip that was not uncommon for them. There was nothing extraordinary about this Monday morning, except that the two of them had come to understand the dangers involved in living out a risky faith in such a violent place.

Kongkoli and Rita had just finished bargaining and were heading back to their van when Kongkoli noticed some interesting tiles on display in the yard outside the store. He started walking toward them. It was then that two masked men approached Kongkoli and shot him in the back of the head at near point-blank range, then fled on a motorcycle.

Rita ran to her fallen husband, adrenaline and shock taking over her body in waves. As a member of the East Palu police force, Rita had been trained to respond in such an incident, but for her this incident became a crisis and soon a tragedy. Kongkoli was rushed to a nearby hospital where doctors battled to save his life, but the wounds were too severe, the blow too violent. Irianto was gone.

It had only been a short time earlier that Kongkoli had taken over as acting head of the Protestant Church in Central Sulawesi, following in the steps of Pastor Rinaldy Damanik. It was a hazardous undertaking. Damanik himself had only been released two years earlier after being imprisoned for twenty-three months on trumped-up charges.

In the late 1990s, fighting erupted in Indonesia through what Damanik has called "corruption and favoritism." Commenting on this violence, he said that "this is not a religious conflict. The real causes are the injustices we live with."

It was for justice and an end to the corruption that Kongkoli fought. He offered life in the form of justice and freedom for the oppressed and victimized. He often spoke out against governing authorities who failed to properly investigate incidents of violence in the region.

He and Damanik had a passion to protect the victims of the violence, beyond the bounds of ethnicity or religion. Amazed by their love, a Muslim refugee wrote a letter stating that he had been a victim of the violence and had received aid by evacuating to one of the Crisis Centers. "Even though we differ in religion," he stated, "their hearts...were extraordinary."

Pastor Irianto Kongkoli bore many titles and lived out many roles: father, husband, pastor, beloved friend, defender of the oppressed, and a voice of justice for the wronged. But perhaps he will be most remembered as one who bore the scars and the wounds that come through suffering, the marks of love.

"A SHADOW OF A DOG CAN'T BITE YOU, AND A SHADOW OF DEATH CAN'T KILL YOU. YOU CAN KILL US OR PUT US IN PRISON, BUT NOTHING BAD CAN HAPPEN TO US."

—A PASTOR WHO WAS FACED WITH THE THREAT OF ARREST AND TORTURE BY POLICE WHO BURST INTO HIS HOME AS HE, HIS WIFE, AND HIS SIX SMALL CHILDREN FINISHED READING PSALM 23

İmmanuel Andegeresgh and Kibrom Firemichel

(October 17, 2006)

ight had fallen as the men left their houses, silently closing the doors behind them. They each stood still a few frozen, breathless seconds and looked cautiously both ways down the street before they dared move. Confident of their concealment, they quietly and carefully set off in the direction of the meeting place, following the contours of shadows and dark lanes to veil their journey.

When they arrived, they were greeted by the warm and familiar faces of their brothers and sisters who had also gathered to fellowship together. For all of them, including two men, Immanuel Andergeresgh and Kibrom Firemichel, this was the only opportunity to worship their Savior together in a community, their only hope for true fellowship, and they were entrusting their lives to all of those present. They had become all too accustomed to the laws forbidding open worship in Eritrea. The fear and hesitation melted away as they began to worship and share together.

It came as both an intrusion and a distress when a loud hammering at the door broke their praise. The singing stopped. The gathered believers exchanged wide-eyed and knowing glances. They knew immediately what it meant: Their meeting had been discovered, and they would be arrested, detained, and possibly tortured for breaking the law.

Since 2002, only the Orthodox, Roman Catholic, and Lutheran churches have been recognized in Eritrea, along with Islam. Numerous evangelical Christians have been arrested for practicing what officials call a "new religion." Since that time, thousands of Christians have been placed in prisons where they face deplorable conditions, some held in metal shipping containers in temperatures that can soar above 100 degrees Fahrenheit or drop below freezing.

Within moments the door was forced open to reveal several uniformed security police, members of a task force specifically established to eradicate all menfesawyan, or "spirituals," a term often used to describe Christians not belonging to one of the recognized churches.

Andergeresgh, twenty-three years old, Firemichel, thirty, and eight others were arrested and taken to a military confinement camp. There they were subjected to torture and "furious mistreatment," according to one of the other believers. At the end of two days, Andergeresgh and Firemichel both died of severe dehydration and injuries sustained in the torture.

In the end, the two men dared to gather with other believers because they understood the life-giving effects of sharing in the bonds of brotherhood. They understood the risks, but could not deny that to be united with Christ meant to be bound to one another in love and encouragement, gifts that far outweighed the risks.

THEREFORE DO NOT BE ASHAMED OF
THE TESTIMONY ABOUT OUR LORD,
NOR OF ME HIS PRISONER, BUT
SHARE IN SUFFERING FOR THE GOSPEL
BY THE POWER OF GOD.

2 TIMOTHY 1:8

2007—2011

CHRISTIANAH OLUWATOYIN OLUSASE
(MARCH 21, 2007)

The day started out like any other school day for teacher Christianah Oluwatoyin Olusase. There was nothing to suggest that anything out of the ordinary might happen, though as a Christian teacher in predominantly Muslim northern Nigeria, she surely understood the risk to her life that daily hovered. Still, Olusase took her work seriously and was open about her faith. It was not a secret that she was a Christian, and this is what eventually led to her death.

It was time for an Islamic Religious Knowledge exam at the Government Day Secondary School in Gombe, Nigeria, where Olusase taught. As was her custom during any test, she collected the students' bags, books, and papers, and set them aside for the girls to pick up after completing their tests. She then handed out the examination papers. Somewhere during this routine activity, one of the girls grew very upset and began spreading the word to the other students that a copy of the Koran—the Islamic holy book—had been in her bag. She supposedly didn't agree with the way her teacher had handled it, and she accused Olusase of desecrating the Koran by touching it since she was a Christian.

The other students in the all-girl class agreed, and the situation soon escalated as they began chanting *"Allahu Akbar!"* (Allah is great!") The girls then got out of their seats and swarmed their teacher. They threw stones from outside at her, used heavy objects to club her, and eventually beat her to death. Afterward, they dragged her body outside the classroom and set it on fire.

The shocking circumstance of Christianah Oluwatoyin Olusase's death is not an isolated incident. A similar incident occurred in February 2006 in the neighboring state of Bauchi when a secondary school teacher, also a Christian, supposedly confiscated a Koran from a student. This teacher also was accused of desecrating the Koran, and a riot ensued in which five people were killed and several churches burned down. Other Nigerian Christians have been beaten, kidnapped, threatened, intimidated, and even killed by Muslims in a country that is sharply divided between Christian and Muslim. Though Islam claims to be a religion of peace, every day is a risk for Christians in Northern Nigeria who seek to spread the Gospel of true peace and love. But it is a risk that will plant seeds of faith and salvation and reap an eternal reward, as testified in the story of Christianah Oluwatoyin Olusase. She certainly knew the stories of fellow persecuted Christians in Nigeria, and she daily understood the risk to her own life. Yet that didn't deter her from making her faith known.

AND DO NOT FEAR THOSE WHO KILL THE BODY BUT CANNOT KILL THE SOUL.

MATTHEW 10:28

Ugur Yüksel, Necati Aydin, and Tilmann Geske martyred in Turkey

Necati Aydin, Tilmann Geske, and Ugur Yüksel
(April 18, 2007)

On the morning of April 18, 2007, two Turkish Muslim men, Emre Günaydin and Abuzer Yildirim, came into the office of Zirve Publishing, a Christian publishing company that distributes Christian literature in Eastern Turkey. Supposedly the young men wanted to learn more about the Christian faith, as they had a few times in the weeks before.

Necati Aydin, the pastor of the Protestant church in Malatya, wanted to use this opportunity to tell the young men about Jesus, even though he had previously told his wife, Semse, that he did not think the men's interest was very genuine. Aydin did not know that they had brought two knives and a blank pistol with them this time.

Besides Aydin, Tilmann Geske was also in the office. He was a forty-six-year-old German Christian who had been living in Turkey for years, and aside from his job as an English teacher, he had been assisting in the church that Aydin led. In addition, Ugur Yüksel, age thirty-two, came to the office. From the nearby city of Elazig, he had been working at Zirve Publishing for about a year.

According to Turkish hospitality, tea was served. After a short conversation the doorbell rang. Günaydin explained that he wanted to have three additional friends there for the discussion. Then Hamit Ceker, Cuma Özdemir, and Salih Gürler came in and joined the three Christians.

They brought three more large knives, adequate clothesline, and plastic gloves—all of which they had hidden in plastic bags. Besides this they had two blank pistols, which at first glance are difficult even for experts to distinguish from real weapons.

The exact sequence of events that followed has not been completely reconstructed. Later, in court, the murderers tried to accuse each other and gave contradictory testimony. A rough outline of the crime seems to be: The young men threatened Aydin, Yüksel, and Geske with the pistols and knives. Then all three Christians had their arms and legs bound and were thrown face-down to the floor. The three Christians were verbally abused, "interrogated," and most likely commanded to reject their beliefs.

When the judge later asked the murderers if the victims had made no replies, the record of their testimony shows how peaceful the three must have been even in the face of death. The record also shows that Yüksel called out to Christ as his brothers were murdered.

One of the murderers tried to strangle Aydin with clothesline. When Semse heard about this later, she was appalled, because one of her husband's greatest fears was that of being in close quarters and unable to breathe.

All three Christians were then tortured; they were stabbed and kicked all over their bodies. The official autopsy report would show strangulation marks and six stab or cut wounds for Aydin, sixteen stab or cut wounds for Geske, and fourteen for Yüksel.

The murderers finished their cruelty by kneeling on the backs of their victims, cutting their carotid arteries, and then letting them bleed to death.

Gökhan, another worker in the Malatya church, and his wife, Özge, arrived at the door of the publishing house just before 1 p.m. After Gökhan realized that the office door was locked and the key was still in the lock on the other side, he tried to reach his brethren in the faith on his cell phone. Aydin and Geske could no longer answer; they were already dead.

The murderers forced Yüksel to speak into the phone: "We're at the Golden Apricot Hotel for a meeting. You can meet us there." Ten days earlier they had celebrated Easter in a room they had rented at the hotel, but what could they have been doing there at that time? Yüksel's voice sounded unusual and pained; Gokhan called the police.

As the police were nearing the crime scene, Yüksel's throat was cut. Despite the transfusion of fifty units of blood, he died at 6:30 that evening.

Christians make up less than 1 percent of the population of seventy million in Turkey, a secular country that claims freedom of religion in its constitution. Most of the population, however, is Muslim, and persecution (including discrimination, death threats, and vandalism) against Christians has risen steadily in recent years, especially with Christians being negatively portrayed in the media. Christian evangelical groups have been presented on the same level as terrorist groups such as al-Qaeda. The National Security Council of Turkey has claimed that evangelical Christians pose a threat to Turkey's national security.

It has been a paradoxical reality throughout history that persecution doesn't destroy Christianity, but instead only serves to expand it. Jesus Himself prepared His followers for such a reality when He said, "If the world hates you, know that it has hated me before it hated you...If they persecuted me, they will also persecute you ... But all these things they will do to you on account of my name, because they do not know him who sent me...Indeed, the hour is coming when whoever kills you will think he is offering service to God...In the world you will have tribulation. But take heart; I have overcome the world" (John 15:18, 20-21; 16:2, 33).

When Tilmann Geske's widow, Susanne, was asked to make a statement regarding her husband's killers, she borrowed the words of Christ by saying, "Oh God, forgive them, for they know not what they do." Semse, too, spoke on national television in Turkey about forgiving the men who had taken the life of her husband. The widows' statement of forgiveness swept through Turkey, on the front pages of all the prominent newspapers and on live national TV, showing the power of God to use even the death of His faithful ones to fulfill His plans of bringing light to all people that they might know the love of Christ.

Even Muslims recognized the effect the murders and the widows' forgiveness had on the nation. The editorial writer of a large Turkish newspaper wrote a couple of days later: "The murderers wanted to hinder the activities of the missionaries. But what these women have facilitated in a few days by their statements is something that a thousand missionaries could not have done in a thousand years."

And most of the brothers,
having become confident in the
Lord by my imprisonment, are
much more bold to speak the
word without fear.

Philippians 1:14

ΠiGisti Haile

(September 5, 2007)

T hirty-three-year-old Nigisti Haile was a determined woman who found strength in Jesus Christ. From the northeastern African country of Eritrea, she daily faced the possibility of threat and danger because of her Christian faith. Years before, in 2002, the country had banned all independent Protestant church gatherings, whether private or public, closing church buildings and in effect outlawing the Protestant religion. Since then it recognizes only Islam, Orthodox Christianity, Lutheranism, and Catholicism as official state religions. Despite this, Haile continued, like many other Eritrean Christians, to maintain involvement in her independent Protestant church group. At the same time, she was dedicated to improving herself; she worked diligently for a relative while studying to achieve a high-school level of education. She lived her life well, working hard and learning all she could. She enjoyed soaking in the truths of Jesus Christ, sharing them throughout her life, gaining joy, strength, and courage for the trial she would face—and which she would overcome.

One day as Haile was gathered with other believers for fellowship and worship in the village of Keren, Eritrean authorities stormed in, broke up the meeting, and arrested her along with nine other single Christian women. For breaking the law by participating in an unregistered church gathering, they were arrested and held at Wa'i Military Training Center for several months. During that time, Haile was tortured and pressured to sign a letter renouncing her Christian faith. She suffered harsh conditions and cruel treatment in prison, with little to no medical attention, and was most likely subjected to forced labor. Through it all she held firm to her belief in Christ, knowing that what was being asked of her was more than just saying or writing a few meaningless words. She was being asked to deny her Lord, and that she would never do. She may have thought of Jesus's words in Matthew 10:32-33: "So everyone who acknowledges me before men, I also will acknowledge before my Father who is in heaven, but whoever denies me before men, I also will deny before my Father who is in heaven."

Her jailers continued to torture her, most likely in hopes that the pain and threat of death would supersede her bold claims of faith and trust in Christ. But they didn't, and after months of persecution, on September 5, 2007, Nigisti Haile was tortured to death. Hers was the fourth such incident in less than a year. Three other Christians within the previous year had also been arrested for unlawful worship. They had died from a combination of torture wounds and medical conditions such as pneumonia and dehydration.

Like the other 2,800 Eritrean Christians who are currently imprisoned for their faith, Haile was held without charge and denied any form of legal counsel or a trial. She refused to give up her belief in Jesus Christ, knowing that her faith was "more precious than gold that perishes though it is tested by fire," and that it would "be found to result in praise and glory and honor at the revelation of Jesus Christ" (1 Peter 1:7).

"THE DUNGEON BECAME TO ME AS IT WERE A PALACE, SO THAT I PREFERRED BEING THERE TO BEING ELSEWHERE."

—PERPETUA, MARTYRED AD 203

Rami Ayyad

(October 6, 2007)

◆

I t was early evening. Rami Ayyad had just stepped out of his Christian bookstore in Gaza City to close for the night when a car pulled up and three men stepped out to grab him. The unidentified men, two of them wearing masks, forced Ayyad into the backseat of the car and drove away. The attack surprised him, but was not fully unexpected, as he had earlier noticed a car with no license plates following him. As the manager of Gaza's only Christian bookstore, he had also received several death threats throughout the course of his work. Though he knew the risks involved, Ayyad had continued to run The Teacher's Bookshop.

Owned and operated by The Palestinian Bible Society, The Teacher's Bookshop was more than just a bookstore offering Bibles and other Christian books and resources. Ayyad's ministry there included computer classes and other educational opportunities for the citizens of Gaza, many of whom are uneducated, jobless, and living in poverty. So beloved was the bookstore that after a small bombing several months before, which caused a temporary closing of the shop, people rallied together in a demonstration to persuade The Bible Society to reopen it. In addition to his work with The Bible Society, Ayyad was also a leader of the Awanas club and the summer children's camp at his church.

Ayyad believed in his work, so he continued on despite the bombings and death threats he received from militant Islamic groups. On the evening of October 6, 2007, those threats became a reality for him. As he sat in the backseat of the car with his kidnappers, Ayyad had just enough time to call his wife, Pauline, to try to encourage her. "I'm going with some young men somewhere, but I'll be home soon," he said, his calm voice expressing his trust in the Lord and peace in the middle of the frightening situation. He later called his mother as well, telling her that he should only be with the "people" for another couple of hours, but if he was not back by then, he might not be back for a long time.

Ayyad was taken just a few blocks from his store, and questioning and torture ensued. His attackers beat him with clubs and the butt ends of their guns, accusing him of evangelizing in order to spread Christianity. Most likely he was told to accept Islam and Islamic law, but he refused. The men continued to beat and stab Ayyad, and when the torture and threats proved futile on the man so resolute and strong in his faith, they finally shot him to death. His body was found early the next morning. His murderers were never identified.

Ayyad's pregnant wife and their two children continued to receive threats to their safety, and were eventually transported out of the Gaza Strip into Israel.

In a place where Islam reigns and the small percentage of Christians are increasingly threatened and pressured to accept Islamic law in return for their safety, the odds were against Rami Ayyad. He didn't let fear for his own life deter him from doing the Lord's work, caring for people, and spreading the message of the Gospel. His life and death will continue to encourage Christians around the world to stand firm in all things. As a Christian worker in Gaza said after Ayyad's death, "All things work together for good. God has a purpose for letting this happen. It will not silence the church."

Tulu Mosisa
(March 2, 2008)

Tulu Mosisa was just a simple farm laborer who loved the Lord. He worked in the remote village of Nensebo Chebi in southern Ethiopia in order to support his wife and five children, who remained at home in another village. He also worshiped at a Protestant church there: Kale Hiwot Baptist Church.

During the regular Sunday morning worship service, as Mosisa and his Christian brothers and sisters were in the middle of prayer, men armed with knives and machetes stormed into the church building. At the same time, about a half hour's walk away at Birhane Wongel Baptist Church, more armed men interrupted the service. They were militant Muslims, charged by their religious beliefs to cleanse the Muslim-dominated area of Christians.

Mosisa had come to church that morning alone—his family was not with him—but the congregation was ,composed of people of all ages, including women and children. The believers looked on helplessly as their attackers barred all the church doors and windows, and then came at them with their weapons.

"Allahu Akbar!" ("Allah is great!") the attackers shouted as they swung their knives and machetes. The people were defenseless; they screamed and ran in all directions to avoid their assailants, but at least twenty-three were injured, two even losing their hands. Mosisa was killed when an attacker swung at him with a machete, nearly beheading him. The violence finally ceased when members of the local militia arrived and drove the men off. Several suspects were arrested, but none of the attackers were officially identified.

At the time of the attack, 45 percent of Ethiopia's population was Muslim, reportedly practicing a tolerant version of Islam. However, according to the Ethiopian Islamic Affairs Supreme Council, Ethiopia's Muslims have been increasingly influenced by Wahhabi Islam. Based on the teachings of Muhammad al-Wahhab, who lived in the eighteenth century, Wahhabism is an extremist sect of Islam that seeks to reinstate a pure, historical Islam that adheres strictly and solely to the original teachings of the prophet Muhammad. Thus, it rejects all things modern and secular, including reinterpretation of the Koran. It opposes the nineteenth- and twentieth-century Muslim reform movements that have sought to reinterpret parts of Islamic law to bring it closer to Western standards. According to Wahhabi Muslims, theirs is the only true Islam. Any other form of Islam is a false path, and Muslims who practice other forms of Islam are not true Muslims.

It takes daily courage and strength—unwavering trust and hope in the Lord—to live knowing that each day might be your last. Tulu Mosisa's dedication to his faith was evident in his life, and his example through his death spread to his family. When his wife, Chaltu Waga, was visited by a Christian support organization after the incident, she greeted them with smiles and enthusiasm.

"God is great," she proclaimed in the local language. Though devastated by her husband's death, she explained how she had been greatly encouraged by visits from Christian friends. She said of her husband, "Although it is painful, I understand that he was killed for his faith."

Jesus said, "And you will be hated by all for my name's sake" (Mark 13:13). Sometimes that hate manifests itself in bodily death to the believer. Tulu Mosisa was not afraid of death. He lived bravely and continued to meet regularly with other believers though it eventually cost him his life, for he knew the promise of his Lord that "the one who endures to the end will be saved" (Mark 13:13).

✠

ORISSA ATTACKS
(AUGUST 2008)

◆

India's Orissa state has frequently been a hotspot of anti-Christian violence by Hindu fundamentalists. One of the worst cases, called a genocide, occurred in August 2008 when Hindu mobs attacked the Christian community in retaliation for the murder of a beloved Hindu religious leader, Laxmanananda Saraswati, and four of his followers. Saraswati was assassinated on August 23, 2008, and local Christians were blamed for it by Hindu extremist groups, particularly those of the World Hindu Council (VHP), which is believed to be behind most of the anti-Christian violence in Orissa state.

The day after Saraswati's assassination, the state's ruling Hindu nationalist party, the BJP, along with the VHP, called for a twelve-hour shutdown to protest the Hindu leader's murder. During this time, speeches were allegedly made accusing Christians of his death even though police cited evidence that linked the murder to Maoist rebels. They then paraded Saraswati's body through the streets of nearby villages, arousing anti-Christian sentiment and inciting the people to avenge his murder.

"Kill Christians and destroy their institutions," they shouted among other slogans and chants.

Defying curfew and other district-imposed regulations, hundreds of angry Hindus gathered and proceeded to attack Christians all over Orissa state. In the ensuing days, pastors and Christian leaders were targeted and killed; Christian homes and churches were burned down; Christian organizations and shops were looted and vandalized; a missionary-run orphanage was set on fire; villagers were pulled from their homes and beaten or killed; and women were raped. In at least three hundred villages, thousands of people were attacked and displaced from their homes, forced to flee and go into hiding. Many found refuge in the surrounding forests and jungles, but were exposed to inclement weather, hunger, and starvation. The violence trickled down through September and into surrounding states, with fewer, though connected, incidents involving church burnings, church leaders receiving death threats, and forced conversions of Christians to Hinduism.

Around ninety-two incidents of violence were reported in fourteen districts around the state, mainly within the Kandhamal district. At least four thousand houses and 115 church buildings were burned or destroyed. Statistics on the death toll differ, but it is believed in total that more than five hundred Christians were killed. Many of the victims were dalits, or "untouchables," on the lowest tier of India's caste system. Making up around 60 percent of India's population, dalits have responded to the call of Christ in overwhelming numbers, making them likely targets for Hindu extremists who hope to preserve India's traditional religious and cultural roots.

The authorities and the media in Orissa downplayed the violence and refused to see the attacks as organized though it was the second such case of mass attacks in Orissa state. December 2007 saw the first when Hindu radicals in Brahmanigaon, Phulbani district, protested the erection of an arch and a tent for a Christmas service, though the Christian community had gained permission beforehand. A riot broke out and twelve Christians were killed, two thousand homes destroyed, Christian shops looted and destroyed, and four Gospel for Asia churches damaged.

Although India's Christian minority constitutes about 2 percent of the country's population, violence against Christians in and around Orissa state continues largely unabated. Not only are Christians harassed, but churches and Christian organizations are looted, vandalized, and set on fire regularly, all acts which aim to strike fear and intimidation into the hearts of believers. But courage and hope remain despite the odds.

GAYLE WILLIAMS

(OCTOBER 20, 2008)

G ayle Williams walked cheerfully to work that morning. It was still early—before eight o'clock. She used a familiar route, one of many that she took partly for a change of scene and partly for safety measures, though she didn't really expect anything to happen. Kabul was, after all, the capital city and relatively safe, and she had worked for SERVE Afghanistan, an aid organization based out of Britain, for two and a half years without incident. For a short time she had been in another city—Kandahar, in the south of the country—but after receiving reports of Taliban insurgents coming in, it was considered too dangerous and she was moved back to Kabul.

Hers was one of many Christian humanitarian aid organizations in the country, and she loved being a part of what God was doing. Her heart beat for the needy of Afghanistan, for the helpless and the marginalized, and so she had come to serve them. She worked primarily with the disabled in their homes, helping to rehabilitate them. She helped direct projects that would allow the disabled to gain better education and better opportunities for their lives. She also helped raise awareness of disabilities and trained Afghan staff on how to work with the disabled.

She walked on toward the office that morning, anticipating all she had to do that day. The sound of a motorbike caught her attention as it came roaring up the street toward her. Williams glanced at it. Two men were on the motorbike, and they seemed to be watching her as they drew closer. Suddenly the motorbike stopped just in front of her, and one of the men drew a pistol, pointed it at her, and fired several shots. Williams was killed almost immediately as bullets pierced her body and her leg.

The Taliban openly claimed responsibility for the attack, saying that Gayle Williams had been targeted because she worked for an organization that preached Christianity. But SERVE Afghanistan, like many other Christian humanitarian organizations in the country, focuses on aid and service, not preaching. Williams would have known that in Afghanistan proselytizing—trying to convert a person from one religion to another—is illegal. She had come to show Christ's love to the Afghan people in a tangible, practical way by serving them and ministering to their needs. The love of Christ was shown through her actions, not through words.

The thirty-four-year-old British aid worker had early on developed a passion for working with the disabled. Having gone to school in both Britain and South Africa (with a dual citizenship), she had completed a sports degree, was a trained fitness instructor, and worked with students with special needs in London, all before volunteering with SERVE Afghanistan. She was a very active and athletic person, which served her well in working with the disabled. Her background, education, and interests all collided into a passion for them. After her death, her mother said of her, "Gayle was serving a people that she loved, and felt God called her to be there for such a time as this…We know her life was blessed and she was a blessing to those around her…She died doing what she felt the Lord had called her [to do] and she is definitely with Him."

AFTER THIS I LOOKED, AND BEHOLD, A GREAT MULTITUDE THAT NO ONE COULD NUMBER, FROM EVERY NATION, FROM ALL TRIBES AND PEOPLES AND LANGUAGES, STANDING BEFORE THE THRONE AND BEFORE THE LAMB, CLOTHED IN WHITE ROBES, WITH PALM BRANCHES IN THEIR HANDS.

REVELATION 7:9

Dora Lilia and Ferley Saavedra

(November 18, 2008)

The small number of children in the village of Santana Ramos in Colombia enjoyed coming to school and learning from their teacher, Dora Lilia Saavedra. She prayed with them every day and told them about Jesus while they learned. She also sometimes traveled for hours to more distant villages, where there were no teachers, to help the children there. She was a good, loving teacher. But one day in November, the children's ordinary school day was interrupted when two men with guns, wearing army fatigues and boots, walked into the one-room schoolhouse and told the children to leave.

"There will be no more school today. Go home and return tomorrow," they said gruffly.

The children quickly gathered their belongings and slipped out of the schoolhouse, wondering what was going to happen.

Dora Lilia and her husband, Ferley Saavedra, who also taught at the school, knew what was going to happen, and they were prepared. These men who had come for them were guerrilla soldiers with the Revolutionary Armed Forces of Colombia (FARC), a Marxist movement characterized by threat, force, and violence. For decades they have terrorized Colombians, targeting Christians in particular. "Christians are dangerous," they say. "Christians cannot lie. If the army asks them about us, they will tell the truth!" They also don't like that Christians stand opposed to violence, which is the principal way of life for the guerrillas. They recruit members at a young age since the life expectancy of a guerrilla is short, and they don't want anything or anyone to stand in their way or to weaken their cause. The Saavedras stood in their way by teaching children, for if the children knew about the love of Jesus and became Christians, they would not join the guerrillas' cause.

Dora Lilia and Ferley Saavedra shot to death in Colombia

Dora Lilia knew the risks when she returned to Santana Ramos to teach. A poor rural farming village marked by violence between the FARC guerrillas and the Colombian government, Santana Ramos was Dora Lilia's home, and she hoped, through her love of teaching, to bring the light of Jesus there. This is exactly what she and her husband did, and it was also why their lives were threatened. But even when Dora Lilia was warned by a neighbor that she and her husband would be killed the following day, the farthest thing from her mind was to take her family and flee the village, though she was advised to do so.

Instead of panic, relief poured over her at the neighbor's words. Earlier, this man had come to tell Dora Lilia that her brother was going to be killed. Now the neighbor was correcting his statement. "I have made a mistake," he said. "It is not your brother who will be killed tomorrow... but it is you and your husband."

"This is better," Dora Lilia told him. "My brother was not ready to meet the Lord. But my husband and I are."

She refused to let fear keep her from her work, and instead drew closer to her family and to the Lord for peace and preparation. That evening the couple led their children in family devotions. They prayed and read the Bible together.

"Mommy may be going to sleep tomorrow for a long time," Dora Lilia told her oldest daughter.

After the kids were in bed, the couple spent much of the night praying and fasting, reminiscent of Jesus's time with His Father in prayer in the garden of Gethsemane when He prayed, "not my will, but yours, be done" (Luke 22:42). When morning came, the Saavedras headed to the school as usual, knowing that their lives, and those of their children, were in the Lord's hands.

After the soldiers marched in and the students had been sent away, the guerrillas told the couple to say goodbye to their own children. Suddenly, more guerrillas entered, their big boots treading heavily on the wooden floorboards. One of them pointed at the oldest child, Marcella. "We will kill her first!" he shouted.

"No, please," Dora Lilia pleaded. She stepped in front of the man to shield her daughter from him. "It is me you want. Take me. Leave her here and take me now."

The crying children were left behind as Dora Lilia and Ferley were taken out of the schoolhouse and led across a field to a river about three hundred yards away. The guerrillas ordered the couple to lie face-down on the ground, where they were each shot to death.

The Saavedras daily lived out the love of Christ. So influential were their lives that just months after their death, twelve-year-old Marcella was able to say, "If I met the men who did this I would forgive them. I know this would be hard, but I know God forgives them. So I have to as well." Through her parents' example, this little girl had learned love and forgiveness in place of hatred and bitterness. It is certain that many other children have learned that lesson as well and will continue to share it because two teachers were willing to risk their lives to bring Christ's love and truth to a place where it was most needed.

RE𝑘OICE IN HOPE, BE PATIENT IN TRIBULATION, BE CONSTANT IN PRAYER. BLESS THOSE WHO PERSECUTE YOU; BLESS AND DO NOT CURSE THEM.

ROMANS 12:12,14

Fatima Al-Mutairi

(December 2008)

atima Al-Mutairi had been locked in her room. Though she was hardly a child at twenty-six years of age, she had been confined to her room by her brother to punish her for her "disobedience." She had just proclaimed to her family that she was a Christian. Though she knew it would likely mean death—a Saudi Muslim abandoning her faith generally equates to the death penalty—Al-Mutairi boldly stood her ground and didn't keep her beliefs a secret. She had returned to her bedroom soon after to find her brother sitting at her open laptop, where, like journal entries, she had kept written notes about her conversion and spiritual journey. He seemed to be looking for proof of what she had spoken to her family about—evidence to use against her. He was, after all, a Muslim cleric and member of Saudi Arabia's Commission of the Promotion of Virtue and Prevention of Vice. He might claim he was merely doing his job, despite the fact that Al-Mutairi was his own sister. Incensed at this new knowledge about his sister, he left Al-Mutairi alone and locked her in her room.

Al-Mutairi didn't know how long she would be locked away or what would happen afterward. She knew her time might be limited. She went to the only place she knew she had any voice and freedom: her computer. The majority of her fellowship with other believers had been found on internet forums. That was where she had learned and been fed with the truths of Christ that had come pouring into her life. Though coming from a strict, traditional Islamic area, she loved her country and her people, and desired that same Light that had illuminated her life to flood Saudi Arabia as well. Instead of keeping the truth about Christ to herself in what could be her last moments on earth, she used her computer as a medium of truth. She considered the words of Psalm 27:1, which say "The LORD is my light and my salvation; whom shall I fear? The LORD is the stronghold of my life; of whom shall I be afraid?" She took comfort in these words as she composed a final letter. She then wrote and posted a poem online.

"May the Lord Jesus guide you, Oh Muslims / And enlighten your hearts that you might love others," she wrote. The words poured out of her as she courageously proclaimed Jesus Christ as the Master of the prophets (a title designated for Muhammad in Islam), the Clear Truth and the Lord of the worlds (terms designated for Allah in Islam). She described the Saudi Christians' love for their homeland and pride in their citizenship. She expressed her sorrow at the cruel treatment of Saudi Christians.

> *There are tears on my cheek, and Oh! the heart is sad*
> *To those who become Christians, how you are so cruel!*
> *And the Messiah says, 'Blessed are the Persecuted'*
> *And we for the sake of Christ all things bear*
> *What is it to you that we are infidels?*
> *You do not enter our graves, as if with us buried*
> *Enough—your swords do not concern me, not evil nor disgrace*
> *Your threats do not trouble me, and we are not afraid*
> *And by God, I am unto death a Christian — Verily ...*
> *We are Christians—in the path of Christ we tread*
> *Take from me this word, and note it well*
> *You see, Jesus is my Lord, and He is the Best of protectors*
> *I advise you to pity yourself, to clap your hands in mourning*
> *See your look of ugly hatred*
> *Man is brother to man, Oh learned ones*
> *Where is the humanity, the love, and where are you?*

And finally, as she sat with her laptop open before her and her fingers hovering over the keys, she wrote her final words to the poem, appealing to her fellow Muslims to embrace Christ.

As to my last words, I pray to the Lord of the worlds
Jesus the Messiah, the Light of Clear Guidance
That He change notions, and set the scales of justice aright
And that He spread Love among you, Oh Muslims.

Al-Mutairi's brother kept her locked in her room for four hours, after which she was killed for her profession of faith in Jesus Christ. Her courage in the face of death and the words she shared will remain as a testimony and inspiration to believers everywhere.

THEY WERE STONED, THEY WERE SAWN IN TWO, THEY WERE KILLED WITH THE SWORD. THEY WENT ABOUT IN SKINS OF SHEEP AND GOATS, DESTITUTE, AFFLICTED, MISTREATED —OF WHOM THE WORLD WAS NOT WORTHY— WANDERING ABOUT IN DESERTS AND MOUNTAINS, AND IN DENS AND CAVES OF THE EARTH.

HEBREWS 11:37-38

NEPAL BOMBING
(MAY 23, 2009)

Morning light flooded through the church windows while people settled into their seats as the service began in Kathmandu, Nepal. The beautifully decorated church hall was a refuge for the three hundred who gathered there that morning to pray and hear God's Word, finding joy, comfort, and wisdom in the fellowship and worship. The officiating pastor took the pulpit and spoke, and people bowed their heads in prayer.

From the entrance in the back of the church hall, a young man and woman entered, their faces grave. The woman, carrying a large black handbag, moved forward quickly and quietly, sitting down next to some of the other parishioners. She set the handbag on the seat next to her and waited, distractedly watching the pastor up front and occasionally glancing around. After a few minutes, she turned to the middle-aged couple sitting next to her.

"Where is the bathroom?" she asked.

"Back near the entrance," the couple informed her.

The woman stood, leaving her handbag behind on the seat, and disappeared from the building with the man. Some of the churchgoers glanced curiously at the bag, though others thought nothing of it and continued in prayer, their heads bowed and eyes closed, their lips moving soundlessly.

Within minutes an explosive blast tore through the hall, shattering windows and tossing worshipers from their seats. Nails and shrapnel flew through the air, piercing and injuring people. Flames and smoke filled the sanctuary. In a split second, the peaceful atmosphere of the church had turned to chaos as women screamed, children cried, and people ran around, trying to find the exit. Several injured people were sprawled across the ground, lying in pools of blood; fifteen-year-old Celeste Joseph's body lay lifeless on the ground. She had been killed immediately by the explosion. Her mother, Buddha Laxmi Joseph, died later of a hemorrhage. Thirty-year-old Deepa Patrick, a newlywed from India who had been visiting her family in Nepal, died on the way to the hospital.

As police and ambulances arrived on the scene, a second bomb was discovered and disarmed. Scattered throughout the debris were several green leaflets from an extremist Hindu organization called the Nepal Defense Army (NDA). A day after the bombing, Bishop Narayan Sharma of the Protestant Believers' Church in Nepal received a call from the leader of this organization. Although the leader "expressed regret for the death of innocent people," the bishop recounted, "he said his organization wanted the restoration of Hinduism as the state religion."

Though the majority of Nepal's population is Hindu, the country abolished its centuries-old Hindu monarchy in favor of a republic, and in 2006 the government declared Nepal a secular state. Christians (and even Muslims) in Nepal have faced persecution from two main sects: extremist Hindu groups hoping to reinstate the monarchial government of the past and/or restore Nepal to an exclusively Hindu state, or Maoist groups wishing to impose an atheistic Communist regime. Hindu converts to Christianity may also be threatened and ill-treated by members of their families or villages for abandoning their faith and for refusing to participate in Hindu religious practices.

Despite all this, the small number of Christians in Nepal continues to thrive and grow, undaunted in the face of persecution and death, choosing to believe that the love and peace of Christ will supersede the hate and violence of their attackers. At a nationwide peace rally held a week after the bombing, Silas Bogati, the pastor leading the service at the time of the attack, said, "We are holding prayers to show our solidarity and religious tolerance...Some armed groups are trying to disturb religious harmony in Nepal but they will never be successful."

Gojra Christians attacked by a Muslim mob

Gojra Attack
(July/August 2009)

On August 1, 2009, thousands of Muslim supremacists, including members of banned terrorist groups, led a demonstration in the town of Gojra in northeastern Pakistan to protest the supposed desecration of the Koran by Christians. The protest evolved into a riot as Muslims swarmed a Christian neighborhood with sticks, clubs, firearms, stones, bricks, and flammable substances, attacking the residents. They pillaged and burned the houses and other property. A church building was set on fire and destroyed. Main roads and railways were blockaded to keep out the fire brigades. Leaders at local mosques began broadcasting messages, saying that those "who love Muhammad and Islam should gather…to defend Islam because it is in danger."

The riot escalated. Women and children were injured in the house fires, but because of all the blockades and road closures, many were unable to make it to hospitals for immediate medical attention. By the end of the riot at least one hundred houses had been looted, fifty homes burned down, one church destroyed, fourteen people killed, and nineteen others injured. Security measures had been taken by police before the riot, but the effect was minimal at best. It was only after Christian survivors placed the bodies of the deceased along railway tracks as a kind of protest that authorities finally filed formal reports against the perpetrators.

Just days before, on July 30, the village of Korian, only seven miles from Gojra, was also attacked. Most of the Christian villagers fled to safety, but at least sixty homes were ransacked and then burned to the ground.

The attacks at Korian and Gojra were fueled by rumors of blasphemy which began with an incident on July 25. During a Christian wedding ceremony, the guests tossed coins and paper currency into the air, letting the children catch the money as it fell, all according to tradition. There was music, laughter, and celebration. Nearby, a Muslim funeral was in progress at the same time, and apparently the noise from the wedding ceremony disrupted the funeral. On the following day, certain Muslims visited with the bride's parents, claiming their sons had cut pages out of the Koran to resemble paper currency, which they had then used as confetti during the wedding ceremony. (Some children may have cut pages out of an old schoolbook, unaware that the pages contained verses from the Koran, as has been reported.) The father of the bride, Talib Masih, assured the Muslims that the incident hadn't occurred, but that he would talk with his sons and have them apologize in case they had done anything offensive. The Muslims then jumped on the man, beating him unconscious. A few days later Muslim clerics sent out a broadcast accusing "infidel Christians" of profaning the Koran and warning them to leave the area unless they wanted to be killed. The Korian and Gojra attacks immediately followed, and are considered one of the worst cases of Christian persecution in Pakistan.

In the mainly Muslim nation of Pakistan, Christians constitute less than 5 percent of the total population, which is around 175 million. Gojra, in Punjab province, is the headquarters of the Anglican Church of Pakistan, and the province itself is home to most of the country's Christian minority. It is also the home base of at least forty militant Islamic groups, some linked to the Taliban and al-Qaeda. Strict and outdated blasphemy laws exist in the country, which are repeatedly misused in order to carry out militant agendas against Christians.

An astounding faith is one that faces death every day for the sake of Christ. Jesus said, "If anyone would come after me, let him deny himself and take up his cross and follow me" (Matthew 16:24). Pakistani Christians follow this mandate literally to the point of death. They die for nothing other than lifting up the name of Christ and bearing the title of Christian; but in their brave sacrifice they find that their story is not over. "For whoever would save his life will lose it, but whoever loses his life for my sake will find it" (Matthew 16:25).

MANUEL CAMACHO

(SEPTEMBER 21, 2009)

Pastor Manuel Camacho, with his wife and children nearby, watched as soldiers with the FARC (Revolutionary Armed Forces of Colombia) stepped out of the surrounding jungle and moved toward his home. They had come on appointment, as he supposed, to discuss his request to have an official Christian church in the area. Though Camacho had been ministering to people in the remote Chopal village in the San Jose del Guaviare region of Colombia for about nine years, there had been many difficulties with the FARC, who had closed and banned several churches and threatened Camacho himself. He hoped, by this meeting, to come to some sort of understanding with them so that they might allow him to keep and pastor an official church.

As the pastor was aware, there are areas in Colombia where the FARC allow churches to operate. For most FARC-controlled areas, though, persecution of Christians reigns in the form of intimidation, vandalism, beatings, and even death. Christianity poses a threat to the violently political regime of the Marxist group, which has been waging a revolution against the Colombian government since the 1960s.

Despite all this, and despite the personal threats he had received, Camacho knew that God was using him to make a difference in the lives of the people of Colombia, including the FARC guerrillas. Just five months earlier he had been instrumental in leading three guerrillas and seven members of the paramilitary militia to trust in Christ during an evangelistic event. He knew God could work miracles, even on the hardest hearts, and he was willing to believe that God would use this meeting with the guerrillas for good.

The FARC guerrillas came, as usual, with their guns. Camacho's family looked on in anxious curiosity as he stepped outside to speak with the men. His wife, Gloria, grew more anxious when one of the guerrillas began walking toward the house, soon joining her and her daughter inside. She was momentarily distracted by his presence as he sat down to talk with her, wondering what it could mean, when gunshots suddenly rang out. She understood almost immediately that they were murdering her husband, and this man must have been sent inside to keep her and the children out of the way.

Five shots rang out as Gloria's heart sank in despair. She stole a glance outside and saw her husband's back redden. After the fifth shot, the soldier in the house called, "Make sure that dog stays dead!" A sixth shot then rang out, and all was silent. Tears ran down Gloria's face and she shook visibly. The guerrilla finally left the house and joined his comrades outside.

"This is the end of the story," the men said to the onlookers, "the story of the evangelical. And he who rises up against us will have the same thing happen. This ends here. We killed him because we don't share the same ideas." With those parting words of warning, the men left.

Gloria ran outside and knelt by her husband's body. He had been shot in the face and neck. She took a cloth and began wiping his face clean of the blood. With her children's help, she dragged his body under the shade of a tree and out of the way. Noticing all the people standing by, she suddenly ran back inside the house, retrieved her Bible, and then returned, still weeping. She gathered some composure and began reading from the book of John to the people who had gathered near, continuing in her husband's footsteps the work he had died for, strengthened by faith rather than disabled by fear at his death.

"This is what my husband believed," she told the people. "He didn't do anything wrong, but he was willing to give his life for what he believed. Satan didn't win the battle here today; God did."

"Mom, don't worry," Gloria's ten-year-old son told her, noting her distress. "Dad died for Christ and now he is with Christ. When I grow up, I'm going to be a pastor like my dad."

Camacho's family continues the faith legacy that he left behind in love and strength, as are many more Christians in Colombia who face the possibility of death every day. Yet they remain steadfast, encouraged and strengthened by the sacrifice and example of people like Manuel Camacho.

Mariam Muhina Hussein
(September 28, 2009)

The paper crinkled softly as Mariam Muhina Hussein turned the page of the Bible, bent over the words as she read them aloud to a fellow Bantu tribeswoman that Sunday afternoon. The woman had come to Hussein's home in the village of Marerey in Somalia requesting to know more about Christianity. The forty-six-year-old woman loved to speak to others about Jesus and share God's Word. She had several copies of the Bible hidden in her home for just such an occasion and was thankful for yet another opportunity to be a witness of God's love and grace.

So Hussein read, interjecting explanations or comments here and there to help her guest better understand the message of the words she spoke. The woman listened quietly; her eyes swept over the words on the page before her. The minutes passed by quickly, and when it was time to go the woman stood up to leave, her hand touching the Bible on the table.

"May I take this with me?" she asked.

Hussein's smile waned slightly and she hesitated. "I am sorry, but it would not be safe for you. Instead, you may come visit me any time to read and discuss God's Word."

"I will come again soon then," the woman agreed before saying goodbye and leaving the house.

The following afternoon Hussein received another visit, but it was not from the woman. Instead, she opened her door to discover a few men standing there. One of them introduced himself as Sheikh Arbow and said he was the husband of the woman who had visited the previous day. He was curious about something in the Bible and hoped Hussein might be able to help him. She ushered the men into her home and went to retrieve one of her Bibles. She handed it to Arbow, whose face suddenly fell as he looked it over. All pretense of friendliness melted as he looked seriously upon Hussein.

"These men and I have been looking for Christians who have defiled the Islamic religion," he stated. "Now we know you have other Bibles. Go get them!"

Her heart beating frantically, Hussein obeyed, knowing she had no other choice though it might cost her life. The men were part of a militant Islamic group in Somalia called al-Shabaab, which had been responsible for the murder of many Somali Christians, including a known Christian leader, sixty-nine-year-old Omar Khalafe, just weeks before. Al-Shabaab controls large areas of central and southern Somalia, and works against the Transitional Federal Government in Mogadishu, as well as laboring to impose Islamic law on all of Somalia. Proselytizing, and especially evangelizing Muslims, is strictly forbidden by the militants. Many Christians have fled for their lives and found refuge in the neighboring country of Kenya.

Mariam Hussein bravely faced the men and obeyed their orders as she retrieved all six of her Bibles and handed them over to Arbow. He then pulled out a gun that had previously been hidden and pointed it at her. He shot her three times, killing her instantly.

Though her Bibles and her life were taken, the Word of God will continue to spread in Somalia. Isaiah 55:10-11 says, "For as the rain and the snow come down from heaven and do not return there but water the earth, making it bring forth and sprout, giving seed to the sower and bread to the eater, so shall my word be that goes out from my mouth; it shall not return to me empty, but it shall accomplish that which I purpose, and shall succeed in the thing for which I sent it." In the terrorized, war-torn country of Somalia, Hussein's dedication to truth and her life sacrifice will be like water to a parched earth, revitalizing it and causing flowers to spring to life in hearts that were once dry and dead.

✳

Nag Hammadi Attack
(January 6, 2010)

The Christmas Eve service at the Coptic Orthodox St. John's Church in Nag Hammadi, Egypt, ended an hour earlier than usual—11:00 p.m. Bishop Kirilos hoped it would be an adequate security measure. Some of his parishioners had received threatening phone calls suggesting Muslims might attack on Christmas Eve in retribution for a crime that had supposedly been perpetrated by a Christian man against a young Muslim woman. The bishop had warned the police about the threatening phone calls, but police had taken no measures to increase security for the worship service. Though Kirilos expected the threats to be carried out in some way, he hoped and prayed they wouldn't.

So he decided to end the service early to give his congregants a chance to get home safely and avoid any trouble. After being dismissed around 11 p.m. on January 6, the people began filing out of church. They were dispersing just as a car sped down the street. As it passed by St. John's, men from within pointed automatic guns out the windows and sprayed the churchgoers with bullets. Several Christians were gunned down; seven were killed and nine injured. The gunmen then continued on into other parts of the city, shooting at other Coptic Christians as well as a convent.

Once Egypt's largest religious group, Coptic Christians make up around 10 percent of the country's eighty million people. Though Egypt's constitution guarantees freedom of religion, Islam is the official state religion, and violence against Christians of the Orthodox Coptic Church is staggering. Muslim extremists often target Christians in unprovoked attacks that largely go unpunished. Copts have protested several times in the past over lack of protection against violence and the unfair treatment received at the hands of the government, including discriminatory laws that favor Muslims over Christians. Christians have been arrested and imprisoned under false charges (or no charges at all), denied political representation and equal employment, intimidated into renouncing their faith, and even killed. Christian girls have been known to be raped and then forced to marry Muslim men.

Egypt's Christians continue to trust God to strengthen and empower them to face suffering and persecution for His sake, knowing that "suffering produces endurance, and endurance produces character, and character produces hope" (Romans 5:3-4). And hope does not disappoint.

"I HATE THE Communist SYSTEM, BUT I LOVE THE MEN. I HATE THE SIN, BUT I LOVE THE SINNER. I LOVE THE Communists WITH ALL MY HEART. Communists CAN KILL CHRISTIANS, BUT THEY CANNOT KILL THEIR LOVE TOWARD EVEN THOSE WHO KILL THEM."

—RICHARD WURMBRAND, WHO WAS IMPRISONED FOR FOURTEEN YEARS IN A Communist PRISON

DOGO NAHAWA ATTACK
(MARCH 7, 2010)

T he villagers of Dogo Nahawa, Nigeria, awoke to the abrupt sound of gunfire outside. It was the middle of the night, early Sunday morning on March 7, and they suddenly realized they were being attacked. The gunshots were a message, the beginning of the ambush. Panic and chaos ensued as hundreds of militant Fulani Muslims, waving knives and machetes, burst into the village huts, cutting people down. They wore military camouflage, and their heads were wrapped in cloth to keep them from being recognized.

"Allahu Akbar!" ("Allah is great!"), they yelled. "The time has come! You will see! We will destroy you!"

The cries of women and children split the air. The villagers, mainly simple farmers and their families, rushed about, trying to escape. Those who made it outside were ensnared in mosquito netting and animal traps—traps that the assailants had planted in the night when all was dark and silent. Some villagers made it to safety, hiding behind bushes or scurrying up trees. Many women refused to flee, attempting to hide within their houses and shield their children with their bodies. They were easily and brutally cut down. Like animals, the people were hunted, trapped, and violently killed. Their houses, property, and bodies were then set on fire.

Two simultaneous attacks took place in the nearby villages of Ratsat and Zot, south of the state capital, Jos. After the attackers had finished their work and left, around five hundred people—mostly women and children—were dead.

Dogo Nahawa, Ratsat, and Zot are all Christian communities composed mainly of ethnic Berom Christians. The villages are part of Plateau state, a predominantly Christian region on the dividing line between Nigeria's mainly Muslim north and mostly Christian south. Political and religious tensions are high, with the south's Muslim

*Families grieve the loss of five hundred residents of Dogo Nahawa, Nigeria, a
Christian village attacked by militant Fulani Muslims.*

minority attempting to gain control of the state. The Muslim Fulani herdsmen, whose cattle graze openly on farmland, have often gotten into clashes with the Christian Berom farmers. Attacks on Christians and churches by Islamic extremists in and around the state capital are frequent. In January 2010, hundreds of Christians from Plateau state were killed in an outbreak of riots, with others forced to flee to nearby Bauchi state to find refuge. On March 17, 2010, just days after the Dogo Nahawa attack, two other Christian villages in Plateau state—Byei and Baten—were attacked, leaving thirteen people dead. On Christmas Eve that year, thirty-one Christians were killed and more than seventy injured in attacks that took place in and around Jos.

Though in some cases the motives for the conflicts are supposedly linked to property or ethnic disputes, the attacks have been described as provocation of Christians, and bear hallmarks characteristic of the Islamic jihad, or holy war, in which all "infidels" are wiped out. The perpetrators of such attacks are seldom arrested, and when they are, they are rarely convicted, usually for lack of evidence. In many cases, suspects uninvolved in the attacks are arrested merely to mollify the bereaved communities and to offer a pretense that the authorities are on the case.

Christians in Nigeria continue to fight for their right to live and worship openly and freely. Though their strength to endure is often challenged, they remain faithful, knowing their plight is seen by God. As Plateau state Governor Jonah Jang said after the attacks, "I have total faith in God because I am a child of God, and because I know there is nothing that happens that God is not aware of, particularly when it happens to His children."

Ishaku and Selina Kadah
(April 13, 2010)

For Pastor Ishaku Kadah and his wife, Selina, the report on Monday morning that their village was going to be attacked caused very little stir. Incidents of Christians being harassed, threatened, and killed were a regular occurrence in northern Nigeria, a Muslim-dominated area. Though panic ensued in Boto upon the rumor, during which some villagers fled, Kadah and Selina remained at their home, which was also the headquarters for the Church of Christ they shepherded in Bauchi state. Whether or not the reports were true, they would not be driven from their home and away from their flock, but would remain strong and steadfast, ready to face whatever was in store for them—even if it meant death. This would not be the first time they had experienced persecution for their faith.

Just a few months before in neighboring Plateau state, several Christians had been killed in a sudden outbreak of violence in and around Jos. Those who survived fled to Bauchi for their lives, and Kadah and Selina gave them refuge in their church. A few days after, suspected extremists set fire to the church building. Because of this and other experiences, the Kadahs understood only too well the cost of living as Christians in such a hostile area of the country.

Though the rumored attack on the village never came, on the following day—Tuesday, April 13—unidentified men came to the Kadahs' church home and abducted the couple, forcefully dragging them away. Their burnt bodies were found the next evening stuffed in some bushes near their home in Boto village.

In Africa's most populous country, which is almost equally divided between Muslim and Christian, radical Islamists are bent on eliminating the name of Christ. Kadah and his wife were bent on proclaiming it, knowing how desperately the people of Nigeria need the hope, truth, and love of Christ to guide them. They now experience the promise of

James 1:12, which says, "Blessed is the man who remains steadfast under trial, for when he has stood the test he will receive the crown of life, which God has promised to those who love him."

"I WILL NOT RUN AWAY. I AM READY TO TAKE A STAND."

—Saratu Turundu, a single thirty-five-year-old who loved the children she taught in Sunday school. She was killed for her faith in Christ by a fanatical Muslim mob in Nigeria.

YUSUF ALI NUR
(MAY 4, 2010)

Yusuf Ali Nur was at home in Xarardheere, Somalia, when at 10:30 a.m. several men wielding guns burst into his house. They were members of the Islamic extremist militia al-Shabaab, which had been fighting a rival rebel group in the area for the last two hours. Having taken control of Xarardheere from their rivals, they were sweeping the area for enemy soldiers, searching in all the houses in case any were being sheltered.

Nur was not hiding enemy soldiers, but he was hiding something else: his Christian faith. The fifty-seven-year-old was a leader of the underground Christian church movement in Somalia. Christians like him were always being hunted by al-Shabaab, which was at war with the government and imposed strict Islamic law on all areas it controlled. Having ties with the terrorist group al-Qaeda, they had vowed to do away with Christianity in the country. As a result, Somali Christians were constantly under threat of death. Even under the Transitional Federal Government headed by president Sheikh Sharif Sheikh Ahmed, there exists a version of Sharia law whereby Muslims who leave the Islamic religion still face the death penalty.

Nur understood that death could be his fate as well, yet still he chose to remain in the country, and moreover, to move to the extremist-controlled area of Xarardheere in 2009. He had previously been a hardworking farmhand in Jowhar, where even then al-Shabaab had their eyes on him as a suspected Christian. Since moving to Xarardheere he had worked as a private school teacher at Ganane Primary School. He also taught English, though the militants objected to the use of English, preferring the traditional Arabic. Despite the growing violence in the region, even though al-Shabaab had forbidden radio stations from playing music and school bells from ringing (because of their resemblance to church bells), Nur remained steadfast and continued his work.

That Tuesday morning, as members of al-Shabaab stormed into his house, he knew he would have to be ready to die. Sure enough, one of the militants immediately recognized him.

"Oh!" he said. "This is Yusuf, whom we have been looking for!"

The men then turned their guns on Nur and fired a volley of bullets at him at close range. He fell to the ground dead, leaving a wife and three children behind.

Yusuf Ali Nur was a minority in his home country—one of just one thousand practicing Christians in the Islamic nation of eight million people. He lived in an area where persecution was strongest, and yet he chose to live humbly and serve others as well as he could in order to be the light of Jesus in the darkness of Somalia. He understood that even in living out our daily lives, we are at war—a war in which the powers and principalities of darkness (Ephesians 6:12) labor to stamp out the light of Christ, to cause believers to lose heart and forget the love and power of God. Nur might have understood this better than most, having seen physical war up close and been a victim of it. And yet, though he had no guns or weapons, he fought. Like Paul's words to Timothy, he was willing to "share in suffering as a good soldier of Christ Jesus" (2 Timothy 2:3). Nur fought to retain his faith and be an example of the love and peace that Christ offers.

ARTUR SULEIMANOV
(JULY 15, 2010)

Artur Suleimanov was very active in the community in which he lived, worked, and taught. Pastor of the largest Protestant church in the Russian republic of Dagestan, his heart beat to bring the good news of Jesus to the mainly Muslim nation. In fact, the majority of Christians in his church were former Muslims. He had begun the church as a small prayer group in 1994 in the capital city of Makhachkala. The people's thirst for Christ had grown, and before long he was shepherding a 1,000-member church, Hosanna House of Prayer. To continue to spread hope and truth to the poverty-stricken people of Dagestan, the congregation established smaller branch churches throughout the country and began a formal Bible study center at the main church. They began outreaches whereby they distributed food and aid to needy people, started a prison ministry, and worked with drug addicts.

A native Dagestani coming from a traditionally Muslim ethnic group, Suleimanov was considered by Muslims to be an apostate of the Islamic religion. But it was from this background that his love for his people came, and because of it he understood the emptiness and need that only Christ could fill. The pastor was well-liked and respected, and for the most part, his work was welcomed and met with positive response.

But then things started to change. A priest of the Russian Orthodox St. Thomas Church in Moscow was murdered. The man, like Suleimanov, was also known for reaching out to Muslims. Then in Makhachkala government authorities suddenly and inexplicably revoked the Hosanna church's five-year permit for their prison ministry, and negative attitudes toward the church's work with drug addicts permeated the atmosphere. The media began calling for action against Suleimanov, drawing parallels between his work and that of the murdered priest, accusing him of being too active in helping convert Muslims to Christianity. The pastor did not balk at these threats, but continued to trust that God would produce fruit from his work, whether by his life or death.

These events came to a head on Thursday, July 15. Suleimanov had just left his church in the early evening and was walking down the street when he was approached by two men. They took out handguns, shot the pastor, and left him dead in the street.

In his letter to the Corinthians, Paul said, "Therefore, my beloved brothers, be steadfast, immovable, always abounding in the work of the Lord, knowing that in the Lord your labor is not in vain" (1 Corinthians 15:58). Artur Suleimanov was involved in one of the most dangerous types of work known—reaching Muslims for Christ—and yet he worked at it with all his heart and soul, knowing it would not be in vain. His death provides an example of faith and courage that other Dagestani Christians will follow. As minister Sergei Ryakhovsky said, "You cannot scare Christians with murders; for Christians, to die for Christ is an honor."

BUT THE LORD HAS BECOME MY STRONGHOLD, AND MY GOD THE ROCK OF MY REFUGE.

PSALM 94:22

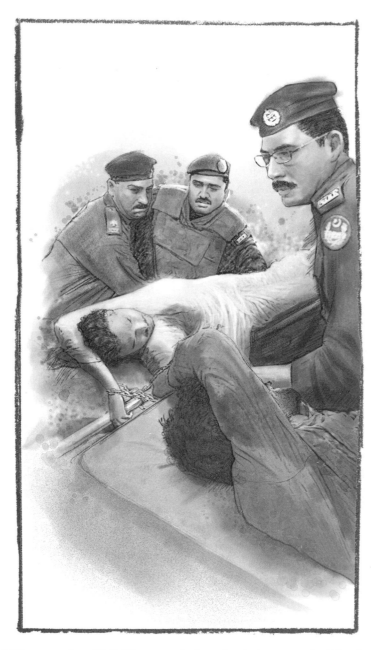

Rashid Emmanuel and Sajid Emmanuel, shot after being accused of blasphemy in Pakistan

Rashid and Sajid Emmanuel
(July 19, 2010)

Thirty-two-year-old Rashid Emmanuel hung up the phone and eagerly prepared to meet the caller at the train station. It was the second time the man had called, describing himself as a school teacher and wishing to meet him in person to speak with him. Emmanuel had earlier declined since he had been about to lead a prayer service in Railways Colony, Faisalabad, in Pakistan. But the insistent man had called again right after the service, and Emmanuel, as a pastor, didn't want to pass up a potential opportunity to help a fellow man. He brought along a Christian friend for support, and having arranged to meet the anonymous caller at the train station, the two headed over there immediately.

When they arrived at the designated meeting place, Emmanuel glanced around to find the man, but encountered something he hadn't expected. A swarm of policeman surrounded him and his friend. They accused Emmanuel and his younger brother Sajid of violating the law by blaspheming the prophet Muhammad. The police produced photocopied papers that the brothers had supposedly distributed—papers that disparaged Muhammad. The names, phone numbers, and signatures of the brothers were also listed on the papers, but Emmanuel had never seen them before. He and his friend were immediately arrested and whisked away to the police station.

The Christian friend was released after a few hours, but Emmanuel's brother, thirty-year-old Sajid Emmanuel, was thrown in jail just days later. Sajid was a graduate student of business, and together with Emmanuel was involved in leading United Ministries Pakistan. Several churches, a school, an orphanage, and a women's program were affiliated with the ministry, which described itself as "a group of believers, committed and dedicated to preaching the Word of God" and "helping the poor and downtrodden people of this area." They had been arrested because of their known Christian faith. In Pakistan, extremist Muslims take advantage of the government's harsh blasphemy laws, often to settle personal disputes and grievances, by wrongfully accusing Christians in order to have them jailed, tortured, or possibly killed. Militant Islamic groups often stage rallies on Friday nights after Mosque, speaking out against Christianity.

The Emmanuel brothers became the target of such treatment as they remained behind bars day after day while their case was investigated.

"Hang the blasphemers to death immediately!" chanted hundreds of Muslim protesters who gathered outside the jail in the predominantly Christian community where the brothers were being held. Led by Islamic extremists, the group hurled bricks, stones, and glass at the main gate of a church in the neighborhood. Christians in the area locked their doors or fled for their lives as the rally threatened to erupt into a full-blown riot. After a couple weeks of imprisonment, handwriting experts informed police that the brothers' signatures on the papers had been falsified. A court hearing was scheduled for their case and they were optimistic about the outcome.

On the afternoon of Monday, July 19, after their court appearance in Faisalabad, the Emmanuels were still on court premises, being escorted by police back to the jail, when five armed, masked men stepped out from the crowds. The gunmen warned the Muslim police officers to step away to avoid being shot, and then they opened fire on the brothers. Sajid caught a bullet in his heart and died right away. Emmanuel was shot in the chest and died later. Physical evidence in the form of cuts and other marks found on the bodies afterward suggested that the brothers had sustained torture while in police custody.

For proclaiming the name of Christ and selflessly loving others, especially the needy of Pakistan, these two brothers were ruthlessly killed. Their work was risky, but they were unafraid of facing consequences for Christ. "Now who is there to harm you if you are zealous for what is good? But even if you should suffer for righteousness' sake, you will be blessed. Have no fear of them, nor be troubled, but in your hearts honor Christ the Lord as holy, always being prepared to make a defense to anyone who asks you for a reason for the hope that is in you; yet do it with gentleness and respect" (1 Peter 3:13-15). The Emmanuels defended the Gospel to their deaths.

AND WE LABOR, WORKING WITH OUR OWN HANDS. WHEN REVILED, WE BLESS; WHEN PERSECUTED, WE ENDURE; WHEN SLANDERED, WE ENTREAT. WE HAVE BECOME, AND ARE STILL, LIKE THE SCUM OF THE WORLD, THE REFUSE OF ALL THINGS.

1 CORINTHIANS 4:12-13

CHERYL BECKETT
(AUGUST 5, 2010)

C heryl Beckett was excited about the opportunity to accompany a medical team on a service trip to remote Afghan villages. During her nearly six years of living there, she had traveled to several places outside Kabul, but this new trip was to an area she had never visited before. It was also an area featured in one of her favorite stories by Rudyard Kipling, "The Man Who Would Be King." She knew in her heart that it would be a memorable, life-changing experience, albeit one that might also hold some danger. Certainly, the thirty-two-year-old humanitarian aid worker never could have foreseen that it would be her last adventure on Earth and the beginning of her eternal adventure in Heaven.

To some degree, living in Afghanistan always held the prospect of danger, yet Beckett had felt a calling from the Lord to serve there, leading community development projects. Mainly, she taught villagers how to provide food for themselves through nutritional gardening, and she also worked in women's clinics, teaching mothers and children how to keep themselves healthy. Whenever the opportunity arose, she shared about her faith in Jesus. This new trip with International Assistance Missions would take her to the province of Nuristan, meaning "Land of Light." Through providing basic dental, eye, and prenatal care to villages in the area, Beckett and her teammates would be bringing the Light of Life to the Afghan people. Besides that, Beckett hoped to entertain any children she met there by making balloon animals for them. For her, it was an experience worth the risk of physical danger. As she once said to a friend, "I want to walk in faith in this place. We are not promised safety...but I know that there will also be beauty and fruit due to walking in obedience to God."

Beckett and her teammates traveled far into northern Afghanistan mainly by foot, at times having to cross very rough terrain involving high mountains and rain-flooded rivers. Day after day they ministered to villagers they met, many of whom suffered physically from their medical issues. They spoke to the people and comforted them, demonstrating Jesus's love with their kindness and service. After three weeks, the team packed up to head back to Kabul. As they were hiking through the mountains, they were suddenly caught off guard when a group of armed Taliban insurgents surrounded them, marched them into the woods, and shot them to death one by one as they stood in a line. The Taliban's accusation against the aid team was that they were spies trying to spread Christianity.

Jesus once said, "If anyone would come after me, let him deny himself and take up his cross daily and follow me" (Luke 9:23). The ten martyrs embodied this mandate to the point of death. They had all left successful businesses or family and friends in their home countries to serve as humanitarian aid workers for Christ. Each of the members contributed needed services and unique skills which caused the entire team to work efficiently as a single unit. They served others as well as one another.

Tom Little, age sixty-one, was the group's leader. He had served as an optometrist in Afghanistan since the 1970s with his wife, providing eye care for anyone in need, even Taliban soldiers. His three daughters were all raised in Afghanistan.

Another veteran aid worker who had arrived in Afghanistan in the 1970s was Dan Terry, age sixty-four. He worked with Global Ministries and was considered a peacemaker who had a heart for the poor and marginalized. He was deeply passionate about the languages and culture of Afghanistan.

Dr. Thomas L. Grams had left a successful dental practice in Colorado in 2007 to serve with Global Dental Relief. His service had taken him not only to Afghanistan, but also to isolated villages up Mount Everest, where he had to carry dental equipment by yak.

Dr. Karen Woo, a Briton, had served in South Africa, Australia, Papua New Guinea, and Trinidad and Tobago. Eventually, after visiting a friend in Kabul, she quit her job with its six-figure surgeon's salary to move there permanently. She was involved in raising money for charities and hoped to eventually promote women's rights in Afghanistan.

Daniela Beyer, a shy German woman, was a minister's daughter whose faith was very important to her. She had worked on translating textbooks into Afghan languages.

Glen D. Lapp was a nurse from Pennsylvania who specialized in eye care and hoped to represent Christ in his vocation while serving in Afghanistan.

Brian Carderelli, one of the youngest of the group at twenty-five, was a videographer from Virginia. He saw beauty in the Afghan people and their country, and had a passion for capturing it on film and sharing it with the world, saying "It's not all war."

Two Afghan members of the team—a cook and a driver—who had come along in support of the aid work were also killed.

In His life on earth, Jesus provided not only for the spiritual needs of people, but for their physical needs as well. He fed many thousands who were hungry after spending all day sitting on a hillside listening to Him preach. To those who were blind He gave sight, and for those who couldn't walk or stand, He strengthened their legs and made them able. During His last earthly meal, He knelt before His disciples in a humble manner and washed their coarse, dirty feet, telling them they ought to follow His example of love and service in similar ways.

That's just what Cheryl Beckett and her fellow International Assistance Missions teammates did when they risked their lives to provide medical care in remote, rural villages in Afghanistan. To know Christ and to make Him known through service in love is what drove this group of martyrs, and it is what they will be remembered for.

Rocio Pino
(ϻarch 6, 2011)

J ames Pino and his wife, Rocio, had already gone to bed for the night when they heard an unexpected knock at the front door. When Pino opened the door, he was met by two men asking for help with their motorcycle. He went outside to help while one of the men stayed by the door, where Rocio stood watching her husband.

"Is your name Maria?" the man asked her.

"No, I am Rocio Pino," she replied.

Suddenly three gunshots shattered the stillness of the night, and when Pino turned around he saw his wife fall to the ground. The attackers then jumped on their motorcycle and sped away.

Because they lived in one of Colombia's red zones, areas controlled by the Armed Revolutionary Forces of Colombia (FARC), no emergency services would respond. The road to their village was heavily mined and guarded by armed FARC guerrillas, so Pino and his daughters were left to watch Rocio die on their front doorstep.

Rocio was known for sharing the Gospel with everyone she met, especially the guerrilla fighters. "All who come here will hear about Christ," she had said. Pino later learned that Rocio's killers were probably retaliating against her for witnessing to a female guerrilla who had stopped by their house a few weeks earlier. "The Lord is waiting for you," she had told the woman, handing her a New Testament.

Pino knew the killers. They had arrived in the community two weeks earlier and introduced themselves as members of the FARC. Like many other guerrillas in the area, they occasionally stopped to talk with James. He struggles now to forgive them. "That step is very difficult to say, when I see [her attackers], 'I forgive you,' knowing that these are scars that never get erased," he said. After the attack, Pino and his daughters moved to a safer area.

Rocio took seriously Jesus' Great Commission, "Go therefore and make disciples of all nations" (Matthew 28:19). Knowing the risks, she and her husband chose to live and share the Gospel in a dangerous area of Colombia. Though it cost Rocio her life, it was a decision that was worthy of Jesus and the advancement of His Gospel.

"BUT IF IT IS DANGEROUS TO DO GOD'S WORK, HOW MUCH MORE DANGEROUS IT IS TO LEAVE IT UNDONE."

—SABINA WURMBRAND

Younis Masih and Jameel Masih
(March 21, 2011)

The residents of Hurr Camp in Hyderabad, Pakistan, gathered amid greetings, smiles, and conversation for their church's anniversary celebration. The Salvation Army Church had been a presence in the working-class Christian community of Hurr Camp for thirty years, and that constituted a special ceremony to celebrate.

Several Pakistani youths—Muslims of the Palari tribe—sat nearby, watching as the Christians gathered. They joked and laughed with each other, throwing insults at the women who passed by on their way to the service. They turned up the volume of the music on their cell phones, which mingled with the sounds coming from the church. Before long they had sufficiently distracted the service.

Forty-seven-year-old Younis Masih and twenty-two-year-old Jameel Masih, as well as two other men from the church, approached the Muslim youths.

"Please stop playing your loud music," they asked. "Please respect the Christian women and the sanctity of the church."

The youths began arguing with the Christian men. Soon they left in frustration, and the four men returned to the church building. The worship celebration continued as the congregants sang, prayed, and gave thanks to God. As it came to an end and people began leaving to return home, the Muslim youths returned, this time with handguns. Shots rang out, and the people ran in all directions to avoid the gunfire. The Masihs were both shot and killed instantly, while the two other men who had confronted the youths were badly injured, suggesting the youths had targeted them specifically in retribution for their earlier altercation. Younis's death left his wife widowed and four children fatherless. Jameel, who had been married only a month before, left behind a new bride.

Pakistan is considered one of the most dangerous places for Christians. Because of the country's harsh and prejudiced blasphemy laws, which are constantly abused, Christians are continually under threat. By merely being perceived as having offended Islam in any way, Christians put their lives on the line.

The Masihs and their friends tried to settle a dispute peacefully, and they were killed for it. The love and peace of Christ continues to threaten those who walk the way of hate and violence. These Christian men fearlessly and openly celebrated the goodness of God, trusting Him to bring transformation to their country and their people. Their lives were an example of Romans 12:17-18: "Repay no one evil for evil, but give thought to do what is honorable in the sight of all. If possible, so far as it depends on you, live peaceably with all." Their sacrifice will open the way of love and peace in Pakistan.

CLARITO DELA CRUZ (July 26, 2011)

Though not a pastor or a missionary, Clarito dela Cruz was a faithful worker in Christ. The Filipino man was involved in his church's evangelism program, which his parents oversaw. It was dangerous work in the Muslim-dominated area of Mindanao where Christians face persecution for sharing the Gospel with Muslims. Filipino Christians have suffered abduction, beatings, and torture, as well as the loss of their homes, livestock, and in many cases their lives.

When not at church, dela Cruz lived out his faith in his daily working life. He helped support his pregnant young wife, three-year-old child, and father-in-law by hiring himself out as a driver. One ordinary day on July 26, 2011, a man and woman claiming to be a married couple hired dela Cruz to take them to a remote village near the town of Linamon. As usual, he took his father-in-law's motorbike to drive them. When they arrived at their destination, the couple, most likely with the help of an accomplice, revealed themselves to be Muslim extremists. Somehow having knowledge that dela Cruz was a Christian, they used an electrical wire to strangle and torture him. They may have tried to force him to convert to Islam, since members of his church had been confronted by Muslims in the past for the same reason. When the torture produced no result, his assailants shot him twice and left him dead, stealing his motorbike to make their getaway.

Though the Philippines can be considered a Christian nation, the Muslim minority resides mainly on the island of Mindanao in the southernmost part of the country. Muslim extremist groups linked to al-Qaeda populate and control the island in their attempt to establish an entirely Islamic state there. Filipino Christians and missionaries in Mindanao face continual threats to their lives. Despite the odds against them, they continue to practice their faith and share the Gospel, trusting that their work will plant and water the seeds of faith that God will cause to grow among those lost in the dark (1 Corinthians 3:6).

MARIO ACIDRE
(AUGUST 27, 2011)

The gunman pointed the pistol at Pastor Mario Acidre and shot him six to eight times. The shots rang throughout the house, startling Acidre's wife, Jum, who sat in their bedroom alone. Frozen in fear and shock, she dared not come out to see what had happened.

The lay pastor had been spending an ordinary evening at home in Jolo, Sulu, in the southern Philippines when the attack happened. The gunman fled, leaving his victim for dead, but Acidre, bleeding profusely, managed to stagger into the bedroom where his wife was. Stunned by what had happened, Jum gathered her wits enough to rush her husband to the hospital. At least fourteen hours passed before he was able to receive a blood transfusion, and though the operation was successful, Acidre's kidneys failed; he subsequently died.

In some respects, Acidre had anticipated the attack. He had in the past received threats to his life for his work. Earlier in the day on which he was killed, some Muslim vendors tried to sell the pastor special amulets they claimed would protect him from bullets. They either targeted him themselves, or knew that he was a target for other extremists. Instead of giving way to fear or intimidation, he refused the amulets, saying he didn't believe in them, and instead asking the vendors to pray to God for his safety and that of his family.

The evening before his death, Acidre had prayed for the safety of all the Christian workers in the area—quite an ordinary and unexceptional prayer in the southern Philippines, where being a Christian means being ready to die at any moment. The area is controlled by Muslim militant groups linked to al-Qaeda who hope to install an independent Islamic state.

Acidre put his life on the line every day in order to bring the truth of God's Word to his fellow Filipinos. A former Muslim himself, he was driven by the love of Christ to share the Good News with his Muslim relatives and neighbors, which he did eagerly. He openly held Bible studies in his home, which eventually evolved into a house church, the Jolo Evangelical Alliance Church.

Knowing the risk, he told Jum on several occasions, "We must always be ready to face death for the work of the Lord."

As a church leader and peace advocate, Acidre boldly and openly proclaimed the truth, and he lost his life for it. Though other leaders have also received threats or been killed since his murder and some churches have been forced to close, the southern Filipino Christians have not all retreated. Many continue to meet and worship in the city's only surviving church. Months after her husband's death, Jum Acidre continued in church ministry in an effort to reach out to her nonbelieving relatives.

Pastor Edilberto Beira of the Christian and Missionary Alliance Churches of the Philippines was also not scared away after Acidre's murder, despite threats to his own life. He found strength and encouragement from Acidre's example, becoming more determined than ever that the church in the Muslim-dominated area would flourish.

"The only thing we can do is help these people grow in the Lord," he said. "If ever we are [killed], we are still confident that the work of the Lord will go on, because that's the promise of the Lord. He said, 'I will build my church, and the gates of hell will not prevail against it'" (Matthew 16:18).

"In spite of the painful
reflections and memories,
I have no time for bitterness.
My life is filled with too much
happiness, too many loving,
caring people to allow myself
to be devoured by the cancer of
hate. I rejoice. I sing. I laugh.
I celebrate, because I know that
my God reigns supreme over
all the forces of evil and
destruction Satan has ever
devised. And best of all—my
God reigns supreme in me!"

—Pastor Nobel Alexander, who was imprisoned
in Cuba for twenty-two years

2012—2018

Africa Inland Church Attack
(July 2012)

◆

It was a typical Sunday morning for four-year-old Melissa and her mother, Sandra. They woke up, got dressed for church and joined the rest of the congregation for worship and fellowship at Africa Inland Church in Garissa, Kenya. Sandra dropped Melissa off at her Sunday School class before joining the adults in the sanctuary.

But worship that morning was far from typical. In the middle of the service, attackers threw grenades into the sanctuary. The panicked congregation ran for the exits amid the chaos and explosions, but they were met with automatic gunfire as they tried to escape the carnage inside the church. Melissa and the other Sunday School students huddled quietly in their classroom, trying to wait out the attack.

When the violence ended, fifteen were dead and more than fifty others wounded. Members of the militant Islamic group al-Shabaab claimed responsibility for the terrorist attack, one of the worst Kenya had suffered in years.

Kenya's Christian population has been an al-Shabaab target ever since the group began its "holy war" against the enemies of Islam in 2006. The group, whose Arabic name means "the Youth," was founded in Somalia before extending its reach into Kenya. Tensions in Kenya intensified after Kenyan military forces invaded Somalia, leading al-Shabaab to vow revenge on the people of Kenya.

Sandra didn't pick Melissa up from Sunday School that morning. When a family friend arrived to take Melissa home, she told the young girl that her mother had been shot and was in the hospital. Sandra died from her wounds the next day, making Melissa one of twelve children orphaned in the attack.

Across town, Christians attending a Catholic church were attacked on the same day; Kenyan security forces believe the attacks were coordinated.

As the churches grieved for those lost in the attacks, they continued to cling to the eternal truths of God's Word. One widow had John 3:16 engraved on her husband's headstone because she knows God's love extends even to the men responsible for the attacks. And though Kenyan Christians continue to face persecution by al-Shabaab, they hold to the promise that the Lord will not leave them nor forsake them in their time of distress.

And I tell you, you are Peter, and on this rock I will build my church, and the gates of hell shall not prevail against it.

Matthew 16:18

MATHAYO KACHİLİ
(FEBRUARY 2013)

As soon as Generosa said goodbye to her husband, Mathayo Kachili, she returned to the kitchen to tend to the rice she was boiling for her twelve children's breakfast. The couple's four-month-old baby, who was strapped to her back, cooed as Generosa stirred a pot of steeping black tea on a burner beside the rice.

Kachili's work as a pastor to a growing Christian church in northwestern Tanzania came with more than its share of difficulties, but God had always provided for him and his family. Still, Generosa worried about Kachili that morning in February 2013, knowing he was going to say farewell to a pastor who had been visiting from another country.

Tensions were high in the city following a recent controversy between Muslims and Christians over butchering meat. Although the Tanzanian constitution did not prohibit Christians from slaughtering livestock for meat, it was traditionally a job reserved for Muslims; the meat was considered "halal," or permissible according to Islamic law, only if a Muslim performed the task.

Kachili had recently spoken out in favor of Christians' right to slaughter livestock and sell the meat, and Generosa worried that his comments may have made him a target for angry Muslims. She knew they had been rioting that day at a nearby butcher shop, but Kachili assured his wife the people in the town of Buseresere knew he meant no harm to anyone.

On his way to meet the visiting pastor, Kachili was stopped on the street by four militant Muslims. "There he is—the Christian pastor!" yelled one of the men, who also happened to be one of the Kachilis' neighbors. The men grabbed him and dragged him down the gravel street, then surrounded him and attacked him with machetes. One tried to behead him, but the blow missed and struck Kachili in the chest. His right hand was nearly severed from trying to block the blows to his head and neck.

Later, after the men left, one of Kachili's church members found him in the street. Although he could not say much, he had enough strength left to identify one of his attackers. "I am finished up by the people I know," he said, "including Abdullah." Abdullah, who had once claimed the Christian faith but had converted to Islam, was seen earlier at the butcher shop with a machete in his hand.

Shortly after the attack, a neighbor rushed to Generosa's home, sobbing as she told her the news of her husband. "I was on my way to the market when I saw a crowd of people gathered around the clinic," the woman said. "Doctors were placing bandages on Mathayo's wounds!"

Kachili was lying unconscious on a stretcher when Generosa arrived at the clinic, and he died soon thereafter.

Despite her great loss, Generosa has forgiven Abdullah and the other men who murdered her husband. "They didn't know what they were doing," she said. "We read in Scripture that God wants us to forgive those who offend us."

While Christians in Tanzania can freely practice their faith, they are oppressed and harassed in predominantly Muslim areas. Persecution ranges from family pressure to violent threats to the burning of churches and homes. Radical Muslims hope this persecution will intimidate followers of Christ and stop the advance of God's kingdom, but it is having a different effect.

Local churches in the country continue their efforts to spread the Gospel in difficult and unreached areas. And like many Tanzanian Christians, Generosa believes the persecution is bringing greater unity to the church. She believes God allowed her husband to die this way "so the Lord can bring harvest into His kingdom."

ALL SAINTS CHURCH BOMBING
(SEPTEMBER 22, 2013)

K halid had been sick for several months, but as he got ready for bed on Saturday night at his home in Peshawar, Pakistan, he told his wife he was feeling well enough to go to church. "Tomorrow is Sunday," he said, "so I will go to church to give thanks to the Lord." Elsewhere in Peshawar, sisters Sumble and Saba went to bed early, anticipating the morning's service at All Saints Church.

The next morning, Khalid, Sumble, and Saba made their way to church, along with hundreds of other Christians. One of the songs they sang that morning included the lyrics, "Who loved him, they drink happily the cup of martyrdom … They took persecution on their body." After the service, the congregation planned to share a meal outside the church.

Meanwhile, two militants linked to the Pakistani Taliban, known as Jandullah, had also made their way to the church that morning, wearing suicide vests. As the congregation gathered for food and fellowship, the militants detonated their explosives. Two blasts ripped through the air, one after another. In a matter of seconds, more than eighty Christians had been killed and 150 injured. Grief-stricken and in shock, church members tried to help their badly injured friends and relatives outside the damaged church building. At the time of the bombing, it was the deadliest known attack on Pakistani Christians in history.

Sumble, who survived the bombing, watched her sister die. Khalid also died from his wounds before reaching the hospital. Another Christian woman injured in the attack, Khalida Merriam, was eight months pregnant at the time. Shrapnel from the explosions fractured both of her legs and one arm, and pierced her abdomen, killing her unborn child. Merriam was taken to a hospital, where they put rods in her legs. They also treated her arm and performed a surgery to remove the unborn baby. She later recovered from her physical injuries.

Christians from other parts of Pakistan worked together to provide relief and aid to the Peshawar bombing victims, offering an example for Christians around the world of what it means to be the body of Christ. The legacy of the faithful believers who were martyred that day will last far longer than the fear the attackers hoped to cultivate in the community. As Khalid's wife said, "Khalid is a martyr, and the whole world will remember him."

IF ONE MEMBER SUFFERS,

ALL SUFFER TOGETHER;

IF ONE MEMBER IS HONORED,

ALL REJOICE TOGETHER.

I CORINTHIANS 12:26

Ehab Gattas
(December 31, 2013)

E hab Gattas had looked forward to ringing in the New Year with other believers at San George Church in Cairo. But shortly after he arrived and settled in for an evening of worship and fellowship, a group of extremists from the Muslim Brotherhood threw a Molotov cocktail into the church and opened fire on the building. He and several other young Christians immediately tried to protect the church and the other members, but Gattas was hit by gunfire and taken to the hospital.

He was turned away from three hospitals before finally being admitted, but by then it was too late. His condition had worsened, and he died shortly afterward.

Gattas, a college student, was a part of Egypt's Eastern traditional Coptic Christian community. Egypt is home to the Middle East's largest Christian minority, and Islamic extremist groups such as the Muslim Brotherhood have specifically targeted Christians, kidnapping their daughters, murdering their sons, burning and looting their homes and businesses, and bombing their churches. Attacks against Christians by the Muslim Brotherhood increased noticeably after the extremist group's political candidate, Mohammed Morsi, was ousted from office as president in 2013.

While Christians in Egypt know they could be attacked at any time, they refuse to give in to fear, instead choosing to gather for worship in a nation dominated by Islam.

Dike Ocha
(February 4, 2014)

When Pastor Dike Ocha discovered the body of a young girl in a building near his home, he immediately contacted the police. The six-year-old child had been missing for four days, and the townspeople of Kankia, in Katsina state, Nigeria, had feared the worst. By calling the police, however, Ocha had made himself an easy target for angry villagers.

False rumors that Ocha was responsible for the girl's death spread quickly through the village. And soon, a mob of more than two thousand youths descended on his home, calling for his death as well as the deaths of all the other Christians in the village. When some members of the mob managed to grab Ocha, they pulled him into the street and beat him mercilessly.

The mob pursued him even as he was being taken to the hospital, and when they found his room, they dragged him into the street and set him ablaze, killing him. The attackers also burned the pastor's home and a local church. Several other Christians' homes were looted and destroyed, forcing the families to flee the village in fear. Having lost everything and fearing for her family's lives, Ocha's wife also fled with their two children.

The local police commissioner later determined that Ocha could not have had anything to do with the girl's death.

Members of the destroyed church gathered in a home for worship the following Sunday, visiting the remains of their church building afterward.

Though located in northern Nigeria, where Christians are routinely persecuted by radical Muslims seeking to create a separate country governed by Islamic law, Katsina state has remained relatively peaceful. However, Christians in the area know that persecution at the hands of Islamists or even their own neighbors can erupt at any time, leaving them without homes or families. Still, many Christians in northern Nigeria maintain their bold witness among their neighbors.

Samira

(June 25, 2014)

O n the morning of September 11, 2001, Khaled (name changed for security) led the call to prayer at his local mosque in Yemen. Although he had been a Muslim his entire life and even taught Islamic studies at a high school, he had recently begun to question his religion after reading a copy of the Gospel of Matthew he had found in a family member's library.

As Khaled watched news reports that day and saw the evil committed in the name of Allah, he decided to walk away from Islam. "Three thousand people were killed," he thought. "What kind of religion is that?"

After one of his students told him about a Christian radio program, Khaled decided to listen to the broadcast in secret. He soon began calling in to speak with the program's hosts, and one night while talking with them he accepted Christ.

Leaving Islam was a big risk for Khaled. In Yemen, Muslims who turn to Christ face threats, beatings and, in some cases, death. Less than 1 percent of the country's population is Christian, and the laws of the country allow the killing of those who leave Islam. It is considered a great shame for a family member to become a Christian, and the church in Yemen operates mostly in secret. Khaled knew he would soon face consequences for his decision.

The change in Khaled's behavior did not go unnoticed by his family. His wife, Samira (name changed for security), became worried. Khaled frequently traveled to a Bible study in another town, and she feared that he may have found another wife.

Telling her that he had become a Christian was one of the most difficult conversations Khaled had ever had. But as he explained that Christ's love had changed his heart and his actions, Samira decided that she wanted this change in her life, too. She then joined her husband in following Jesus.

Khaled, Samira, and their four children stopped going to mosque, but they kept their new faith a secret. They lived that way for two years, until members of Khaled's Bible study asked if he would like to be baptized. At that point, he felt that it was time to declare his faith in Jesus. He and his family traveled to the coast for the baptism, and when they arrived, Samira decided that she, too, wanted to be baptized.

Somehow, members of a terrorist organization called the Muslim Brotherhood obtained photos of their baptisms and posted them on a Facebook page targeting evangelists in Yemen. Days later, DVDs were distributed with the baptism photos, the family's address and the address of the school where Khaled worked. His co-workers lashed out at him, throwing rocks at him and beating him on several occasions. His car tires were slashed and the windows shattered, and neighbors poisoned their family dog.

Samira was also targeted. While walking down the street one day in 2013, Khaled's nephew attacked her, breaking her arm. When Khaled tried to file a police report, he was told that his wife deserved the beating because she was a Christian.

The persecution became so intense that Khaled began to look for a way out of Yemen, making plans to move at the end of the school year.

On the morning of June 9, 2014, Khaled was awakened by his son, who was shaking him and shouting, "Father! Mother is on fire in the kitchen!"

Someone had broken into their home and replaced her cooking oil with gasoline. Khaled and his son put out the flames and rushed Samira to the hospital.

The doctors determined that Samira had suffered third-degree burns on the upper half of her body. But when the staff became aware of Samira's Christian faith, they began to neglect her care. Her nurses stopped changing her bandages, and the doctor forced Khaled to buy Samira's medicine from the pharmacy with his own money. The hospital also assigned an imam to Samira's room; he read to her and Khaled from the Koran and pressured the couple to return to Islam.

By the end of June, Khaled had seen enough. He told hospital administrators that he wanted to have his wife transferred to receive treatment elsewhere. They insisted, however, that they would treat her better. The doctor gave Khaled a prescription for potassium chloride and assured him that the medicine would heal her.

The pharmacist asked Khaled what the drug would be used for, and when Khaled told him he immediately called the doctor. An argument ensued, but the doctor had the final word. The prescription was filled, and the doctor injected Samira with the drug. Khaled and Samira then spoke briefly and prayed together before Khaled left so she could rest.

When he returned two hours later, Samira was dead. While the exact contents of the last injection are unknown, high doses of potassium chloride can stop the heart.

After Samira's death, villagers tried to discredit her and Khaled by spreading rumors that she had set herself on fire because Khaled had refused to let her return to Islam. Students from Khaled's school even told him they had heard that he was the one who tampered with the cooking oil.

While admitting that it wasn't easy, Khaled said by God's grace he has forgiven those who persecuted his family. In 2018, he made it public with this social media post: "Everyone who persecuted me verbally, with their actions, by encouraging others to persecute me—any way direct or indirect—I forgive you." In their final conversation, Samira told Khaled that she had forgiven all those who had persecuted them, including whoever had caused her burns.

Khaled and his late wife, Samira, exemplified the words of Jesus to His disciples in Matthew 6:15: "If you do not forgive others their trespasses, neither will your Father forgive your trespasses."

KENYAN COAST ATTACKS
(JUNE-JULY 2014)

C hristians in coastal Kenya were targeted in multiple Islamic attacks during June and July 2014. While Christians comprise the majority of the population in Kenya, Muslim influence has grown, and Christians have faced increasing persecution from Islamic militants in recent years, notably from the Somali-based al-Shabaab.

Al-Shabaab first targeted the village of Mpeketoni in June. Nearly fifty militants stormed the village, going door-to-door asking villagers if they were Muslim or Christian, and then killing the Christians. "My husband told them we were Christians, and they shot him in the head and chest," said attack survivor Samantha. The attack lasted five hours, leaving sixty people dead.

Days later, Poromoko, Kenya, was targeted in an attack in which fifteen were killed and twelve women abducted. As in the Mpeketoni attack, armed men went door-to-door in the middle of the night, dragging people outside and ordering them to recite the Islamic creed. Those who couldn't or wouldn't were killed.

Almost two weeks later, fourteen were killed in an attack on the village of Hindi. Militants again went house-to-house and dragged Christians out of their homes. They tied up the Christian men before shooting them or slitting their throats. One man who refused to deny his faith in Christ was left face-down in the dirt with a Bible on his back.

While many Kenyans face persecution from Islamic extremists determined to eradicate Christianity from the country, members of the body of Christ there persevere and continue to serve as His witnesses.

TERRY TUMBA

(SEPTEMBER 17, 2014)

As Terry and Elizabeth Tumba heard the attackers approaching their Nigerian village, they quickly gathered their children together to pray. Tumba urged Elizabeth to take their children and run, but it was too late. Boko Haram fighters caught them as they fled over the back fence.

Founded in 2009, the Islamic group Boko Haram seeks to rid northern Nigeria of Christians and to form a Muslim nation based on Islamic law.

The attackers immediately began threatening Tumba. "Do you want to follow us?" they demanded at gunpoint. "Do you want to become a Muslim?"

Elizabeth's husband didn't waver. "I will not become a Muslim," he replied.

The attackers then proceeded to loot the small store the family operated to support themselves, hoping the loss of income would entice Terry to join their cause. When they finished, they again offered him the chance to become a Muslim. And once again he refused.

Finally, the militants ordered the family outside. Elizabeth watched in horror as one of them threw an explosive into their shop while another shot her husband.

In his final moments of life, Tumba called out to his Savior. "Jesus, it is in Your name that I am killed!"

Elizabeth gathered her children and fled into the countryside. They walked for a week before finding a Christian, who offered to help them.

Even when faced with death, Terry Tumba held fast to his faith in Christ. Countless Christians across northern Nigeria have been killed at the hands of Boko Haram and other radical Muslims for refusing to turn their backs on their Savior, Jesus Christ. But their steadfastness will be rewarded.

SHAHZAD AND SHAMA
(NOVEMBER 4, 2014)

Shahzad and his wife, Shama, clung to each other and prayed as more than five hundred Muslims surrounded their house, shouting insults and threats. The mosque leader had accused the couple, over the loudspeaker, of burning a Koran, fueling the mob's rage. "They have burned the Holy Koran!" they shouted. "We will teach them a lesson!" It didn't take long for the accusation to spread.

After entering their house through a hole in the couple's thatched roof, the angry Muslims dragged them outside. Despite their pleas for mercy and Shama's pregnancy with their fourth child, the mob beat them ruthlessly, breaking both Shahzad's and Shama's legs. Next, the mob tied them behind a tractor and dragged them for more than thirty minutes.

Shahzad had moved to the Pakistani city of Kot Radha Kishan in 2000 with his brothers and their father, Nazar. Because of their Christian faith, they had difficulty finding work. In Pakistan, Christians are treated as second-class citizens and often must work as street cleaners or sewage workers. Shahzad and his family found work at a brick kiln. It was hard work but provided enough money for food and a place to live, even though they lived as slaves and owed a large debt to the brick kiln owner.

Six years later, Shahzad married a Christian woman named Shama. Together, they devoted themselves to the Lord and to the Christian community, meeting with local Christians twice a month for prayer. However, Shahzad's father, Nazar, had befriended some local Muslims and even began joining in some of their rituals. This disturbed Shama, who pleaded with him to stay true to Christ. Nazar later heeded his daughter-in-law's advice and stopped participating in the Muslim rituals, and it did not go unnoticed in the community. Muslims in the village thought Shama had converted him from Islam to Christianity, and their resentment toward her grew.

When Nazar became ill, Shahzad took time off work to find treatment for him. When Nazar died at the end of October, Shahzad returned to his job at the kiln, only to be beaten by his superiors for missing work. Shahzad then decided they could no longer stay at the kiln. But they owed the owner a large debt, passed on from Nazar, and Shahzad wanted to leave on good terms. "Tell us how much money we owe you," he told the owner. "We will return it and leave your brick kiln."

The kiln owner and his clerk did not want the couple to go free. They already resented Shahzad for not letting his wife work there, for fear the men would take advantage of her. The kiln owner and his clerk devised a plan: If they accused Shahzad and Shama of burning a Koran, they would be beaten and thrown in jail. So early on the morning of November 4, 2014, the kiln owner and his clerk went to the local mosque and accused the Christian couple of the crime, creating outrage in the Muslim community.

After the mob dragged Shahzad and Shama around the kiln yard, their lifeless bodies were stuffed into the vent holes above the brick kiln oven and burned. The vicious attack had lasted four hours.

Police reported that there was no evidence of Koran burning, and local politicians condemned the killings. Four hundred people were arrested and jailed for their actions that day, and a movement was begun to change the country's blasphemy laws, which have been widely used against Christians and others by anyone who has a grievance against them. Under the laws, Christians have been falsely accused of blaspheming Islam, the Koran and Muhammad. Shahzad and Shama clung to their faith in Jesus in their final moments, and their deaths were not in vain.

Werner, Jean-Pierre, and Rodé Groenewald

(November 29, 2014)

Roughly a month before Werner Groenewald and his two children were killed by Taliban fighters in Afghanistan, he delivered a passionate conference message on the topic of counting the cost of living for Christ. He ended his message with these words: "We die only once. It might as well be for Christ." Werner did not realize that weeks later, he and his children would be martyred.

Werner sensed the Lord leading him to leave his comfortable life in South Africa to become the hands and feet of Christ while on a mission trip to Pakistan in 2002. When he returned home to his family, he told his wife, Hannelie, that he felt they should go to Afghanistan on a short-term trip. She agreed, and during the trip, Hannelie, too, felt the Lord leading them to long-term work in Afghanistan.

"It was the first time in my life I had experienced this specific touch from the Lord in this way," Hannelie said. "I just started crying and knew that Afghanistan and Pakistan, wherever in the world the Lord calls you, can be your home."

The decision to move was not an easy one, especially as the couple considered what life in Afghanistan might look like for their two children. Afghanistan was the home of the terrorists who had planned the September 11, 2001, attacks on the United States, and life for Christians was difficult and dangerous there. They discussed the possibility of dying in the war-torn country and, as loving parents, worried about how they would educate their five-year-old son, Jean-Pierre, and three-year-old daughter, Rodé. But they trusted the Lord, knowing His call was just as real as the dangers they might face, and they knew that obedience to God mattered more than their fears.

Werner Groenewald and his son, Jean-Pierre, and daughter, Rodé,
martyred by the Taliban in Afghanistan

When they moved to Afghanistan in 2003, they experienced culture shock; they struggled to connect with their new neighbors and felt like they were always being watched. Over the years, Werner served with various humanitarian organizations, providing leadership training and English-language education. He gradually began to develop relationships with the Afghan people, and he enjoyed his work as a teacher.

In the weeks preceding the attack on the Groenewalds, several bombings occurred in the area. They knew the security situation was deteriorating as the Taliban gained more ground, and suicide bombings increased following the inauguration of the new Afghan president. On two occasions, while Hannelie was driving to the clinic where she served as a doctor, she almost found herself in the middle of an explosion. However, no one expected their family to be targeted that Saturday afternoon.

On the morning of November 29, 2014, Hannelie and the medical staff from her clinic were placed on standby at a U.N. meeting in case of a terrorist attack. Jean-Pierre spent the day in his room listening to music, playing the guitar and chatting with friends on social media, while Rodé spent time crocheting, working on her computer and playing video games. Werner went to his office in their apartment complex at 8 a.m. to prepare for leadership-training classes he was teaching that morning and afternoon.

At about 3:30 p.m., three armed men arrived at their compound. One climbed onto the other two men's shoulders before jumping over the wall. Once inside, he opened the gate and let the others in. When the unarmed Afghan gatekeeper confronted the intruders, the men immediately shot him to death.

As soon as Werner heard the gunshots, he ordered the students in his class to take shelter in Hannelie's consulting room next door. Then he sprinted upstairs, but encountered the attackers, forcing him to return downstairs.

"Lord, please help us!" Werner said. He was shot three times and died almost instantly. The attackers continued their assault, killing both

Jean-Pierre and Rodé. Two Afghan Christians hiding in the conference room survived the attack, but one of the men suffered a wound to the leg when the terrorists fired blindly into the room with an AK-47. The other students in the consulting room barricaded the entrance, but one was killed as an attacker fired through the door.

When Hannelie arrived home from work, she found the street blocked by armored cars and police officers. She fervently tried to call Werner and the children on their phones. A crowd had gathered outside their apartment complex, which was surrounded by Afghan police, but no one would tell Hannelie what was going on.

At 5:45 p.m., the eerie silence was shattered by the sound of gunfire, followed by an explosion. One of the Taliban fighters had detonated a bomb in the hallway of the building, killing himself and others. The remaining two fighters were killed in a skirmish with police. Then, Hannelie learned the worst: Her husband and children were dead.

"We had a clear calling," Hannelie said. "We had a mandate with this; we counted the cost. We knew that something like this could happen. God allowed that for a reason.

"I know that they are actually chasing me on to finish the race as well, to finish well," she continued. "I believe one day Jean-Pierre will say, 'Mom, what took you so long to get here?' I believe they are where they are supposed to be, on Jesus's lap, and I cannot wait to be there as well. But I have to finish this race for the Lord."

Twenty-One Christians Martyred by ISIS

(February 2015)

The world watched in horror at the widely publicized video of Islamic militants executing twenty-one Christians on a beach in Libya. All but one of the men were Coptic Christians from Egypt. The militants, who had pledged loyalty to the self-proclaimed Islamic State (ISIS), wore black clothing and covered their faces for the video. They marched the Christians, dressed in orange jumpsuits, out onto the beach, ordered them to kneel, placed them face-down in the sand, and beheaded them. When the video was released to the world, the jihadists made it clear their victims were "people of the cross, followers of the hostile Egyptian church."

The twenty-one Christians, most of whom were from the same village in Upper Egypt and had been working in Libya, were taken captive in a series of raids along the Libyan coast in the months prior to the beheadings. When their families learned they had been abducted by ISIS, they hoped and prayed they might see their loved ones again, but most of all they prayed they would remain faithful.

While ISIS claimed the massacre as a victory for Islam, the Christians' families understood that Christ could use even this tragic event for His eternal glory. "When we heard they died in the name of Christ, we were very happy," said Bebawy Alham, whose brother, Samuel, was among those killed. "We were very comforted, because these were God's children."

In the end, the video did not have the effect ISIS had intended. Many Muslims in Egypt spoke out against it. A prominent Sunni university in Cairo, Al-Azhar, called the beheadings "barbaric," and others noted that the Christian men were saying "Lord Jesus Christ" in Arabic as they knelt in the sand. They died with the name of Jesus on their lips.

Twenty-one Christians, beheaded by the self-proclaimed Islamic State (ISIS)

Several of the men's family members later said they were praying for the militants who had killed their husbands, sons, and brothers. "We forgive them, and we hope that they can come to know Jesus," Bebawy Alham said. And Mariam, the widow of Malak Ibrahim Sinyout, had a similar reaction upon seeing the video. "I was very proud that he stood firm in the faith and that he didn't deny Jesus," she said.

INDEED, THE HOUR IS COMING WHEN WHOEVER KILLS YOU WILL THINK HE IS OFFERING SERVICE TO GOD. AND THEY WILL DO THESE THINGS BECAUSE THEY HAVE NOT KNOWN THE FATHER, NOR ME.

JOHN 16:2-3

Pastor Han Chung-Ryeol, murdered for his ministry to North Koreans

PASTOR HAN CHUNG-RYEOL
(APRIL 30, 2016)

H e was warned that his life was in danger. Chinese police and South Korean intelligence officers had told Pastor Han Chung-Ryeol of Changbai, China, that he was at the top of a North Korean "hit list." He, his wife, and other Christian leaders had even agreed on security precautions designed to protect him while allowing him to continue his ministry to North Koreans. But after receiving a phone call one afternoon at his church, the pastor uncharacteristically disregarded those precautions and left alone. His body was found that evening in a rural area along the North Korean border.

Han and his wife moved to Changbai in 1993 to lead a small church of ethnic Koreans, who compose about 25 percent of the population in that part of China. Han himself was a Chinese citizen of Korean ancestry.

One thing they hadn't expected was that their ministry would expand to include North Koreans. When they arrived, they found the border controls between China and North Korea relaxed, with many Chinese and North Koreans crossing back and forth regularly to visit friends or family. Having suffered crippling economic woes and food shortages during the 1990s, North Korea had left its citizens with little choice but to cross the border into China in search of food, medical help, and a better life. Word spread among those seeking help that churches were one of the best places to go. Soon, Han and his wife were helping a growing number of North Koreans, and as a result, many were also placing their faith in Christ.

Han faithfully taught these new believers, many of whom returned to North Korea to share the Gospel with their families and neighbors. Though the pastor and his wife knew they were doing dangerous work, he felt strongly that the best way to get the Gospel into North Korea was through North Koreans evangelizing their own people.

Among North Koreans, Han became known as the man who could be counted on when help was needed. Even as other churches stopped ministering to North Koreans for fear of backlash from the Chinese government, Han continued to greet them with open arms. The work was dangerous, but the ministry was successful and growing steadily. When he learned that he was on a hit list, specific security precautions were put in place to keep him safe. For example, he never left his house or the church alone, and he stopped driving along the border.

On April 30, 2016, when Han received the phone call and left so abruptly, his wife did not think of it as especially out of the ordinary. She grew concerned, however, when he didn't come home that evening. And when he didn't answer his phone, she called the police.

By 7 p.m. that night, Han's body had been found in his car in a remote area near the North Korean border. He had been stabbed in the heart, and his neck was slashed—a common calling card of North Korean government assassins. Additional wounds to his head indicated the degree of his attackers' anger.

The seeds that Han planted continue to bear eternal fruit. Many North Koreans who met him share God's love with their friends and family inside North Korea, bringing the light of the Gospel into one of the most restricted countries for Christians.

Monica Ogah
(October 15, 2016)

Monica Ogah's grandmother was dying, and all she wanted was to return to her home in the village of Godogodo, Nigeria. Ogah's younger brother, Zwandien, urged them not to go; militant Muslim Fulani herdsmen, who had been radicalized by the Islamic terrorist group Boko Haram, had attacked the village just six weeks earlier. But wanting to honor her grandmother's request, Ogah and her mother decided to take her back to Godogodo.

On October 15, 2016, Zwandien's fears were realized when the militant Islamic Fulani herdsmen returned to Godogodo, shooting villagers and setting homes ablaze. Ogah, her mother, and her terminally ill grandmother hid in a small room inside their home as the sound of gunfire and shouting grew louder. They waited in silence, hoping the attackers would soon pass.

Then, during a pause in the gunfire and shouting, Ogah's grandmother coughed uncontrollably, alerting the attackers to their hiding place. Five men barged into the room and surrounded the women, pointing their weapons and shouting threats. Ogah and her mother begged the men to spare their lives, to allow them to care for Ogah's aging grandmother in her final days. Finally, the attackers agreed to a compromise: They would kill only one of them—Ogah.

"Are you a Christian or a Muslim?" one man asked her.

"I'm a Christian," she responded.

When the attackers could not convince Ogah to convert to Islam, they ordered her to lie on the ground in front of her mother and grandmother. One of the men raised his gun and shot her in the head, and then the attackers left the house.

Ogah was one of more than twenty Christians killed in the attack. Adding to the family's anguish, Ogah's grandmother died two days later, grief-stricken from seeing her granddaughter murdered.

In the years leading up to Ogah's death, anti-Christian violence had escalated in northern Nigeria, leaving children without parents and husbands and wives without their spouses. But amid the ongoing persecution, Christians in Nigeria are taking comfort and finding strength in the Lord. "We have our consolation in Jesus Christ," Zwandien said. "Whatever happens in this life, our faith in Him, my salvation in Him, our belief and trust in Him, will always help us to overcome."

FOR AS WE SHARE ABUNDANTLY IN CHRIST'S SUFFERINGS, SO THROUGH CHRIST WE SHARE ABUNDANTLY IN COMFORT TOO.

2 CORINTHIANS 1:5

Li XinHenc and Lu Linc Lina
(June 2017)

They moved to an area of Pakistan known to be influenced by the Taliban. Despite the danger, Chinese citizens Li Xinheng and Lu Ling Lina felt compelled to share the Gospel in the radicalized area. While studying Urdu, the language spoken in Pakistan, and starting a school in one of the poorest parts of the country, they built relationships with their neighbors. But their witness was not welcomed by some in the city of Quetta.

In late May, Li and Lu were taking their lunch break when three armed men dressed as police officers forced them into their vehicle. A third woman, also Chinese, was kidnapped along with them, but it is unclear whether she was released because there wasn't room in the vehicle or because she escaped and called for help. A Pakistani man saw what was happening and tried to help, but he was shot in the foot by the kidnappers.

Li and Lu were held hostage for several days before their executions, which were recorded on video. The self-proclaimed Islamic State (ISIS) claimed credit for their deaths, and the Pakistani government eventually carried out a raid on the ISIS hideout. However, by that time the Islamists had fled.

The Chinese government did little to aid in the investigation or the retrieval of the couple's bodies. In fact, the Chinese government declared their work illegal and blamed Korean churches affiliated with other missionary work in Pakistan. Some Chinese Christians who spoke out against their government's handling of the case were detained or pressured to remain silent. The official government stance was that the language school where the couple studied was merely a front for illegal religious activities.

The Pakistani government also accused Li and Lu of "preaching" during their time in the country. Following their deaths, a South Korean

Chinese Christians Li Xenheng and Lu Ling Lina, kidnapped and killed in Pakistan

instructor at their language school was ordered to leave the country. The Pakistani government accused Jean Won-seo of using his school as a cover for preaching. Christians in China and around the world were perplexed by the responses of both the Chinese and Pakistani governments, which focused more on the couple's activities in the country than on the fact that ISIS had murdered two Chinese nationals.

Despite being ignored by earthly governments, the sacrifice of Li and Lu will not be ignored by the King of their eternal home. The writer of Hebrews tells us that "God is not ashamed to be called their God, for he has prepared for them a city" (Hebrews 11:16).

"PRAY THAT GOD WOULD BE SANCTIFIED IN MY LIFE, AND IN THE LIVES OF ALL HIS CHILDREN HERE... I LONG TO LIVE A POURED-OUT LIFE UNTO HIM AMONG THESE CHINESE, AND TO ENTER INTO THE FELLOWSHIP OF SUFFERINGS FOR SOULS, [AS HE]...POURED OUT HIS LIFE UNTO DEATH FOR US."

—MILDRED CLARKE IN HER JOURNAL IN 1894. SHE WAS MARTYRED IN 1900 IN CHINA.

QUETTA CHURCH ATTACK
(DECEMBER 17, 2017)

Fazal's wife, Shahnaz, smiled as she watched her husband put on his new shoes, excited to attend church that morning. Christmas was just a week away, and he looked forward to taking communion that day at Bethel Memorial Methodist Church in Quetta, Pakistan. Shahnaz quietly chided him for running late, then kissed Fazal and their son goodbye, not realizing it would be the last time she would see her husband.

Fazal and his son arrived at a church packed with people who had come to watch the children's Christmas celebration. But as the congregation lined up to receive the elements of communion, four men wearing suicide vests approached the church. Seeing their intent, security personnel tried to prevent the men from entering, shooting one as he entered the compound. Two of the others fled the scene, but the fourth man managed to push his way through the entrance and detonate his explosives. Fazal's son was preparing to receive the elements when the explosion occurred, and the woman next to him was injured in the blast.

Eleven Christians, including Fazal, were killed in the attack, and many others were wounded. The self-proclaimed Islamic State (ISIS) later claimed credit for the bombing.

While composing less than 1 percent of the country's population, Christians are marginalized by the Muslim majority and must often work menial jobs for minimal pay. Christian communities receive little protection from the government and are often easy targets of Muslim extremist attacks. Large gatherings of believers on Christian holidays are also often targeted by the extremists.

While church members mourned for those killed in the bombing, they also had reason to praise God. If the other attackers had managed to get inside the church and detonate their explosives, the death toll would have been far greater.

Pakistani Christians endure great hardships for their Christian witness. They are hated by their neighbors and treated as second-class citizens for worshiping Jesus, who promised, "Blessed are you when people hate you…on account of the Son of Man" (Luke 6:22).

HE WILL WIPE AWAY EVERY TEAR FROM THEIR EYES, AND DEATH SHALL BE NO MORE, NEITHER SHALL THERE BE MOURNING, NOR CRYING, NOR PAIN ANYMORE, FOR THE FORMER THINGS HAVE PASSED AWAY.

REVELATION 21:4

PASTOR GIDEON PERIYASWAMY
(JANUARY 2018)

Hindu radicals in the area had warned him to leave. Pastor Gideon Periyaswamy and his church were attracting a lower caste of people to the area, and that was unacceptable to the high-caste villagers living nearby. "Leave this village, or else we will make life difficult for you," they had told him. But Periyaswamy knew the risks of serving the Lord in his homeland of India. "If the Lord permits it, I would die as a martyr for Christ," he had told a fellow pastor.

Periyaswamy had left Hinduism for Christ when he was a young man and served in ministry for most of his life. In 2015, he planted a church in a high-caste Hindu area near the city of Chennai in Tamil Nadu state, India. Unsurprisingly, he was not welcomed by local Hindu activists. Radical Hindus harassed him nearly every Sunday, and in 2017 they even beat him. Still, Periyaswamy urged his congregation to try to live peacefully with their neighbors.

Then, on the morning of January 20, 2018, members of Periyaswamy's congregation discovered his body hanging from the ceiling of his home. Upon closer investigation, it was apparent that the unmarried pastor had been murdered and then hanged in order to make it look like a suicide.

Persecution at the hands of radical Hindus has intensified since the 2014 election of Prime Minister Narendra Modi, who has ties to the Hindu nationalist Bharatiya Janata Party (BJP)—the political arm of the Rashtriya Swayamsevak Sangh (RSS) Hindu nationalist organization. At the time of Periyaswamy's martyrdom, RSS informants were known to live in nearly every village in India, reporting on the activities of Christians.

The surge in persecution is also related to the increased efforts of bold evangelists and pastors like Periyaswamy who are leading Hindus to Christ, undeterred by threats and beatings intended to stop their witnessing. Radicals are enraged when Hindus turn to Christ, disrupting their plans for a purely Hindu nation. Despite this, Christians continue to courageously and faithfully share the Gospel in India, seeing many Hindus turn to Christ.

But Peter and John answered them, "Whether it is right in the sight of God to listen to you rather than to God, you must judge, for we cannot but speak of what we have seen and heard."

Acts 4:19-20

SURABAYA CHURCH BOMBINGS
(MAY 13, 2018)

◆

I t was 7:30 on a Sunday morning when two brothers, ages sixteen and eighteen, rode their motorcycles to the Santa Maria Catholic Church in Surabaya, Indonesia, and detonated their explosives, killing themselves and six others in the blast.

Five minutes later, the boys' father drove a car filled with explosives into the Surabaya Center Pentecostal Church. The bombs detonated outside the building, killing the driver and six churchgoers.

In another part of town, the boys' mother and two sisters, ages nine and twelve, approached the Diponegoro Indonesian Christian Church with explosives strapped to their bodies. When a security guard stopped them, they detonated their explosives, killing themselves and the security guard. No church members were killed in the blast.

A single family attacked three separate churches within a span of ten minutes. Twelve Christians were killed, and more than forty men and women were injured.

Shortly after the attacks, the self-proclaimed Islamic State (ISIS) claimed responsibility for the bombings. Investigators eventually learned that the family had spent time in Syria and was working with the group Jemaah Ansharut Daulah, an Indonesian militant group with close ties to ISIS.

Indonesia is the most populous Muslim nation in the world. Although attacks against Christians there have become less common in recent years, radicalization is a growing problem. The bombings in Surabaya, generally known as a peaceful community, marked the first incident of church bombings in the city.

Instead of instilling fear in local Christians, however, the bombings have brought them together. "What they expect is that we will suspect each other, hate each other, and close ourselves so they can easily do more terror," said one church leader. But the church members stood together, taking care of their wounded and even starting the rebuilding process. They will not be driven away by fear. "Father, forgive them, for they don't know what they are doing," said the church leader, echoing the prayer of Jesus on the cross.

IF ONE MEMBER SUFFERS,

ALL SUFFER TOGETHER;

IF ONE MEMBER IS HONORED,

ALL REJOICE TOGETHER.

I CORINTHIANS 12:26

Fulani Islamic Militant Attacks Near Jos, Nigeria
(June 2018)

Dalo arrived at the hospital with second-degree burns over most of his body. He had been left for dead by Fulani Islamic militants after one of a series of attacks that June that killed hundreds, including his parents and siblings, while leaving thousands homeless. But eight-year-old Dalo did not despair. Though he had lost everything, the words on Dalo's lips were not filled with anger or revenge. He was praying for those who had attacked him and his family.

Life for Christians like Dalo in central Nigeria had not been considered especially dangerous, relative to what believers faced in the north. Muslims in northern Nigeria have long desired to create a separate country governed by Islamic law, and the extremist group Boko Haram has served as the primary weapon in that fight, recently enlisting the help of Fulani Islamic militants. But violence from the northern states has gradually crept southward, and in late June 2018, five hundred armed Fulani Islamic militants attacked the areas of Barkin Ladi and Jos South, killing two hundred and displacing ten thousand—mostly Christians.

The attacks ripped apart families and left thousands grieving. One young girl arrived home from school to find that her entire family had been killed. A woman lost her husband and two of her children, barely escaping with her own life; her family was specifically targeted because they had left Islam to follow Jesus Christ. A pastor was tied up in his own home while four men abused his wife. And attackers burned the house of a Christian widow and stole produce from her garden to feed their animals.

After the attacks, the Fulani Nationality Movement released a statement in which they took credit for the attacks and threatened more in the future. "Our men are waiting," the group warned. "We are eager to fight. We are boiling with the zeal to actualize our dream. *Insha Allah* [God willing], we shall take this battle across the sea, on the land, in the air, on the mountains, in every territory currently occupied by the *kafirs* [unbelievers]." And as promised, more attacks continued for months, creating more martyrs and leaving many more displaced, widowed and orphaned. Amid the bloodshed, many are forgiving their attackers and choosing to remain steadfast in the Lord, refusing to deny Christ even in the face of great loss.

BLESSED ARE YOU WHEN PEOPLE HATE YOU AND WHEN THEY EXCLUDE YOU AND REVILE YOU AND SPURN YOUR NAME AS EVIL, ON ACCOUNT OF THE SON OF MAN! REJOICE IN THAT DAY, AND LEAP FOR JOY, FOR BEHOLD, YOUR REWARD IS GREAT IN HEAVEN; FOR SO THEIR FATHERS DID TO THE PROPHETS.

LUKE 6:22,23

THEN THEY WERE EACH GIVEN
A WHITE ROBE AND TOLD TO REST
A LITTLE LONGER, UNTIL THE
NUMBER OF THEIR FELLOW SERVANTS
AND THEIR BROTHERS SHOULD BE
COMPLETE, WHO WERE TO BE KILLED
AS THEY THEMSELVES HAD BEEN.

REVELATION 6:11

About
The Voice of the Martyrs

The Voice of the Martyrs (VOM) is a nonprofit, interdenominational Christian missions organization dedicated to serving our persecuted family worldwide through practical and spiritual assistance and leading other members of the body of Christ into fellowship with them. VOM was founded in 1967 by Pastor Richard Wurmbrand and his wife, Sabina. Richard was imprisoned fourteen years in Communist Romania for his faith in Christ, and Sabina was imprisoned for three years. They were ransomed out of Romania in 1965 and soon established a global network of missions dedicated to assisting persecuted Christians.

To be inspired by the courageous faith of our persecuted brothers and sisters in Christ who are advancing the gospel in hostile areas and restricted nations, request a free subscription to VOM's award-winning monthly magazine. Visit us at vom.org, or call 800-747-0085.

To learn more about VOM's work, please contact us:

United States	vom.org
Australia	vom.com.au
Belgium	hvk-aem.be
Brazil	maisnomundo.org
Canada	vomcanada.com
Czech Republic	hlas-mucedniku.cz
Finland	marttyyrienaani.fi
Germany	verfolgte-christen.org
The Netherlands	sdok.nl
New Zealand	vom.org.nz
Poland	gpch.pl
Portugal	vozdosmartires.com

Singapore	gosheninternational.org
South Africa	persecutionsa.org
South Korea	vomkorea.kr
United Kingdom	releaseinternational.org

SCRiPTURE iⅡDEX

TOPICAL INDEX

A

a Beckett, Thomas, 100
Abdullah, 453
Aberdeen, Scotland, 124, 186
Abubakar Tafawa Balewa University, 357–58
Abuja, Nigeria, 310
Abwehr, 267–68
Acidre, Jum, 446
Acidre, Mario, 446–47
Adams, Hendrick, 158
Adolphus, Gustavus, 192
Adrong, Y Ngo, 384
Aegaeas, 30
Afghanistan, 256, 350, 405, 405, 435, 439, 440, 465–67
Africa, 16, 42, 62, 69, 81, 205–09, 215, 233, 235–36, 241–43 256, 259, 277, 279, 286, 302, 357, 397, 406, 428, 439, 450, 465, 490
Ahmed, Sheikh Sharif Sheikh, 430
Akaluka, Gideon, 327
Al–Azhar, 469
Al–Mutairi, Fatima, 411–13
al–Qaeda, 395, 418, 430, 445–46
al–Rifa, Jamil Ahmed, 330–32
al–Shabaab, 302, 422, 430–31, 450–51, 461

al–Wahhabm, Muhammad, 401
Alexander the Great, 11
Alexandria, Egypt, 20, 42
Alham, Bebawy, 469, 471
Ali, Shokat, 343
Alison, Isabel, 188–89
Amin, Idi, 201, 286
Ananias, 18
Andegeresgh, Immanuel, 387–88
Andes Mountains, 215
Andover Seminary, 210
Andrea, Santoro, 376–77
Angus County, Scotland, 159
Antwerp, Belgium, 105, 121, 123, 139
Aquinas, Thomas, 161
Arabia, 27
Aragon, Catherine of, 123, 129, 154
Arbow, 421–22
Aristotle, 161–62
Armenia, 33, 36–37
Arundel, Earl of, 99, 168
Asia, 53, 81, 90, 255–57, 303
Atta, Emmanuel Allah, 311
Atta, Kinza, 311
Atta, Sarapheen, 311
Atwater, Lizzie, 247
AUC (United Self–Defense of Colombia), 326